Editions SR / 13

EDITIONS SR

Volume 13

Religion in History
The Word, the Idea, the Reality

La religion dans l'histoire
Le mot, l'idée, la réalité

edited by / sous la direction de
Michel Despland and/et Gérard Vallée

Published for the Canadian Corporation for Studies in
Religion/Corporation Canadienne des Sciences Religieuses
by Wilfrid Laurier University Press

1992

Canadian Cataloguing in Publication Data

Main entry under title:

Religion in history : the word, the idea, the reality = La Religion dans l'histoire : le mot, l'idée, la réalité

(Editions SR ; 13)
Text in English or French.
Papers presented at a conference held in Oct. 1989 at McMaster University.
Includes bibliographical references.
ISBN 0-88920-211-7

1. Religion − Philosophy − History − Congresses. 2. Religion − History − Congresses. I. Despland, Michel, 1936- . II. Vallée, Gérard, 1933- . III. Canadian Corporation for Studies in Religion. IV. Title: La Religion dans l'histoire. V. Series.

BL51.R45 1992 200'.1 C91-095676-6E

Données de catalogage avant publication (Canada)

Vedette principale au titre:

Religion in history : the word, the idea, the reality = La Religion dans l'histoire : le mot, l'idée, la réalité

(Editions SR ; 13)
Textes en français ou en anglais.
Textes présentés à une conférence ayant pris place en octobre 1989 à McMaster University.
Comprend des références bibliographiques.
ISBN 0-88920-211-7

1. Religion − Philosophie − Histoire − Congrès. 2. Religion − Histoire − Congrès. I. Despland, Michel, 1936- . II. Vallée, Gérard, 1933- . III. Corporation canadienne des sciences religieuses. IV. Titre: La Religion dans l'histoire. V. Collection.

BL51.R45 1992 200'.1 C91-095676-6F

© 1992 Canadian Corporation for Studies in Religion/
Corporation Canadienne des Sciences Religieuses

Cover design by Michael Baldwin, MSIAD

Printed in Canada

Religion in History: The Word, the Idea, the Reality / La religion dans l'histoire : le mot, l'idée, la réalité has been produced from a manuscript supplied in electronic form by the editors.

All rights reserved. No part of this work covered by the copyrights hereon may be reproduced or used in any form or by any means—graphic, electronic or mechanical—without the prior written permission of the publisher. Any request for photocopying, recording, taping or reproducing in information storage and retrieval systems of any part of this book shall be directed in writing to the Canadian Reprography Collective, 379 Adelaide Street West, Suite M1, Toronto, Ontario M5V 1S5.

Order from:
WILFRID LAURIER UNIVERSITY PRESS
Waterloo, Ontario, Canada N2L 3C5

Contents / Matières

Contributors / Collaborateurs vii

Acknowledgments ix

Introductions

1. The Conference
   Gérard Vallée 3

2. W. C. Smith : son apport, son oeuvre
   Michel Despland 7

Première partie : Retours en arrière
Part One: Looking Backward

3. Retrospective Thoughts on *The Meaning and End of Religion*
   Wilfred Cantwell Smith 13

4. *La religion en Occident* : Rétractations
   Michel Despland 23

Deuxième partie : Les mots, l'histoire
Part Two: The Words, The History

5. From the Classical *Religio* to the Modern *Religion*: Elements of a Transformation between 1550 and 1650
   Ernst Feil 31

6. The Reified Heart in Seventeenth-century Religion
   J. Samuel Preus 45

7. La religion au XIXe siècle : quelques particularités françaises
   Michel Despland 57

8. Le concept de religion chez Ernst Troeltsch : pour un dépassement du positivisme et de l'empirisme
   Jean Richard 71

| 9 | An Ambivalent Relationship to the Holy: Gerardus van der Leeuw on Religion *Richard J. Plantinga* | 93 |

| 10 | An Asian Starting Point for the Study of Religion *Michael Pye* | 101 |

| 11 | World Religions: A Category in the Making? *Katherine K. Young* | 111 |

Troisième partie : Les idées, la réalité
Part Three: Ideas and Reality

| 12 | Anthropological Perspectives on Popular Faith: Catholicism in Brittany *Ellen Badone* | 133 |

| 13 | Is it a Crime to be Interdisciplinary? A Different Approach to the Study of Modern Jewish Law *Simcha Fishbane* | 145 |

| 14 | Religion, religieux, croyance, imaginaire *Roger Lapointe* | 157 |

| 15 | Foi et religion : une relecture sémiologique *Raymond Lemieux* | 169 |

| 16 | Prolégomènes à une définition sémiotique de la religion *Jacques Pierre* | 193 |

| 17 | W. C. Smith, Hermeneutics, and the Subject-Object Syndrome *John C. Robertson, Jr.* | 209 |

| 18 | In Search of an Open Concept of Religion *Jacques Waardenburg* | 225 |

Appendice / Appendix

Wilfred Cantwell Smith: A Chronological Bibliography
Compiled by Richard T. McCutcheon 243

Contributors / Collaborateurs

Ellen Badone is Assistant Professor of religious studies and anthropology, McMaster University, Hamilton.

Michel Despland est professeur de sciences religieuses à l'université Concordia, Montréal.

Ernst Feil is Professor of theology, University of Munich, Germany.

Simcha Fishbane is researcher in Judaic studies, Bar Ilan University, Israel.

Roger Lapointe est professeur de sciences religieuses à l'université d'Ottawa.

Raymond Lemieux est professeur de sociologie de la religion à l'université Laval, Quebec.

Richard McCutcheon is a Ph.D. candidate in the Department of Religious Studies, McMaster University, Hamilton.

Jacques Pierre est professeur de sciences religieuses, à l'université du Québec à Montréal.

Richard Plantinga is Assistant Professor of religion, Calvin College, Grand Rapids, MI.

J. Samuel Preus is Professor of religious studies, University of Indiana, Bloomington, IN.

Michael Pye teaches Religionswissenschaft, University of Marburg, Germany.

Jean Richard est professeur de théologie systématique et philosophie de la religion à l'université Laval, Québec.

John C. Robertson is Professor of religious studies, McMaster University, Hamilton.

Wilfred Cantwell Smith is Professor Emeritus of history of religions and lives in Toronto.

Gérard Vallée est professeur de sciences religieuses, McMaster University, Hamilton.

Jacques Waardenburg is Professor of science of religion, University of Lausanne, Switzerland.

Katherine Young is Associate Professor of religious studies, McGill University, Montreal.

Acknowledgments

The 1989 Religion in History/La religion dans l'histoire conference was made possible by an SSHRCC conference grant and by grants from the Faculty of Social Sciences and the Department of Religious Studies, McMaster University, and from the Faculty of Arts and Sciences and the Department of Religion, Concordia University.

This book has been published with the help of a grant from the Canadian Federation for the Humanities, using funds provided by the Social Sciences and Humanities Research Council of Canada.

Introductions

CHAPTER 1

The Conference

Gérard Vallée

The idea of the October 1989 conference was suggested by a concourse of events that were not entirely coincidence: three scholars, W. C. Smith, M. Despland, and E. Feil had virtually written the same book. More precisely, they had written a work on the same topic, the history of the concept "religion." It appeared highly desirable, therefore, to have the same three persons sit around the same table to talk about the ways they see the subject matter now, confess their *errata*, and incorporate various *corrigenda*, but also hear from other colleagues who, though not having written the same book, have nevertheless read our three authors and would have fruitful things to interject from their respective positions in the field of religious studies. Such colleagues were chosen not only for their competence but also for the diversity of perspectives they represent, in the hope that the encounter of a wide variety of views would produce some longed-for insights. A single purpose, therefore, brought together all the participants.

As a way of introducing the three colleagues whose work constituted the main focus of the conference, it might be useful to recall the nature of the contribution each of the three was in a position to offer. This will be done briefly, at the risk of oversimplification.

All three have dealt substantially with the same issue: the history of the concept "religion" in the Western tradition. All three begin their investigation in the Greco-Roman period, which soon becomes for all three the Latin West and eventually the Christian Latin West. All three look at literary material that was produced in the course of sixteen to nineteen centuries. Their work is cumulative in the sense that Despland knew of Smith, and Feil knew of both Smith and Despland. So far the elements common to the three.

Methods of enquiry, approaches, and interests are, however, distinct. The main differences between the three can be outlined as follows.

Writing in 1963, in the chapters of *The Meaning and End of Religion* dealing with the history of the concept, Wilfred Cantwell Smith expressly used the "history of ideas" method, scrutinizing the ways the word "religion" has been used [especially but not exclusively in book titles], reflecting various ways of thinking about the subject matter and leading to a wide variety of meanings. Smith, the historian of religions, was haunted by the question: How are we to understand that many cultural worlds are religious without having a distinct idea of religion, still less our modern idea? In fact, our modern idea itself means so many discrete things that he proposed to replace it with the duet: personal faith and cumulative tradition[s]. As a historian of religions, he thought that such a distinction afforded satisfaction to his overall interest, which is, How do we study religious traditions? His work witnesses both to a wide experience in the field of history of religions and a distinctive religious passion.

In 1979 Michel Despland published *La religion en Occident: Évolution des idées et du vécu*. The method used might appear similar to that of history of ideas. But a double interest bears and transforms that method: the work is seen, on the one hand, as a first step toward an "histoire des mentalités" in the manner of recent French historical research; on the other hand, it is conceived as prolegomenon to a philosophy of religion, which is Despland's main interest; in fact, the first volume ends with the late eighteenth century, that is, with the emergence of philosophy of religion as a distinct field of research. The second volume will deal with the golden time of philosophy of religion, the nineteenth and twentieth centuries. The work so far combines objective care and historical-mindedness at its best. This happy combination is seen, for instance, in the list of forty typical ideas of religion or on religion which has been wrought through a constant look at historical contexts and lived experiences.

In 1985 the first volume of Ernst Feil's *Religio: The History of a Modern Fundamental Concept from Early Christianity to the Reformation* appeared in German. Assuming a certain continuity through the centuries, aware of the hermeneutical requirements of such investigations, and making use of the avenues opened by the *begriffsgeschichtliche Analyse* Feil outlined the history of the concept *religio* from the first Christian writings in Latin on, and developed his analysis on the basis of an abundance of texts given in their contexts. The analysis of the concept *religio* was deliberately conducted in the light of its modern usage, i.e., first of all philosophical and German, thereby verifying the axiom that it is always in the light of contemporary thought that we understand the past, reading the book of history backward from the last to the first page. Since we cannot ignore the present standpoint from which we need to start, Feil spelled out his initial understanding of religion as follows: Religion is a meta-concept signifying, in a given form of expression, the sum of all that is assumed and/or done by humans in relation to a reality which is qualitatively superior to them. We have inherited this conception, which appeared with increasing clarity since the fourteenth-fifteenth century humanism. Feil's work takes its place within a larger project as well; he is interested in the idea of religion to the extent that its analysis constitutes a prolegomenon to the study of the triad faith-reason-religion and of the tensions within modern reason, the whole seen from a theological perspective.

It is not surprising, then, that our three authors, working within three distinct disciplines, were led to adopt three distinct approaches to the subject matter and to offer different ways of determining the turning-point in the emergence of the modern concept of religion. For Wilfred Cantwell Smith the break in the tradition is seen in the seventeenth to eighteenth centuries, when the interest in religion switches from inner piety to historical-empirical expressions of it, from personal commitment to intellectual views of beliefs and practices or, in the words of Samuel Preus, from a religious to a naturalistic framework. Here the development culminates in David Hume. For Michel Despland the mature concept of religion appears around 1800, with the constitution of philosophy of religion as an independent field and the beginning of a truly scientific study of religions, i.e., with the "anthropological reduction" of religion. Kant and Fichte could be seen as exemplifying this movement. But Ernst Feil discovers the emergence of the modern concept already in fourteenth-fifteenth century humanism, when *religio* progressively replaces the concepts of *fides-lex-secta*, and is used as *Oberbegriff*, as umbrella encompassing all religious manifestations. Nicholas of Cusa is one representative of this transformation.

These are the three authors whose work called us to the October 1989 conference. We now had our three authors at this table. In their own persons, they verified the medieval definition of the term "analogy": *simpliciter alii, secundum quid similes*; they are absolutely different but relatively similar. They were now to interact between themselves and with the assembly in an effort to help us both to a better grasp of the usefulness of such studies and to a more adequate approach to their subject matter.

It seems that much work still remains to be done in order to attain the necessary clarifications beyond all prejudices. The conflicting views of the past centuries on the topic of religion are no more conflicting than the modern ones. In the past, before religion became for Barth opposed to faith and for Bonhoeffer opposed to this-worldliness, it was held, in sequence from Cicero to Schleiermacher, to be the *opposite* of superstition, of ignorance, of irreligion, of atheism, of ceremonies, of lack of love, of lack of moral seriousness, and was thought to be distinct from knowing, willing, and doing. To define religion, then, we have the choice between the referents of those negatively marked items; but one doubts that an eventual synthesis will be able to subsume them all under a single umbrella.

The modern perceptions are no less diverse or confused. It is said, in sequence, that religion is more than knowledge, *more than* doctrine, more than personal faith, more than devotion, more than religiosity, more than experience, more than feeling, more than gnosis. What is it then? Have we said anything transparent when we say that religion refers to a relation of the finite being to the Infinite? Or have we said anything true when we declare that religious consciousness has collapsed in this world of ours?

It comes as no surprise, then, that the words "religion" and "gnosis" belong to the most widespread boo-words on the nineteenth-twentieth century critical and theological scene. Religion is all that is detestable in the eyes of the enlightened naturalist; gnosis is all that is execrable in the eyes of a Christian theologian or philosopher.

We are about to cease branding gnosis as being cheap heretical dreaming and to try to understand it for what it is; are we about to cease branding religion as being unthinking blindness? as unteachable subject in a secular society? Any academic step that might contribute to lifting the thick veil over the reality of religion and to giving back to religion its *droit de cité* will have to be considered a positive step amidst the uses and abuses of religion in our world.

CHAPTER 2

W. C. Smith :
son apport, son oeuvre

Michel Despland

Une tradition intellectuelle qui remonte à Socrate persiste non seulement à se poser des questions au sujet de la vertu (ou de la piété), mais aussi à s'interroger sur les questions mêmes que l'on soulève au sujet de la vertu. C'est alors que le travail de la pensée devient vraiment sérieux : il suffit en effet d'avoir des parents pour être muni d'idées sur la vertu, et il suffit de sortir ensuite de sa famille et de son village pour commencer à s'interroger sur ces idées. Mais avec la deuxième interrogation, celle qui est proprement réflexive, la pensée ressent comme une espèce d'effroi : qui suis-je en effet pour me poser des questions non seulement sur la vertu mais aussi sur les doutes communément acquis quant à elle ? Jusqu'où ce questionnement va-t-il me mener ? Cette deuxième interrogation ouvre ainsi, béante, une très grande question : quelles sont les ressources sur lesquelles la pensée peut compter afin de ne pas s'engager dans une spirale infinie de retours sur elle-même, afin aussi de ne pas retomber dans de vieilles ornières prétendues vertueuses ? et quels frais la pensée doit-elle envisager si, à l'instar de celui qui rassemble des matériaux pour bâtir une tour, elle entreprend d'ériger un édifice pensé qui soit constamment réflexif, et se veut prête à rendre compte de chacun de ses gestes ?

Depuis sa publication, *The Meaning and End of Religion* fut un rappel lancinant : ceux qui font des «sciences religieuses» doivent s'interroger sur la pertinence et l'adéquacité de l'idée même de religion qui délimite le champ de leurs efforts intellectuels. L'ouvrage soulève une question autre que celle, technique et pourtant fort importante, portant sur les outils que l'on se donne, et que l'on emploie si naturellement que l'on oublie qu'ils furent une fois des outils façonnés (bien ou mal) par l'inventivité humaine. En effet «la religion» prise globalement, trop globalement certes, est l'un des lieux obligés de notre réflexion sur la modernité telle qu'elle a été constituée depuis 1800 – à moins que ce ne soit depuis 1550. Cette

---

Le note et références concernant ce chapitre se trouvent aux pages 9-10.

réflexion, pour le mieux ou pour le pire, est aujourd'hui globalisante, et donc a besoin d'une notion «globale» de la religion, une notion qui donne un objet apparemment bien défini que les modernes peuvent attaquer avec zèle — ou défendre avec dévouement.[1]

À ce carrefour, Smith me semble avoir apporté une double contribution.

1. La première est d'ordre critique, analytique; elle relève de la philosophie dans sa version la plus incrédule: aucun mot n'est indispensable; aucune idée ne mérite d'être reçue une fois pour toutes. Ce que l'on pense de la religion (ou ce que l'on pense grâce au recours à ce concept) doit être examiné *sine ira et studio*, car toutes les habitudes intellectuelles doivent être situées dans le contexte qui les a vues naître, puis soupesées et critiquées. Il y a même lieu de réexaminer de temps en temps les nouvelles habitudes que l'on a réussi, à force de perspicacité, à substituer aux anciennes. Après avoir montré en 1969, avec force, qu'il faut situer la vie religieuse des personnes dans des traditions, Smith en 1980 souligne les écueils des approches purement diachroniques et nous invite à nous pencher sur des phénomènes synchroniques. «Traditions in Contact and Change: Towards a History of Religion in the Singular» reprend à zéro l'entreprise de reconceptualisation et déplore la tendance historiographique qui voit des traditions religieuses parallèles, parfois en contact, et ainsi en train de changer au contact les unes des autres. (Cette tendance, qui fait remonter chaque religion à l'oeuvre de son fondateur, devint une stratégie historiographique raisonnable une fois qu'il semblait difficile d'écrire l'histoire de la religion en commençant avec les communications que Dieu avait eues avec Adam.) L'article, partant de l'exemple le plus notoire, celui de l'époque hellénistique, établit une liste de huit moments (et lieux) dans l'histoire religieuse de l'humanité où l'historien sans préventions ne voit pas des «contacts» entre des «traditions» mais une matrice confuse où sont mêlés (avec bonheur) des thèmes qui, par la suite, seront déclarés incompatibles par des «traditions» ayant achevé leur oeuvre d'auto-définition. En d'autres termes, les traditions, dans ces huit cas, n'ont existé qu'après les contacts. Celui qui aborde l'étude de ces lieux et moments muni de l'idée de «tradition religieuse» ne voit pas la religion que les personnes y vivent.

Smith, à ma connaissance, n'a jamais parlé d'archéologie du savoir et il y a certainement quelque chose de piquant à placer dans la compagnie des déconstructionnistes parisiens un homme qui ne cesse de rappeler (encore est-ce avec un ton de voix particulier) qu'au fond il est un presbytérien de l'Ontario. Mais son travail est un modèle de grande hardiesse intellectuelle. Il a, par exemple, appris à de nombreux Nord-Américains à se méfier des constructions livresques qui font le jeu de regroupements d'intérêts (et de pouvoirs et savoirs aptes à protéger ces intérêts) prétendûment progressistes et certainement occidentaux. L'approche de Smith lui a permis d'accueillir la problématique marxiste; elle me semble aussi accueillir la problématique psychanalytique dans ce qu'elle peut avoir de plus déroutant.

2. Ceci dit, Smith ne nous laisse jamais perdre de vue un autre fait: quand on s'interroge sur les questions communément soulevées sur la vertu, ce n'est pas pour rivaliser avec d'autres hommes, qui, eux aussi, s'interrogent mais posent des questions qui sont moins bonnes que les nôtres; c'est plutôt pour en arriver à connaître la vertu (ou la piété) et surtout à la pratiquer. La réfléxivité, le doute sur le doute, ne doivent pas devenir des fins en soi. Si captivant que puisse être le jeu de la chasse, et le dialogue ou la rivalité avec les autres chasseurs, il ne faut perdre la proie de vue. Ainsi, s'il y a quelque chose de post-moderne dans les interventions écrites ou orales de W. C. Smith, il y a aussi quelque chose de si franchement théologique que j'en suis réduit à dire que ses déclarations ont une saveur proprement archaïque, encore que je doive préciser que ce quelque chose d'archaïque est toujours présenté dans sa fraîcheur et sa jeunesse. On apprend à écarter le recours commode à la notion de religion, pour sortir des ornières d'une modernité trop sûre d'elle-même, et ainsi pour réapprendre à parler de Dieu. Derrière le brouhaha des idées sur la vertu ou sur l'homme, sa voix répète l'appel à la vertu, à la piété, et à la nécessité d'être humain. C'est alors que l'étonnement ironique, amusé, voire ahuri, devant l'étrangeté de nos habitudes intellectuelles (et leur bizarres prétentions à l'autorité), cède la place à l'étonnement au sens fort, celui qui tient de l'émerveillement.

W. C. Smith fut, depuis la fondation de la société, un membre assidu aux réunions de la Société Canadienne pour l'Etude de la Religion et cela même durant les années où il assumait d'importantes charges aux Etats-Unis. Les membres francophones n'y ont jamais eu le plaisir de l'entendre parler français lors de réunions où les deux langues étaient en usage, mais ils ont eu la satisfaction, plus rare, et peut-être plus précieuse, de savoir rapidement qu'il avait parfaitement compris tout ce qui avait été communiqué en français. Nous sommes heureux de noter, par le biais de ce volume, son apport au bilinguisme fonctionnel. Le magnifique *Festschrift* qui lui fut offert en 1984 (*The World's Religious Traditions: Current Perspectives in Religious Studies*, Edinbourg: T. and T. Clark) est signé par un groupe d'auteurs britanniques et américains. Nous n'oserons certes pas parler ici de correction, mais un ajout pouvait sembler nécessaire. De même pour une bibliographie mise à jour.

Note

1 Voir Strenski 1989.

Références

Smith, Wilfred Cantwell. 1983. «Traditions in Contact and Change: Towards a History of Religion in the Singular.» In *Traditions in Contact and Change: Selected Proceedings of the XIVth Congress of the International Association for the*

History of Religions, edited by Peter Slater and Donald Wiebe, 1-23. Waterloo, ON, Wilfrid Laurier University Press, 1983.

Strenski, Ivan. 1989. «Louis Dumont, Individualism and Religious Studies.» *Religious Studies Review* 15, 1 (January) : 22-29.

PREMIÈRE PARTIE :

Retours en arrière

PART ONE:

Looking Backward

CHAPTER 3

Retrospective Thoughts on The Meaning and End of Religion

Wilfred Cantwell Smith

First, a word on the phrasing of my title. Originally, "Second Thoughts on *The Meaning and End...*" had been proposed, and seemed natural enough. Yet I have had twenty-five and more years to mull over that work (1963 et seq.), so that if I was to come up now with something new and fresh about it I thought of changing that to "third thoughts." I realized, however, that "seventeenth" or "umpteenth" would have been still more appropriate. Moreover, even "second thoughts," in a usual sense of that phrase, could be misleading, for I confess that at a fundamental level I have in fact not changed my mind on the basic thesis of the book. On the contrary, my subsequent work, which I should like to think has led me gradually to wider horizons, deeper awareness, further insight, has been both a development from and served as a confirmation of the underlying orientation, which perhaps I have summed up in my continuing theme song, "The study of religion is the study of persons." Later books, from my *Questions of Religious Truth* (1967) to *Belief and History* (1977, 1985), *Faith and Belief* (1979, 1987), *On Understanding Islam* (1981b, 1984, 1985), *Towards a World Theology* (1981a, 1989), are all in line with this "orientation," as I have just called it. So too are my most important recent articles: "Philosophia" (1984b); my presidential address to the American Academy of Religion (1984a); my recent Ingersoll lecture at Harvard (1988b); and much else. All these in a sense grow out of *The Meaning and End*, and its roughly simultaneous companion piece *The Faith of Other Men* (1962, 1963, 1965, 1972) (nowadays, given the ever-changing history of language and of the meaning of words, *The Faith of Others*; or as its recent Korean translation [1989] happily put it, *Faith in the Global Village*). These later publications grew out of the early two, carried the outlook further, and confirmed it. I am pleased that the present volume will carry the investigation still further in certain directions, critically or corroboratively.

References for this chapter appear on pages 20-21.

I have elsewhere remarked that, of my two categories proposed as alternatives to "the religions," one of them, "tradition," has been much more widely accepted than has the other, "faith." In academic circles it has by now become relatively standard to speak of "the Hindu tradition," "the Confucian tradition," "the Jewish tradition," and the like; and even in general parlance to some extent one hears such wording. In "faith," on the other hand, academics, at least, have proven themselves much less ready to be interested, explicitly interested. I have not claimed, of course, to have coined the "tradition" usage, although perhaps my book did something to popularize it. (I got it, by the way, from attempting to understand China.) Certainly, of course, I did not coin the notion "faith." Yet it can be said, perhaps, that in choosing "tradition" I hit upon a congenial and potentially highly serviceable term (though the "cumulative" bit has been less stressed, even less noticed); whereas in selecting "faith" I may have guessed wrongly. (My *Faith and Belief* perhaps demonstrates that the choice was logically, if not sociologically, valid.)

Some may be interested to learn that for a moment I had thought of using, rather, "piety." Certain of my friends urged me for heaven's sake to drop that idea, the word having become from the nineteenth century far too unctuous and sanctimonious to have any future in the twentieth. I certainly underestimated, however, with regard to "faith," the degree to which even intellectuals, let alone the general reading public, had and insisted on keeping a firm sense of what the term meant to them: an idea definitely formed and rather rigidly jelled. They were unwilling, it seemed, to entertain suggestions as to developing a new and open understanding for it — or to modify it in the light of new evidence. Some critics also seemed to feel that I was speaking of faith in a reified sense — which showed me with considerable force how woefully I had failed to make myself clear.

Other critics insisted on presuming that by "faith" I of course must and did mean faith in a traditional Protestant sense: that I was imposing my particular background on the world scene. In fact, however, I was brought up like others in modern Western culture — not least, other Protestant Christians — to imagine that "faith" is more or less synonymous with "belief," or at least has primarily something to do with it. It was a consideration of the Islamic case that freed me from this error. In the course of writing a review that I had been asked to do of the translation by a reputable Western scholar of a medieval Arabic work by a Muslim theologian, I found myself forced to realize that the English version made no sense in rendering the Muslim word *iman* by "belief," in the contexts where it occurred. (No one doubted that this Arabic term might also be translated as "faith.") This set me to thinking about what Islamic theology did classically understand faith to be, since it was inescapable that it was not belief" for this particular writer, and I gradually discovered that the same was true for other Muslims, and later for Hindus, Jews, Sikhs, and others and finally also for pre-modern Christians. Thus it was this wrestling with Islamic faith—and its discontinuity with current Christian thinking—that proved the basis for my eventually working out and presenting, twenty years later, a concept of faith that would enable us to understand intellectually the whole range of the world scene. It perhaps required that later book to make the argument of the earlier one clear enough to be persuasive.

When I admit that on the fundamental outlook I have not changed but have gone on further, I do not of course mean that on certain details of the overall thesis I have not been open to revision; and I have of course been flattered, and felt grateful, that Despland (1979) and Feil (1987) have taken the trouble to elaborate in imipressive books what I sketched in part of one chapter. It is clear that these substantially enrich my chapter. Careful study of their work and discussions with the authors have left me happy to see it enriched but not refuted.

Readers may be interested to know, too, that the work was markedly slow in getting going. In fact the book might be considered to have been at the start a failure. The original edition was "remaindered" within a year, and drew some pretty disparaging, even hostile, reviews. Gradually, however, the situation changed, and five editions have now sold out (about fifty thousand copies); a sixth is currently being undertaken (by Fortress Press).

The two most striking new insights that the new orientation has since enabled me to develop are, perhaps, the recognition of the Greek legacy in Western civilization as one of the "great religious traditions of humankind," to quote my "Philosophia" article (1984b); and secondly the recognition that "religion" in its modern sense is at heart a secular concept: that modern secularism is not a vision of the world free from bias—so-called religious bias—but is rather one more ideology among others, to be understood and interpreted as peculiar, both in the sense of being particular, *sui generis*, and peculiar in the sense also of being odd—an aberration, as I have called it; and an intellectual error, there are strong empirical and rational grounds for contending.

Both of my two new "developments," as I call them, are, of course, comparativist insights, like the original one. From seeing it in the context of world history, I have gained new understanding of Western civilization, and of the two traditions that have jointly informed it over the centuries, and that I see as mutually comparable: the one from Greece and Rome, the other from Palestine; the one with humanism, idealism, justice, reason, as the chief forms for its apprehension of transcendence, the other with, primarily, God as its chief form. These two traditions of ours have been conspicuously different from each other, both in pattern and in content; yet no more different than the one from Palestine, in both its Christian and its Jewish branches, has been from the Hindu; nor than the Shinto has been from the Islamic; and so on; and at the same time no less similar, so far as personal involvement goes, than these others have been among themselves. It was an error, when the West became aware of other civilizations, to universalize the distinction that it saw between its own two heritages, Graeco-Roman and Palestinian, lumping all the others under its rubric for one of them, as if that distinction could be generalized for the world. The Confucian case in China appeared to be special, a matter on which we have a paper in this volume, and on which I have spoken in Japan (1988a). So far as the West itself is concerned, it is not only the comparativist perspective that enables one to see that the Western classic tradition was for long just as "religious" as its Palestinian; it is also the personalist perspective. If one looks at the effect on persons, on their living of their lives, on the faith generated, on the role played in society, rather than focussing on the traditions themselves as objects, one sees the spiritual convergence. To think of one of the Western, and all of the Asian, traditions — except perhaps the Confucian — as falling in some different category, is an accident of history based eventually on the West's unawareness of the rest of the world, and on its consequent inadequate analytic awareness of itself.

The other development from *The Meaning and End*'s outlook on "religion" as a category that is unnecessary and misleading is closely linked with this. I have come to recognize how pervasively modern conceptions harboured under the term "religion" — Feil has emphasized how novel those modern conceptions are, how different from those of its traditional Western use — are *au fond* secularist. When I wrote *The Meaning and End* I knew that "religion" was a Western and a modern notion. I had not yet seen, but now I do see clearly, that "religion" in its modern form is a secular idea. Secularism is an ideology, and "religion" is one of its basic categories. Like all such conceptual categories thus far in human history, it is time-bound and culture-bound, and is legitimately meaningful only for insiders, for those who pretty much accept all the other basic categories of that particular worldview, or anyway accept their overall framework. (It is illuminating to observe the extent to which even many Christians have been brainwashed by their secularist milieu.) The secular *Weltanschauung* postulates, and then presupposes, a particular — indeed an odd — view of the human, and of the world: namely, the secularist view. It sees the universe, and human nature, as essentially secular, and sees "the religions" as addenda that human beings have tacked on here and there in various shapes and for various interesting, powerful, or fatuous reasons. It sees law, economics, philosophy (things that we got from Greece and Rome) as distinct from religion. And so on.

I do *not* mean — if I may quote from my American Academy of Religion talk (1984a: 9) — that humanity is basically *homo religiosus*.

That is an error that further illustrates my thesis, by its perpetuating the idiosyncratic outlook that the Modern West has defensively constructed. It took [me] some time to detect this. The concept "religion" has itself been developed by Western secularism as naming something that is supposedly over and above the standard everyday. Religion [, however,] is in fact not something special, the [comparative] historian can now see; it is secularism that is odd. [The notion "religion" sets up a dichotomy that secularists need in order] to justify their own separate peculiarity; but normal people do not and cannot. The dichotomy is retained, in inverted form, in that phrase *homo religiosus*. In fact, there is rather just plain *homo sapiens*, with a minority, of those not *sapientes* enough to have sensed what kind of universe we live in and what kind of being we are

—or from another perspective: one more minority whose *sapientia* is of a different form from their fellow's, with that difference requiring to be explained.

A third avenue along which my thinking has been led by my subsequent study of world history develops the anti-reifying thrust of *The Meaning and End* in additional realms beyond simply "religion." One example is language. I have gradually come to feel that the study of language, and of languages, must also be a study of persons who speak and write and think. My own understanding of language, and of such of the world's languages as I have learned, has become deeper and more illumined as I have moved beyond the meaning of words and texts to the meaning of the persons who use them. Each instance of language in use is a juncture of a cumulative tradition on the one hand, and on the other, of the personal activity of the heart and mind of some human being or beings.

This kind of consideration leads in the end to a sensitivity to the extent to which our whole modern culture is coloured by, and I have come to think is significantly skewed or even distorted by, our inveterate reifying or objectivizing of almost everything we touch or think about: our objectivity mania, and its objective-subjective dichotomy, our impersonalism. My sense is that the objective-subjective mind-set is a vast problem, and that I shall have long since died before our culture solves it, so deeply has it penetrated our outlook, and so richly has it served our culture in innumerable areas before its limitations began to surface.

Finally, let me touch on the two elements in that early book of mine — one that elicited perhaps the most significant outside criticism, the other my own querying—about which my later studies and thinking have led me to cogitate most carefully, without yet having reached a clarified articulation.

First, in proposing "tradition" and "faith," I was accused of underestimating the central, foundational importance of community, especially in religious life. I wrote of the Church and other social groups as both products and an engenderers, and nurturers, of faith. Yet I have come to see that nonethless I no doubt underplayed it, to say the least; underplayed the importance in human life, I would characteristically rather say, of our participating in community: the community-ness of being human. I have wrestled with this problem, and I am interested to hear comments. The reasons for my error — if error it was — are not far to seek. I hammered out my ideas on religion not in solidarity with the Christian Church, my religious community, from whom in fact at that time I felt myself relatively isolated; and indeed throughout, I have developed my ideas — not least, religious ideas — fairly much with a sense of solitariness; not to say, of being beleaguered. Only quite recently have I grown out of this. Another facet of this dilemma, however, less idiosyncratically mine, and indeed one in relation to which I could perhaps be perceived as rather representative of our modern world, is that the community of which I fundamentally felt a part is not the Church or an other formalized religious grouping; rather, it is undefined. In principle it is humankind as a whole, an ideal that has powerfully shaped my feeling and thinking and writing. In practice it is liberal intellectuals throughout the world — to whatever institutionalized group they may ostensibly belong.

This hesitation about identifying (that word is these days used far too glibly, too loosely; but I mean it here seriously) — this hesitation about identifying myself with my specifically religious community, indeed in general a distaste for people's identifying themselves with their specific boundaried communities, had been given powerful emotional as well as intellectual force by my experience in Lahore in the forties and the ensuing Partition of India, when a million people were massacred and ten million uprooted in inter-communal conflict. The continuing bitterness and hatred and devastation of this sort of conflict are still being vividly illustrated among Christians in Northern Ireland; with the Sikhs in the Punjab; in Palestine, in Lebanon, in Sri Lanka — but need I go on? I see uncritical social, or religious, conformism as an index of lack of deep faith. Yet so is lonely solipsism.

Despite this distrust of devoted or blind loyalty to one's mundane circumscribed group, I take community among persons very seriously indeed — religiously, one might say; more seriously, I should think, than do many intellectuals. This comes out, for instance, in my incorporating community among persons as a central factor in a theory of language; my including friendship as an integral element in epistemology (surely that is rare); love as constitutive of rationality; mutual understanding and "corporate self-consciousness" (*not* "inter-subjectivity"), as an avenue out of the subjective-objective polarity. I see modern secular individualism as pitiable and forlorn. Thus it was gravely awry if my writing gave an impression of embracing it. I deem human community as exceedingly important, and the striving to establish it as central to the moral and spiritual imperatives that faith lays on us.

Although admittedly there is an as yet unresolved, or at least unarticulated, issue here, my feeling is that it lends itself to solution, and with a little more work even to articulation, on the basis of my personalism, and my vigorous rejection of the subjective-objective polarity. I have been at pains to say that for me personal does not mean individual: "an individual becomes a person only in community; and a society can be either personal or impersonal."

The other point in the book about which I have had genuine second thoughts, and uncertainty, is my having rejected "religion" as a noun yet been willing to retain "religious" as an adjective, qualifying persons. My further studies and reflection have pushed me to doubt any final legitimacy or validity to the concept even for characterizing human beings, although I certainly recognize, of course, why one is tempted to dub one person more religious than another, or one phase of one's own or anyone else's life as more religious than another phase. Nonetheless it has become clear to me not only that what moderns wish to separate — by calling it "religion" — from what they regard as the straightforward everyday, has itself been in fact for most people at most times in most places straightforward and everyday; has been simply human. Being Hindu is not a way of being religious, but a way of being human, as I put it in *Faith and Belief*. So increasingly clear has this become as I have enlarged my study of world history that I have become restless with thinking that even the adjective "religious" has any viable meaning. Yet one cannot reasonably claim that there is no significant difference between those human beings, on the one hand, who are indifferent and those, on the other, who to varying degrees and at varying moments take seriously the great matters of life and of meaning and of morality and worth.

Recently I have found a solution to this problem, a profoundly humanist solution. It is this: that some people are more truly human than are others.

Since there is no universal agreement as to what constitutes being *truly* human, this puts us all — including those of us who are scholars, observers, secularists — nicely in our place. Would-be scientific types might hold that science is incapable of dealing with truth, and must therefore leave out of consideration what it means to be truly human. (In passing, that would force them to give up the view that secularism is true.) In any case, they should be compelled to recognize that the science of religion, as they would call it, is precisely a science endeavouring to make systematic, rational sense of the observable fact that most human beings at most times in most places have lived and thought in relation to the aspiration to be or to become truly human. Ours is the science of observing and trying to understand the answers that humankind has in theory and in practice given and is today giving, has tried to give and is today trying to give, to the question of what it means to be truly human, and how this is to be done.

I could go on. Whether or not one is ready to take seriously these later reflections, in any case may we not say that to see, as I did already in the book, the religious as an aspect of what it means to be human — and the study of religion as part of the general inquiry as to what it means to be human; and so the study of language, or economics, and so on — raises ramifying questions, of both metaphysics and history; and certainly, of academe. Some of those ramifying questions have kept me going for much of a lifetime, and could keep me going for many pages here. As that lifetime draws towards its end, it is more interesting to listen carefully to what others have, and will have, to say on the matter.

Références

Despland, Michel. 1979. *La religion en Occident: Évolution des idées et du vécu.* Héritage et projet, 23. Montréal: Fides.

Feil, Ernst. 1986. *Religio: die Geschichte eines neuzeitlichen Grundbegriffs vom Frühchristentum bis zur Reformation.* Forschung zur Kirchen- und Dogmengeschichte, 36. Göttingen: Vandenhoeck and Ruprecht.

Smith, Wilfred Cantwell. 1962 et seq. *The Faith of Other Men.* Toronto: Canadian Broadcasting Corporation. Rev. ed.; New York: New American Library, 1963; Mentor, 1964. London: New English Library, 1965. New York and London: Harper & Row, 1972. (Swedish trans., 1965. Korean trans., see below.)

———. 1963 et seq. *The Meaning and End of Religion.* New York: Macmillan, 1963. New York: New American Library; Mentor, 1964. London: New English Library, 1965. San Francisco: Harper & Row, and London: S.P.C.K., 1978. Minneapolis: Fortress, 1990. (Korean and Chinese translations are currently in process.)

———. 1967. *Questions of Religious Truth.* New York: Scribner's, and London: Victor Gollancz. (Also in Japanese, 1971.)

———. 1977. *Belief and History.* Charlottesville: University of Virginia Press. Paperback, 1987.

———. 1979. *Faith and Belief.* Princeton, NJ and Guilford, Surrey: Princeton University Press. Paperback, 1987.

———. 1981a. *Towards a World Theology.* London: Macmillan, and Philadelphia: Westminster. Paperback: London: Macmillan; and Maryknoll, NY: Orbis, 1990.

———. 1981b. *On Understanding Islam: Selected Studies.* Religion and Reason: Method and Theory in the Study and Interpretation of Religion, 19. The Hague, Paris, London, New York: Mouton. Delhi: Idarah-i Adabiyat-i Delli, 1985. Paperback: Berlin and New York: de Gruyter, 1984.

———. 1984a. "The Modern West in the History of Religion." *Journal of the American Academy of Religion* 52: 3-16.

———. 1984b. "Philosophia, as One of the Religious Traditions of Humankind: The Greek Legacy in Western Civilization, Viewed by a Comparativist." In *Différences, valeurs, hiérarchie: textes offerts à Louis Dumont*. Edited by Jean-Claude Galey, 253-79. Paris: Éditions de l'École des Hautes Études en Sciences Sociales. (Maisons des Sciences de l'Homme — Bibliothèque.)

———. 1988a. "Shall Next Century be Secular or Religious?" In *Cosmos, Life, Religion: Beyond Humanism*, 125-51. Tenri International Symposium '86. Tenri, Japan: Tenri University Press. (Also in Japanese.)

———. 1988b. "Transcendence." The Ingersoll Lecture. *Harvard Divinity Bulletin* 18, 3 (Fall): 10-15.

———. 1989. ["Faith in the Global Village."] Korean translation of *The Faith of Other Men*, translated by Kim Sung-Hae. Waegwam, Korea: Benedict Press.

CHAPTER 4

La religion en Occident :
Rétractations

Michel Despland

Il fallait s'y attendre : les travaux préparant la suite de *La religion en Occident* ainsi qu'une étude plus poussée des phénomènes religieux propres à la modernité ont amené des retours en arrière. La modernité, d'ailleurs, parvient-elle à se définir autrement que par rapport à ce qui l'a précédée ? Aidé aussi par les auteurs de compte-rendus, j'en suis donc arrivé au point où je peux mieux voir les défauts de l'ouvrage de 1979.
    1. Une première carence a été fort bien notée par J. S. Preus au terme de la recension publiée dans la *Religious Studies Review* (1986). À la fin du XVIIIe siècle, les horizons intellectuels du livre, subitement, se restreignent, et je n'y examine, au fond, que l'émergence, en Allemagne, de la philosophie de la religion, passant sous silence la montée de la science des religions. Après avoir examiné Bodin, Spinoza, Vico, Fontenelle, je ne mentionne pas Hume ! Ainsi je noue la gerbe pour tout ce qui, par le biais de la théologie naturelle, prépare l'une des deux grandes approches modernes, l'approche herméneutique, celle qui s'efforce de *comprendre* la religion, mais n'examine pas les antécédents historiques de l'autre approche, celle qui vise à *expliquer* la religion. Heureusement l'ouvrage de J. S. Preus *Explaining Religion* (1987) est venu combler cette carence et la lecture de son travail m'a aidé à rééquilibrer ma vision ou mieux régler mes jumelles avant de m'enfoncer dans la jungle qu'est le XIXe.
    2. Une deuxième carence m'est devenue apparente depuis que je suis allé plus loin dans le recours à l'histoire des mentalités et aux travaux d'anthropologie culturelle.[1] Il me semble qu'en 1979, je ne cernais pas vraiment la singularité culturelle de la France, comme on était alors en mesure de le faire.[2] Cicéron (*De legibus* I,24) faisait allusion aux choses *quibus cohaerent homines*; il est clair à mes yeux maintenant que la France médiévale puis moderne offre un exemple frappant de l'histoire de ces choses-là. Je voudrais donc maintenant mieux montrer la lente construc-

---

Les notes et références concernant ce chapitre se trouvent aux pages 26-27.

tion d'un ensemble culturel où moeurs, religion et politique se mettent à fusionner pour former un tout, qui est à la fois une volonté de vivre ensemble et la pratique heureuse d'une vie commune. Je voudrais, par exemple, me mettre à l'école de Paul Alphandéry, pour mieux montrer l'impact qu'ont eu les croisades, surtout celles qui sont allées par voie de terre, sur les mentalités populaires. Reprendre aussi les pages sur les «réalisations médiévales», en particulier sur «le processus d'extension de la religion» pour mieux souligner la variété et surtout la profondeur des phénomènes. J'aurais dû mentionner l'importation massive de reliques, qui amène en Occident les sacralités de l'Orient et répand de manière générale le droit de toucher au sacré. Et l'apprentissage généralisé des gestes rituels du pèlerinage. J'aurais pu signaler aussi le rituel d'entrée en léproserie, qui permet à des individus qui ne deviennent pas des moines, de passer par un rite d'initiation et d'entrer dans une fraternité. J'aurais pu examiner la montée des nombreuses associations pieuses et fraternelles (guildes marchandes ou confraternités), et mieux montrer ainsi comment se généralisent, en milieu urbain, des associations où des êtres se lient les uns aux autres par serment, des associations qui doivent donc être comptées (avec le processus de sacramentalisation et moralisation du mariage que je mentionnais déjà) au nombre des ramifications sociales du processus de «démocratisation» de la religion et de ses engagements et voeux. J'aurais pu enfin montrer la montée de la prière domestique : celle de laïcs qui, seuls ou en groupe, prient à la maison. J'aurais ainsi mieux illustré les montages culturels profonds qui ensemble constituent le processus que Georges Duby (1979:172) a si bien ramassé dans sa formule éloquente : «il n'y a plus de religieux dès que tous les chrétiens doivent l'être».

Tout au long du moyen-âge français, les chrétiens sont bel et bien devenus quelque chose de nouveau : un corps organique où coopèrent des individus qui ont profondément intériorisé leurs pratiques et leurs obligations et qui sont devenus à la fois liés intérieurement et ouverts les uns aux autres. L'histoire religieuse et civile de la France médiévale montre que le champ sémantique des mots *religio* puis *religion* s'est incarné dans un tout de pratiques culturelles généralisées. Le signe verbal a pris une puissance réelle : un peu à la manière du *hoc est corpus meum* de la messe, où le mot, en disant, crée.[3] La religion est ainsi entrée dans les moeurs nationales : des comportements caractéristiques ont été adoptés par les populations d'un vaste territoire; ils ont marqué de manière étonnamment cohérente tous les niveaux de la population, du roi jusqu'aux occupants des chaumières; ils se sont enfin installés dans l'histoire apparemment pour toujours; ils ont duré. La notion chrétienne de sainteté s'est emparée de l'espace, du temps, des modèles sociaux, et des modèles de perfection individuelle.[4] En d'autres termes, la religion est devenue une *civilisation*.[5]

Cette singularité culturelle peut aussi être signalée en parlant de *moralisation* de la foi, en ce sens que l'appartenance chrétienne assure dans le quotidien une certaine qualité de vie pour la collectivité historique.[6] Saint

Louis, pour dire qu'il préférait le chrétien, qui a acquis des vertus morales à celui qui n'en a pas, avait recours à la formule — qu'il faisait approuver par son chapelain — selon laquelle «prud'homme vaut mieux que béguin» (Joinville 1952:207). Le prud'homme n'est pas tant quelqu'un qui a intériorisé une loi; mais un être plutôt qui a la pratique des hommes, qui connaît le commerce humain et qui a de l'entregent (terme clef du premier des moralistes, Montaigne). Précisons donc bien qu'en parlant de moralisation, je veux signaler la construction dans l'histoire d'une conscience morale intersubjective: les rites, gestes et codes sociaux appris sont de ceux qui permettent la communication. En France les consciences sont toujours à la fois *Gewissen* et *Bewusstsein*; elles sont toujours conscientes les unes des autres (Despland 1987). Tout au long de l'histoire intellectuelle, il semble toujours aller de soi, selon la belle formule de Montesquieu, que les hommes «naissent tous liés les uns aux autres» (*Lettres persanes* 44).

L'amour courtois, la légende de Tristan et Iseut en particulier, nous offre un exemple éclatant d'accès généralisé à l'intersubjectivité. Le vin herbé diffère de tous les philtres amoureux que les soupirant(e)s administraient à l'objet de leurs désirs: il n'opère son sortilège que lorsque le couple le boit ensemble. Le désir érotique s'ajoute à l'obscure démangeaison du besoin; la tempête des passions s'enrichit à partir de la magie intersubjective de la séduction mutuelle. On retrouve d'autres indices du processus de socialisation dans la théologie des savants. L'insistance sur le caractère civil du bon chrétien se retrouve tout au long des siècles. À l'époque classique, les théologiens, toutes tendances confondues, saint François de Sales, Moïse Amyraut et Pierre Nicole, observent les moeurs, veulent les former et écrivent des traités de morale.

Il y a lieu aussi de parler dans le cas de la France d'un processus de *politisation* de la foi. Après avoir présidé à la création de l'unité nationale, la Couronne fait au XVIᵉ un choix politique: séduite par la musique de la formule «un roi, une loi, une foi», elle se prononce pour la vieille Église et contre les Réformés; il faut dire que par le Concordat de 1517 le pape avait accordé au roi le choix des évêques. L'État français en voie de constitution sous sa forme moderne trouve donc son intérêt à s'imbriquer de plus près avec l'institution écclésiastique. Un autre mot royal précise les arrêtes du phénomène: Louis XIV apprenant que le duc d'Orléans s'est lié avec le fils d'une janséniste est rassuré quand le duc ajoute que ce fils est athée: mieux vaut, dit-il, un athée qu'un janséniste, car on peut «le mener» (Saint-Simon 1952, II:980). L'expression médiévale «religion du roi» jouait avec bonheur sur l'ambiguïté entre le génitif subjectif et l'objectif; cette religion devient maintenant celle que le roi exige plus que celle qu'il partage avec ses sujets. (Les jansénistes qui se recrutaient dans la classe où le roi allait chercher les serviteurs dont avait besoin le nouveau type d'État, sont par leur indépendance religieuse une rude menace politique. Les athées, par contre, sont, croit-on, incapables de constance ou de fidélité; de toute façon au XVIIᵉ ils ne constituaient pas un parti.)

Mais une partie de la religion demeure en France indépendante de l'institution royale et écclésiastique. Quelque chose dans la civilisation nationale, dans la vie que partagent les populations, échappe au quadrillage serré établi par les lois du roi et celles de l'autorité en matière de foi. Ce reste on peut le nommer proprement religion. On le rencontre dans la religion populaire qui, selon la jolie expression de Dupront (1987:425) poursuit sur la lancée «agro-monastique» acquise au moyen-âge, et cela en dépit de la lutte serrée que mène la réforme catholique contre toutes les «superstitions». On la rencontre dans la religion que les Réformés diffusent, et maintiennent dans l'adversité. On la rencontre aussi chez les Jansénistes, qui refusent de s'incliner devant les pouvoirs, c'est-à-dire devant le roi, la Cour, et le pape, et acquièrent petit à petit, malgré leurs errances théologiques, une noblesse morale devant laquelle s'inclinent Voltaire, qui a été éduqué par les Jésuites, et Stendhal, qui est athée et anti-clérical.

En résumé, si je récrivais *La religion en Occident*, je voudrais mieux montrer comment en France la religion est devenue partie intégrante de la civilisation nationale, ciment, ou, mieux, levain de la vie collective, intimement imbriquée avec les phénomènes d'union sociale et de pratique du pouvoir, bref réalité morale et nationale à partir de laquelle les Français peuvent résister aux pouvoirs qui violentent l'unité nationale.

Une telle lecture des particularités de l'histoire française me placerait vraiment à pied d'oeuvre, prêt à bien saisir les caractéristiques de cette scène nationale au cours du XIXᵉ, mieux préparé en tout cas que le lecteur ne l'est au terme de sa lecture du texte de 1979. (Je rappelle que le livre s'achevait avec le contraste entre la «solution française», la laïcisation de l'État et des moeurs, et la «solution allemande», la constitution de la philosophie de la religion.) Comme nous le verrons ci-dessous, ces caractéristiques sont de deux ordres : il y a tout d'abord la manière dont les Français vivent la religion; il y a aussi la façon qu'ils ont d'y penser, de la penser, et donc d'organiser leurs entreprises «scientifiques» de connaissance de la religion.

Notes

1 Robert Muchembled (1988a) assure que la saisie des mentalités, «situées à la croisée des phénomènes quotidiens et des pratiques culturelles» en est arrivée à prétendre pouvoir décrire «la spécificité générique d'un groupe social précis dans un temps et un espace donnés». Son livre *L'invention de l'homme moderne* (1988b) recueille des articles qui montrent, dans le sillage de l'oeuvre de Norbert Elias, la lente organisation des cadres de vie modernes.

2 Jean Doré notait dans son compte-rendu (1982) que j'avais trop négligé les apports de la sociologie et de l'ethnologie.

3 Ce que dit Alphonse Dupront (1987:28) du mot *croisade*. Je rappelle que *La logique de Port-Royal* invoque dans sa cinquième édition (1683) la formule eucharistique pour

illustrer sa théorie de la représentation signifiante : l'énoncé crée la réalité. Voir L. Marin 1986 :35.
4 W. Oxtoby note (1987) qu'en anglais «holy» désigne ce que le locuteur vénère, alors que «sacred», qui ne se dit ni de Dieu ni des personnes, devient vite le qualificatif auquel ont recours ceux qui observent les attitudes religieuses de l'extérieur. On trouve en français un autre contraste. Il faut attendre le nationalisme républicain pour voir entrer l'adjectif «sacré» dans l'usage quotidien : l'«amour sacré de la patrie». Le langage de la piété chrétienne n'y connaît que ce qui est saint : sainte bible, sainte table, sainte vierge, saint ciboire, sainte ampoule, saint nom de Jésus et ainsi de suite. Ce sont les savants qui parlent d'espaces ou de temps sacrés : les fidèles parlaient et parlent encore de lieu saint et de semaine sainte; ils connaissent la différence entre un saint homme et un sacré bonhomme. Vases sacrés et Sacré Collège sont des usages savants. Quant au Sacré-Coeur, il s'agit d'une dévotion récente et l'adjectif ne s'applique qu'à une partie du Christ. L'usage québécois semble respecter la sainteté d'une manière particulièrement durable : les blasphèmes évitent l'adjectif : ciboire! vierge!
5 Notons, en passant, que pour ce dernier mot aussi, l'étude de l'histoire du mot débouche sur une histoire des idées et de la vie.
6 Roger Lapointe (1982) trouve que la morale est «le sous-thème» du livre.

Références

Despland, Michel. 1987. «Conscience». Dans *The Encyclopedia of Religion*. Vol. 4, 45-52. New York: Macmillan.

Doré, Jean. 1982. Recension de Michel Despland, *La religion en Occident*. Dans *Recherches de science religieuse*, 423-30.

Duby, Georges. 1979. *Saint Bernard. L'art cistercien*. Paris : Flammarion.

Dupront, Alphonse. 1987. *Du Sacré. Croisades et pèlerinages. Images et Langages*. Paris : Gallimard.

Joinville, Jean de. 1952. *Histoire de saint Louis*. Dans *Histoires et chroniqueurs du moyen-âge*. Paris : Gallimard, Pléiade.

Lapointe, Roger. 1982. «Le sous-thème d'un thème : perspective morale sur le livre de Michel Despland *La religion en Occident*». *Studies in Religion/Sciences religieuses* 11, 4 : 403-17.

Marin, Louis. 1986. «La parole mangée ou le corps divin saisi par les signes». Dans *La parole mangée et autres essais théologico-politiques*, 11-35. Montréal : Boréal.

Muchembled, Robert. 1988a. «Avant-Propos». Dans *Affaires de sang*, collection Mentalités. Paris : Imago.

———. 1988b. *L'invention de l'homme moderne* Paris : Fayard.

Oxtoby, Willard. 1987. «Holy, idea of». Dans *The Encyclopaedia of Religion*, Vol. 6, 431-38.

Saint-Simon, Claude Henri de Rouvroy. 1952. *Mémoires*. Vol. 2. Édition Truc. Paris : Gallimard, Pléiade.

DEUXIÈME PARTIE:

Les mots, l'histoire

PART TWO:

The Words, The History

CHAPTER 5

From the Classical Religio *to the Modern* Religion: *Elements of a Transformation between 1550 and 1650*

Ernst Feil

Introduction

The following presentation can be little more than a brief statement of the results which I have extracted so far from the period 1550 to 1650. I intend to carry the project on as far as 1800, that is, up until Hegel's philosophy of religion. And by far the greatest effort here, as far as I can see, would be to attempt to trace the beginnings of post-Enlightenment "religion." As far as my method is concerned, I can only say that each branch of knowledge develops a usable picture of its subject matter, like a mapmaker who is given a number of trigonometrical points from which to try and draw a map, in the hope that it will correspond with reality.

Michel Despland's work is unfortunately catalogued in the Munich State Library under the title of "history of religion." Its real subject is therefore very efficiently hidden from the library user. Had I, perhaps, known of the book by 1982-83, I might never have made a start on my own work. But since I only became aware of Despland's work when my first volume was completed, and since our working methods are very different, I decided to publish my own work as well. Despland's investigations are based on an extraordinarily large number of authors, whereas I restrict myself to a selected few, whom I can then study more thoroughly, and exclusively on the basis of original texts.

References for this chapter appear on pages 42-43.

The Conclusions Published in my Studies on "Religio. Die Geschichte eines neuzeitlichen Grundbegriffs vom Frühchristentum bis zur Reformation"

As far as conclusions are concerned, the main difference between me and Michel Despland is that I find, up to the middle of the sixteenth century, which is as far as my first volume goes, an astonishingly strong attachment to a classical and Roman concept of *religio*. I am therefore unable to discover different understandings of *religio* in the more than thousand-year history of the concept up to this point. *Religio* means the careful and even fearful fulfilment of all that man owes to God or to the gods. In this sense, *religio* means something very neccessary to man. It is by no means that which very generally lies at the bottom of all different opinions and persuasions, but on the contrary, something very concrete. It involves the careful enacting of rituals before political and military action, as well as, in fear and trembling, attending to every sacrifice and to other demands, handed down from the past to be passed on to future generations. Therefore, I will use the Latin word *religio* without translating it whenever it occurs in the original Latin text and meaning.

We can add, completely within this framework of meaning, that quite early (according to my research, already in the 7th century) *religio* became a designation for the communities of those people who dedicated their whole lives to the scrupulous and withdrawn service of God, the *religiosi*, which gave rise, of course, to the English expression "religious" for one belonging to such an order (R 76f.).

The first significant departure from this concept is to be found in a context far removed from the above, namely in the letters of Martin Luther (WA 9,24; R 244). Here we find a text from Melanchthon, a petition addressed to the Duke of Saxony. He says that various "worldly-wise" people — by which he means humanists and philosophers — hold every "argument about religion to be a playing with words," whereas in truth "every people of every age do hold one religion" and "the names alone changed." According to this there is only one "Religion," which bears different names, and, we may conclude, has different external manifestations. So far this is in fact the same concept we find in Goethe's "Faust," where we are told that, in religious argument, names are no more than "Schall und Rauch," "noise and smoke."

With Melanchthon it seems to me that we are not immediately dealing with a new meaning of "Religion," but in fact with the expression of a new structure: The essence of "Religion" is held in common; the names change; and it is not at all worth it to fight over them.

So far, I have discovered no one who actually held the position Melanchthon describes. We still do not even know whether those humanists and philosophers really existed, quite apart from determining which of them would have fallen under Melanchthon's condemnation. What his verdict hints at cannot be verified historically. We find again and again that accusations, such as that of "atheism," were brought far too easily against people who were under suspicion at that time, but these days seem to us to deserve no such suspicion.

The upshot of this research so far is that nowhere is *religio* used primarily as a generic term. It remains throughout on a level with other terms, frequently, even as early as Cicero, being used as part of a pair: *religio et pietas, religio et cultus*, and others, which suggests that on its own it does not express everything necessary to appropriate service of the gods. Furthermore, the term is not yet so abstract that it can take in the different forms of service and worship to be found among people of different nations and persuasions. A Roman would not have been able in this sense to speak of "Greek religion," since in his own land he would already have to deal with different *religiones*, that is, the cult due to each individual god.

Of course we have to keep in mind that the Greeks had no expression for *religio* in their language, and in fact saw no need for one. This disproves the assertion of the well-known Greek scholar Ulrich von Wilamowitz-Moellendorff (1848-1931) who, in his significantly named book *Der Glaube der Hellenen (What the Greeks Believed)* of 1931-32, maintained that we are able to talk of "Religion" in the Greek world, and that the Greeks themselves must have made use of the concept. He based his conclusion on the false premise that we cannot talk about humanity without at the same time talking about "religion."

Even in Christian usage, *religio Christiana* was not used as universal description for everything Christian, but only in relation to its claims that the Romans possessed no *religio*, but a *superstitio*, an idolatry. Christians made a point of designating their own belief as *fides*.

The Mid-Sixteenth Century

The next step was to use these results as a background for a closer analysis of the period immediately following to see if such a concrete and narrow concept of *religio* was to be maintained, for it is often said that *religio* is already being used in the modern universal sense by Giovanni Pico della Mirandola, if not by Nicholas of Cusa.

From the authors studied I have chosen Cardano, whose work I shall briefly analyze before summarizing the results of work on the Spanish Late Scholastics and on political writers, perhaps more correctly writers on political science.

Girolamo Cardano

I might not have dared to publish my examination of *Religio* if I had not happened upon Girolamo Cardano (1501-76). He was a doctor, a mathematician, a philosopher, and a humanist; and what we call a "cardanjoint" or "cardanshaft," is named after him. His unusually broad academic output includes a work on astrology. Of course, he leans on the traditions he knew well, referring to ideas held by Roger Bacon (1220-92 or later) and others, that the different persuasions we call "religions" are a result of stellar conjunctions. Bacon, when speaking of this theory, systematically places the different persuasions on the same level as regards their origins, and treats them even-handedly. He does not, however, speak of them as *religio* and *religiones*, but uses the expressions *sectae* (in the sense of schools of followers, from *sequi*, to follow, not *secare*, to cut) and, in particular, *leges*, laws. This term, *lex*, served as a matter of course to designate Jews, Christians, and Mohammedans, and occasionally heathens, too, whenever he wanted to speak of them in common.

In coming to grips with this astrological speculation, Cardano, too, does not use the term *religio* as a basic designation of separate persuasions. What he declines to accept is the traditional theory that there existed six such *leges*, and that the *lex Antichristi* was either contained in the six or was added to them as a seventh *lex*. Cardano's use of language is confirmed in his book *De subtilitate*, in which he also broaches our subject, but here in a way that was to make him many enemies, so much so that Gotthold Ephraim Lessing (1729-81) felt obliged to write in his defence. Cardano's book of 1552 presents us, in as clear a way as we could wish, with what he sees to be the four major persuasions: those of the heathens, the Jews, the Christians, and the Mohammedans. In Latin: *leges autem quatuor, idolorum, iudaeorum, christianorum et mahumetanorum*.

Neither here nor anywhere in this context does Cardano use the designation *religiones*, but *leges*. This expression is completely neutral. A *lex* can be found in every persuasion, and, surprisingly, in the case of the heathens, can for these purposes be used as a general term to include every aspect of whatever heathens, Jews, Christians, and Mohammedans have to do with God, or what he has to do with them. It may be used on the other hand to show what they have in common, so that the term is useful in making comparisons.

For me, this passage is a key proof that at this time, 1552, an author who was unusually well acquainted with tradition simply did not have at hand a general and universal usage for the word *religio*. If our usage were based on his, then we should find ourselves saying—instead of "the history of religions," "the philosophy of religion," "religious science"—"the history of lex," "philosophy of lex," "science of lex." *Lex* is genuinely for Cardano a common generic term. It is, by the way, used far more correctly to designate different persuasions, since *religio*, for Cardano's time and still later, implied the idea of *religio vera*, and thus, for Christians, can be said only of their Christian belief.

The Spanish Late Scholastics

Francisco de Vitoria

Of this theological school, I shall name two representatives, the first being its actual founder, Francisco de Vitoria (1482-1546). He was a Dominican, and was principally occupied with the problems which had been raised by the discovery of America. His particular contribution was the formulation of legal principles to be observed by the Spanish in relation to the aboriginal inhabitants of the continent. However much Vitoria worked for real rights for these people, he still considered them as "barbarians" who were in all respects inferior to his own culture. Despite this, he laid down that no one should be forced to embrace the faith, which was therefore no reason for waging war against them.

Vitoria's arguments use the expressions *fides* and *religio* basically only in regard to Christians, and the others are lumped together as unbelievers, heretics, or idolaters. In standing up for their rights, therefore, he was clearly not doing so because of his Christian belief, but rather simply because they were human beings. Since they are human, they have rights, and however barbarian they may be, they still possess institutions which are the result of human reason: they have a state and government; they marry; and finally, they have a sort of *religio*. As human beings they can participate in salvation, and thus they deserve to be treated as human, as was directed by Pope Paul III in 1537.

Francisco de Suárez

The second representative I have chosen from Spanish Late Scholasticism is Francisco de Suárez (1548-1619). He was a Jesuit, born almost twenty years after Bodin and a little more than a decade before Francis Bacon. In his time he decidedly took up the pen in defence of the true Christian faith against the Church of England. He also made a very clear study of *religio* in a very comprehensive book, the title of which already presents *religio* as possessing the two meanings, first of a virtue and then of a religious order. From one side we can see in this work Suárez's wish to follow Thomas Aquinas in defining *religio* as a virtue. But he goes beyond his master in giving up the strict subordination of this virtue to that of justice, which had been held obligatory over the centuries since Thomas. He was thus able to designate *religio* as *supernaturalis*, which would have been impossible for Aquinas and for the tradition which depended upon him. At the same time he gives this virtue of *religio* concrete meaning, by restricting it, in line with medieval tradition, to things which have to do with the honouring of God rather than with God directly. In this sense it has no link with the theological virtues of faith, hope, and love, which have directly to do with God and therefore with salvation. These are supernatural virtues, which consequently human beings cannot achieve all on their own.

In the end, Suárez's work remains ambivalent. He holds on quite fundamentally to the medieval tradition, but also seems to have sensed the limits of this tradition, which he tries to take into account. But, like it or not, this only serves to underline that Suárez's concept of *religio* as a virtue has nothing to do with the post-Enlightenment understanding of it. A virtue cannot be taken as an anthropological given, and Suárez does not use the term in connection with any other persuasion. For example, in his dispute with the Church of England, he prefers to call the Christians there *Anglicana secta*, *secta* again not so much meaning sect here as a group of followers.

Writers on Politica

Of course, authors dealing with political questions are of special interest here. For it is in this context that those—mostly civil—wars are discussed, which were the bloody result of the deep confessional divisions.

Those reflections on political themes are particularly interesting because it is frequently held that divisions of faith and the consequential civil upheaval were the main reason for the neutralisation of "religion," as a step on the way to reducing it to a private phenomenon. What has been claimed here is that various authors demanded and encouraged the removal of "religion" from public life in order to reduce conflict within a common society, if not to remove it altogether.

The authors I have dealt with are Jean Bodin (1529/30-96), Lambertus Danaeus (1530-95), Justus Lipsius (1547-1606), Johannes Althusius (1557-1638) and Bartholomäus Keckermann (1571-1609). Each of the authors believes unreservedly in God, and that God is both Creator and Preserver of the world. They are further one in the belief that there is only one true God and that therefore there should only be one appropriate form of worship. With a surprising unanimity they reject any form of atheism, not, though, on theological grounds, but rather political, in that an atheist is simply considered politically untrustworthy. A believer will always try to follow the laws of God—which are basically identical with the laws of nature—for any transgression brings with it fearful and eternal punishment. This moment of fear of eternal damnation becomes for these authors an important and even indispensable support for the common life in any society. Althusius's conclusion is that no atheist should under any circumstances be allowed to become a magistrate.

Although united on this point, the authors differ in the way they legitimate the political system. For Bodin, Lipsius, and Keckermann, the system develops from the ruler down, instead of finding its legitimation in the whole of the people, as in Althusius. Looking at the relevant works of these writers, however, it is surprising to find that there is little awareness of our particular problem. Only Lipsius holds the attitude of humanity to God important enough to give it a place of its own in his *Politica*. His immediate and basic approach to this attitude, however, is under the heading of *pietas*. Only later, looking at its public face, does he use the term *religio*. *Religio* would hence not appear to be a dominant concept, but rather one ordered alongside others, and this is the case throughout these authors. For example, Danaeus's key term is that of *cultus*, or *verus Dei cultus*. In these authors' writings, therefore, *religio* remains as a concrete attitude and lifestyle best understood in continuity with the classical meaning of the term, that is, the careful observance of everything owed to God by the human race.

These authors are also united in believing that the only way to worship the one God is the one *religio*, the *religio vera*. They then have the difficulty of coming to terms with what to do when the unity of faith is broken. Overwhelmingly they look to bring every citizen to this one true worship through example rather then by force, quoting a passage from Cassiodorus which maintains that people cannot be brought to *religio* by order.

Whenever it comes to this question of inner peace, the authors seem, however, rather helpless. Frequently they assign considerable competence in the area of worship to the ruler or magistrate. Beside the one true worship established, others may at most be tolerated, but would of course not be acceptable to the authors themselves. And they do not even make it entirely clear which one is really true, but rather tacitly seem to accept that it must be their own. As a criterion of the truth of their own persuasion reference is made to Scripture, but practice shows its inadequacy as a source of final proof.

To summarize: each author's arguments are based on an express belief in God. This belief has political consequences, creating a fear which prevents the infringement of divine and natural law. There is no innovation in the question of *religio* or its associated concepts *pietas* and *cultus*. There is no suggestion that worship be considered politically neutral, as in this case the magistrate would be expected merely to ensure that each individual community meet only privately and organize its own services and other practical elements of its particular belief. But this is not the case. We must then conclude that the stuff of *religio* remains the same for these authors as for their predecessors, that is, they consider it to be a concrete attitude and lifestyle revolving around the worship of God, and we have no reason to go beyond this. A serious attempt to designate different beliefs and groups with the term *religio* is nowhere to be found.

The Transition to the Enlightenment: Bodin's religio naturalis

The authors dealt with so far are still only from the sixteenth century. Suárez and Lipsius were born just before the middle of the century, and Althusius just after. Only Keckermann was born after 1570, but by 1609 he was already dead. Of the others, Suárez survived the turn of the century, living until 1619, and most notably Althusius, who died in 1638, saw a good part of the seventeenth century. We have seen, however, that there is no reason to set the beginning of transition with them.

However, it has long been known that Jean Bodin, some twenty years older than Suárez and Lipsius, put together an influential *Colloquium heptaplomeres* in 1593, three years before his death. This work therefore appeared twenty years before the last work of Suárez, only four years after the *Politica* of Lipsius, and about ten years before Althusius came into circulation. I need not say that we are dealing here specifically with *religio naturalis*; since no earlier use of the term was known, he was said to have invented it. (Thus the articles on Deism in the *Brockhaus-Encyclopaedia* IV, 379, and, more cautiously, in *Lexikon für Theologie und Kirche* III, 296.) At this point, I want to stress that in his *Six livres de la République*, which were written twenty years earlier, the term *religio naturalis* is not to be found.

Christoph de Cheffontaines

But the very developed account of *religio naturalis* in Bodin's *Colloquium* suggests that he is not its inventor. Detailed research has so far not brought to light any satisfactory answer to this problem. However, in the figure of Christoph de Cheffontaines (c. 1532-95) — his name translated into Latin as *de Capite fontium* — we find in a Catholic theologian and near contemporary of Bodin a very important first indication of the use of the formula as if taken from an earlier source. This Franciscan Archbishop of Caesarea produced in 1586 a tract on *Novae illustrationes christianae fidei* against libertines, atheists, epicureans, and other sorts of unbelievers. He consistently makes use of the concept *naturalis ratio*, and maintains that its conclusions are the same as those of Christian faith, or at least point in the same direction. His own reflections on the topic are under the title of *fides* and not *religio*. Toward the end of his argument, he says as a matter of course, that the basic contents of Christian faith, that is, the *vera religio* are the same as those of the *naturalis religio*. In his summing up he uses this term quite routinely to designate those of his opponents against whom he is defending the Christian faith, and to whom he has been trying to point out that what they put forward as *naturalis religio* is in fact at base the same as the Christian faith.

From the way he uses the term it would seem well within the bounds of possibility that such a term existed and was used in the French philosophical tradition toward the end of the sixteenth century. The impression is that Cheffontaine, unlike Melanchthon earlier, is not developing his own term to apply to his adversaries.

In view of the absence of reference to the term *naturalis religio* in Bodin's six books on the state, as well as by all the authors we have looked at, up to and including the writers on *Politica*, its appearance seven years before Bodin's *Colloquium* is outstandingly significant.

Bodin's Colloquium heptaplomeres

Without doubt this text of Bodin's overshadows the previous and more or less incidental opinions expressed up to then on the theme of *religio*.

Bodin's *Colloquium* is sufficiently well known that I shall restrict myself to making just a few remarks. Bodin presents us with a disputation in the great tradition of the Middle Ages, dating from patristic times, and popular especially since Abelard. This old tradition always involved the demonstration of the truth of one's own belief against other, untrue persuasions. It took precedence over the other early medieval tradition of the three rings: One was real and the other two such perfect forgeries that the real ring could not be distinguished from the other two. This parable was in fact given a late lease on life by Lessing in his *Nathan der Weise*. However, instead of the usual two, or at most three, disputants, Bodin goes beyond tradition by presenting us with seven. There are three who present Christian beliefs, one former Christian who has converted to Islam, a Jew, and two additional figures, both of whom represent *religio naturalis*, although it is difficult to tell the difference between the two. Bodin designates all of these persuasions not just *religiones* but *sectae* as well, the latter in the classical Latin sense not of "sects" but of parties of followers. They are judged by the criterion of age, that is, whether they correspond to the *religio* that existed before the Flood. Of course, each persuasion claims this period for its own, the representatives of *religio naturalis* just as much as the Jews.

The debate begins hesitantly, as the participants are worried about whether it is appropriate to debate the subject at all. It yields no conclusions, insofar as no one is persuaded of the truth of another's position. The disputants nevertheless wish to remain in friendly contact with each other, but want no further debate on this subject.

Religio performs the same function here as *secta*. The term may be made use of by different persuasions, and each of them may claim to be the *religio vera*, in comparison to which all the others are merely *superstitio*. In contrast, the ring parable allows no more for classification of any one of the three as idolatry. In addition, Bodin uses the word *religio* in conjunction with other terms, for instance *fides*. This is a sign that we are still not looking at a generic term which would include *fides* in itself. The term then might still mean the same as in classical tradition: "the careful observance of what has to be done with regard to the gods."

What is remarkably new about Bodin's *Colloquium* is that it contains not one, but two new and unusual sorts of *religio naturalis*. This is where questions arise which I intend to take up further, and eventually hope to make at least a little clearer. What is the precise difference between these two, and to what, or whom, precisely do they refer? In addition, I would be interested to know why the dialogue takes place in Venice. Is this just an accident? I came across a text of Henri Etienne (Henricus Stephanus), the sixteenth-century French humanist and publisher, according to which Guillaume Postel made in Venice a statement on *religio* which Etienne is very concerned to counter, because it is heretical. Now I ask myself whether this much respected and much disputed author was in Bodin's mind as a participant in his disputation. In short, as far as I can see, this *Colloquium* presents us with a whole lot of questions which as yet have no answer. It is clear, anyway, that somehow a decisive new start is being made here, though how new remains to be seen.

Francis Bacon and Tommaso Campanella

As we have to be brief, two completely contrasting authors must be dealt with here together. But as near contemporaries they demonstrate the very different ways in which *religio* was treated in this period.

The thinking of Francis Bacon (1561-1626), both in his *Novum organum* and in his reflections on knowledge and science, as well as elsewhere, can be summarized as follows. The existence of God is unwaveringly accepted, even in the framework of philosophy, with the result that Bacon considers it appropriate to see *theologia naturalis* as *divina philosophia*. What God has to say to us can be read by means of two books, that of Revelation and that of Nature. In deciding to work with the latter, Bacon leaves Revelation entirely to theology and insistently argues against any mixture of the two, and any attempt to derive scientific knowledge from Revelation. Thus the position of *religio* remains ambivalent. An important passage in the last book of his *De dignitate et augmentis scientiarum* separates the principles of *religio* from reason in such a way that not only *fides* but also *religio* with it takes up a separate compartment alongside that of reason. He can therefore name both "healthy reason and religion" as the two requirements for the right use of the discoveries of natural science.

In contrast, Tommaso Campanella (1568-1639) is the first writer I have come across to have written genuinely on the theme of *religio*, in his *Metaphysica*. The result is that *religio* belongs to the study of philosophy and lies squarely within the purview of reason. To say this is not quite enough, however, since Campanella at the same time characterizes *religio* as being something revealed by God, thus based on *fides*. But Campanella is also aware of a *fides naturalis*. He is one of the first writers after Bodin explicitly to accept a *naturalis religio*, as different from Bacon, where this term cannot be found. Campanella also speaks of a *religio politica*.

But neither he nor Bacon allow *religio* to move out of the concrete and practical. Campanella even names the different "acts" of *religio*: adoration; sacrifice; prophetic direction; blessing; oath; prayer. This is precisely the same as Thomas Aquinas's approach to the separate acts of the virtue of *religio*. It is also significant that Campanella does not oppose *religio naturalis* to a *religio supernaturalis*, but to one *artificialis*: *religio* that requires set forms of observance. *Religio naturalis* for Campanella is hence one and the same in every case. Nonetheless he also speaks of *superstitio*. It seems to me very significant that he is the first to revive the idea of three different persuasions that are so similar they cannot be distinguished, a fable which he claims to have found in Boccaccio. I want to emphasize that in this context Campanella is taking up the old term *leges*.

Edward, Lord Herbert of Cherbury and Thomas Hobbes

The last figures in this survey of my recent studies are again contemporaries whose positions differ considerably.

Edward, Lord Herbert of Cherbury (1583-1648), is well known for his intensive studies on truth as well as on *religio*. He is the first author expressly to argue for an idea of *religio* which is now entirely a matter of reason and separate from *fides*. In theology, and more importantly, in history, *fides* is founded on the evidence of witnesses, and hence does not lead to the truth, but to probability, in the sense of the nearest appearance to truth (*veri-simile*) that can be achieved at least on earth.

In contrast to this, Cherbury places *religio* with the general principles (*communes notitiae*) which derive from universal truth itself and represent the truth that can be found by understanding and intellect. *Religio* is characterized by Cherbury through five principles: that God exists; that he must be worshipped; that religion is the highest virtue found in worship; that it frees from sin; and that after this life it is the giver of reward and punishment. This very comprehensive list, fundamentally identical, of course, with Christian beliefs, is firmly placed by Cherbury in the realm of human knowledge and certain truth, not in the realm of faith, which, as has been said, ends up in probability.

Lord Herbert of Cherbury is looked on by historians of philosophy as the father of deism. But this is, as I shall point out at the end, by no means so definite. Let it simply be said here that Cherbury, significantly, used the expression *religio naturalis* only once, in a manuscript, the published version of which has the phrase removed. In enumerating the general principles characterizing *religio* he is still moving within the framework of the *theologia naturalis*, which was believed to be arguable philosophically. Cherbury's specific contribution is not in fact this description, but the considerable distinction he makes between reason and faith.

In contrast, Thomas Hobbes (1588-1679) works out for himself a different concept of *religio*. My comments are based on his book, *De Cive*, of 1642. Alongside the worship of God which results from natural reason, there exists a form of revelation such as that given to Abraham. The worship which comes from this is not a *cultus rationis* but *religionis et fidei*. But the concept *religio naturalis* appears only once; normally, *religio* in this book means a revealed one, in a special pact of God with us. We can summarize, then, that Hobbes, in this book mainly speaks of *religio et fides*, deriving from God's revelation.

Conclusion

The positions presented here serve as a sufficiently clear warning to avoid exaggerated schematisation and interpretation. There is no continuous development to be discerned, but rather, the co-existence of concepts alongside and also in opposition to one another. Among all these separate pieces in the mosaic there is but one new one to be found, the significant contribution of Bodin in his *Colloquium heptaplomeres*. But even here we must be careful, since *religio* still retains its fundamental concrete meaning, that is, the careful fulfilment of what God has commanded. *Religio* preserves in itself this relevance to the external, as we see particularly in Hobbes. But against this we can see the first signs of an inner *religio*. This remark of Bacon is about the most progressive element of the thoughts we have been dealing with. The formulation of a *religio naturalis* seems to me to be a significant forerunner to the Enlightenment, but from Bodin until about 1650 this concept made no real breakthrough. And it is suprising, too, that Descartes hardly touched on the topic. These results suggest extreme caution in reading a "philosophy of religion" into this historical scene. The nearest thing to it can be found in Campanella, apart from which there is nothing that would fit the bill.

The caution required becomes evident in the case of Cherbury being called the father of "deism." Now "deism" is universally taken to be a philosophy which acknowledges God as creating the world in order then to have nothing more to do with it. The term is first attributed — and I have been able to find nothing to the contrary — to Pierre Viret (1511-71). Only a few years later, in 1569, a certain Gabriel Prateolus Marcossius uses the term *deistae* to designate the Sociniani, the followers of Fausto Sozzini (1539-1604), who denied the Trinity. But to do this is not to reduce God to one who has nothing more to do with creation, nor has it any link with a *religio naturalis*. And the source and original meaning of this term was still known in the eighteenth century, in Heinrich Zedler's *Groaes Universallexikon*. A final instructive example, maybe, showing that we should pay heed to the precise and confined meaning of the words we use. For only in this way will the work we do be convincing.

Hinweise

I would like to give a sincere vote of thanks to Gérard Vallée: He first of all drew my attention to Michel Despland's book while on a visit to Munich in 1984. Then, as soon as my own book appeared, he wrote a review of it, which inspired Michel Despland to suggest we should have a conference. Finally, he invited me to this conference and did a great amount of preparatory work.

The foregoing explanations refer first of all to E. Feil, *Religio. Die Geschichte eines neuzeitlichen Grundbegriffs vom Frühchristentum bis zür Reformation* (= Forschungen zur Kirchen- und Dogmengeschichte 36), Göttingen 1986.

The studies on the subsequent authors will be published soon by Vandenhoeck and Ruprecht.

References

Althusius, Johannes. 1610. *Politica, methodice digesta* (1603). Arnhemii.
Bacon, Francis. 1858-61. *The Works of Francis Bacon*, hg. von James Spedding, Robert Leslie Ellis und Douglas Denon Heath. London.
Bodin, Jean. 1576. *Les six livres de la République* (1576). Paris, 1583, Reprogr. Nachdruck Aalen, 1961.

Bodinus, Joannes. 1857. *Colloquium Heptaplomeres de abditis rerum arcanis.* Edited by Ludovicus Noack. Schwerin, 1857; reprogr. Neudruck Hildesheim 1970.
Campanella, Tommaso. 1967. *Metafisica,* ed. Giovanni di Napoli (= Collana di Filosofi moderni). Bologna.
Cardanus, Hieronymus. 1663. *De Libris propriis.* In ders., *Opera Omnia.* Lugduni, Reprogr. Neudruck Stuttgart-Bad Cannstatt, 1966.
———. *De Subtilitate.* In ebd.
Lord Herbert von Cherbury, Edward. 1645. *De Veritate.* London: Reprogr. Neudruck Stuttgart-Bad Cannstatt, 1966.
Christoforus de Capite-fontium. 1586. *Archiepiscopus Caesariensis, quondam generalis Minister ordinis Minorum, Novae illustrationes Christianae Fidei adversus impios Libertinos, Atheos, Epicureos, et omne genus infideles.* Paris, 1586.
Danaeus, Lambertus. 1596. *Politicae Christinae libri septem,* o. O.
[Henri Estiene/Stephanus]. 1568. *L'introduction au traité de la conformité des merveilles anciennes avec les modernes ou traité préparatif à l'apologie pour Hérodote.*
Hobbes, Thomas. 1642. *De Cive* (Orig. Title: *Elementorum Philosophiae Sectio tertia de Cive,* Titel der weiteren Auflagen: *Elementa philosophica de Cive*), edited by Howard Warrender. Oxford 1983.
Keckermann, Bartholomäus. 1606. *Systema Disciplinae Politicae, publicis praelectionibus Anno 1606 propositum in Gymnasio Dantiscano.* Francoforti 1625.
Lipsius, Justus. 1589. *Politicorum sive Civilis doctrinae libri sex.* Lugduni.
Prateolus Marcossius, Gabriel. 1569. *De vitis, sectis, et dogmatibus omnium haereticorum, qui ab orbe condito, ad nostra usque tempora, et veterum et recentium authorum monimentis prodidi sunt.* Elenchus Alphabeticum, Coloniae.
Suárez, Francisco. 1859. *De virtute et statu religionis.* In ders., *Opera omnia,* edited by von Carolus Berton. Paris.
———. *De virtute religionis.* In ebd.
———. *Defensio fidei Catholicae adversus Anglicanae sectae errores* (1613). In ebd.
de Vitoria, Francisco. 1952. *De Indis recenter inventis et de jure belli Hispanorum in Barbaros Relectiones. Vorlesungen über die kürzlich entdeckten Inder und das Recht der Spanier zum Krieg gegen die Barbaren.* Edited by Walter Schätzel (= Die Klassiker des Völkerrechts in modernen deutschen Übersetzungen 2). Tübingen.
Viret, Pierre. 1564. *Institution Chrestienne en la doctrine de la loy et de l'Évangile: et en la vraye philosophie et théologie tant naturelle que supernaturelle des Chrestiens . . . ,* 1: *Briefs et divers Sommaires et Catéchismes de la doctrine Chrestienne. . . .* Genève; 2: *Exposition de la foy Chrestienne, touchant la vraye cognoissance et le vray service de Dieu . . . .* Genève.

CHAPTER 6

The Reified Heart in Seventeenth-century Religion

J. Samuel Preus

Introduction

The appearance of powerful trajectories of thought running in two opposite directions is a puzzling seventeenth-century paradox: one trend is "reification" — the objectifying of many aspects of culture, such as politics and religion, as well as the realm of nature itself. On the other hand, when we look at the movements within religious life peculiar to that century, we cannot fail to notice that the real action is taking place in the interior: religious vitality is expressing itself simultaneously across Europe in pietistic movements. Consider the intensely inward-oriented writings of Spener, Pascal, and Bunyan — all writing about the same time. These and dozens of other writers testify to the continued vitality of seventeenth-century religion alongside and in spite of the gathering power of sceptical and critical analyses of religion (e.g., from Hobbes, Spinoza, LaPeyrère, Bayle, etc.).[1]

Originally, I took this paradox to be evidence simply of the intellectual fragmentation of European culture into separate spheres no longer in conversation with one another — one devoted to objectification, the other to subjectivity. Furthermore, guided both by contemporary sources and secondary studies, I uncritically assumed that the truly vital signs of religiousness belonged exclusively to the latter side of this disjunction.

What follows is a revision of that view. I am much more inclined now to see the objectifying tendencies of the century to be quite indifferent to the question of religious commitment or detachment, or even to the distinction between the inner and outer. Consider for instance the appearance, historically, of new terms, new cultural universals: how are we to explain and understand them? One example is particularly pertinent: the expression "religious experience." One could hardly think of a more

---

Notes and references for this chapter appear on pages 52-56.

familiar term today than this reification of an inner event, or series of events. Everyone uses it, seems to know what it means. Nobody questions its usefulness. And yet one will not find it in Calvin or Luther, Aquinas or Augustine, Paul or Jesus, or even the Psalms.

I don't know when the term "religious experience" first appeared (it was, of course, decisive for Schleiermacher, c. 1800, and canonized by William James, c. 1900), but the seventeenth century is certainly its generative context. Whenever exactly one does locate it, once it becomes part of common speech, it signifies that a certain zone of experiences has been seen in a new way, and congealed in people's minds sufficiently that a new universal has been created — an abstraction that stands for things concrete and particular, an expression that can henceforth be used without explanation. Somehow everyone knows what it refers to; ordinary discourse cannot seem to get along without it. My general point is that one finds such new terms emerging at the end of a process of development in which it has come to stand for "something" whose reality is commonly acknowledged (comparable in the early eighteenth century is the arrival of a new literary genre called "the novel" — see McKeon).

To come quickly to my thesis: the motivation and significance of the intensely inner-oriented religiousness of the seventeenth century (at least in England) is not its *opposition* to reification of "religion."[2] Rather, we witness there a novel reification of inner religious events, of the innermost reaches of religious life. It is this reification that eventually gives rise to the modern term "religious experience" as our obligatory identifying term for the generative spring of religiousness. Furthermore, reification in this instance is obviously not a signal of alienation from religion, but, on the contrary, an aspect of its intensification, featuring relentless analysis and answering to specific, identifiable religious needs.

My focus here is English Puritans of the seventeenth century, although I think this line of inquiry could be extended to parallel inward-oriented or pietistic movements elsewhere in Europe.[3] More particularly, I shall focus on the Puritans in their use of the Bible, because there one can watch this process — this reification of interiority — developing, exemplified in the works of Baxter and Bunyan but evidenced in thousands of seventeenth-century sermons, pamphlets and books. I am interested in discovering how, at this time and place, the great Protestant experiment of reforming individuals, as well as social and religious life in general, on the basis of a book — how that theory worked in actual use — in the lives of devout and literate Protestants — of whom there were suprisingly many at this time! In other words, my focus here is not hermeneutics, but the more unequivocally religious act of divination (cf. J. Z. Smith, and Loewe and Blacker).

The Bible and Protestantism

Protestant Christians proposed to stake their relationship with God on the claim that the Bible was both sufficient and sufficiently clear to instruct them in all the necessities of faith and life.

This astonishing innovation engendered a new form of religiousness on this planet. Insufficient attention has been paid in our circles to the momentous impact of the prior technological innovation that made this innovation possible — printing. Consider: without Martin Luther, there would have been a Reformation, more or less, in the sixteenth century. But without the printing press, not a chance. No wonder Luther himself referred to the invention of printing as God's "greatest grace." Could Luther have sat drinking beer with Melanchthon, and said "I did nothing; the Word did it all" in the age of hand-copied manuscripts? Not likely. In John Foxe's judgment as well, printing was a miracle (Haller 1963:110).

Recent scholarship has shown how profoundly the reform movements depended on the presses, while the growth of the printing business in turn depended on the new demand for Bibles, hymnals, and other religious literature for an increasingly literate laity (Stone, 1969).

Printing may, in fact, be the decisive causal factor in the phenomenon of reification for, as Michael McKeon observes, writing reifies memory. Furthermore, he says, "The physical preservation of knowledge produces not only documents and archives but also the conditions for the 'objective' comparison of data, even the inclination to regard knowledge [itself] as a collection of discrete 'objects' " (McKeon 1987:29). (The scientific revolution, as well as the Reformation, depends on this.) In the religious sphere one could instance the great polyglot Bibles of the time, the massive chronicles of the German Centuriators, the beginnings of comparative studies of non-European cultures, comparative studies of ancient myths and chronologies, collections of martyr stories (Foxe's great book) — all "reifications" of hitherto unavailable material poised to make a permanent impact on religious life and thought. Through the medium of print, in an unprecedented way, objectified materials bearing on or even mediating the reader's very salvation, were laid out in full array.

Above all, of course, the Bible. Among English Puritans we find Bible reading already firmly established as a necessity for salvation in the sixteenth century (Haller, 1963:52). Several scholars have, with considerable justification, dubbed this activity the "sacrament" of Protestantism. Bible reading was indeed a "means of grace," the very medium and instrument of interaction by which the Spirit conveyed to the person's expectant heart the knowledge and assurance of God's favour.[4]

And just as the sacraments had been seen as real instruments of interaction, so now the very speaking of God or Jesus to the heart could occur through reading, hearing, or remembering the Word. The Biblical word in the Spirit's hand took on what Knott aptly calls a "kinetic" quality for the faithful. In *Grace Abounding*, Bunyan portrays the Word (not always a Biblical text, and by no means always conveyed in the act of reading) coming upon him when it will: it "falls" on him with "great weight" or like a "hot thunderbolt"; it "darts from Heaven" into his soul, "bolts," "pinches," "tramples," "breaks in," "seizes, tears and rends" his soul. In *The Pilgrim's Progress* as well, the Word is reified as a separate character with a will and plan of its own.[5]

This leads to the central matter of this paper — what I call the "reified heart."

The Emergence of the Self as the "Text"

As previously noted, I am interested here in actual use of the Bible rather than in hermeneutical theory. Rereading *The Pilgrim's Progress* recently in hopes of understanding it as biblical commentary, I was captivated by the closing lines of its opening section, wherein the author teases his readers with the question, "Wouldst *read thyself* . . . ? Oh, then come hither, and lay my book, thy head, and heart together" (italics mine).

Just as Socrates held the aim of the dialectic to be "Know thyself," Bunyan saw *his book* as an instrument for "reading" the self. So also did he and his co-religionists view the Bible. Now, simply reading *The Pilgrim's Progress* as a literary text is easy on one level: the lessons are direct and clear, and Bunyan glosses the margins lest anyone should miss the point — just as the Geneva Bible glossed the text lest any lay reader should fail to grasp its obvious Calvinist sense. But *using* these books is another matter. Increasingly, the entire problem for Puritan reading was to learn how to apply the clear threats, laws, promises of the text to one's own life through spiritual analysis of experience.[6]

Why was the "reading of the self" so important? The prime reason in these cricles seems to have been that the self had to be rigorously examined to discover evidence of one's election. Dozens of texts can be quoted to this effect, accompanied by excruciatingly detailed spiritual inventories.[7]

Especially important to notice here is the necessity of rigorous objectivity — detachment even — in this analysis. At your soul's peril, you had better see yourself *as God sees you*, not as your wishes and desires dictate. Cultivating such objectivity, one had to learn how to reify one's very heart — as a thing, an "it": "Reader," Baxter demands, "when was the time . . . that ever thou solemnly tookest thy Heart to task, as in the sight of God, and didst examine it by Scripture, whether it be renewed or not? whether it be holy or not?" (Baxter 1825:135f.). Again: "If thy heart draw back from the work, force it on. Lay thy command upon it," etc. (147). An introspective trial of one's own heart, with full examination of all evidence, was only a preliminary to the Last Judgment; one could not afford to be anything but absolutely clear headed and detached,[8] and there must be no tampering with the evidence.

God had given the Scriptures as the instrument and criterion for conducting this inquiry. A common metaphor was Scripture as mirror, or looking-glass, in which to discover the state of one's soul and the rule for living (Knott 1980:77). But, Haller notes, "telling people to look for the rule of life in a book which mirrored life with such variety and intensity was like telling them to look in life itself" (Haller 1963:53). The result was that their own lives became their "text" — the *interpretandum* — while the inspiring Scripture functioned as the *interpretans* — the instrument for extracting the spiritual significance from the most mundane occurrences.[9]

A further aspect of this exercise bears our attention: since God's decree was eternal and unchangeable, there was nothing they could do but watch: "They were only the witnesses of a drama which moved to its predetermined end according to a law they could do no more than marvel at.... They watched its unfolding, therefore, with the most absorbed attention" (Haller 1972:90f.). Observers, as it were from outside, of the reified soul.

What readers looked for was evidence that would match their own spiritual experiences to those of the biblical figures such as Paul, David, Job, following "by intense introspection the working of the law of predestination within their own souls" (Haller 1972:90f.). Their "reading" could not be a scholarly one, but every Christian could learn to read spiritually what was available to each and all — their own everyday experience.

Haller aptly compares spiritual writers to the natural scientists. In England, where people were predominantly empiricists, the language shows that the religious writers were in some respects as rigorous, demanding, sceptical, and experimental as the early scientists. Spiritual theory was, as Haller observes, "inevitably subjected to the testing of observation and experience" (Haller 1972:135). One had to accomplish the verification of Scripture in the laboratory of one's own heart.

Indeed, Bunyan reports periods of desperation in trying to grasp the Scriptural promises — desperation not because he couldn't understand them, but because he couldn't believe that they were meant *for him* (Bunyan 1962:77). This nearly drove him mad, for he was under the influence of a fairly typical Puritan teacher who, Bunyan reports, "pressed us to take special heed, that we took not up *any truth on trust*, as from this or that or another man or men, but to cry mightily to God, that he would convince us of the reality thereof... for... if you do otherwise, when temptations come,... you not having received them with *evidence from heaven*, will find you want [lack] that... strength now to resist" (Bunyan 1962:37; italics mine). Like a scientist, Bunyan searches for the causes of severe temptation and gives careful consideration to alternative explanations. He conducts an empirical test of whether God can read his inner thoughts; he examines — with frightening results — "my *Evidences* for that blessed world to come," while Satan at his elbow taunts him with lack of such "*evidence*" (Bunyan 1962:75, 79, 100; italics mine).

"Experience" and "experiment" are used interchangeably in this literature. Puritan preachers were trained (especially at Cambridge) "to subject all doctrine to the test of experience. Thus the preachers made experiment a familiar word on the plane of religion and morals long before it became supreme on that of natural science" (Haller 1972:299).

It was Protestant dogma that the literal meaning of Scripture was not problematic, at least regarding matters necessary for salvation.[10] The problem was particular application, the difficulty of which was heightened because the Puritan/Protestant stood alone before God. He had no authoritative tradition, no mediating institution, no massive ritual reinforcement to fall back on. Everything depended on inner, individual verification of the objectively given word. For that reason, these writers would refer to experience as "a second Scripture" (Lewalski 1979:160) — even as better than Scripture[11] because it revealed God's particular will.[12] The very "truth" of Scripture, then, could come to depend on the Christian's ability to verify its personal applicability.[13]

This whole trend of biblical usage constitutes an epochal change in the history of interpretation, because making one's self the text involves a reversal of traditional allegorical interpretation of Scripture. The Puritan, driven into the world to pursue his God-given vocation, must learn to "allegorize" his own *experience* rather than the scriptural text — that is, must learn to construe his everyday *life* as a spiritual narrative, to grasp the spiritual depths beneath the literal surface meaning — not of his Bible, but of his experience, new every day and never stable.[14] Scripture provided the "construing book," as Isaac Ambrose called it, "to the book of God's Providences" (Kaufmann 1966:210). McKeon perfectly captures the religious sense of the Puritan's reflexive allegory when he says, regarding Christian in *The Pilgrim's Progress*, "life for Christian and his readers is a matter of perpetual and self-conscious interpretation. It entails a responsibillity not to 'demystify' experience, but on the contrary to disabuse it of its material self-sufficiency" (McKeon 1987:295).

Bunyan may be the master "reifier" of the century, for in *The Pilgrim's Progress* his vividly concrete imagination renders profound spiritual and moral situations and attributes as physical objects, events, and characters. The inner world is turned utterly inside out, and laid before our eyes as a physical landscape, through which the soul must make its pilgrimage.

We noted earlier the impact of printing on the reification of memory, and of culture generally. Not just reading, but the new-found ability to *write* also contributed to the reification and routinization[15] of religious experience. Christians were encouraged to keep diaries: "When night comes," Henry Vaughan (a lyric poet) advised, "list thy deeds; make plain the way / Twixt Heaven, and Thee" (quoted by Lewalski 1979:172). And Isaac Ambrose advises readers to "gather" experiences; "to treasure up . . . observations" for purposes of verification (quoted by Kaufmann 1966:206f.). Beyond that, he teaches them how to systematize the record of what happens to them "under such heads as Promises, Threatenings, Deceits of the Heart; then to consider what Scripture texts are verified thereby" (quoted by Lewalski 1979:161). In this way, the individual creates personal objects of meditation, Hunter observes, "without violating the stricture against making graven images, for the objects they contemplated were made by God, who alone was responsible for all their significations" (Hunter 1966:97).

Further evidence of the reification of inner life lies in the celebration by the Puritans, not of traditional holy days of the church year, but of significant dates in their own spiritual biographies—a sign of the radical individualizing of the framework within which Christian life was lived and the Bible interpreted.[16] Not the nativity of Jesus, but that of the New Man, was marked out for observance.

Concluding Reflections

Across the board, the seventeenth is a reifying century in ways that profoundly affect religious life and the way it is understood. We have already mentioned printing. The impact of exploration of the world could be elaborated further: travel literature promoted an objectified view of one's own culture as well as others. Montaigne pioneered this genre; a vivid seventeenth-century example is the fictional work *L'Espion Turc* (1684; Marana), first of a new genre, which discovers (in eight volumes!) a Turkish spy living in Paris and critically evaluating European religion, philosophy, politics and manners (Popkin, 115). Reification with a vengeance! Or consider Fontenelle's *Conversations on the Plurality of Worlds* (1686): its speculation about other inhabited worlds puts the entire planet on a comparative level.

Thus we see the term "religion" rising of necessity to describe an increasingly complex world, beginning with the internal religious rivalry among Christians (as a result of which rival forms of Christianity are referred to as "religion[s]"); added to it the growing realization that Christianity is only one among the world's religions, or possibly, one among the universe's! Bunyan's colourful recognition of this new reality (new at least to the ordinary layperson) is expressed thus: "Everyone doth think his own Religion rightest, both Jews, and Moors, and Pagans; and how if all our Faith, and Christ, and Scriptures, should be but a think-so too?" (Bunyan 1962:31).[17]

Reification has nothing *necessarily* to do with alienation from religious life, with an outsider's perspective, or with attention only to externals.[18] In fact, it is a fundamental mistake to drive a wedge between "inner" and "outer," as though the essential subject matter for the study of religion is the inner life, while externals are peripheral. This dualism accurately reflects a certain kind of theology, of course, but it radically falsifies the data of religion,[19] and tends to inject normative considerations prematurely into the study of the facts.

The complexity of the picture is deepened when we reflect that the very same authors who passionately documented the inward life of the Christian pilgrim could also write about "religion" in the most externalized way; for example Richard Baxter, whose *Saints Everlasting Rest* and *Christian Directory* are two of the century's spiritual classics, also wrote books whose titles include the phrases "vain religion," "the old religion," "modern religion," "the protestant religion," and, of course, "true religion" (W. C. Smith 1964:220f., n. 23 and 25).

Reification is here, and often, a necessary linguistic/conceptual event signalling some object (or objects) of thought, inner or outer, that has captured the attention of a culture, or of a religious community, at a particular time and circumstance. Consider such other examples as the careful medieval distinction between *fides quae* and *fides qua creditur* (the faith which is believed and the faith *by* which it is believed),[20] the mechanics of sacramental grace (the *ex opere operato/operantis* distinction), the "atonement," states of the medieval *viator's* soul under various forms of grace, and so on. All of these items held, we may presume, intense existential religious significance to individual believers who knew nothing of the theories attendant upon them. But all these same items were at certain moments subject to the most intensive analysis by the learned community.

The process of reifying seems to me similar to the creation of universals (such as "religion" in its new seventeenth-century connotations, or "religious experience," mentioned at the beginning). They are a necessary part of our language, and useful so long as we remember (*pace* medieval realists) that universals like "religion" and "Buddhism" do not exist, except as creations of imagination and/or mind by which we organize and interpret experience.[21]

Finally, we are now coming to understand how the early-modern type of rigorous spiritual observation and documentation — biography, autobiography, diaries, and so on — contributed decisively to the rise of *the* modern literary genre *par excellence*, the novel. Studying this development, recent scholarship draws a fairly direct line from writers such as John Foxe, Baxter, and Bunyan to Daniel Defoe, that is, from spiritual biography and autobiography to the novel, wherein a human life is reified, that is, rendered with "narrative completeness" (McKeon 1987:280) as a coherent and meaningful whole in which inner and outer are all of a piece.

Notes

1 As a result of mounting criticism, the Bible was no longer able to sustain itself as a source of knowledge to explain and order the world. Despite these setbacks, biblical authority sustained itself with vigour in explaining and shaping the *inner* world.

2 Such a thesis might fit the rise of German Pietism as a protest against Orthodox "reification," and its tendency to reduce essential Christian religiousness to "pure doctrine."

3 Pascal, for example, says that God "gives" people "religion through a sentiment of the heart" (according to Despland 1979:270). This seems to be more likely a Catholic than Protestant usage, parallel to the notion of infusion of grace. For Spener, the purpose of self-scrutiny is to rouse from spiritual lethargy rather than to achieve certainty (Hirsch, 149f. Cf. Hausammann). Yet another motivation and framework for introspection lies in Boehme's view that "the way to God and to the understanding of the universe lay through the scrutiny of the human soul, for man, as microcosm, contained within himself the epitome of nature" (Thomas 1971:376).

4 Properly speaking, "the Word" was the only means of grace for most Protestants; it could be mediated, however, in more than one form—e.g., not only through reading, but through hearing of sermons, or [for some] various sorts of extraordinary divine visitations. The "sacrament" of reading could be "received" anywhere, of course, without mediation of priest. It also signals that individual divination, rather than communal participation, is perhaps the quintessential religious "moment" of Protestant religiousness. (See Haller 1063:80). Kaufmann (1966:55f.) explains clearly the basic Puritan idea of the Word as *the* primary means of interaction with God (superior to images and events).

5 At the same time, however, the Word has to be *remembered*, being easily and disastrously forgot in an emergency. Cf. Fish 1972:259f., on *The Pilgrim's Progress* as a trial of memory. At a crucial moment: "My brother, you have quite forgot the text...."

6 Remarking on how combinations of biblical verses providentially "make up some Christians destinie," the poet George Herbert addresses the Bible as follows: "Such are thy secrets, which my life makes good, / And comments on thee: for in ev'ry thing / Thy words do finde me out, and parallels bring, / And in another *make me understood*" (quoted by Lewalski 1979:105; italics mine).

7 This from Richard Baxter's *Saints Everlasting Rest*, quoted by Kaufmann, 197f.: "Remember what *discoveries* of thy *state* thou hast made formerly in the walk of *self-examination*; how oft God hath convinced thee of the *sincerity* of thy *heart*: Remember all the former Testimonies of the *Spirit*; and all the *sweet feelings* of the Favour of God; and all the prayers that he hath heard and granted; and all the rare *preservations* and *deliverances*; and all the progress of his *Spirit* in his workings on thy Soul; and the disposals of *Providence*, conducing to thy good: . . . And though one of these considered alone, may be no sure evidence of his special love (which I expect thou shouldst try by more infallible signs) yet lay them altogether, and then think with thy self, Whether all these do not testifie the good-will of the *Lord* concerning thy *Salvation*, and may not well be pleaded against thine unbelief?" (italics in text). See also Kaufmann 1966:205.

8 "Why then do I not search into every corner, till I know my state? Must I so shortly undergo the trial at the bar of Christ? and do I not presently try myself?" (Baxter 1825:146).

9 John Hieron lists 14 events that became to him divine deliverances, including getting hooked, then unhooked, from a cow's horns; falling out a window unhurt, falling out of a boat and surviving, etc. Related by Hunter 1966:84f.

10 One can find among Protestants astonishing rejections of the idea that one "interprets" Scripture at all: interpretation is something wily Papists do in order to wrest Scripture's true and obvious meaning. For examples, see Harris.

11 Cf. Daniel Burgess, quoted by Hunter 1966:78: "The Holiness that is in God's children is of a more excellent kind, than that which is in His Holy Bible."

12 So also Kaufmann 1966:201: "Life was a second Scripture by which to understand the written word . . ." and "experience . . . was the final authority of the Puritan."

13 All outward proofs of Scripture authority, John Preston confesses, are "not enough, unless God infuseth an inward light by his Spirit to worke this faith" (quoted by Kaufmann 1966:65). Cf. John Owen: proofs can only lead to an opinion; it takes "divine and supernatural" faith to be utterly convinced (ibid., 65f.).
14 Bunyan's instability in *Grace Abounding* is astonishing: just when one spiritual crisis is solved, something else happens and he is worse off than before! Lewalski offers a perceptive contrast to Roman Catholic meditation, wherein "the meditator typically seeks to apply himself to the subject, so that he participates in it; he imagines a scene vividly" and then "stirs up emotions appropriate" to it. Protestant procedure is "very nearly the reverse: instead of the application of the self to the subject, it calls for the *application of the subject to the self* — indeed for the subject's location in the self" (149; italics mine).
15 I am grateful to my conference colleague, Professor Roger Lapointe, for suggesting the appropriateness of the Weberian notion at this point.
16 This whole development is significant in terms of Hans Frei's important idea that a "great reversal" takes place with regard to the conceptual framework within which biblical interpretation is carried out in our period. This reversal occurs when some other framework replaces the biblical myth of creation-final judgement as the framework within which one's personal experience is fitted (Frei 1974:esp. 130).
17 Cf. George Fox (1963:479): In a period of spiritual crisis, "I was brought into the deep, and saw all the religions of the world, and people that lived in them. And I saw the priests that held them up; who were as a company of meneaters, eating up the people like bread, and gnawing the flesh from off their bones. But as for true religion, and worship, and ministers of God, alack! I saw there was none amongst those of the world that pretended to it."
18 This qualifies Despland's observation (1979:228), correct in its own context, that in the seventeenth century "the idea of religion is en route to reification: 'a religion' begins now to designate an ensemble of practices and beliefs which are observed as exterior realities and are distinct from the *intériorité* of the religious person who practices or believes them. From now on, to be religious signifies, for the great majority of European minds, to have a religion, that is to say, to identify oneself with one or the other of these groups."
19 An example from the seventeenth century: Hunter (1966:123) comments on Robinson Crusoe, whose physical and spiritual activities "are all of a piece in a world where secular activity is meaningful, where history (even the history of every man's trivialities) is somehow the record of divine activity."
20 This distinction in usage is at least as old as the so-called Athanasian Creed, which begins, "Quicumque vult salvus esse, ante omnia opus est, ut teneat catholicam fidem.... Fides autem catholica haec est, ut unum Deum..." (Denzinger #75). W. C. Smith's second chapter of *Meaning and End* thus misrepresents medieval "faith" by ignoring this fundamental distinction in usage.
21 An interesting parallel to the rise of "religion" is the rise of "the human," as noted by Roof (1988:298), in a discussion of the emergence of the human sciences (anthropology, sociology, psychology, and *Religionswissenschaft*): "the human sciences did not inherit a cognitive domain already outlined; the object of the new sciences, the human, had not existed before as the object of a science." The type of reification to be avoided involves the hypostatization of theoretical constructs ("progress," "chain of being," "modernity") which may conceal ideological commitments: cf. Skinner 1969:10-12.

References

Baxter, Richard. 1825. *The Saint's Everlasting Rest* (1650). London: Caxton Press.
Bunyan, John. 1962. *Grace Abounding to the Chief of Sinners* (1666). Edited by Roger Sharrock. Oxford: Clarendon Press.
———. 1955. *The Pilgrim's Progress* (1678-84). New York: Rinehart.
Denzinger, H. and Schönmetzer, A. 1963. *Enchiridion Symbolorum*. 32d ed.; Rome: Herder.
Despland, Michel. 1979. *La Religion en Occident. Évolution des Idées et du Vécu*. Montréal: Fides.
Fish, Stanley E. 1972. "Progress in *The Pilgrim's Progress*." In *Self-Consuming Artifacts: The Experience of Seventeenth-Century Literature*, 224-64. Berkeley: University of California Press.
Fox, George. 1963. *The Journal of George Fox* (1694). Edited by R. M. Jones. New York: Capricorn.
Frei, Hans. 1974. *The Eclipse of Biblical Narrative*. New Haven: Yale University Press.
Haller, William. 1963. *Foxe's Book of Martyrs and the Elect Nation*. London: Jonathan Cape.
———. 1972. *The Rise of Puritanism*. Philadelphia: University of Pennsylvania Press.
Harris, Victor. 1966. "Allegory to Analogy in the Interpretation of Scriptures." In *Philological Quarterly* 45: 1-23.
Hausammann, Susi. 1971. "'Leben aus Glauben' in Reformation, Reformorthodoxie und Pietismus." *Theologische Zeitschrift* 27,4: 263-89.
Hirsch, Emanuel. 1949. *Geschichte der Neueren Evangelischen Theologie*. 2 v. Gütersloh: Bertelsmann.
Hunter, J. Paul. 1966. *The Reluctant Pilgrim: Defoe's Emblematic Method and Quest for Form in "Robinson Crusoe"*. Baltimore: Johns Hopkins Press.
Kaufmann, U. Milo. 1966. *The Pilgrim's Progress and Traditions of Puritan Meditation*. New Haven: Yale University Press.
Knott, John R. 1980. *The Sword of the Spirit: Puritan Responses to the Bible*. Chicago: University of Chicago Press.
Lewalski, Barbara K. 1979. *Protestant Poetics and the Seventeenth Century Religious Lyric*. Princeton: Princeton University Press.
Loewe, M. and C. Blacker, eds. 1981. *Divination and Oracles*. London: Allen & Unwin.
Lukin, Henry. 1669. *Introduction to the Holy Scripture*. London.
Marana, Giovanni Paolo. 1734. *The Eight Volumes of Letters Writ by a Turkish Spy*. London: G. Strahan et al.
McKeon, Michael. 1987. *The Origins of the English Novel, 1600-1740*. Baltimore: Johns Hopkins University Press.
Popkin, Richard H. 1987. *Isaac La Peyrère: his Life, Work and Influence*. Leiden: Brill.
Roof, Wade Clark. 1988. "On Bridging the Gap Between Social Scientific Methodology and Religious Studies." *Soundings* 71: 295-314.

Skinner, Quentin. 1969. "Meaning and Understanding in the History of Ideas." *History and Theory* 8: 3-53.

Smith, Jonathan Z. 1982. "Sacred Persistence: Toward a Redifinition of Canon." In *Imagining Religion: From Babylon to Jonestown*, 36-52. Chicago: University of Chicago Press.

Smith, Wilfred Cantwell. 1964. *The Meaning and End of Religion*. New York: Mentor.

Sommerville, C. John. 1977. *Popular Religion in Restoration England*. Gainesville: University of Florida Press.

Stone, Lawrence. 1969. "Literacy and Education in England, 1640-1900." *Past and Present* 42, 69-139.

Thomas, Keith. 1971. *Religion and the Decline of Magic*. New York: Scribner's.

CHAPTER 7

La religion au XIXe siècle : quelques particularités françaises

Michel Despland

Introduction

À partir de la Révolution française, les Français se mettent à vivre la religion d'une manière bien particulière. Ces particularités, conséquences inévitables des crises en matière de religion causées par la grande Révolution, seront l'objet premier de cet article. Mais je tiens à montrer aussi que les Français se mettent à penser à la religion d'une manière qui leur est propre. (L'article comportera donc des ouvertures sur l'apport français à la science des religions qui se constitue au cours du XIXe siècle.) J'ajoute qu'une deuxième partie s'efforcera aussi de tirer quelques conclusions d'ordre méthodologique.

La Révolution mise en marche en 1789 entreprend de renégocier tous les rapports de pouvoir dans la société. Le sérieux des confrontations qui s'ensuivent est bien exprimé par l'opinion de Quinet (1845:273): en France l'Église la plus ancienne (par quoi il faut entendre celle qui a plongé les plus profondes racines dans les atavismes des moeurs) fait face à la révolution la plus moderne, celle qui attaque les hiérarchies le plus radicalement. Ici encore le vocabulaire et les pratiques de la religion gardent leurs liens avec ceux de l'unité nationale et du pouvoir. L'État et la religion collaborent ou entrent en conflit; ils s'avèrent incapables de s'ignorer mutuellement.

Dès 1789 une succession de propos doctrinaux et de démarches politiques prétendent établir un nouvel équilibre entre la religion et la vie nationale. L'abbé Grégoire, évêque constitutionnel, se fait le théoricien de la chrétienté républicaine. Il définit (1794) la religion comme «principe actif», «qui place les qualités sociales dans le cercle des devoirs; et qui en les faisant chérir, en facilitant les moyens de les accomplir, mettra du prix,

---

Les notes et références concernant ce chapitre se trouvent aux pages 66-69.

du plaisir aux sacrifices que l'on fait pour la chose publique». «Ne comptez donc pas, lance-t-il aux législateurs, sur l'existence d'une république sans religion». Survient alors ce que Michel Lagrée (1989) a fort bien appelé «la déchirure» : en Vendée le peuple trouve des chefs pour affronter les armées de la République et défendre roi et religion derrière l'étendard du Sacré-Coeur. Les Vendéens furent massacrés sur le terrain. Grégoire perdit sa bataille au sein de la Convention. Les Républicains abandonnèrent l'Église constitutionnelle au profit de cultes révolutionnaires façonnés sur des modèles antiques puis au profit d'un laisser-aller qui ouvrit la porte à un jeune général qui avait manifestement des dons et de l'ambition. La question religieuse fut alors «résolue» au niveau politique. Le premier consul et le pape s'arrangèrent pour rendre le catholicisme comme religion publique aux Français.

Chateaubriand prend alors la plume pour expliquer à nouveau comment la religion est un fait de société. *Le Génie du christianisme* (1802) présente le catholicisme comme un fait d'histoire, ami des arts et des moeurs, moteur de la civilisation et ferment de liberté.[1] Lamennais lui donne la réplique dès l'*Essai sur l'indifférence* : il veut que le catholicisme enseigne une philosophie sociale et instaure l'ordre; mais, d'allégeance ultramontaine, il croit, à la manière de l'Ancien Régime, qu'entre vrais catholiques, prêtres, aristocrates et paysans, aucune difficulté d'ordre politique ne saurait surgir. L'évêque Frayssinous, Grand-Maître de l'Université sous Louis XVIII, formule (1821) le compromis gallican dans sa conférence «Sur l'union et l'appui réciproque de la religion et la société». Le protestant Guizot entre dans le concert: la religion, écrit-il dans son *Histoire de la civilisation en Europe* (1828:113, 133-36, 152, 161), veut être considérée du point de vue de la civilisation. Elle n'est pas «purement individuelle», mais entre dans «le gouvernement des sociétés»; «puissant et fécond principe d'association», elle permet le fonctionnement d'un gouvernement persuasif plutôt que coercitif. Les questions et les sciences religieuses, ajoute-t-il, sont maintenant entrées dans le domaine public; la religion doit dorénavant se faire accepter de la liberté humaine. Ainsi, à partir du XIXe siècle, conclut le professeur de la Sorbonne, le gouvernement ne saurait être exercé ni par des fanatiques ni par des libertins. Une fois aux commandes de l'État, Guizot corrige son tir; il accepte la religion catholique et cherche son alliance, non pas au nom de la liberté, mais par conservatisme; il faut accepter le poids de l'histoire et admettre que la composante catholique est une présence durable dans l'équation politique (Rosanvallon 1985:238-40). Tous les premiers théoriciens socialistes, enfin, se veulent des analystes compétents du phénomène religieux. Leur volonté de résoudre les problèmes sociaux les amènent à examiner de près tous les phénomènes associatifs (Biéler 1982). Que la religion relie les hommes entre eux est le cliché le plus répandu sous la Monarchie de Juillet.

De telles perspectives ne sont pas le fait des seuls théoriciens de la religion ou de la société. F. P. Bowman a montré (1987:69, 343, 356) comment chez les théologiens et les littéraires la réfléxion christologique après la Révolution et jusqu'en 1848 ne cesse de suggérer des conséquences historiques issues des événements de Nazareth et de Golgotha. Sa démonstration retient quatre thèmes: le sacrifice de la crucifixion amène la rédemption de toutes les formes du mal; Jésus était un maître d'amour et de charité fraternelle; l'incarnation du verbe assure la présence de Dieu en nous; le christianisme a une fonction de verbe dans l'histoire. Ainsi la christologie situe l'humanité dans une histoire christique et élabore une figure christique d'espérance.

Les choses se compliquent après 1848. Apeurés par le comportement des ouvriers parisiens, les Catholiques sont rassurés (ou manipulés) par le Prince-Président qui fait appel aux «couches saines» de la société; ils acceptent de lier la cause de la religion, qui pour eux est alors celle de leur Église, à celle de la classe possédante. Le régime de suffrage universel les amène à se constituer en parti politique de droite. En 1789 le clergé avait rallié le Tiers-État; en 1802, il avait encensé le Premier Consul; en 1814, il avait accueilli Louis XVIII avec joie; chaque fois, même lorsque, dès 1815, il rêvait à la reconstitution d'une société de trois ordres, il croyait vouloir le bien de la nation toute entière. En 1852 l'Église songe à son propre intérêt et lie son sort aux intérêts d'une classe. Il y a une autre différence, tout aussi importante. En 1802 la paix religieuse vint d'en haut: deux souverains signèrent un concordat que le peuple accepta. Cinquante ans plus tard, la pacification des esprits est issue d'une majorité électorale qui s'oppose à une partie de la nation. Le compromis entre souverains ne discrédita pas la religion aux yeux du peuple. Le coup de force de 1849-52 se fait aux dépens d'une partie du peuple, lequel, à cette date, c'est là l'essentiel, se conçoit comme le souverain; ce coup de force ouvre donc beaucoup d'yeux sur les compromissions politiques de la religion dans la société industrialisée. L'adjectif «clérical» devient une insulte dès 1860.

En résumé, jusqu'en 1848, les Catholiques français croient à l'unité de la civilisation chrétienne et épousent l'idée d'un pouvoir qui serait bon pour tous. Dans la société moderne diversifiée, où politique, économie, art et religion se développent de manière autonome, un tel pouvoir n'est facile ni à concevoir ni à implanter. Tous y tiennent néanmoins. Quand l'alliance du trône et de l'autel se discrédite sous Charles X, les Catholiques, hormis les nobles légitimistes, se rallient derrière Lacordaire et Montalembert pour s'installer dans un régime libéral dont ils ne pressentent que mal les conséquences. Quand Lamennais voit sa vision de l'alliance entre les peuples et la papauté refusée par cette dernière, il préfère quitter l'Église plutôt que renoncer à sa vision d'un pouvoir bon pour le peuple. Par contre, après 1852, quand les Catholiques se rallient à un pouvoir qui ne sert que l'intérêt des «bons», et promet de les protéger contre les «méchants», les républicains deviennent anti-cléricaux et ne tardent pas à forger une contre-religion, c'est-à-dire l'idéal d'un pouvoir national laïque qui serait bon pour tous les citoyens. Cette fois les athées sont entrés dans un parti, avec les agnostiques, les protestants, les Juifs et quelques autres. En 1905, ce parti vote les lois de séparation de l'Église et de l'État.

Ces grands traits de la situation religieuse propre à la France affectent l'essor français des sciences religieuses. Cet essor est apparemment lent.[2] Il a de la peine à trouver ses bases institutionnelles; celles-ci ne sont assurées, encore que peu nombreuses, qu'en 1880. Durkheim (1887 :486) s'étonne du faible développement de ces études dans une nation qui veut se gouverner elle-même et compare l'Allemagne favorablement à la France. Loisy (1911) souhaite une meilleure vulgarisation de l'enseignement de l'histoire des religions. Plus récemment, Eric Sharpe note (1975 :122-23) que la tendance radicalement sécularisante de la vie publique française affecte les démarches des sciences religieuses et trouve que le positivisme d'après 1880, positivisme dont il cite des formules outrancières, représente l'essentiel de l'apport français. On explique d'ordinaire une telle situation par le sérieux des conflits politico-religieux dans la France du XIXe. Le système scolaire, du primaire au Collège de France, est l'objet de luttes serrées. Les facultés de théologie catholique dans les universités végètent à cause de conflits entre l'Église et l'État. Quinet et Renan voient leur enseignement suspendu au Collège de France en 1846 et 1862, sous l'effet de pressions catholiques. Et quand vers la fin du siècle, des institutions se mettent en place, qui prétendent aborder l'étude de la religion librement et scientifiquement, celles-ci semblent devenir l'apanage exclusif des positivistes. On en vient donc vite à conclure que l'étude des religions en France est tombée victime des aléas d'une politique nationale tourmentée.

Je voudrais proposer ici que tous ces faits devraient être lus différemment. Ce qui singularise la France du XIXe n'est pas le faible développement des études religieuses, mais l'absence d'une notion de religion qui soit libre de toutes résonnances et implications politiques et sociales, bref d'un concept de religion qui serait comme une case vide que des savants objectifs et détachés pourraient remplir de connaissances dénuées de conséquences pratiques. Aucun discours théorique en effet ne réussit à accréditer d'une manière durable les mérites d'études portant, disons, sur le sentiment religieux comme donnée universellement présente dans l'histoire. Une succession de discours théoriques établit plutôt des types de liens entre religion et politique. Puis le devenir politique discrédite chacune de ces théories à son tour. Tout discours sur la religion comporte donc des conséquences morales et politiques. Ce qui explique le mieux les particularités de l'essor des sciences religieuses en France n'est donc pas tant le fait qu'une politique partisane mette les nerfs particulièrement à vif, c'est plutôt qu'en France depuis le moyen-âge on ne peut parler de religion sans toucher aux moeurs de la nation et aux pratiques du pouvoir.

Tout le monde s'accorde sur le fait que depuis le XVIIIe siècle de Semler, l'université allemande a fourni les locomotives du progrès dans le domaine de l'érudition historique en matière de religions. On s'accorde aussi pour dire que le romantisme et l'idéalisme allemands, avec leurs théories du langage et des mythes, avec la théologie de Schleiermacher, ont fourni une anthropologie qui favorisait l'étude des phénomènes religieux tels qu'ils se manifestaient dans toutes les cultures (Despland 1985). Les milieux savants avaient ainsi un programme de recherches commun et bien défini : il fallait étudier les textes, faire ressortir la diversité des formes, et retrouver partout une unité de sentiment ou d'aspiration; l'*homo religiosus* devenait ainsi un concept stable, apparemment légitime aux yeux de la philosophie (et de la théologie), et manifestement utile aux historiens et à tous ceux qui visaient à l'accroissement du savoir.[3]

Or je crois être en mesure de montrer que les savants français, tout au long du XIXe siècle, ont refusé d'accorder une hégémonie intellectuelle à une telle anthropologie. Depuis Victor Cousin jusqu'à Durkheim, en passant par Quinet, Littré et Renan, on trouve des universitaires qui étudient avec zèle les auteurs allemands, veulent introduire leur savoir dans les débats d'idées français, et les offrent à leurs compatriotes comme objets d'émulation.[4] Depuis Germaine de Staël jusqu'à Albert Réville on trouve aussi des Protestants pour répéter à la fois que le sentiment religieux est une réalité pérenne qui ne cessera de se donner de nouvelles formes, quitte à abandonner les vieilles, et que le christianisme n'est pas aussi figé que les théologiens catholiques veulent le faire croire. Les traités de Benjamin Constant, publiés durant les dernières années de la Restauration, expriment dans un français limpide, qui a tous les mérites du style des philosophes, ce que les protestants allemands avaient élaboré sur le rapport entre l'individu et les institutions religieuses. Pour un moment, sous la Monarchie de Juillet, on a l'impression que cette anthropologie est en train de faire école. Malgré celà, on retrouve sans cesse l'idée que le sentiment religieux est un phénomène passager et insignifiant.[5] Et surtout les événements de 1848-52 rappellent aux Français, avec force, que la religion est liée à l'exercice du pouvoir en société, que les mentalités religieuses reposent sur des atavismes sociaux qui restent opaques aux yeux des agents et n'ont ni la luminosité ni l'innocence que les piétistes et les romantiques allemands attribuent à la conscience religieuse.

C'est donc par le biais d'un contraste avec le modèle allemand que je vais achever le portrait de la voie française en science des religions. Schleiermacher enseigne dans les discours *Über die Religion* que le sentiment existe dans le for intime, oscille entre le secret et l'expression; il explique aussi que les exercices spirituels ne jouent aucun rôle à l'origine du sentiment religieux, mais en sont la conséquence; Otto écrit *Le Sacré* pour prouver que, si une expérience religieuse peut être expliquée, elle n'est plus religieuse (Proudfoot 1985 : 113, 118). On trouve chez les théoriciens allemands les formules les plus dures pour affirmer l'autonomie de la religion : la religion a des causes religieuses et des conséquences religieuses. Les Français, en contraste, définissent le sentiment comme ce qui se dit quand on s'exprime sincèrement (*Encyclopédie*, article «Sentiment»); ils admettent le rôle de causes secondes dans la formation des émotions religieuses; ils n'ont pas de honte à reconnaître qu'il y a en nous une bête qui apprécie les rituels mécaniques; et ils ne dressent pas de contrastes absolus entre les apprentissages sociaux et les sentiments intimes, entre l'artifice (ou l'art) et la sincérité (Starobinski 1989). Hegel affirme que «chacun entend et ressent sa force d'obligation lorsqu'il lui prête attention». Il y voit là à la fois une marque de la raison humaine universelle, et une preuve du caractère religieux de l'homme; une occasion aussi de souligner que la religion n'a rien de positif en soi.[6] Devant la même affirmation, un Français du XIXe verrait une marque de socialisation; le phénomène relèverait pour lui de la morale et non de la religion, qui, toujours, comporte du positif. Bref les philosophes et théologiens allemands du XIXe siècle accordent à l'expérience religieuse une valeur cognitive: elle révèle l'existence de Dieu ou le rapport de l'homme à l'Absolu. Ils sont donc portés à examiner les mythes plus que les rites; et ils interprètent les symboles de manière à leur donner une signification absolue, métaphysique.[7] La religion est associée au sentiment, à la pensée; le langage religieux est perçu comme cognitif, plutôt que rhétorique ou performatif. Les Français, au contraire, sont portés à insérer naturellement la vie religieuse dans les réalités de l'histoire sociale et ne se passionnent guère pour les débats sur l'essence de la religion.[8]

Ainsi quand Chateaubriand et Guizot[9] affirment que le christianisme est une grandeur historique, ils en soulignent le poids et la valeur. Ils sont loin de le relativiser. Quand les théologiens protestants allemands se penchent sur le caractère historique du christianisme à la fin du XIXe siècle, ils considèrent avec effroi que celui-ci est en train de perdre son caractère absolu. Avoir le Jésus de l'histoire, c'est, à leurs yeux, risquer de n'avoir que le Jésus de l'histoire et de perdre le Christ de la foi, et c'est surtout prendre pour acquis que le Jésus de l'histoire manque de l'épaisseur et de la consistance nécessaires à la religion.[10] Quand Edgar Quinet évoque les travaux qui lui ont permis d'écrire *Le Génie des religions*, il signale sa dette aux auteurs allemands, mais il ajoute: «les Allemands qui avaient tant examiné les symboles, n'en avaient déduit aucune conséquence sur le développement moral des peuples».[11] Royer-Collard définit les croyances de l'esprit comme «les forces de l'âme et les mobiles de la volonté».[12] Fustel de Coulanges (1864, 1984:149) affirme que «pour instituer le commandement, il faut la croyance». La croyance donc institue le commandement. Quand Durkheim évoque les mérites de l'université allemande, il note (1887:461-62) qu'en Allemagne on sépare la morale théorique de la morale pratique. On commence (selon lui) par inculquer des moeurs à l'école primaire, pour ensuite, à l'université, enseigner la *Critique de la raison pratique* sans se mêler des moeurs. En France, par contre, ajoute-t-il, un «penchant de notre caractère national nous pousse à traduire aussitôt les doctrines en faits». Loisy en effet se soucie de la vulgarisation de son savoir: il souhaite que la science des religions élaborée à Paris ait des rétombées, sinon à l'école primaire de Clocher-les-Bécasses, du moins dans les écoles secondaires; il sait qu'une telle science a de quoi inquiéter l'opinion. En utilisant les expressions que Durkheim emploie pour parler de la morale, on peut proposer que la science allemande des religions a pu se développer tôt «avec une entière indépendance», parce qu'elle «était dégagée de toute préoccupation utilitaire et de toute responsabilité sociale» (Durkheim 1887:461).[13] On pourrait évoquer ici le fait que cette science a trouvé ses bases épistémologiques autour de 1800 auprès de philosophes et de théologiens installés dans des chaires universitaires. La science française, par contre, était en contact avec l'érudition espagnole et reposait sur des travaux remontant au XVIe produits par des missionnaires et des voyageurs (Bernand et Grucizinski 1988) : ceux-ci ne faisaient pas que lire des textes; ils rencontraient des hommes et cherchaient à décrire des civilisations tout en étant partie prenante à l'instauration de rapports de pouvoir.

La démonstration est, je crois, faite : le peuple et les savants français au XIXe siècle jusqu'en 1880 ont tendance à croire que la religion comporte toujours un élément d'*extériorité*. Ils s'attendent toujours à y trouver du factuel, du traditionnel, du positif, du social, de l'hétérogène à la conscience claire, voire de l'hétéronomie. «La religion, écrit Ernest Renan (1857: 18), n'existe qu'à la condition d'être très arrêtée, très claire, très finie et par conséquent, très critiquable». Les Français se divisent entre ceux qui trouvent que leur religion comporte trop d'éléments extérieurs, et ceux qui trouvent que la dose est à peu près la bonne. En d'autres termes, les Français s'attendent toujours à voir dans la religion un système culturel qui s'est mis en branle, s'est installé dans le temps et l'espace, et se reproduit presque de lui-même.[14] Tous à la Restauration s'accordent pour dire que, quand il n'y a plus de cérémonies, il n'y a plus de religion. B. Plongeron (1984:113) signale le témoignage du général Lacuée à son retour d'une mission dans l'Orléanais : à la campagne, assure cet observateur, les gens «aimeraient mieux des cloches sans prêtres que des prêtres sans cloches». On trouve même un abbé Bletton (1829:39) pour contredire carrément et posément le témoignage unanime des Écritures : Dieu, écrit-il, «ne se laisse fléchir le plus souvent que par le culte extérieur». Claude Geffré n'est pas du tout dans la lignée de cet abbé, mais la préface qu'il écrivit pour *La religion en Occident* contient une observation qui va quand même dans le même sens et qui, maintenant, me semble fort sage : il se dit «résister à la séduction de la notion de réification»; «La tentation consisterait à recourir une fois de plus à la dialectique entre une foi anhistorique et une religion irrémédiablement mêlée aux vicissitudes de l'histoire». Car je m'inscris bel et bien dans la tradition de pensée pour laquelle l'extériorité nourrit autant que brime l'intériorité, et n'est pas aliénante pour celui qui est au fait des pratiques de l'inter-subjectivité.

Tirons maintenant quelques conséquences d'ordre méthodologique

Précisons pour commencer que l'anthropologie romantico-idéaliste n'exerce plus d'hégémonie en Allemagne depuis au moins 1918. La laïcité en France n'a plus ni la force politique ni les robustes assurances de 1905; les entorses à sa règle y sont devenues nombreuses et l'on parle ouvertement d'une solution "européenne» des rapports entre l'Église et l'État. On trouve aussi en France l'oeuvre d'un Gilbert Durand (1964) qui s'avance hardiment dans les voies ouvertes par la veine romantico-idéaliste. Mes observations d'ordre méthodologique n'entendent donc pas nous insérer dans les carcans de typologies qui ne sont appropriées qu'à l'histoire du XIXe siècle.[15] J'ajoute néanmoins, enracinement culturel oblige, que comme Protestant francophone, je tiendrai toujours haut les deux flambeaux de la liberté et de l'intériorité religieuses.[16] Je me félicite que de nombreux lecteurs français ont apprécié le côté personaliste de *La religion en Occident*, et que ce livre (qui en est à sa deuxième édition) aide à diffuser le tournant que W. C. Smith a fait prendre à l'histoire des religions en insistant qu'on ne trouvait de religion que chez des personnes.

En tant que savant, j'ajoute néanmoins que maintenant que je suis mieux informé sur l'histoire et sur la pensée religieuses modernes et sur leur insertion dans la longue durée, je souhaiterais que les historiens de la religion portent aussi une attention froide sur les extériorités de la religion.

Le processus de civilisation de la religion, celui que j'ai pu analyser dans le cas de la France à partir de l'ère médiévale, me semble être au moins aussi intéressant et important que le fameux processus d'hellénisation de l'Evangile. Or ce processus a construit des encadrements culturels et créé des rites et des codes qui à la fois favorisent la communication intersubjective et instaurent des pratiques de pouvoir; ces rites et ces codes ont disparu en Occident, mais seulement dans la mesure où ils ont donné naissance à d'autres encadrements culturels, lesquels règlent à leur tour nos propres jeux de pouvoir. Le pouvoir doit être distribué chaque fois que des hommes veulent vivre ensemble et il l'est grâce à des pratiques établies que ceux-ci n'ont jamais le loisir de toujours réexaminer à nouveau et de renégocier sur chaque front. Et la distribution qui permet à la société de durer et de se reproduire doit être légitimée. Il est bon que le pouvoir, qui se prétend bon pour tous, soit un pouvoir auquel tous peuvent consentir. Le principe marxiste selon lequel, tout rapport de domination est religieux, charrie avec lui deux erreurs : d'une part il confond autorité et domination; d'autre part, il prétend que ces rapports peuvent être abolis. Mais ce principe, une fois bien compris, a le mérite de signaler qu'il n'y a pas société sans ordre, ni ordre sans légitimation. Louis Dumont (1983, 1987, Collins 1989, Strenski 1989) nous lance ici des avertissements incontournables. L'*homo oeconomicus* est très différent de l'*homo hierarchicus*, mais lui aussi instaure et légitime des hiérarchies. L'Ancien

Régime européen est bel et bien mort et la religion ne vit plus de la même manière. Des constellations de valeur, qui comme les constellations sont lointaines, froides et durables, — les sociétés ne sont pas des personnes, rappelait Lévi-Strauss (1983 : 215) — continuent néanmoins à accomplir des travaux de consolidation/construction ou de transgression de l'ordre du monde. Le pouvoir politique en particulier continue à posséder l'étrange caractéristique de n'être ni tout à fait hors de la société, ni tout à fait dans la société (Lefort 1986). Le roi qui a la même religion que le peuple n'en est pas moins le roi. Et le roi, qui se croit en mesure d'imposer une religion au peuple, fait quand même partie de la même société. Le pouvoir républicain et démocratique continue à se constituer dans une espèce d'écart qui doit se légitimer dans la durée et qui maintenant se légitime en faisant appel à une histoire en amont et en aval de celle que peuvent vivre les personnes auxquelles il s'adresse.

La pratique du dialogue humanise le pouvoir. Le dialogue interreligieux est une des réussites de l'humanité moderne. Mais le savant attentif aux extériorités et aux pratiques d'écart doit rappeler que la pratique du dialogue — qui doit être étendue — ne peut être généralisée ou universalisée. La pratique du dialogue n'abolit pas la réalité du pouvoir. C'est un théologien engagé dans l'oecuménisme qui m'a mis sur cette piste de réflexion : selon lui, les seules rencontres oecuméniques qui attirent aujourd'hui des participants autres que les bureaucrates ecclésiastiques, sont celles où l'on passe rapidement sur ce qui unit les chrétiens pour examiner les différences, bref ce qui les sépare. Au même moment, bien des philosophes proposent, je cite Bouveresse (1984 : 133, 170), que l'enjeu de la pensée est peut-être «le différend plus que le dialogue». La parole, ou l'écriture, ne saurait devenir une fin en elle-même. Le verbe peut éclairer la nature des désirs qui nous différencient et nous opposent; ou il peut devenir le lieu où se replient nos désirs pour s'accomplir en paix. Je préfère attribuer au verbe le premier de ces deux rôles et répandre le soupçon quant au second. Qu'a-t-on accompli quand on a bien parlé, si l'on n'a instauré qu'une union dans le verbe?

Tout donc me semble indiquer que la notion de religion entièrement intériorisée, exclusivement personaliste, héritée de la matrice culturelle romantico-germano-protestante est loin d'être la plus utile pour nos travaux contemporains. J'avancerai deux exemples pour signaler des auteurs qui ne travaillent pas du tout à l'intérieur de ce modèle et qui me semblent ne pas avoir encore reçu dans notre milieu professionnel toute l'attention qu'ils méritent.

J'ai déjà cité Louis Dumont. Il nous force, nous les Occidentaux, qui parlons toujours *dans* l'individualisme, de nous mettre à parler *de* l'individualisme, et donc de prendre dans l'intellect la distance par rapport à notre culture que permet le détour par la compréhension des celles des autres. Et je mentionnerai aussi Alphonse Dupront. *Du Sacré. Croisades et pèlerinages. Images et langages* constitue ouvertement son matériau. C'est l'ethnohistoire qui fournit les données : des fêtes[17], des cultes de saints, des pratiques de pélerinages, et ainsi de suite, bref des «sacralités» durables, souvent silencieuses, qui sont entrées dans la vie des sujets, servent de fonds «irrationnel» à l'existence collective, et permettent à la foule de «trouver son âme». Dupront reste dans l'histoire mais nous fait pénétrer dans des profondeurs mentales étonnantes : on rencontre dans son étude de l'*homo religiosus occidentalis* un sacré qui manifestement existe en dehors de l'acte de sacralisation. Grâce aux extériorités, les sujets entrent dans une inter-subjectivité heureuse : la «vie du sacré» apporte à la fois un accomplisssement individuel et rajeunit la vie collective. Et l'historien qui en recueille les matériaux en Occident observe la genèse d'individus qui font corps avec les autres individus qui vivent sur le même territoire, avec les générations mortes aussi, et celles à venir.

Un plaidoyer qui souligne l'importance des extériorités et signale les insuffisances du dialogue risque d'apparaître suspect. Que le savant marque sa propre distance par rapport à ce qu'il étudie pourrait passer pour du positivisme. Remarquez cependant que je ne plaide que pour un changement d'accent. Et j'ajoute que le positivisme attribuait à l'homme de science une distance souveraine par rapport aux objets religieux qu'il épinglait avec ses mots, et que je suis loin de proposer une distanciation si altière. Appuyés sur un rationalisme désuet, ces hommes de science ignoraient le lieu d'où ils parlaient. Contre eux je tiens à rappeler que le savant parle toujours d'un lieu précis, qu'il n'y est pas confiné et qu'il peut communiquer avec ceux qui parlent d'un autre lieu, s'ils n'y sont pas confinés. Contre eux aussi, et contre leur volonté de plier la vie aux exigences de leur raison professorale, je rappelle que la distanciation inhérente au savoir moderne implique une hétérogénéité entre celui-ci et les pratiques quotidiennes. Mais, s'il est vivant, ce savoir hétérogène conserve, voire établit, des ponts avec la vie concrète. Sur ce point, la vérité donc me semble se trouver quelque part entre Durkheim et les professeurs allemands qu'il critique. La distanciation dont je parle n'est pas constituée une fois pour toutes; c'est une distanciation, un mouvement, qui ne sauraient être que relatifs, si impérieusement nécessaires soient-ils, une fois que nous avons découvert que nos vérités, au fond, sont très peu vraies, et que nos procédures d'approche de la vérité doivent être agiles et rusées.

Notes

1 Il accentuera et sa conception de la perfectibilité humaine et les exigences de la liberté au cours de son oeuvre. Voir surtout le dernier chapitre des *Mémoires d'outre-tombe*.
2 Je dis «apparemment», car je crois que ceci est dû à nos grilles de lecture.
3 J'ajoute que ce concept servait aussi à une stratégie apologétique (pas toujours menée ouvertement) : de Schleiermacher à Max Müller (Olender 1989 : 124-27) la science allemande des religions se porte à la défense de la religion en assurant qu'elle est une composante essentielle de la culture, et que le christianisme (une fois réinterprété) en est la forme la plus haute.

4 Après 1870-71 les Français regardent de plus près l'organisation des institutions universitaires allemandes mais rompent avec la tradition enthousiaste, issue de Mme de Staël, qui se tournait vers l'Allemagne pour y trouver des pensées généreuses et émancipatrices (Digeon 1959).

5 Stendhal est particulièrement éloquent sur ce point : cet athée est fort sensible à la beauté du sentiment religieux, qu'il peint avec délicatesse. Cette tête froide sait aussi montrer comment le sentiment religieux est manipulé sous la Restauration à des fins politiques. Voir Albérés 1980.

6 Cité par Habermas (1988 :31). La notion hégélienne de religion est issue d'un contexte culturel précis : le piétisme luthérien.

7 Claude Lévi-Strauss (1985 :255) reproche à Freud de croire que derrière un nombre illimité de signifiants, le signifié est toujours le même.

8 Une illustration, classique, sur ce point : la réaction d'Alfred Loisy aux efforts d'Adolf von Harnack pour définir "l'essence du christianisme»; deux citations (1902 :ix, 274) suffiront : comment une religion qui a tenu tant de place dans l'histoire pourrait-elle, demande Loisy, avoir eu son point de départ «dans une seule pensée»? «Les critiques protestants, lorsqu'ils s'étonnent que l'esprit chrétien se rencontre encore dans le catholicisme malgré l'Eglise, la foi malgré le dogme, la vraie piété malgré la multiplication des pratiques extérieures, prennent pour des obstacles, les garanties réelles et les conditions normales des biens que l'Evangile, devenu religion, a donnés au monde, et que leurs spéculations sur la pure essence du christianisme sont impuissantes à lui procurer». Plus récemment et dans un tout autre contexte, Jean-Paul Vernant (1976) déplore que des théories sur la religion, issues, soit de l'étude du christianisme (par des philosophes ou des théologiens), soit de celle des primitifs (par des sociologues), fournissent des cadres interprétatifs qui sont tout à fait inadéquats à l'étude de la religion grecque.

9 «Le christianisme est bien autre chose qu'un système; c'est une histoire» (Guizot 1869).

10 Il y a lieu de rappeler ici les diagnostics des deux critiques les plus acerbes de l'anthropologie romantico-idéaliste, formulés au moment de sa plus grande hégémonie. Marx écrit dans l'*Idéologie allemande* (1846 :39, 72), que les Allemands n'ont jamais eu de bases terrestres pour l'histoire et que, sous le nom d'histoire, ils se représentent tout sauf la réalité. Selon Nietzsche (*Seconde considération intempestive* 1874 :108-12, 172) les Allemands veulent la fleur, sans la racine ni la tige, et vivent dans la crainte que leur être intime (le seul précieux à leurs yeux) se volatilise.

11 Préface à l'édition italienne (1864) reproduite dans l'édition Hachette.

12 En exergue à l'édition 1913 des *Fragments philosophiques*.

13 Marilyn Chapin Massey (1983) a su montrer qu'il n'en était pas ainsi dans l'Allemagne des années 30, si le discours portait sur le christianisme. Strauss y fit scandale parce que son discours sur la religion (qui était sur les origines chrétiennes) avait des ramifications sociales.

14 Le mysticisme évidemment est autre chose; ou, plutôt, pour l'autre chose, ils parleront de mysticisme.

15 Je tiens néanmoins à souligner que la langue est fort conservatrice. L'ouvrage de W. C. Smith *Faith and Belief* (1979) serait difficile à traduire en français. Le traducteur serait tenté de traduire *belief* par *croyance*; le lecteur aurait de la peine à admettre que ce que Smith dit des *beliefs* soit aussi vrai des *croyances*.

16 Pour éviter les malentendus, je précise bien que mon intérêt pour les phénomènes collectifs ne relève pas d'une quelconque idéologie collectiviste, mais d'un intérêt pour la genèse de l'intersubjectivité.

17 Étrange ce silence sur les fêtes dans les *Discours* de Schleiermacher, oeuvre qui pourtant se veut chaleureuse. Ou plutôt : étrange, ce rétrécissement du regard qui ne porte que sur les célébrations qui ont lieu dans des salons bourgeois! La fête, qui supprime la production et affirme le vouloir vivre du groupe (Dupront 443), illustre au mieux l'expérience religieuse collective.

Références

Albérés, Francine Marill. 1980. *Stendhal et le sentiment religieux*. Paris : Nizet.

Bernand, Carmen et Serge Gruzinski. 1988. *De l'idolâtrie. Une archéologie des sciences religieuses*. Paris : Seuil.

Biéler, André. 1982. *Chrétiens et socialistes avant Marx*. Genève : Labor et Fides.

Bletton, Abbé. 1829. *Abrégé des preuves de la religion mises à la portée de tout le monde*. Lyon.

Bouveresse, Claude. 1984. *Rationalité et cynisme*. Paris : Minuit.

Bowman, Frank Paul. 1987. *Le Christ des barricades*. Paris : Cerf.

Collins, Steven. 1989. «Louis Dumont and the Study of Religions». *Religious Studies Review* 15, 1 (janvier).

Despland, Michel. 1985. «La pensée idéaliste sur les religions». *Studies in Religion/Sciences religieuses* 14, 4 : 455-63.

Digeon, Claude. 1959. *La crise allemande de la pensée française*. Paris : PUF.

Dumont, Louis. 1983. *Essais sur l'individualisme. Une perspective anthropologique sur l'idéologie moderne*. Paris : Seuil.

———. 1987. *Homo aequalis. Genèse et épanouissement de l'idéologie économique*. Paris : Gallimard.

Dupront, Alphonse. 1987. *Du Sacré. Croisades et pélerinages. Images et Langages*. Paris : Gallimard.

Durand, Gilbert. 1964 (1989). *L'imagination symbolique*. Quatrième édition révisée. Paris : PUF.

Durkheim, Emile. 1887 (1975). «La philosophie dans les universités allemandes». *Textes*. Vol. 3. Paris : Minuit.

Frayssinous, Denis. 1821. *Défense du christianisme, ou Conférences sur la religion*. Paris.

Fustel de Coulanges, n.d. 1864 (1984). *La cité antique*. Paris : Flammarion.

Grégoire, Abbé. 1794 (1989). «Discours sur la liberté des cultes» (an III). Dans F. P. Bowman, *Grégoire évêque des Lumières*. Paris : France-Empire.

Guizot, François. 1828 (1985). *Histoire de la civilisation en Europe*. Paris : Hachette.

———. 1869. «Christianisme et spiritualisme». *Revue des Deux Mondes*.

Habermas, Jürgen. 1988. *Le discours philosophique de la modernité*. Paris : Gallimard.

Lagrée, Michel. 1989. *Grégoire et Cathelineau. La déchirure*. Paris : Editions sociales.

Lefort, Claude. 1986. «Permanence du théologico-politique». In *Essais sur le politique. XIXe-XXe siècle*. Paris : Seuil.

Lévi-Strauss, Claude. 1983. *Le regard éloigné*. Paris : Plon.

———. 1986. *La potière jalouse*. Paris : Plon.

Loisy, Alfred. 1902 (1930). *L'Évangile et l'Église*, cité d'après la cinquième édition. Paris : Nourry.

———. 1911. «De la vulgarisation et de l'enseignement de l'histoire des religions». Dans *À propos d'histoire des religions*. Paris : Nourry.

Marx, Karl et Friedrich Engels. 1846 (1968). *L'Idéologie allemande*. Paris : Éditions sociales.

Massey, Marilyn Chapin. 1983. *Christ Unmasked : The Meaning of the «Life of Jesus» in German Politics*. Chapel Hill : University of North Carolina Press.

Nietzsche, Friedrich. 1874 (1988). *Seconde considération intempestive : De l'utilité et de l'inconvénient des études historiques pour la vie*. Paris : Flammarion.

Olender, Maurice. 1989. *Les langues du paradis. Aryens et Sémites : un couple providentiel*. Paris : Gallimard et Seuil.

Plongeron, Bernard. 1984. «Échec à la sécularisation des lumières? La religion comme lien social». Dans Michèle Mat, *Sécularisation*. Bruxelles : Éditions de l'Université libre de Bruxelles.

Preus James Samuel. 1986. Recension de Despland, Michel *La religion en Occident*. *Religious Studies Review* 12, 2 (avril) : 112-18.

———. 1987. *Explaining Religion : Criticism and Theory from Bodin to Freud*. New Haven : Yale University Press.

Proudfoot, Wayne. 1985. *Religious Experience*. University of California Press.

Quinet, Edgar. 1845 (1984). *Christianisme et révolution française*. Paris : Fayard.

Renan, Ernest. 1857. *Études d'histoire religieuse* dans *Oeuvres complètes*. Vol. 7. Paris : Calmann Lévy, s.d.

Rosanvallon, Pierre. 1985. *Le moment Guizot*. Paris : Gallimard.

Sharpe, Eric. 1975. *Comparative Religion : A History*. Londres : Duckworth.

Smith, Wilfred Cantwell. 1979. *Faith and Belief*. Princeton, NJ : Princeton University Press.

Starobinski, Jean. 1989. *Le remède est dans le mal*. Paris : Gallimard.

Strenksi, Ivan. 1989. «Louis Dumont, Individualism and Religious Studies». *Religious Studies Review* 15, 1 (janvier).

Vernant, Jean-Paul. 1976. *Religion grecque, religions antiques*. Leçon inaugurale de la chaire d'études comparées des religions antiques (Collège de France 1975). Paris : Maspéro.

CHAPTER 8

Le concept de religion chez Ernst Troeltsch : pour un dépassement du positivisme et de l'empirisme

Jean Richard

Cette communication voudrait répondre à une double question. La première concerne Troeltsch lui-même dans l'évolution de sa pensée : qu'en est-il du Troeltsch philosophe de la religion? Qu'est devenue chez lui la philosophie de la religion? La question se trouve soulevée par l'ouvrage de Jean Séguy, *Christianisme et société*, qui constitue dans les cercles francophones comme la somme de la recherche actuelle sur Troeltsch. Dans un mini-chapitre de deux pages, intitulé justement : «De l'organisation a priori de la conscience à l'historicité», Séguy soutient que Troeltsch aurait connu là-dessus une évolution assez radicale. Il aurait d'abord conçu la religion comme une catégorie autonome de la conscience, distincte des catégories théorique, éthique et esthétique. Mais, dans la mesure où son intérêt se porte de plus en plus sur l'historicité des religions, l'idée d'un a priori religieux et d'un concept de religion perdrait chez lui son importance. Finalement, c'est l'aspect sociologique de la religion qui retiendrait surtout son attention, les considérations d'ordre philosophico-psychologique sur l'essence de la religion étant alors plus ou moins évacuées (Séguy 1980 : 49-50). Voilà donc une thèse qui mérite un examen plus approfondi, et tel sera précisément l'objet premier de notre étude.

Mais nous sommes par là même aussi confrontés à une autre question fondamentale, celle soulevée en 1962 par Wilfred Cantwell Smith, quand il suggérait de laisser tomber toute considération sur la nature de la religion, puisque loin de favoriser la compréhension de la situation religieuse de l'humanité à travers son histoire, une telle recherche philosophique constitue plutôt un obstacle (Smith 1964 : 16). Cela semble bien s'opposer directement à cet aspect de la recherche de Troeltsch qui nous intéresse

---

Les notes et références concernant ce chapitre se trouvent à la page 91.

plus particulièrement ici, et qui s'exprime au mieux dans un essai de 1906, revu et augmenté en 1909, intitulé justement : «L'essence de la religion et de la science de la religion». Évidemment, tout conflit disparaît, si l'on admet avec Jean Séguy que Troeltsch a lui-même, au cours de sa carrière, abandonné cette recherche philosophique sur la nature de la religion. Mais on pourrait aussi comprendre les choses en sens exactement inverse, et penser qu'on a ainsi interprété l'évolution de Troeltsch parce qu'on était convaincu qu'un homme aussi lucide que lui, aussi conscient de la réalité concrète, historique et sociologique, des religions, ne pouvait pas faire autrement que laisser tomber une recherche aussi inutile et encombrante que celle de la philosophie de la religion.

On voit par là que les deux questions soulevées ici sont plus étroitement reliées qu'on serait d'abord porté à croire. Je commence par la première : qu'en est-il de l'évolution de Troeltsch en philosophie de la religion? On peut répondre de façon assez précise à cette question, car on trouve toute une série d'écrits, échelonnés sur une vingtaine d'années, qui montrent assez manifestement que ce fut là pour lui une préoccupation constante. Pour les fins de la présente étude, je retiens plus spécialement les textes suivants. Le texte central de 1906-1909, que j'ai signalé, suivait immédiatement une autre étude d'une cinquantaine de pages, qui portait pour titre : «Psychologie et théorie de la connaissance en science de la religion». Cet opuscule, paru à Tübingen en 1905, était le fruit d'une conférence donnée à Saint-Louis, aux États-Unis, lors du Congrès international des arts et sciences en 1904. Suivent, encore en 1909, une réponse à des critiques intitulée : «Sur la question de l'a priori religieux», et en 1912, l'année même de la publication des *Soziallehren*, un article paru dans la revue théologique de Harvard sous le titre : «Empirisme et platonisme en philosophie de la religion». Il faut noter enfin un article plus ancien, publié en 1895 dans une revue théologique allemande de renom. Cette longue étude, intitulée : «L'autonomie de la religion», peut être considérée comme le point de départ de la réflexion de Troeltsch sur le sujet.

Nous avons là, sans doute, une documentation suffisamment abondante pour répondre à nos questions sur Troeltsch. Mais pour cela, il faut nous demander d'abord quelles étaient les propres questions de Troeltsch, à quels problèmes il se trouvait lui-même confronté. Or, nous pouvons assez facilement discerner ici deux problèmes principaux, qui caractérisent assez bien chacun des deux continents auxquels Troeltsch s'est adressé, l'Europe et l'Amérique. Quand il publie en Allemagne, pour des lecteurs allemands, il s'intéresse d'abord à la question du positivisme, alors que c'est l'empirisme qui le préoccupe surtout dans ses études de 1905 et de 1912, où il réagit aux travaux de William James pour des lecteurs et des auditoires américains. Quant à l'article de 1906-1909, sur «L'essence de la religion et de la science de la religion», il peut être considéré comme la synthèse où ces deux points de vue sont intégrés dans une théorie générale de la religion et de la science de la religion. Je propose donc de considérer successivement chez Troeltsch chacun de ces deux problèmes du positivisme et de l'empirisme, en partant dans chaque cas de l'article qui en traite plus spécifiquement, et en voyant aussi chaque fois comment la position de Troeltsch se trouve intégrée dans l'article central de 1906-1909.

Au-delà du positivisme

Voyons d'abord la thèse fondamentale soutenue par Troeltsch, dans son article de 1895 sur «L'autonomie de la religion». Elle se trouve bien formulée par lui dans les termes suivants : «La religion est un phénomène qui possède son identité propre, qui se produit en étroite relation avec l'ensemble de la vie de l'esprit, mais selon ses lois propres, qui maintient une relative autonomie face aux autres domaines de la vie, qui contient en lui-même sa substance de vérité et qui reçoit et manifeste son plein contenu dans son actualisation et sa particularisation historique» (1895 : 369-70).

Cette thèse s'oppose à toute réduction de la religion à quelque autre domaine de la vie de l'esprit, comme par exemple aux fonctions éthique et esthétique (1895 :392-97). Mais elle vise plus directement encore et tout spécialement le positivisme. Dans son auto-bibliographie de 1922, Troeltsch avoue que la grande question, que ses études théologiques avaient laissée ouverte, était celle de la justification de la religion face au naturalisme moderne dominant, qui semblait tout engloutir. C'est la raison pour laquelle il s'est tourné vers des philosophes comme Kant, Fichte, Schleiermacher et Dilthey (1922 :5-6). Et c'est précisément à cette question centrale du naturalisme positiviste que s'attaque l'article de 1895.

Comme tout phénomène psychique, la religion comporte des représentations qui donnent lieu à des sentiments et à des impulsions de la volonté vers l'agir. Or, les représentations religieuses ont ceci de particulier qu'elles portent sur des puissances ou réalités suprahumaines qui commandent la vénération. Tout le débat vers le positivisme consistera donc dans la question de l'origine de ces représentations. Il faudra pour cela considérer plus profondément la structure de la psyché. On pourra ainsi préciser le lieu d'origine de la religion, et finalement répondre par là à la question de sa nature et de son essence (*Wesen*) (1895 :381-82).

Le positivisme a d'abord fait remonter les représentations religieuses à la tendance profonde de tout expliquer par mode de causalité. À l'origine, ces représentations signifieraient donc tout simplement les causes des phénomènes naturels et elles répondraient par là à notre besoin d'explication, notre besoin de comprendre. Troeltsch réfute longuement cette réduction des représentations religieuses à la pensée causale. D'abord, l'histoire ne présente aucun cas de religion, qui soit ainsi née du besoin d'explication causale. Et l'on pourrait présenter l'argument en sens inverse : la simple représentation d'une cause n'engendrera jamais une religion. L'essentiel d'une représentation religieuse ne consiste donc pas dans sa capacité de satisfaire le besoin de comprendre. Sa signification réside en elle-même, dans la valeur de son contenu propre, dans son rapport au sens idéal de l'existence, au désir du coeur et au sentiment d'une réalité suprahumaine infinie. Les grands maîtres et prophètes religieux n'étaient pas tellement intéressés par les questions de causalité, mais ils étaient passionnés par le contenu vivant des représentations religieuses et de l'expérience qu'ils en faisaient. Troeltsch en conclut que la pensée logique est d'une immense importance pour la compréhension de toutes choses et pour la compréhension de la vie religieuse elle-même, mais elle ne constitue pas le fondement ni l'origine de la religion. La pensée religieuse jouit d'une signification propre, indépendamment de la pensée logique, à laquelle elle ne peut d'aucune façon être réduite (1895 : 384-85).

Mais cela même ouvre la porte à une autre explication, par le désir humain. Il ne s'agit plus alors du besoin d'expliquer le monde, mais du besoin d'être délivré des maux de la vie, en d'autres termes, du besoin de salut. Stimulée par ce désir, pour répondre à ce besoin, l'imagination construit spontanément des représentations de puissances suprahumaines, qui ne sont que les copies agrandies des forces humaines, ou encore des personnifications de forces naturelles impressionnantes. Telle serait l'origine des représentations religieuses, selon la théorie de l'illusion religieuse. Notons qu'il s'agit là encore une fois d'une réduction de la religion à quelque chose d'autre que ce qu'elle prétend être. Le monde idéal de la religion se dissout alors dans le monde sensible; il n'en est qu'une réduplication, qu'une pâle image. Ceux qui proposent une telle explication reconnaissent pourtant habituellement l'autonomie des valeurs morales et esthétiques. Le monde de la morale et le monde de l'esthétique ne sont pas pour eux de simples mirages. Ce sont d'authentiques créations de l'esprit humain, auxquelles correspondent des fonctions spécifiques de l'esprit. Sans doute, nos représentations des idées morales et esthétiques comportent-elles aussi des éléments du monde sensible, mais on ne les soupçonne pas pour autant de n'être rien d'autre que de faux semblants. Pourquoi n'en serait-il pas de même pour les représentations religieuses? Ne pourrait-on pas supposer qu'elles possèdent elles aussi leur valeur propre, qu'elles répondent à une fonction spécifique de l'esprit et que sous le revêtement des images sensibles, elles portent un contenu idéal qui est le fruit d'une authentique perception de l'esprit? (1895 : 385-88 et 397-99).

Tel sera précisément l'objet de la recherche de Troeltsch : indiquer, préciser, exprimer autant que faire se peut, ce noyau irréductible de la religion, toujours présent au milieu des représentations religieuses, même les plus fantaisistes apparemment. Troeltsch croit donc pouvoir affirmer que l'analyse découvre toujours au coeur du besoin religieux un élément objectif et réel, qui constitue sa véritable origine. Sans doute, toute religion s'exprime-t-elle dans des images qui proviennent de l'expérience humaine, mais quand on parvient à pénétrer plus profondément au coeur d'une religion donnée, on perçoit sous cette représentation d'une puissance suprahumaine le pressentiment de quelque chose d'infini, d'inconditionné et d'absolu. Et ce sens de l'infini n'est pas produit par nous pour répondre à quelque besoin. C'est un donné originel de la conscience (*Urdatum des Bewusstseins*), qui accompagne tout sentiment religieux (1895:406). Il y a donc dans toutes les représentations religieuses un élément fondamental, qui seul explique la permanence de la religion : c'est l'idée indéductible et irréductible d'un inconditionné. Voilà précisément ce que Schleiermacher appelait le sentiment de dépendance absolue (1895:401-02).

Par ailleurs, ce sentiment de l'absolu n'est pas sans rapport avec notre vision du monde. Il implique, en effet, que notre monde terrestre et humain est soumis à un ordre rationnel (1895:403). D'où le caractère existentiel du sentiment religieux. Ce que cherche le croyant, c'est avant tout un fondement à son existence, grâce auquel il ne se trouve pas seul dans l'affreux fouillis des choses. Ce qu'il cherche, c'est une certitude sur le sens et la rationalité de la vie, c'est une communion avec la source de toute vie (1895:404-05). Il y a bien là encore l'expression d'un besoin et d'un désir, mais cette quête du sens est d'un tout autre ordre que les visions préscientifiques du monde, auxquelles on a voulu réduire les représentations religieuses. La foi religieuse implique sans doute une option, celle du sens du monde et de la vie. Mais cette option vaut bien l'option contraire pour le non-sens. Ce sont là deux options aussi radicales l'une que l'autre, et, en ce sens, aussi préscientifiques l'une que l'autre.

L'essence de la religion

En précisant ainsi l'origine ou le contenu fondamental des représentations religieuses, Troeltsch a conscience d'avoir, par le fait même, indiqué leur essence, et par conséquent aussi l'essence de la religion elle-même. Ainsi, l'essence des représentations religieuses ne consiste pas à répondre aux questions théoriques portant sur les phénomènes naturels. Ce sont plutôt essentiellement des expressions de la foi en une puissance suprahumaine et suprasensible. Troeltsch dira aussi qu'elles sont l'expression de l'expérience que nous faisons d'une puissance dominant la nature et notre propre vie. Ces représentations religieuses seront donc toujours accompagnées de forts sentiments d'espoir et d'inquiétude concernant notre destinée. Cependant, même si ces sentiments ont une importance capitale pour la vie concrète de la religion, ce n'est pas d'eux que procèdent les représentations, mais plutôt l'inverse (1895:422). Cela signifie que les dieux ne sont pas les simples produits du sentiment religieux; c'est plutôt l'expérience du divin, l'impression du divin dans l'esprit humain qui suscite le sentiment.

Mais la religion n'est pas non plus simple perception, réception du divin; elle est aussi réaction de l'homme sur la divinité. Et tel est précisément le fondement du culte, qui constitue la forme principale de la religion. Le culte singifie vraiment la réaction humaine à l'action divine sur l'homme. C'est l'actualisation solennelle de la relation de l'homme à la divinité, et c'est par là principalement que le sentiment religieux trouve à s'exprimer (1895:424). Or le culte est lui-même intérieur tout autant qu'extérieur. Il est réponse intérieure, offrande de soi à la divinité, avant d'être célébration extérieure. Troeltsch pourra donc conclure que la foi et le culte sont l'âme de la religion pour autant qu'ils sont expérience intérieure, et qu'ils constituent plutôt sa forme et son corps pour autant qu'ils s'expriment en représentations, en doctrines, en rites et en liturgies (1895:427).

Nous avons jusqu'ici résumé la pensée de Troeltsch sur l'essence de la religion, en insistant sur la problématique et sur le contexte bien précis dans lequel la question s'est posée pour lui. Il faut noter maintenant, dans cet article de 1895, une certaine réticence de sa part concernant l'idée même d'une définition de l'essence de la religion. De façon assez inattendue, Troeltsch soutient «qu'on n'a besoin d'aucune 'essence' construite de la religion, que ce soit le sentiment absolu de dépendance (au sens métaphysique-psychologique qu'y attache Schleiermacher), l'idée moniste et panlogiste d'une élévation du fini jusqu'à l'esprit infini, l'auto-affirmation éthique, ou quelque chose de la sorte». Et il indique immédiatement le sens de cette critique : «Nous considérons l'infinie variété de la vie, qui ne se soumet à aucune définition» (1895:419). Troeltsch s'oppose donc à une définition qui viendrait restreindre à un seul de ses aspects le sens très riche de la religion.

Une dizaine de pages plus loin dans le même article, il reconnaît cependant la nécessité de concepts fondamentaux (*Grundbegriffe*), «qui rendent possible une compréhension unifiée de la religion, dans le sens qui lui est propre, en ramenant à une racine commune la variété prodigieuse et apparemment si contradictoire du monde merveilleux de la religion» (1895:428). Il en est ainsi dans toutes les sciences, où les concepts fondamentaux, soigneusement construits, sont nécessaires pour découvrir, sous la multiplicité du réel, un élément fondamental commun. Ces concepts ne doivent pas prendre la place du réel; ils sont là pour l'élucider. La tâche de la science n'est donc pas terminée avec la découverte d'un tel concept universel. C'est à partir de là, au contraire, qu'on peut en arriver à une nouvelle compréhension de la réalité concrète. Il en va de même en science de la religion. L'élément fondamental et universel doit servir à mieux comprendre les phénomènes concrets et à percevoir le fil qui relie la complexité des phénomènes particuliers (1895:429). Voilà pour Troeltsch le sens d'une recherche sur l'essence de la religion en science de la religion.

Il n'y a donc aucune incohérence de fond dans la pensée de Troeltsch concernant l'essence de la religion. L'hésitation que nous avons pu noter chez lui s'explique avant tout, il me semble, par le fait que sa préoccupation première n'est pas de déterminer en quoi consiste précisément l'essence de la religion. Il s'en remet volontiers pour cela aux formulations des philosophes et des théologiens. Ce qui le préoccupe avant tout, c'est plutôt de montrer qu'il y a une essence de la religion, c'est-à-dire que la religion possède son essence propre et qu'elle est une fonction de l'esprit irréductible à toute autre. Le titre de l'article de 1895 indique bien son objectif: «L'autonomie de la religion» (*Die Selbständigkeit der Religion*). En conclusion, Troeltsch rappelle alors le sens de sa démarche: il a voulu montrer «que la religion, en son centre, constitue quelque chose d'entièrement autonome, qui repose sur la relation de l'homme avec le monde suprasensible» (1895:431).

Le présupposé idéaliste critique

Maintenant, concernant le statut épistémologique de cette thèse de l'autonomie de la religion, Troeltsch reconnaît qu'il ne s'agit pas tant d'une conclusion que d'un présupposé: «Le présupposé que la religion constitue un domaine autonome de la vie, et non pas l'épiphénomène (*Begleiterscheinung*) de quelque chose d'autre, est une simple évidence» (1895:376). Il avait d'ailleurs lui-même indiqué, dès le début de l'article, la nature de ce présupposé. C'est le point de vue idéaliste (*idealistische Grundanschauung*), qui, par opposition au matérialisme, permet une reconnaissance universelle de la religion. Troeltsch précise cependant qu'il ne pense pas alors à un système idéaliste particulier, mais à une vision fondamentale des choses, qui reste elle-même ouverte à différentes systématisations philosophiques (1895:362). Cela ne signifie pas cependant qu'il mette sur le même pied tous les systèmes idéalistes. Car il manifeste toujours une grande réserve face à l'hégélianisme, et il recommande par contre un retour au point de départ que sont Kant et Schleiermacher (1895:366-69).

La même thèse est reprise de façon plus systématique une dizaine d'années plus tard, dans la grande étude sur «L'essence de la religion et de la science de la religion». Dès le départ, Troeltsch indique le présupposé qui doit orienter toute la recherche en science de la religion. C'est le présupposé idéaliste, selon lequel les grandes formations culturelles, telles l'éthique, l'esthétique et la religion sont essentiellement des créations de l'esprit humain. Or ce principe idéaliste fondamental s'oppose directement au positivisme, qui ne voit rien d'autre dans l'esprit que le pouvoir de comprendre objectivement les faits, tel qu'il s'exerce au mieux dans les sciences de la nature, selon un processus de coordination des faits et de généralisation dans des concepts, des lois et des théories (1909a:452-57 = 1977:82-84). On voit par là l'importance d'être bien au clair sur ses présupposés en science de la religion. Si l'on opte au départ pour le présupposé positiviste, la religion ne peut être qu'un épiphénomène, qu'une déviation, une maladie de l'esprit, ou du moins l'expression d'un stage encore infantile de l'esprit humain. En effet, si la seule connaissance véritable est celle qui est mise en oeuvre dans les sciences de la nature, la connaissance religieuse ne peut être qu'une infirmité de l'esprit, puisqu'elle ne respecte manifestement pas cette logique. Mais alors, la religion se trouve jugée dès le départ, car on sait dès l'abord ce qu'elle est, un faux semblant, une illusion. Le présupposé positiviste apparaît ainsi comme un préjugé, qui ferme la voie de la recherche (1909a :457-60 = 1977 :84-86). Voilà pourquoi Troeltsch opte résolument pour le présupposé idéaliste. Car en reconnaissant la créativité de l'esprit en matière culturelle, l'idéalisme ouvre la possibilité d'autres modes de connaissance, d'autres modalités de la raison. On peut alors aborder la religion sans préjugé, considérant ce qu'elle dit d'elle-même, laissant ouverte la possibilité qu'elle soit elle aussi une authentique fonction de l'esprit et remettant à plus tard le jugement final sur la question de son authenticité, de sa vérité et de sa validité (1909a :460-61 = 1977 :86-87).

Troeltsch précise cependant que son option est celle de l'idéalisme critique, qui tient toutes les formations de la vie de l'esprit comme des productions de la conscience, et qui fait une démarcation critique entre ces différentes créations de la conscience (1707a :461 = 1977 :88). La notion d'idéalisme critique constitue une référence manifeste à Kant. Effectivement, c'est bien dans la ligne de la théorie kantienne, que Troeltsch définit l'idéalisme critique par l'analyse de la raison humaine et de ses lois dans la connaissance de la réalité. Cependant, Kant ne reconnaît pas pleinement le domaine autonome de la religion; il la réduit plutôt à la sphère éthique, comme son présupposé, comme un simple postulat pour l'éthique. Voilà pourquoi Troeltsch se range plutôt ici du côté de Schleiermacher, qui reconnaît lui-même une fonction religieuse de l'esprit, un a priori religieux indépendant de la morale (1707a :479-80 = 1977 :103-104).

Conclusions

1. Il apparaît dès lors bien manifestement que, par cette fameuse thèse de l'a priori religieux, Troeltsch ne soutient rien d'autre en fait que le principe de l'autonomie de la religion, qu'il défend fortement, depuis ses premières publications, contre toutes les formes du positivisme. L'idéalisme critique, et plus particulièrement l'a priori kantien, n'est qu'une nouvelle forme d'expression plus systématique pour cette même autonomie ou irréductibilité de la religion. Il faudrait poursuivre la recherche et voir plus précisément si Troeltsch a renoncé par la suite à cette expression kantienne de son principe fondamental. On sait qu'il défend encore en 1909 l'application de l'a priori kantien au domaine de la religion tout autant qu'à ceux de l'éthique et de l'esthétique. Il y reconnaît un héritage essentiel de Kant (1909b :757-58). Quoi qu'il en soit de cette question plus particulière et secondaire de l'a priori religieux, on peut affirmer sans crainte ici que Troeltsch a toujours tenu le principe de l'autonomie de la religion, et qu'il a toujours combattu le positivisme sur cette question essentielle de l'irréductibilité de la religion.

2. On voit aussi par là quel est le sens de la recherche de Troeltsch sur l'essence de la religion dans le contexte de sa lutte contre le positivisme. Il

nous prévient lui-même du danger de perdre la richesse infinie de la réalité religieuse dans le cadre trop étroit de définitions philosophiques. S'il tient tout de même à soulever la question de l'essence de la religion, c'est qu'il y est forcé par la démarche des positivistes. Leur application univoque du concept de connaissance scientifique à la réalité religieuse ne peut que l'étouffer en la réduisant à un genre qui n'est pas le sien. Troeltsch doit donc insister sur l'essence de la religion, pour montrer son caractère propre et sa distinction essentielle des autres fonctions de l'esprit, telles la science et l'éthique.

3. Ce contexte de la question de l'essence chez Troeltsch comporte dès lors une dimension épistémologique assez manifeste. Celle-ci apparaît d'ailleurs dans le titre même de l'article de 1906-1909: «L'essence de la religion et de la science de la religion». Le rapport entre les deux est immédiat. Si la religion est une fonction autonome de l'esprit, au même titre que les fonctions logique, éthique et esthétique, il y aura aussi une science de la religion, comme il y a une science de l'éthique et de l'esthétique: «Ainsi, dans la science moderne s'est constituée peu à peu une science de la religion comme science particulière autonome, semblable à la logique, à l'éthique et à l'esthétique" (1909a:461 = 1977:87).[1] Aussi, dès les premières lignes de l'article, la science de la religion se trouve-t-elle située parmi les sciences de la culture (1919a:452 = 1977:82). Il n'y a là d'ailleurs rien d'essentiellement nouveau par rapport à l'article de 1895, où Troeltsch exprime déjà son intention de procéder à l'analyse objective des phénomènes psychologiques et historiques de la religion à partir d'une vision générale idéaliste. Et il se réfère alors aux indications de Dilthey dans son introduction aux sciences de l'esprit (1895:415).

4. Mais cette science de la religion, qui constitue un plus par rapport au positivisme, signifie elle-même un moins par rapport à la dogmatique traditionnelle et à l'ancienne philosophie de la religion. Cela apparaît au mieux dans le brillant exorde de la conférence de Saint-Louis, où Troeltsch présente une brève esquisse historique de la science de la religion. Jusqu'au dix-septième siècle, elle s'identifiait à la théologie dogmatique, qui construisait ses dogmes à partir de la Bible et de la tradition ecclésiastique, en les appuyant d'une part sur les miracles de la révélation biblique, d'autre part sur les spéculations métaphysiques de l'apologétique ancienne. Au cours des deux siècles suivants, elle est devenue une théologie naturelle, qui construisait elle-même des dogmes rationnels avec ses preuves de l'existence de Dieu et de l'immortalité de l'âme. Or ces deux formes de science de la religion sont aujourd'hui révolues. La nouvelle science de la religion a ceci de spécifique qu'elle porte sur la religion elle-même comme phénomène spirituel. Ainsi, la philosophie de la religion n'est pas détruite, mais elle sera désormais philosophie sur la religion (1905:5; cf. 1895:374; 1909a:485-87; 1909b:766-67).

5. Qu'en sera-t-il maintenant de la théologie? Est-elle appelée à

disparaître, ou à devenir elle-même science de la religion, c'est-à-dire science de l'expérience religieuse? Nous ne pouvons répondre ici qu'à un aspect plus particulier, mais fondamental de cette question fort complexe. C'est la question bien précise de la révélation. Cette façon de concevoir la religion comme un a priori, comme une fonction autonome de l'esprit, supprime-t-elle toute possibilité de garder un sens quelconque aux notions de révélation et de foi? On sait que telle fut précisément la principale objection soulevée par la théologie dialectique, qui surgit en Allemagne dans les années 20, en réaction contre la théologie libérale de la génération précédente. Quand on replace l'enseignement de Troeltsch dans son contexte, il devient évident que l'objection ne porte pas. Cela apparaît tout particulièrement dans l'article de 1895. Troeltsch signale alors explicitement «le danger de concevoir le processus religieux comme une pure activité de l'esprit humain, en laissant tomber tout fondement de la religion dans son facteur divin» (1895 :369). La transcendance divine de la religion doit donc être sauvegardée. Aussi, Troeltsch répète-t-il qu'il entend «fonder toute la vie de la religion sur la pure factualité de la révélation, ainsi que sur l'énergie pratique de la foi qu'elle suscite». Car «il est impossible d'atteindre l'objet de la religion par une voie extérieure à la religion» (1895 :432-33). Comment cela peut-il se concilier avec l'idée d'un a priori religieux? Troeltsch l'insinue encore ici en notant que le pressentiment ou l'inclination vers quelque chose de suprahumain et d'inconditionné précède l'expérience de phénomènes déterminés (1895 :412). L'a priori religieux, la fonction religieuse de l'esprit, serait donc comme un sens de l'infini, de l'absolu, qui donne la possibilité de le percevoir quand il se manifeste.

Au-delà de l'empirisme

Passons au second versant de notre étude. Après avoir établi le bien-fondé d'une science de la religion, il s'agit maintenant de distinguer et de relier entre elles les différentes démarches qu'elle comporte. Dans sa conférence de Saint-Louis, aux États-Unis, Troeltsch en mentionne tout spécialement deux, qui constituent comme le noyau essentiel de toute science de la religion : la psychologie empirique de la religion et la théorie critique de la connaissance religieuse. La tâche principale de la science de la religion consistera alors à montrer comment les éléments empiriques du phénomène religieux sont reliés aux éléments rationnels que découvre l'analyse des déterminations universelles de la conscience religieuse (1905 :27-28).

La psychologie empirique de la religion

La science moderne de la religion considère d'abord la religion elle-même, plutôt que Dieu ou la révélation. Cette conviction a conduit Troeltsch à porter une attention spéciale à la psychologie empirique de la religion. Car la nouvelle science de la religion doit s'en tenir aux faits, à ce qui peut faire l'objet d'une véritable expérience. La méfiance générale contre toutes les positions dogmatiques tant rationalistes qu'ecclésiastiques a rendu aujourd'hui toute autre considération impossible. Ici comme ailleurs, c'est l'esprit de l'empirisme qui a triomphé. Mais l'empirisme en ce domaine signifie l'analyse psychologique, puisque l'objet d'expérience est ici la conscience religieuse elle-même (1905 : 6).

Alors, l'occasion est belle pour Troeltsch d'attribuer aux Américains le mérite d'avoir appliqué la psychologie moderne aux phénomènes religieux. Écartant toute théorie métaphysique préconçue, ils ont cherché à montrer la riche diversité des faits selon leur propre sens, dans une perspective pratique plutôt que spéculative, pour le plus grand bien de l'humanité. De toute la littérature américaine sur le sujet, une étude ressort plus spécialement : c'est l'ouvrage magistral de William James, *Les variétés de l'expérience religieuse*, qui montre de façon typique les réalisations comme les limites de la psychologie moderne de la religion (1905 : 13-14). Troeltsch retient surtout deux traits caractéristiques de la méthode empirique de James. D'une part, il procède de façon tout à fait indépendante des normes théologiques et ecclésiastiques de la vérité, en considérant l'expérience religieuse partout où elle se manifeste et non pas seulement à l'intérieur du cercle de la foi chrétienne (1912 : 402). Mais d'autre part, William James se veut tout aussi libre du positivisme matérialiste illustré par Comte et Spencer. Il reconnaît aux expériences religieuses la même valeur qu'aux autres, car il admet l'autonomie et la spontanéité de l'esprit (1909a : 485 = 1977 : 108; cf. 1909a : 457, n. 34 = 1977 : 84, n. 2).

La première question que soulève la méthode empirique est celle du point de départ : comment délimiter le champ de l'analyse et par où commencer? Troeltsch propose d'abord ce qu'on pourrait appeler la cartographie du champ. À l'extrême limite, il y a le domaine d'investigation des anthropologues, qui sont comme les psychologues du passé, qui considèrent aussi les peuplades primitives d'aujourd'hui, mais pour comprendre l'âme religieuse des peuples préhistoriques. Au centre même du terrain, tout autour de l'observateur, c'est l'expérience religieuse du présent, celle de l'observateur lui-même, celle des personnes qui l'entourent et qui rendent témoignage de leur vécu religieux, celle aussi dont témoignent de façon plus générale les grandes religions d'aujourd'hui, comme le christianisme, le bouddhisme et l'islam. Entre ces deux points extrêmes, il y a tout le domaine de l'histoire des religions hindoues, chinoises, sémitiques, helléniques, etc. (1905 : 67).

Avec cette description du champ des phénomènes religieux, la question du point de départ se pose avec plus d'acuité encore. Certains mettent l'accent sur le domaine de l'anthropologie. Car c'est dans le contexte de la culture primitive qu'apparaît le vrai sens de la religion. Celle-ci n'est rien d'autre, en effet, qu'un témoin de l'âme primitive, avec sa propension à tout personnaliser, à considérer toutes choses dans ses rapports personnels, bienveillants ou non, avec l'individu humain. La science moderne a mis fin à cette vision du monde, en considérant les liens matériels de causalité qui englobent toutes choses dans une complète indifférence par rapport à la destinée humaine. La religion a donc perdu tout son sens à l'époque moderne. Ce n'est plus qu'un vestige du passé, appelé tôt ou tard à disparaître. Troeltsch note immédiatement que c'est la psychologie religieuse du positivisme qui parle ainsi, elle qui mesure toute vérité à l'aune de la science moderne de la nature. Ce qu'on trouve ici, c'est une métaphysique positiviste qui s'oppose à une métaphysique religieuse. Ce n'est pas une analyse psychologique de la religion, mais une polémique contre la religion sur la base d'une métaphysique positiviste. En un mot, c'est du positivisme, non de l'empirisme.

La véritable psychologie empirique de la religion procède tout autrement. Son point de départ est plutôt la religion actuelle, pleinement vivante, qui peut fort bien se comprendre par elle-même. Il est en effet plus facile d'interpréter la religion primitive à partir d'aujourd'hui, que de procéder à l'inverse, car il nous est très difficile de connaître les sentiments et la vie intérieure des primitifs. Troeltsch reconnaît bien qu'une authentique psychologie empirique de la religion pourra bénéficier du matériel accumulé par les anthropologues, pour comprendre les complexités et les raffinements de la religion d'aujourd'hui à partir de formes primitives plus simples. Mais il reste convaincu que l'essence même de la chose (*das Wesen der Sache*) doit être cherchée et découverte par l'analyse de la religion vivante du présent, qui seule est pour nous un véritable fait (1905:7-9; cf. 1912:411-12).

À ce premier principe méthodologique, on doit joindre cependant un second, pour rétablir l'équilibre. Il faut observer autant que possible la religion «naïve», c'est-à-dire la religion dans sa pureté originelle, en tant que simple religion, non encore contaminée, mêlée aux autres activités de l'esprit, telles la science et l'art. Si l'on suppose, en effet, que la religion est une fonction spécifique de l'esprit, il importe de l'analyser en elle-même, dans sa forme la plus pure, comme dégagée des autres fonctions scientifique, éthique ou esthétique. Mais comme toutes ces activités de l'esprit ne s'exercent pas indépendamment les unes des autres, Troeltsch sait fort bien qu'on n'arrivera jamais à isoler un phénomène religieux chimiquement pur. C'est tout de même vers cet objectif qu'il faut tendre autant que possible (1909a:463-64 = 1977:89-90).

À la lumière de ce second principe, la religion primitive retrouve son intérêt et son utilité pour l'analyse empirique. Elle constitue en effet un cas typique de religion naïve, car la science et la technologie sont alors trop peu développées pour restreindre et obscurcir le sentiment religieux. Il n'en reste pas moins que certains développements mythiques d'intuitions religieuses à l'origine dépassent amplement le domaine strictement religieux et peuvent déjà être considérés comme des tentatives préscientifiques d'explication du monde. Ainsi, tout le matériel découvert par l'ethnographie et l'anthropologie ne doit pas être porté au compte de la religion naïve, sans plus de discernement. On ne doit retenir de tout cela comme authentiquement religieux que ce qui se trouve directement inspiré par la révélation divine et ce qui est directement relié au culte divin (1909a :464-65 = 1977 :90-91).

Si tout dans la religion primitive ne s'identifie pas à la religion naïve, il faut reconnaître aussi bien que la religion naïve ne se trouve pas elle-même seulement chez les peuples primitifs. On la retrouve aussi tout au cours de l'histoire dans les grandes personnalités religieuses, tels les fondateurs de religions nouvelles, les prophètes, les réformateurs, les missionnaires. Ces gens sont complètement consacrés à une idée religieuse. Ils sont inspirés, portés par elle, et ils ne sentent pas le besoin de la corroborer par la réflexion et la systématisation. Mais ces grandes personnalités religieuses sont en général encore assez loin de nous. Nous n'y avons accès que par l'intermédiaire des documents et des institutions. Troeltsch propose donc comme dernière source pour l'étude de la religion, la propre expérience religieuse du chercheur. Encore là cependant l'introspection devra discerner soigneusement la pure expérience religieuse, en se référant aux moments religieux les plus intenses de la vie, tels ceux de la prière et de la méditation (1909a :465-66 = 1977 :91-92; cf. 1905 :9-10).

Le champ de l'analyse étant ainsi délimité et balisé, reste maintenant à préciser la tâche d'une psychologie empirique de la religion. Elle consiste, somme toute, à déterminer la propriété caractéristique de l'expérience religieuse. Cela suppose qu'on distingue d'abord dans le phénomène religieux ce qui est central et ce qui est périphérique. Troeltsch dira aussi qu'il faut discerner la forme commune de ses divers contenus. Les contenus sont identifiés ici comme les éléments symboliques et doctrinaux, éthiques, liturgiques et institutionnels de la religion. Tous ces éléments matériels varient grandement d'une religion à une autre et parfois même à l'intérieur d'une même religion. Ils ont quand même cette propriété commune d'être des phénomènes «religieux». Et c'est justement cette forme commune que la psychologie tâche de déterminer (1905 :10-11; cf. 1909a :492-93 = 1977 :114-15).

Troeltsch se réfère encore ici à William James, qui définit l'expérience spécifique à la base de tous les phénomènes religieux comme un état d'âme particulier caractérisé par le sentiment de la présence du divin, impliquant la perception de toute réalité dans son rapport avec l'infini (1905 :35-36). Troeltsch en conclut que l'analyse psychologique conduit à reconnaître finalement que l'élément fondamental de toute religion est la mystique, c'est-à-dire la foi en la présence active d'une puissance suprahumaine, avec la possibilité d'une relation intérieure avec elle. La psychologie de la religion montre en effet avec évidence que c'est dans l'expérience mystique que se fait entendre la pulsation propre de la religion (1905 :46-47; cf. 1909a :493 = 1977 :115). On pourrait penser que la détermination de cette forme commune à tous les phénomènes religieux constitue l'équivalent d'une définition de l'essence de la religion. Ce serait là cependant une grave méprise, contre laquelle Troeltsch prend bien soin de nous prévenir. Car, dans la psychologie empirique de James, tout concept universel, toute essence de la religion, se trouve écartée dès l'abord (1905:15).² La conscience se trouve alors conçue comme un flot d'occurences psychiques, comme une suite d'expériences en motion constante. Il n'y a donc aucune unité a priori de la conscience, aucun lien entre la conscience individuelle contingente et la conscience en général. Par conséquent, chez William James, la détermination de ces expériences ou faits de conscience qu'il appelle «religieux» ne s'identifie d'aucune façon à une recherche de l'essence de la religion, ou à la construction d'un concept de religion. La caractérisation qu'il fait des expériences religieuses est purement empirique et approximative. Elle accumule indéfiniment les marques caractéristiques, et elle laisse ouverte la question de l'unité spécifique réelle des phénomènes religieux (1912:412-13). Pour James, il n'y a donc que de l'individuel, et l'individu n'est qu'un élément dans le flot continu qui relativise tout. La recherche ne peut rien faire d'autre que d'analyser ce flot des phénomènes, les classifier et vérifier empiriquement les hypothèses qui en ressortent (1912:410).

À la question de l'essence se trouve intimement liée celle de la vérité et de la validité du phénomène. Et c'est aussi dans le même sens qu'on doit y répondre, d'après William James. Puisqu'il n'y a pas d'essence universelle, il n'y a pas non plus d'idéal absolu d'après lequel on pourrait juger de la vérité et de la validité de la religion. Par ailleurs, toutes les manifestations religieuses n'ont pas la même valeur. Il faudra donc un certain critère pour pouvoir en juger. Et ce critère sera pour James ce qui favorise la vie. Par exemple, sera considéré comme le plus valable ce type d'expérience religieuse qui embrasse la vie de l'âme dans toute sa complexité pour l'unifier par la puissance d'un unique principe. Ainsi, l'idée de «valeur pour la vie» se substitue à celle de vérité et de validité (1912:415-16). C'est en ce sens que James qualifiera lui-même sa position de «pragmatisme». Quant à Troeltsch, il en parlera volontiers comme d'un utilitarisme (1912:410-11).

La théorie de la connaissance religieuse

Tout cela, dira Troeltsch, n'est encore que de la psychologie empirique. Celle-ci détermine le caractère particulier des phénomènes religieux, leur contexte, leurs rapports. Elle montre la variété illimitée des phénomènes et elle fait ressortir les principaux types. Mais là se limite le domaine de sa compétence. Elle ne peut rien dire du contenu substantiel (*Gehalt*) de ces formations religieuses, de leur vérité, de leur validité. C'est là un tout autre problème, qui ne concerne pas simplement les faits comme tels, mais aussi le sens et la valeur de ces mêmes faits. Or cette question de la validité des phénomènes ne peut être traitée et résolue qu'au niveau des concepts universels de la raison. Il faut donc passer ici du niveau de l'«empirisme» à celui du «rationalisme» (1905:17-18).

Notons que ce dépassement de l'empirisme se fait en deux temps. Il faut d'abord que soit posée la question de la validité et de la vérité des phénomènes religieux. Or plusieurs empiristes manifestent déjà ici une certaine résistance. Ils jugent par trop philosophique et spéculative cette question de la valeur et de la vérité, et ils cherchent à l'éviter autant que possible. Troeltsch s'efforce donc de montrer que la question est incontournable, et qu'elle se pose avec plus d'urgence encore à celui qui poursuit des recherches de psychologie religieuse. Car devant la variété infinie des phénomènes, qui semble contenir pêle-mêle le meilleur et le pire, on ne peut s'empêcher de chercher un critère de discernement. Mais ce critère ne peut lui-même se trouver ailleurs que dans l'a priori de la raison, et dans la coordination de cet a priori religieux avec les autres dimensions de la conscience humaine. Tel est justement le second moment du raisonnement par lequel Troeltsch s'efforce d'amener le psychologue à dépasser sa position purement empirique pour se situer à un niveau plus strictement rationnel. Car c'est seulement à ce niveau que peut être fondée la vérité de la religion et, par là même, discernées de façon critique, les multiples productions de la vie religieuse (1905 : 51).

Ces deux niveaux de la recherche, empirique et rationnel, distinguent effectivement deux disciplines à l'intérieur de la science de la religion : la psychologie et la théorie de la connaissance (*Erkenntnistheorie*). Tandis que la première regroupe les faits selon l'analogie, la simultanéité et la succession, en indiquant les relations fonctionnelles qui les unissent, la seconde vise la validité la plus universelle possible à l'aide de concepts rationnels universels (1905 : 21). L'étude de 1906-1909 détermine plus précisément la tâche de cette théorie critique de la connaissance religieuse. Elle doit montrer, dans la nature même de l'esprit humain, la loi a priori de la formation des idées religieuses, en indiquant aussi comment cet a priori religieux se trouve relié aux autres principes a priori de la raison. En d'autres termes, c'est le propre de la théorie de la connaissance de définir la fonction religieuse par rapport aux autres fonctions de l'esprit. La question principale sera donc ici celle du contenu spécifique de cet a priori religieux et de la nature essentielle de cette fonction religieuse. Elle consiste effectivement dans la relation à l'absolu qu'établit l'esprit, grâce à laquelle toute réalité et toute valeur sont rattachées à une substance absolue comme à leur origine première et à leur norme ultime. Et par là même se trouve indiqué aussi le rapport étroit qui unit la fonction religieuse aux autres fonctions de l'esprit, puisque celles-ci atteignent leur unité profonde dans le fondement divin où elles s'enracinent toutes (1909a : 494-95 = 1977 : 116).

L'idée même d'une théorie de la connaissance nous fait immédiatement penser à Kant. Effectivement, c'est bien à Kant que se réfère ici Troeltsch. Car la méthode critique qu'il a suivie pour la connaissance théorique des sciences de la nature, Kant l'a aussi appliquée aux différentes sphères de la raison pratique. Comme il avait montré les lois réglant la raison théorique, il a aussi cherché celles qui gouvernent la conscience éthique, esthétique et religieuse. Et c'est au coeur même des phénomènes de la vie concrète qu'il a trouvé ces lois a priori de la raison, car c'est dans l'expérience concrète de la vie qu'elles se manifestent (1905 : 26).

Ce dernier point est tout particulièrement important. Ce que Troeltsch entend définir par là, c'est le rationalisme propre à Kant, qu'il distingue d'une part du rationalisme spéculatif caractéristique de la scolastique néoplatonicienne et de l'hégélianisme, et d'autre part du rationalisme régressif typique de la scolastique de tradition aristotélicienne. Les premiers déduisent la réalité — le monde et Dieu lui-même — à partir de concepts nécessaires. Les autres, partant de la réalité empirique du monde et par l'effort de l'argumentation rationnelle, tentent de poser l'existence d'un fondement divin du monde. Le rationalisme de Kant est d'un ordre tout différent. Troeltsch l'appelle ici un rationalisme formel, immanent à l'expérience. Car c'est dans l'expérience la plus élémentaire qu'il découvre le règne de l'a priori de la raison. Or cette loi rationnelle, interne à l'esprit et à l'expérience, ne permet d'aucune façon de conclure à l'existence de Dieu. Mais comme elle constitue la forme structurante de l'esprit et de l'expérience, elle permet par là même de diriger l'esprit dans son expérience de la réalité, et de discerner la valeur des différentes expériences disponibles (1905 : 21-22).

Ce qui fait la supériorité de Kant, d'après Troeltsch, c'est qu'il est en même temps un empirique et un rationaliste s'efforçant d'unir la vérité de Hume et celle de Platon. Il possède le même sens aigu pour l'élément empirique-factuel que pour l'élément rationnel-conceptuel de la connaissance humaine, et il conçoit la science comme un équilibre de ces deux éléments. Cela signifie plus précisément qu'il a perçu dans la science moderne un élément rationnel et un élément irrationnel, et qu'il a tenté de faire la synthèse entre les deux. Son grand mérite est d'avoir bien posé le problème, en faisant ressortir cet aspect rationnel a priori présent au coeur de toute science. Voilà ce sur quoi ferme les yeux le pragmatisme de James, lui qui rejette «l'essence rêveuse» (*das grüblerische Wesen*) de Kant. Mais si Kant a bien posé le problème, la solution qu'il en propose est déjà datée, vu son étroite dépendance de la mécanique classique, d'une psychologie encore à l'état embryonnaire et d'une pensée historique tout juste naissante. Troeltsch est donc bien conscient lui-même des aspects périmés de l'oeuvre de Kant (1905 : 24-26).

Troeltsch cependant ne se contente pas d'opposer l'empirisme de James au rationalisme kantien. Prenant plus d'altitude encore, remontant encore plus haut dans l'histoire, c'est au platonisme finalement qu'il rattache la philosophie européenne de la religion, par contraste avec son pendant américain. On trouve d'ailleurs, au temps de Platon, une analogie avec le débat contemporain. Car les sophistes peuvent eux-mêmes être considérés comme les ancêtres de l'empirisme moderne. Leur relativisme et leur subjectivisme viennent justement de ce qu'ils s'en tiennent à la multiplicité du réel. Et c'est là ce que Platon s'efforce de dépasser, en montrant la présence d'un élément nécessaire, rationnel, conceptuel au coeur même du réel. La philosophie kantienne suit là-dessus la ligne du platonisme, quand elle tente d'établir la correspondance entre la loi naturelle et la nécessité rationnelle de l'esprit (1912 :404-05).

La philosophie de la religion, telle qu'elle se trouve pratiquée en Europe, constitue à cet égard une simple application de la conception philosophique platonicienne à la compréhension critique de la religion (1912 :405). Troeltsch résume ainsi en quelques traits ses principaux éléments. La religion est un produit nécessaire de la conscience humaine, selon une loi a priori de l'esprit. Cette loi consiste dans la relation de l'individu à un absolu immanent dans l'esprit. Tel est le coeur du phénomène religieux, telle est l'essence de la religion, qui dans l'actualité de l'histoire apparaît sous une forme toujours différente. Un rationalisme tant soit peu ferme ne se contentera pas ici de classifier les phénomènes; il tentera de comprendre le mouvement de l'histoire, en y voyant les étapes d'une évolution, les différents stages du développement de la conscience religieuse dans sa relation avec le monde de l'expérience. Cela conduit nécessairement à la question d'une réalisation finale et parfaite de cette essence de la religion, en d'autres termes, à la question de la religion absolue. Et le théologien prend alors la relève pour montrer comment le christianisme constitue précisément la religion finale, absolue. Toute cette construction repose évidemment sur un fondement métaphysique, qui consiste dans le rapport de la conscience individuelle, finie et contingente, à la conscience universelle, infinie, nécessaire et absolue, la première tirant son origine de la seconde, pour y retourner finalement au terme de son évolution historique (1912 :407, 409).

Ce que Troeltsch vient de décrire ici, c'est évidemment la philosophie de la religion du XIXe siècle, telle qu'illustrée tout spécialement par le système de Hegel. Il l'a fait sans atténuer les traits les plus extravagants, les plus intempérants de l'idéalisme classique. Lui-même reconnaît cependant que, dans un tel système, le rationnel, le nécessaire, absorbe l'empirique et le contingent. La réaction radicale de William James, qu'il présente immédiatement après, se comprend d'autant mieux dans ce contexte. James aime s'appeler un empiriste radical. Cela signifie qu'il se présente comme un antiplatonicien radical. Il s'oppose à tout a priori et à toute théorie rationaliste de la connaissance. Il ne veut rien faire d'autre que d'analyser les faits, refusant d'y voir toute nécessité ou validité rationnelle qui proviendrait de l'essence de ces mêmes faits. Par là, James a fait plus qu'ajouter tout simplement un nouveau champ à la philosophie de la religion, soit la psychologie empirique de la religion. Il a vraiment converti la philosophie de la religion en psychologie de la religion. Plus exactement, il s'est fait le protagoniste d'un nouveau type, un type opposé de philosophie de la religion (1912 :409).

Entre ces deux voies extrêmes de l'idéalisme hégélien et de l'empirisme de James, Troeltsch réaffirme finalement sa propre position. Il se situe résolument du côté de la philosophie transcendantale a priori, dans la ligne de Platon, de Kant et de Schleiermacher. Car c'est seulement dans ce contexte philosophique que peut être reconnu un élément de validité inconditionnelle, provenant de la nature même de la conscience, dans les domaines de l'éthique et de l'esthétique autant que dans celui de la religion. Il s'est sans doute éloigné de Hegel, et beaucoup rapproché de James, avec sa critique de l'absolu dans l'histoire, telle qu'élaborée dans son essai sur l'absoluité du christianisme. Même alors cependant, il est demeuré dans les limites de la philosophie transcendantale. Il voit même difficilement comment il pourrait incorporer dans la structure de cette philosophie de Kant et de Schleiermacher ce qu'il reconnaît de juste dans la philosophie de la religion de James. Car il ne s'agit pas là simplement d'une psychologie de la religion, mais d'une philosophie de la religion née du «psychologisme» (1912:419-20).

On ne peut donc assumer en même temps ces deux types opposés de philosophie de la religion, mais à l'intérieur de son propre système. Troeltsch entend bien faire la synthèse de la psychologie empirique et de la théorie rationnelle de la connaissance (1905:21 et 23). Telle était déjà d'après lui, nous l'avons vu, la position de principe de Kant lui-même. Cela signifie appliquer successivement deux méthodes de recherche pour saisir deux niveaux différents du réel: le donné-factuel et le rationnel-nécessaire, le psychologique déterminé par la causalité et le valide perçu par la critique rationnelle (1909b:757 et 759).

Cette synthèse signifie par ailleurs beaucoup plus qu'une simple juxtaposition ou application successive des deux méthodes. Il s'agit vraiment d'une corrélation, d'une interdépendance. L'analyse empirique suscite des questions de valeur et de vérité qui ne peuvent être résolues qu'au niveau de la théorie critique de la connaissance. Par contre, les lois rationnelles qui définissent les fonctions de l'esprit ne peuvent être tirées que des faits, que des formations concrètes de la conscience humaine. Ainsi, l'analyse psychologique est le présupposé nécessaire de la compréhension des lois rationnelles; la psychologie constitue la porte d'entrée pour la théorie de la connaissance (1905:34). Il s'ensuit que la découverte des lois a priori de la conscience religieuse est un processus en évolution constante. Les théories de la connaissance ne sont toujours que des approximations, car la créativité inépuisable de la vie est toujours plus riche que tous les systèmes de la raison. Troeltsch critique ici le caractère beaucoup trop rigide du système kantien des concepts a priori. Ce système doit être ouvert, toujours en croissance, en voie d'autocorrection constante (1905:30-31). Par contre, le système ne peut se contenter de suivre le cours de la vie, d'être le simple reflet de la vie, car on reviendrait par là au niveau de la pure analyse empirique. Les lois rationnelles qu'on découvre dans le cours de la vie doivent pouvoir elles-mêmes diriger le cours de la vie. Troeltsch exprime ainsi la tension inhérente à cette corrélation: «Il faut toujours distinguer l'illusion de la vérité par la réduction à une loi universelle, mais en évitant que la loi prenne la place de la réalité vivante. La loi se trouve en elle, elle demeure en elle et elle agit sur elle contre l'illusion et la confusion» (1905 : 24).

Conclusions

1. En conclusion, soulignons encore une fois l'idée centrale d'une synthèse de la psychologie empirique et de la théorie rationnelle de la connaissance, qui doit, pour Troeltsch, constituer le noyau solide d'une authentique science de la religion. C'est par là qu'il conclut lui-même son étude de 1905 : «C'est seulement quand on fait droit à ce double élément, l'empirisme et le rationalisme, la psychologie et la théorie de la connaissance, que la science religieuse (*Religionswissenschaft*) est vraiment une science de la religion (*Wissenschaft von der Religion*), et non pas une substitution de la religion par la science, ou une science contre la religion, ou encore une simple description de la religion sans science» (1905 : 53).

2. On pourrait fort bien maintenant définir la personnalité scientifique de Troeltsch par ce double pôle de l'empirisme et du rationalisme. C'est ce qui le caractérise parmi les chercheurs en science de la religion au début du siècle : au cours des recherches les plus empiriques, il garde toujours vivant le souci des questions philosophiques. Ce serait gravement méconnaître le sens de son oeuvre que de croire qu'il est passé du pôle de l'a priori philosophique à celui de l'a posteriori empirique. Sans doute, le jeu de ces deux pôles s'est-il manifesté de différentes façons au cours de sa carrière. Dans son grand article de 1895, la polarité est celle de la psychologie de la religion et de l'histoire de la religion. La première se trouve alors comprise comme une discipline philosophique qui soulève les questions du lieu, de l'origine et du sens de la religion dans la conscience humaine, pour répondre finalement à la question de la vérité de la religion. Quant à l'histoire de la religion, elle porte sur les réalisations particulières de la religion au cours de l'histoire, représentant ainsi le pôle de la recherche positive (1895 : 370). La même polarité réapparaîtra ensuite au sein même de la psychologie, quand Troeltsch distinguera une psychologie philosophique au sens de Dilthey, et une psychologie expérimentale, telle qu'elle se retrouve chez James (1922 : 6). La première s'appellera désormais «théorie de la connaissance». En tout cela, on le voit bien, autant Troeltsch ressent la nécessité de la recherche empirique, autant est-il soucieux de dépasser ce point de vue purement empirique, pour aborder directement les questions philosophiques sous-jacentes à l'analyse des phénomènes. On pourrait même supposer que le probleme de l'historicisme met en oeuvre chez lui la même tension : d'une part la nécessité de passer par le creuset de la critique historique; d'autre part l'urgence de dépasser une vision purement séculière de l'histoire (cf. Dumais 1988).

3. C'est dans le contexte de cette problématique qu'il faut replacer la recherche de Troeltsch sur l'essence et le concept de religion. On refuse le

plus souvent de soulever ces questions par crainte des positions dogmatiques — en philosophie autant qu'en théologie — qu'on associe habituellement avec ce genre de recherche. Et Troeltsch avoue lui-même : «Pour les purs psychologues et les purs positivistes, ma théorie de la religion est une superstition tout aussi crasse qu'une encyclique papale" (1909b :755). Pourtant, Troeltsch n'est pas moins critique que quiconque face aux déterminations dogmatiques de l'essence de la religion, à partir de données révélées ou de pures théories philosophiques. Ainsi, la recherche sur la nature de la religion ne peut s'effectuer ailleurs que sur le terrain même de l'analyse empirique. Voilà pourquoi Troeltsch se réfère toujours à la théorie kantienne de la connaissance, qui découvre l'a priori de la raison au coeur même de l'expérience sensible. Cette référence à Kant montre cependant qu'on ne peut s'en tenir à l'analyse objective des phénomènes. Et ce n'est pas là pour Troeltsch simplement une question de goût personnel. C'est la situation du temps présent qui l'exige. Celle-ci se caractérise, en effet, par le triomphe de l'historicisation, de la psychologisation et de la relativisation de toute réalité, fermant ainsi l'accès à toute pensée normative (1909b :755). Voilà précisément ce que Troeltsch veut retrouver : l'accès à la question de la vérité et de la validité dans le domaine de la religion. Or cela ne peut se faire sans poser d'abord la question de l'essence de la religion. On comprend dès lors pourquoi l'effort principal de Troeltsch consiste ici à justifier la légitimité de ce genre de question, à montrer son urgence pour la situation présente de la culture, et à faire voir surtout par quelle voie nouvelle une réponse peut y être donnée aujourd'hui.

4. On devine maintenant que cette recherche de la nature, de la vérité et de la validité de la religion n'a pas qu'un intérêt théorique. Troeltsch est bien clair là-dessus : «Comme toute autre science, la science de la religion a un but pratique, soit la régulation et la clarification des productions naïves et barbares, l'harmonisation et l'équilibre des tendances unilatérales avec les autres tendances de la vie» (1909a :468 = 1977 :93). Cet objectif pratique ne se limite pas d'ailleurs aux seules dimensions de l'individu pour assurer l'équilibre et la croissance de la personne. Il s'étend à tout le domaine de la culture, pour l'harmonisation de la religion avec les autres sphères de la culture, pour permettre là encore l'unification de la culture à partir de sa source spirituelle profonde. Enfin, la science de la religion devrait avoir une influence interculturelle dans le sens de la paix mondiale, en favorisant une rencontre et un dialogue harmonieux des religions, à l'abri de toute intolérance. Mais alors, la science de la religion doit-elle prendre la relève des Églises et plus particulièrement de la théologie, considérée jusqu'ici comme l'instance doctrinale régulatrice à l'intérieur de chacune des confessions? Certains textes de Troeltsch pourraient être interprétés en ce sens, quand il exprime son impatience face au dogmatisme des Églises et de leurs théologies, dont il semble parfois désespérer. Mais il reconnaît finalement que seules les religions positives sont vrai-

ment vivantes, et que par conséquent l'influence pratique la plus importante de la science de la religion sera celle qu'elle pourra exercer sur la théologie des confessions chrétiennes (1909a :497-99 = 1977 :119-20).

Notes

1 Notons que le titre de l'article, «L'essence de la religion et de la science de la religion», s'éclaire lui-même par là : s'il y a une essence propre de la religion, la science de la religion aura aussi son essence propre; elle sera essentiellement distincte des autres.
2 Dans l'article «L'essence de la religion et de la science de la religion», Troeltsch se fait plus conciliant. Il admet que l'expression «essence de la religion» peut singifier les traits caractéristiques de ce phénomène psychique qu'est la religion, tels que la psychologie les rassemble dans un concept universel de religion. Mais elle signifie aussi et surtout «l'essence réelle, par opposition au simple phénomène, c'est-à-dire le contenu de vérité de la religion». Et ce n'est plus là l'objet de la psychologie, mais d'une recherche d'un tout autre ordre, celui de la théorie de la connaissance (1909a :489 = 1977 :111).

Références

Dumais, Alfred. 1988. «Ernst Troeltsch et la sécularisation de l'histoire». *Laval théologique et philosophique* 44 : 279-92.
Séguy, Jean. 1980. *Christianisme et société. Introduction à la sociologie de Ernst Troeltsch.* Paris : Cerf.
Smith, Wilfred Cantwell. 1964. *The Meaning and End of Religion. A New Approach to the Religious Traditions of Mankind.* Toronto : The New American Library of Canada.
Troeltsch, Ernst. 1895. «Die Selbständigkeit der Religion» 1-2. *Zeitschrift für Theologie und Kirche* 5 : 361-436. — Nous n'utilisons ici que ces deux premières parties de l'article; les deux autres parties ont paru l'année suivante dans la même revue.
———. 1905. *Theologie und Erkenntnistheorie in der Religionswissenschaft. Eine Untersuchung über die Bedeutung der Kantischen Religionslehre für die heutige Religionswissenschaft.* Tübingen : J. C. B. Mohr (Paul Siebeck).
———. 1909a. «Wesen der Religion und der Religionswissenschaft». *Gesammelte Schriften* 2, Scientia Verlag Aalen (1962) : 452-99. — Nous nous référons ici à cette seconde édition, revue et augmentée, de l'essai paru d'abord en 1906. C'est l'édition qui a été reprise dans les G. S. et traduite par Michael Pye.
———. 1909b. «Zur Frage des religiösen Apriori." *Gesammelte Schriften* 2 : 754-68.
———. 1912. «Empiricism and Platonism in the Philosophy of Religion». *Harvard Theological Review*, 5 : 401-22.
———. 1922. «Meine Bücher». *Gesammelte Schriften* 4 (1966) : 3-18.
———. 1977. *Writings on Theology and Religion.* Translated and edited by Robert Morgan and Michael Pye. Atlanta : John Knox Press. — Nous renvoyons à ce recueil pour la traduction de l'essai de 1906-1909 : «Religion and the Science of Religion».

CHAPTER 9

An Ambivalent Relationship to the Holy: Gerardus van der Leeuw on Religion

Richard J. Plantinga

Introduction

In turning one's attention to the word, the idea, and the reality of religion in history in order to understand the significance of religion and estimate its usefulness in scholarly investigation — particularly in the history of the Occident — it is appropriate and particularly instructive, it would seem, to turn to that period in Western history when religion became a particular object of research. I naturally have in mind the period from the eighteenth century to the present — the time in which *die Religion* came to be associated with its very own *Wissenschaft*. Under the rubric of this new science, various kinds of scholars have investigated religion from philological, historical, anthropological, sociological, psychological, philosophical, phenomenological, and theological points of view.

I would like to take this opportunity to present the view of religion of a major representative of one important tradition within *Religionswissenschaft*, namely, that of the Dutch scholar Gerardus van der Leeuw (1890-1950). Van der Leeuw is an interesting case study, it seems to me, because as a twentieth-century historian and phenomenologist of religion, he had a good overview of the world of religion, ranging from so-called primitive religion to Christianity, from Indian religion to ancient Greek religion, from ancient Egyptian religion to German Romanticism.

I will thus sketch van der Leeuw's view of religion in this essay. I will not, however, discuss his view of method in the study of religion: this would go beyond the necessary limitations of space imposed upon the present study. Nor will I attempt to draw large and systematic conclusions about religion in Western history. This I leave to Professors Smith, Des-

---

Notes and references for this chapter appear on pages 98-100.

pland, and Feil, who have dedicated much scholarly energy to this matter (see Smith 1978; Despland 1979; Feil 1986).

Van der Leeuw's Conception of Religion[1]

Before turning to van der Leeuw's view of religion, a word about his view of the business of offering definitions of religion is in order. One can, he notes, adopt the view of religion found in any one religion—most often one's own—and allow this to stand for religion in general, explaining other religions as falsehoods. A much better approach, van der Leeuw says, is to attempt the very difficult task of seeking what is common in the many different conceptions of the object of religion. One then seeks a term that is as "colourless" as possible, a term that will do justice to all the forms of religion which it is intended to summarize. However, this approach, too, is riddled with difficulties. Van der Leeuw points out that such definitions of religion often tell us more about the intentions and opinions of the person doing the defining and the period in which they were written than they tell us about the phenomenon of religion itself. For, as Schleiermacher argued in *Über die Religion*, one finds religion only in religions—and thus by implication not in definitions of religion (see van der Leeuw 1930:1860-61; 1935a:346; 1941:1-2; 1956:669-70).

Having thus drawn attention to the precarious character of that which he was about to undertake, van der Leeuw sought to characterize religion—a phenomenon rooted in human experience—by preliminarily defining it as a relationship of a person to something or someone "other." The world of religion displays a variety of ways of conceiving this "other" by which one is touched, which one encounters in experience, which intrudes into one's life. Because of this intrusive nature of the other, van der Leeuw notes, life is a dangerous affair filled with critical moments. In thus stressing the experiential character of the human encounter with the other, van der Leeuw writes: "The essence of all religions ... is a relation to a power or to powers—a real relation and real powers, a relation which is felt to be stronger, more real and more living than the relation we have with our fellow human beings" (van der Leeuw 1960:168). The power (*Macht*—one of the central notions in van der Leeuw's *Phänomenologie*) referred to here may be impersonal. It may also be personal; that is, it may be combined with will and form. In fact, van der Leeuw says, in "the three words power, will and form is contained almost the entire concept of the object of religion" (van der Leeuw 1956:83).

In discussing the concept of religion, van der Leeuw called for circumspection with respect to the term "God." While many people are prone to think of religion in terms of belief in and worship of God, such a view of religion is problematic for more than one reason. First of all, van der Leeuw notes, if one chooses to think about religion in terms of God, the term must be so carefully circumscribed as to die the death of a thousand qualifications and so cease to say anything significant. In the second place, in thinking about religion in terms of God, one often does so with a particular conception of God in mind. Naturally, doing so has great potential for distortion where one's own conception of God does not obtain or where God is not a part of religion. God is, if not a Christian, then at least a Greek representation of the object of religion which is not applicable everywhere in the world of religion. Instead of this Graeco-Christian conception, one ought to think of God as the indication of that to which human religious striving directs itself. Notions of God thus arise out of the experience of power encountered in life to which one seeks a relation. In this connection, van der Leeuw speaks of the "double experience of form": numinous experience (experience with power and encounter with will) is formless and without structure; the double experience of form produces representations—power and will acquire name and form as demons, gods, or God. In this way, humanity overcomes its painful solitude. Van der Leeuw hastens to add that this is no Feuerbachian or Freudian process: what one sees here is not projection, theorizing, or abstraction but rather something concrete and empirical—giving name and form to the experience of power and will. It is in light of this that one should understand van der Leeuw's prima facie strange remark that "God" is a latecomer to the history of religion.

Thus, instead of God, one would do better to speak of *numen*, which is a less personal designation for half-formed power with an element of will. Likewise, the Dutch term *religie*, derived from the Latin *religio*, is a less precise and hence more desirable term than the Dutch term *godsdienst*, which is widely used in the Dutch language as a synonym for *religie*. The former indicates only a relation while the latter rather narrowly fixes the object of the relation and focusses on only one religious form (see van der Leeuw 1930:1860-61; 1935a:346-47; 1935b:351; 1941:1-2; 1956:3-4,72,103,155-56,160,168-69).

The encounter with the object of the relation constitutive of religion is characterized by van der Leeuw as wholly other, different, out of the ordinary, strange, marked off, *tabu*, *mana*-like, greater than oneself, superior, powerful, numinous, sacred. All of these terms can be summed up in the terms "holy," "holiness," and "the Holy," which van der Leeuw borrowed from two scholars for whom he had very high regard: Nathan Söderblom and Rudolf Otto (see Söderblom 1913:731-41; Otto 1932; van der Leeuw 1931:136-44; 1935c:113-14; 1938:71-81). In summarizing this impressive encounter with the other, van der Leeuw expresses himself in rather pregnant fashion by saying that "in religion one interprets one's experience as revelation" (van der Leeuw 1930:1861). Thus, religion is a relationship to the Holy or "le rapport existentiel, voire l'unité entre l'homme et l'objet de son expérience, qu'il appelle monde, forces surhumaines ou Dieu" (van der Leeuw 1935d:494).

The human reaction to this encounter is one of awe, amazement, wonder. This the most basic of religious feelings, is not at all straightforward. That is, one's relationship to the other can take various forms. One may seek to dominate the other, or serve it, or love it, or fear it, or seek unity with it. Whatever the form, one's relation to the other or the Holy is two-sided. In the presence of this uncanny other, one has feelings of fear,[2] dread, repulsion, terror, horror, apprehension, *tremendum* — as well as love, longing, attraction, surrender, adoration, reverence, *fascinans*. Thus van der Leeuw writes: "Religion is an ambivalent relationship to the Holy" (van der Leeuw 1941:4). Why this is so one cannot say: the essence of religion is a mystery. However, one can say that the person seeks a relationship to the Holy because he or she is impelled by it.

An encounter with the Holy does not leave one unchanged; after this experience, the religious person feels a demand and the necessity of fulfilling a task. In other words, awe develops into observance. This, according to van der Leeuw, is the significance of the Latin *religio*, which may mean the bond of a person to something or the fact that a person pays attention to something. In fact, both meanings are possible: "Religion is the phenomenon whereby one binds oneself or knows oneself to be bound to something or someone; one pays attention to something, one reckons with something" (van der Leeuw 1941:2). Thus, the opposite of *homo religiosus* is *homo neglegens* (and the modern feeling is one in which awe has become formalized and hence meaningless) (see van der Leeuw 1956: 35-37).

Life is thus a given and a possibility. That is to say, one does not accept life the way it is — one is concerned with one's world and one's relationship to the Holy. One is thus on the alert; one seeks to flee the Holy, or to dominate it, or to form habits in regard to it (rites and customs) — or one adopts a posture of faith. In other words, existential concern develops into a certain type of conduct, which often has a celebratory character. Thus it is that one observes various religious expressions, the chief of which are cult, myth, doctrine, and inner religious life (see van der Leeuw 1930:1862-63; 1935a:346-47; 1941:5; 1956:533-37).

With such a conception of religion, it is not difficult to see why van der Leeuw was uncomfortable with Schleiermacher's famous definition of religion (shared by van der Leeuw's teacher, W. B. Kristensen) as "das schlechthinnige Abhängigkeitsgefühl" (see Schleiermacher 1960:14-30; Kristensen 1962:24-30; van der Leeuw 1930:1861-62; 1941:3-4).[3] On the one hand, this definition says too much: fear, terror, and rebellion against the Holy, which one finds in the history of religion, are screened by the notion of dependence. On the other hand, this definition does not say enough: the feelings of surrender, devotion, and love, which one also finds in the history of religion, are not properly expressed.[4]

Finally, van der Leeuw notes the limitations of conceiving religion as a human phenomenon.[5] That is to say, religion is not merely human experience, feeling, action, and so forth. For the religious person (as opposed to the scholarly investigator of religion), religion is something quite different. "To the person who experiences, religious experience is precisely not experience in the first place, but an act of God" (van der Leeuw 1928a:256). As he notes time and again in the *Phänomenologie*, the object of the science of religion is the subject, the primary agent for religion itself. Van der Leeuw says: "The peculiar relation that is built between oneself and the Other does not seem to one to proceed from oneself but from the Other, from God. Religion is not a human attempt, a human gesture, a human cultural possession but a gift from God to humanity, a change which God brings about in humanity through revelation" (van der Leeuw 1941:4).

Thus, it is necessary to speak, not of religion, but of faith. Faith, however, is hidden from historical conception. The task of its investigation belongs to philosophy of religion and theology. The historian of religion must thus bear in mind that the truly religious person conceives his or her religion in such a way that history can only speak of the human and least important part of it (see van der Leeuw 1930:1862-63; 1935a:346-47; 1935b:351; 1941:4-5; 1956:3,208,382,778-81). One must not forget that "the basic marvel of all religion is that the other becomes one's own. This is what justifies summarizing all religions under one concept, even though the means and way in which revelation takes place is different time and again" (van der Leeuw 1942:6-7).

Conclusion

Ever since I read Professor Smith's *The Meaning and End of Religion* several years ago, I have been somewhat queasy about the use of the term "religion." Is it a useful concept? To focus this question a little more to suit the present investigation and apply it to van der Leeuw's conception of religion: does the notion of an ambivalent relationship to the Holy help one understand Buddhist meditation, *The Bhagavad-Gita*, or Azande witchcraft? It seems to me that it does. In Gadamerian terms, one might say that van der Leeuw's conception of religion is a useful pre-judgement, one that fosters understanding and hence one that has a rightful place in an operational definition of religion. Others have concurred with this view: van der Leeuw was a highly influential figure in the study of religion between roughly 1925 and 1950, and his influence can be seen beyond the middle point of this century in, among others, the work of Mircea Eliade, who in turn has had a sizeable influence on the study of religion in the latter half of this century (see Eliade 1987).

But certainly not everyone has found the van der Leeuw approach to religion congenial. There is also a counter-tradition within *Religionswissenschaft* that seeks to adopt a rather "scientific" attitude to religion. To this tradition, terms such as "holy," "sacred," "transcendence," and the like are too theological and hence not useful for objectively and empirically studying and explaining the cultural phenomenon of religion. While I cannot develop this tradition's sometimes explicit and sometimes implicit critique of the van der Leeuw tradition here, I would like to draw attention to the work of some of van der Leeuw's successors in the Netherlands as well as to certain theorists in North America, who seem united in their agreement that the van der Leeuw approach to religion must be overcome in order for the study of religion to remain academically respectable and "scientific" (see van Baaren and Drijvers 1973; Wiebe 1984; 1985; 1988; Penner 1989).[6]

And so the questions about the word, the idea, and the reality of religion in history have been asked and answered and debated by scholars in the twentieth century—as they will be in the twenty-first. As Professor Smith eloquently put it in *The Meaning and End of Religion* more than a quarter century ago:

> The world is in flux, and we know it. Like other aspects of human life, the religious aspect too is seen to be historical, evolving, in process. Any modern endeavour to clarify what religion is, must now include a question as to what at various stages of development religion has been. And if it does not venture on some speculation as to what it may become in the future, at least there is recognition that, like everything else that we know on earth, religion may be expected to continue to change (Smith 1978:2-3).

Notes

1 Van der Leeuw's conception of religion is most clearly expressed in the following: 1930:1860-63; 1935a:346-47; 1941:1-6; 1956 passim (especially sections 1.2, 1.5, 1.6, 2.1, 3.1, 4.1-4.4, 5.1, 7.1, 7.2, 8.1, 9.1, 9.3, 15.2, 17.1-17.3, 18.4, 19.1, 20.1, 21.1, 22.1-22.3, 23.1, 25.1, 32.1, 32.2, 37.1, 48.1-48.3, 67.4, 68.1-68.4, 69.1, 76.1, 81.2, 83.3, 86.2, 89.1, 99.1, 110). See also: 1928b:839-40; 1935b:351; 1935c:113-14; 1942:6-7, 18,23. Translations from Dutch and German sources in this essay are my own.

2 Van der Leeuw distinguishes primary from secondary fear. The latter is post-experiential and objectively determined: one fears being run over by a car or being attacked when walking in the forest. This has little if anything to do with religion. The former is pre-experiential, unconscious, intuitive: one fears or dreads the otherness of machines or the depths of the forest. This is intimately connected to religion (see van der Leeuw 1928b:839-40; 1956:527-31,579-80).

3 Of Schleiermacher, van der Leeuw remarked: "Everything later in theology and the science of religion proceeds from him in that his ideas are either opposed or further developed" (van der Leeuw 1928a:255).

4 Van der Leeuw was also unhappy with the definition of religion of his teacher P. D. Chantepie de la Saussaye: "belief in superhuman powers and their worship" (Chantepie 1887:51; see van der Leeuw 1941:2).

5 About the human phenomenon of religion, van der Leeuw notes two further characteristics: religion is not individual but communal; and the goal of religion is salvation (see van der Leeuw 1956:81-83, 208-10, 270-72, 610, 778-81).

6 A very different critique of the van der Leeuw approach to religion could be generated from George Lindbeck's provocative *The Nature of Doctrine: Religion and Theology in a Post Liberal Age*.

References

van Baaren, T. P. and H. J. W. Drijvers, eds. 1973. *Religion, Culture and Methodology: Papers of the Groningen Working-group for the Study of Fundamental Problems and Methods of Science of Religion*. Religion and Reason 8. The Hague: Mouton.
Chantepie de la Saussaye, P. D. 1887. *Lehrbuch der Religionsgeschichte*. Vol 1. Freiburg i. B.: Akademische Verlagsbuchhandlung von J. C. B. Mohr (Paul Siebeck).
Despland, Michel. 1979. *La Religion en Occident: Évolution des Idées et du Vécu*. Montreal: Fides.
Eliade, Mircea. 1987. *Traité d'histoire des religions*. Paris: Payot.
Feil, Ernst. 1986. *Religio. Die Geschichte eines neuzeitlichen Grundbegriffs vom Frühchristentum bis zur Reformation*. Göttingen: Vandenhoeck and Ruprecht.
Kristensen, W. B. 1962. "Schleiermacher's opvatting van de godsdienst geschiedenis." In *Symbool en werkelijkheid: Godsdiensthistorische studiën*, 24-30. Zeist: Uit-geversmaatschappij W. DeHaan, N. V.
Leeuw, Gerardus van der. 1928a. "Erlebnis, religiöses." In *Die Religion in Geschichte und Gegenwart*. Edited by Hermann Gunkel and Leopold Zscharnack, 254-56. 2nd ed. Vol 2. Tübingen: J. C. B. Mohr (Paul Siebeck).
―――. 1928b. "Furcht." In *Die Religion in Geschichte und Gegenwart*. Edited by Hermann Gunkel and Leopold Zscharnack, 839-40. 2nd ed. Vol. 2. Tübingen: J. C. B. Mohr (Paul Siebeck).
―――. 1930. "Religion: I. Erscheinungs- und Ideenwelt." In *Die Religion in Geschichte und Gegenwart*. Edited by Hermann Gunkel and Leopold Zscharnack, 1860-63. 2nd ed. Vol. 4. Tübingen: J. C. B. Mohr (Paul Siebeck).
―――. 1931. "Söderblom's wetenschappelijke beteekenis." *Stemmen des Tijds* 20:136-44.
―――. 1935a. "Godsdienst, 1." In *Winkler Prins Algemeene Encyclopaedie*. Edited by J. De Vries, 346-47. 5th ed. Vol. 8. Amsterdam: N. V. Uitgevers-Maatschappij "Elsevier."
―――. 1935b. "Godsgeloof." In *Winkler Prins Algemeene Encyclopaedie*. Edited by J. De Vries, 351. 5th ed. Vol. 8. Amsterdam: N. V. Uitgevers-Maatschappij "Elsevier."
―――. 1935c. "Heilig, Heiligheid." In *Winkler Prins Algemeene Encyclopaedie*. Edited by J. De Vries, 113-14. 5th ed. Vol. 9. Amsterdam: N. V. Uitgevers-Maatschappij "Elsevier."
―――. 1935d. "La mentalité primitive et la religion." *Revue d'histoire et de philosophie religieuses*:485-94.
―――. 1938. "Rudolf Otto und die Religions-geschichte." *Zeitschrift für Theologie und Kirche*, N.F. 19:71-81.
―――. 1941. "Inleiding." In *De godsdiensten der wereld*. Edited by Gerardus van der Leeuw, 1-6. 2nd ed. Vol. 1. Amsterdam: H. Meulenhoff.
―――. 1942. "Religionsgeschichte und persönliches religiöses Leben." In *In Deo Omnia Unum* [Essays for Friedrich Heiler]. Edited by C. M Schröder. *Eine Heilige Kirche: Zeitschrift für Kirchenkunde und Religionswissenschaft* 23: 4-24.

———. 1956. *Phänomenologie der Religion.* 2nd revised ed. Tübingen: J. C. B. Mohr (Paul Siebeck).

———. 1960. "De betekenis van de religie in de ontwikkeling der moderne wereld." In *De onrust der mensheid.* Edited by W. J. Kooiman, 155-74. Amsterdam: W. Ten Have.

Lindbeck, George. 1984. *The Nature of Doctrine: Religion and Theology in a Post Liberal Age.* Philadelphia: The Westminster Press.

Otto, Rudolf. 1932. *Das Heilige.* 22nd ed. Munich: C. H. Beck'sche Verlagsbuchhandlung.

Penner, Hans. 1989. "Accounting for Origins." *Journal of the American Academy of Religion* 57, 1: 173-80.

Schleiermacher, Friedrich. 1960. *Der christliche Glaube nach den Grundsätzen der Evangelischen Kirche im Zusammenhange dargestellt.* Edited by Martin Redeker. 7th ed. Vol. 1. Berlin: Walter De Gruyter & Co.

Smith, Wilfred Cantwell. 1978. *The Meaning and End of Religion.* New York: Harper & Row.

Söderblom, Nathan. 1913. "Holiness, General and Primitive." In *Encyclopedia of Religion and Ethics.* Edited by James Hastings, 731-41. Vol. 6. Edinburgh: T. & T. Clark.

Wiebe, Donald. 1984. "The Failure of Nerve in the Academic Study of Religion." *Studies in Religion/Sciences Religieuses* 13, 4: 4-22.

———. 1985. "A Positive Episteme for the Study of Religion." *Scottish Journal of Religious Studies* 4, 2: 78-95.

———. 1988. "Postulations for Safeguarding Preconceptions: The Case of the Scientific Religionist." *Religion* 18: 11-19.

CHAPTER 10

An Asian Starting Point for the Study of Religion

Michael Pye

It is true to say that the study or science of religion in an investigative, descriptive, and theoretical sense, as opposed to the intellectual promotion of a specific religious tradition or theology, has been mainly a feature of Western culture in modern times. On the other hand, it would be a mistake to radicalize this assumption and to assert that such a science of religion is inherently linked to Western culture alone and hence in principle alien to other cultures. The following paragraphs are intended to provide an antidote to this error by adducing the ideas of an eighteenth-century Japanese thinker, Tominaga Nakamoto (1715-46). Tominaga made a profound contribution to the historical, descriptive, and theoretical study of religion without seeking to provide a normative statement on behalf of any one tradition to which he was beholden.

The sheer honesty and self-watchfulness of some Western specialists in religious studies in recent decades has led to special emphasis being placed on the otherness of the main Asian traditions, on the otherness of the religious consciousness and of the accompanying intellectual patterns. As a result it has usually been supposed that there is little room in these cultures for an autonomously reflective science of religions, standing apart from the religions themselves. It is well known that not a few Western scholars, whether orientalists or theologians, have shown a strong tendency to impose their own assumptions on other cultures which they have attempted to interpret. In reaction to this it has mainly fallen to specialists in religious studies to question the very appropriateness of their own discipline in the face of the autonomous strength of diverse religious traditions. Wilfred Cantwell Smith, to take a clear, leading example, in order to take seriously the self-understanding of Islam in particular, has sought to develop new models of interpretation, even to the extent of avoiding the very term religion and emphasizing instead the concepts tradition and

---

Notes for this chapter appear on pages 108-109.

faith. Thus, precisely within that circle of scholars whose professional activity is consciously focussed on the study of "religion," the application of this very term has been kept under critical review. Yet the very modesty of this self-critical discipline, which has certainly led to a more finely tuned understanding of religions previously caricatured in some European writing, has led to the uncritical view that the study of religion is itself essentially alien to most cultures. In particular it is often supposed to be alien to those complex Asian cultures which have given birth to many of the religions under study. This view, however, itself needs to be overhauled. It is in principle inaccurate.

Admittedly the detached, analytical study of religion is of marginal significance in most cultures, even if it appears at all, and it is particularly fragile where religion itself is a dominant force. As a result Islamic Studies, Buddhist Studies, and the like, tend to become established rather than an autonomous, historical, comparative, or phenomenological discipline. Such a scientific study of religion may be regarded as potentially misleading or even hostile to religion. This reaction is not exactly unknown in the Western world, not to speak of other cultures. On the other hand, it is important, with all respect for the various religious systems themselves, not to lose sight of the attractiveness and value that such an investigation may seem to offer to thinkers whose formation was not dependent on modern Western culture.

That this is so may be clearly seen from the example of Tominaga Nakamoto, a Japanese thinker of great, if not indeed of fundamental, importance in the development of modern critical thought about religion. His two major extant works display modern ways of thinking about the subject which represent an entirely autonomous achievement within the context of Japanese thought. Specifically, Tominaga was concerned with the dominant religions of his place and time: Buddhism, Confucianism, and Neo-Confucianism, Shinto, and more incidentally, Taoism. His historically oriented critique included a critique of origins, a theory of religious development, and a detached assessment of the puzzle of religious pluralism (a traditional theme in Chinese and Japanese thought about religion, but hitherto usually handled from a decisively religious viewpoint).

The very fact that his historical and theoretical critique of three religious traditions, advanced from a standpoint of neutrality, was developed in the context of the urban culture of mid-Tokugawa Japan means that the evident parallels with aspects of European deism (though without Deus) and the European Enlightenment take on a significance of which he himself could not but be unaware. The parallelism inescapably suggests that there is a tendency, given certain intellectual and social presuppositions, for a historical and theoretical (and in this sense rational) critique of religion to emerge, regardless of the widely differing patterns and specific content of the religious systems in question.

The very existence of Tominaga's works, hitherto greatly underestimated, indicates that it is appropriate to speak of an Asian starting point for the study of religion. It is "Asian" and not isolatedly Japanese in that he works with Mahayana Buddhist materials (as far as sources are concerned, Chinese, but in historical projection, Indian), with a wide range of Confucian and Neo-Confucian topics, and also with the Chinese derived "three teachings" question.

That his work has gone relatively unnoticed is probably because his major extant work, *Emerging from Meditation*, had previously remained untranslated into any Western language. Since it has now appeared in a full English translation,[1] the following paragraphs will draw attention to a few salient points of this work, thus complementing earlier articles.[2] The work consists of twenty-five chapters of *kanbun* (here meaning *text* in Chinese, used as a literary language by Japanese scholars). In translation it amounts to 110 pages of printed English text. The title is Tominaga's own abbreviation of the fuller title "Emerging from Meditation and Afterwards Speaking," which implies that the Buddha himself, after attaining enlightenment under the bodhi tree, emerged from his meditation and re-entered the world of articulated discourse. This led to diversity in the forms of his preaching and above all in the forms in which it was transmitted by others. The monks themselves diversified his teaching in the course of the generations, even while claiming authoritative consistency with the original. In fact, however, Tominaga says, the claims to consistency are spurious, at least in secondary matters. Diversity naturally arises because of the point of view and indeed the self-importance of particular groups or religious leaders. Since the same can be said for Confucianism and for Shinto, this assessment amounts to a theory of tradition. This comes out clearly enough in brief in the other work on religion which has been preserved, namely, *Writings of an Old Man*.[3] A detailed exposition relating to Confucianism, entitled *Setsuhei*, has, unfortunately, not been preserved for posterity.

As for Buddhism, Tominaga's main argument is advanced in the first two chapters of *Emerging from Meditation*, entitled "The sequence in which the teaching arose" and "Differences in what the sutras say." He saw clearly, on the basis of a thorough grasp of the contents of a very large number of Buddhist writings, and contrary to the widely current dogmatic orderings of the texts favoured by different schools, that it was these schools themselves who had produced rival versions of the sutras and commentaries in order to compete with each other. "Thus the appearance of the divisions among the various teachings came about because they all first arose by superseding others."[4]

We disputed claims to a special transmission favouring the authority of particular sutras supposedly deriving personally from the Buddha. Thus "the scholars of later generations vainly say that all the teachings came directly from the golden mouth (of the Buddha) and were intimately transmitted by those who heard him frequently."[5] On the contrary, "Everybody renewed the teaching according to their opinions and passed it on orally."[6]

As a result Tominaga challenges the trustworthiness of the phrase with which the sutras always begin, namely "Thus I have heard," a phrase which he uses as the title of the third chapter of *Emerging from Meditation*. He pounces on the improbable arguments advanced within the sutras themselves to come to terms with their own variety. Thus according to one sutra, "Ananda four times entreated: 'May the Buddha please expound again the sutras which I have not yet heard.'" Another says, "The Buddha stretched forth his golden arm from within the golden coffin, and repeated his teaching (for Ananda)."[7] Tominaga simply rejects the view that the sutras were all collected up by Ananda (the Buddha's closest disciple). "The reality of it is that the sutras collected by Ananda were just a few chapters of the Aqamas.... As to the rest, not only do they not stem from Ananda, but they represent the claims of later parties."[8]

Thus the problem known in Japanese as the *daiiobussetsu-hibussetsu no mondai* (the problem as to whether the Mahayana was the teaching of the Buddha or not) was launched by Tominaga in the early eighteenth century, and was not first raised by Western scholarship in the nineteenth.

It should be noted that the above view is both a historical assessment, which (it should not be forgotten) is in general correct, and a theory about the generation of diverse forms in a religious-textual tradition. The theory lies in the term "superseding" (*kajo*), which *explains* the diversified sequence of texts in a manner not drawn from Buddhist teaching itself. In *Writings of an Old Man* this theory is applied to Confucianism and Shinto as well.

This theme may be conveniently illustrated from Chapter 22 of *Emerging from Meditation*, entitled "Heterodoxies." Tominaga here takes up the view widely current in Buddhist writings that there were ninety-six heterodoxies or literally "external ways," that is, paths other than the path of Buddhism. As is clear from the *Fa Hsien Record*, he argues, these heterodoxies have also been handed down over many centuries and at least in this respect are parallel to the teaching of the Buddha.[9] The style of Tominaga's reflection on the different points of view within the Buddhist writings can easily be illustrated by quoting the opening paragraph of this chapter:

> There were probably ninety-six heterodoxies. *The Great Treatise* says, "The ninety-six kinds of heterodoxy once conspired together to debate against the Buddha." In the *Sarvastivada Vinaya* it says, "The six teachers of heterodox ways each gave way to fifteen kinds, which makes ninety-six altogether." The *Daiju Sutra* says, "In the three jewels the mind is held in respect, and this surpasses all the ninety-five ways." Then again the *Bunbetsukudoku Treatise* says, "Among the ninety-six ways the Bud-

dha way is regarded as the greatest." This is the utterance of yet another group who made it ninety-six including the Buddha. The *Lankavatara Sutra* refers to one hundred and eight heretical views. They are not all given in detail. The *Vimalakirti Sutra* lists six teachers of heterodoxies.... The Nirvana Sutra lists six heterodoxies of asceticism as follows: fasting, frequenting a precipice, fire-walking, sitting in solitude, maintaining a tranquil silence, living like a cow or a dog. The *Great Treatise* lists sixteen kinds of false subjectivity, the *Yuga Treatise* lists sixteen divergent theories of existence, the *Dainichi Sutra* lists thirty kinds of heterodoxy, and the *Gedoshojonehan Treatise* lists twenty kinds of Hinayana heterodoxy. These are all convenient summaries and do not amount to the full number of ninety-six. They are not handed down in the *Vedas*, nor did their people enter China.[10]

As is well known, Buddhism was characterized as the Middle Way between self-mortification and self-gratification. As the *Great Treatise* says (quoted by Tominaga): "If Sakyamuni Buddha had not first practised asceticism for six years the people would not have trusted him when he reproved those not following the way. Hence he himself practised asceticism more than other people."[11]

But as the *Inga Sutra* says: "The prince (i.e., the Buddha) said of himself, 'I have now been doing ascetic practice for a full six years. If I now attain the way with an emaciated body I will have to say that self-starvation is the cause of nirvana. I must take food and then complete the way.'"[12]

For Tominaga this statement betrays the real drive behind religious change or development. He writes: "Hence we say that Sakyamuni's double practice of pleasure and of asceticism was in order to bring the heterodoxies to submission. Thus the exposition of what is called the middle way is also something which emerges at one level above."[13] He finds this view directly confirmed in the *Chu-agon* which says: "There are two kinds of practice, that of the five passions and that of asceticism; departing from these two is called the middle way."[14]

Thus the mode of origin of Buddhism is in principle no different from that of the heterodoxies on the one hand or of the later sectarian divisions of Buddhism on the other hand. Tominaga regards it as important to realize this. Otherwise innumerable problems of interpretation arise when the attempt is made to justify one trend over against another or to achieve an apparent harmony between those expressions of Dharma deemed to be orthodox. That the historical Buddha, Sakyamuni, himself played this game of relating dialectically to teachings which he considered inadequate is not in itself reprehensible; but since it has to be understood in terms of the context of other teachings and the intention to go one better than these it implies a relativization of the new teaching which is to be regarded as one teaching among others and part of a normal process of religious innovation.

This fundamental perception by Tominaga was of course quite at odds with the normal Buddhist view, according to which the "heterodoxies," even if not so perniciously misleading as wrong views (*jaken*) within Buddhism, nevertheless were of distinctly secondary value and in principle to be avoided or displaced by the Buddhist way. Not that Tominaga found it inappropriate, in itself, that Buddhists should mount a claim to the superiority of their teaching. This is normal. At the same time such a claim tends to lead to a misreading of the historical development and to presentations of the relations between the different teachings which are oversimplified, for dogmatic purposes, and thus simply not correct. Such errors in retrospective view can be avoided if one realizes that Buddhism, that is, the victorious and now dominant tradition, itself arose as one among several or many alternatives.

This is in fact the very starting point of *Emerging from Meditation*. At the beginning of Chapter 1 Tominaga writes: "If we first consider the sequence in which the teaching (of Buddhism) arose we see that in effect it began among the heterodoxies."[15]

The various teachings rivalled each other in the presentation of a realm lying beyond this world, and since all the possibilities had been exhausted, right up to the idea of a state of "nor-non-conception" which was arrived at by transcending the "realm of nonexistence," there was nothing left over for Sakyamuni but to opt out of this competition and to teach "detachment from the characteristics of birth and death, adding to this the remarkable power of great supernatural transformations."[16] Tominaga concludes dryly: "Pointing out that this was very hard to achieve, he got the heretics to submit and converted the Indians. This was how Sakyamuni's teaching arose."[17]

The supernatural transformations referred to here are considered in more detail in Chapter 8 which, interestingly enough, contains close parallels to the idea in *Writings of an Old Man* that particular countries (we would now say, cultures) have their own special propensities when it comes to the elaboration of systems of teaching. Thus he opens by saying: "The common people of India are very fond of magic, and similarly the people of China are fond of literature. All those who establish a teaching and expound a Way find they must put it forward in terms of such things, for if they do not the people will not trust them."[18] This was unavoidable even for a profound teaching such as Buddhism. "As the other teachings of the time all made use of magic in their promotion, even though Sakyamuni surpassed them in his teaching, he could not avoid using magic provisionally when making it known."[19]

Under "magic," though thinking first of miraculous feats performed by exponents of Buddhism to impress people, Tominaga includes here a wide variety of secondary religious forms, notably "teachings like karmic retribution and heaven and purgatory, originally started in non-Buddhist schools." Making use of such teachings implies a dialectical relationship with forms of teaching which do not themselves represent the ultimate intention of the teacher. "Sakyamuni used them to lead people with, thereby winning over people of the lower kind. He then set up the teaching of attaining Buddhahood by detachment from particulars, and leaving the lower level he won over people of the higher kind. This was possible because those teachings were not originally bad, and moreover the Indian people like them. Nevertheless the reality is that it was a skilful means."[20]

This statement shows that Tominaga's perception of the dynamics of religion is drawn in part from Buddhist self-understanding, in the following sense. The term "skilful means" is a technical term in Buddhism which refers to the presentation of the teaching in a manner which is at once acceptable and understandable to its hearers and true, given a satisfactory devolution of the sense, to its own inner intention. Thus in Buddhism, to regard an element of teaching as "skilful means" is to imply that some dialectical progression is still required in order to lead into the full meaning. This reflective acceptance of the value of particular forms of teaching within Buddhism while at the same time proposing a spiritual departure from them clearly implies a high level of self-conscious detachment from the system of teaching even while this is being propounded. It seems evident from this and other places in Tominaga's work that the degree of abstraction achieved here was one of the seminal features in his own formulation of a theory of the way in which religions work.

The same point may be documented from Chapter 4, which is devoted to a discussion of the diversity of teachings about the cosmos. Tominaga begins:

> The teachings about Mount Sumeru were all handed down by brahmans. Though Sakyamuni used them to expound his Way, they are to be regarded as cosmic theory. Later scholars (i.e., Buddhists) have made much of this teaching while criticising others, and lost sight of the Buddha's intention. This is because the Buddha's intention is not to be found in such matters. He was urgently seeking people's salvation and had no time for such petty matters. What he did is what is known as skilful means.[21]

The implication is that the Buddha (Sakyamuni) expressed his teaching in cosmological terms without intending to assert any particular theory about the cosmos for his own part. The divergences about cosmology between the different texts of Buddhism, adduced in detail in *Emerging from Meditation*, are therefore not of any importance in themselves if Buddhism is properly understood. What they do show, however, is that the Buddhist writings themselves are secondary products of the tradition seeking to outdo each other. Thus Tominaga: "Those discrepancies between what the sutras and treatises say are just there for the sake of giving names to the various divisions (of Buddhist teaching) and providing sayings for each school."[22]

In the same chapter such divergences are linked with the idea of superseding (*kajo*).[23] This is significant in that it represents a displacement of the Buddhist idea that teachings of secondary importance may be understood dialectically in terms of skilful means. This is replaced, for Tominaga, by a more general theory about the relations between a series of teachings, viewed now as rival systems following on each others' heels. The idea of skilful means is internal to the Buddhist system and is in principle subordinate to the intentionality of that system. The idea of "superseding" sidesteps the normative interest of the Buddhist system in itself and helps Tominaga to formulate an independent theory of tradition formation which can be applied to the origins of Buddhism, as one system among many, and to the diversity within Buddhism. This theory conflicts with many specific statements found in Buddhist writings, whether polemical or eirenic, which Tominaga correctly perceived to be inconsistent with each other and thus in many cases historically inaccurate. Whether, as an intellectual theory about religion, it conflicts fundamentally with Buddhism in a more profound sense must remain a question for Buddhists. It is a question to which Tominaga did not directly address himself, though the indications are that he did not consider that a more reliable historical assessment would prejudice the value of Buddhism properly understood.

With these few examples enough has been said to show that a historically and theoretically reflective study of religion has clearly emerged in the context of an Asian culture. This simple fact in the history of ideas should be given due weight. Taking cognizance of it may help to readjust the equilibrium which is sometimes lost when undue weight is given to the supposedly impervious otherness of other cultures. The emergence of a science of religion is not exclusively linked to a set of postulates available only in Western culture, as is often supposed. On the contrary, it can only really come to itself when it ceases to be bound to one culture alone. Although by the nature of the case he could not foresee this at the time, the writings of Tominaga Nakamoto provide mighty assistance in the development of a truly independent and hence intercultural science of religion.

Notes

1 Tominaga Nakamoto, *Emerging from Meditation* (London, 1990). This volume contains a full translation of *Emerging from Meditation* (original Japanese title: *Shutsujokogo*) and of *Writings of an Old Man* (*Okina no fumi*), with an introduction by the present writer.
2 Relevant articles by present writer: "Aufklärung and religion in Europe and Japan," *Religious Studies* 9 (1973): 201-07; "Religion and Reason in the Japanese Experience," *King's Theological Review* (Spring 1982): 14-17; "The Significance of the Japanese Intellectual Tradition for the History of Religions," in D. Slater and D. Wiebe, eds., *Traditions in Context and Change*, Proceedings of the XIVth Congress of the International Association for the History of Religions (Waterloo, Ontario, 1983), 565-77;

"Tominaga Nakamoto (1715-1746) and Religious Pluralism," in G. Daniels, ed., *Europe Interprets Japan* (Tenterden, England, 1984), 191-97.
3 See note 1 above.
4 Nakamoto, *Emerging from Meditation* (hereafter *EFM*), p. 81.
5 *EFM*, p. 81.
6 *EFM*, p. 83.
7 *EFM*, p. 86.
8 *EFM*, p. 87.
9 See *EFM*, p. 157.
10 *EFM*, p. 156.
11 *EFM*, p. 159.
12 *EFM*, p. 159.
13 *EFM*, p. 159.
14 *EFM*, p. 159.
15 *EFM*, p. 73.
16 *EFM*, p. 74.
17 *EFM*, p. 74.
18 *EFM*, p. 105.
19 *EFM*, p. 105.
20 *EFM*, p. 107.
21 *EFM*, p. 88.
22 *EFM*, p. 89.
23 See Pye (1982) (note 2 above).

CHAPTER 11

World Religions: A Category in the Making?

Katherine K. Young

In 1951 Joachim Wach used the term "world religions" in his *Types of Religious Experience: Christian and Non-Christian*, albeit with the more explicit compound formation "world-religions." Wach argues for a concept of the "classical" (the typical, normative or essential) as the best way to guide description, selection, and presentation of the "well-nigh infinite amount of material unearthed by comparative studies during the nineteenth and twentieth centuries" (48). In this context he mentions in passing that:

> The quantitative principle is represented as a regulative norm: the *so-called world-religions* are *more important than less widely spread cults* simply because they command a *larger number of followers*. This fact may justify a more thorough preoccupation with their beliefs. The religions of nations which have played a *larger role in the history of the world* seem to deserve more careful study than those of less active peoples. But this criterion, which may suffice from a purely historical point of view, is unsatisfactory in other respects (50-51, emphasis added).[1]

It is striking that Wach refers to the "so-called world-religions" as if he does not know what is really meant by this category. Nonetheless he mentions three basic characteristics: large size, wide geographical distribution, and big impact on history. He suggests that a category based on such criteria is vague and inadequate to the task of studying religions.

A positive use of the term, however, appears several years later in the preface of Huston Smith's *The Religions of Man* (1958). Smith refers to

> the *great* faiths that have motivated and continue to motivate the peoples of the world ... [and] the need for a different kind of book on *world religions*, a book which without sacrificing depth would move more rapidly than the usual survey into the *meaning* these religions carry for the

---

Notes and references for this chapter appear on pages 128-30.

lives of their adherents.... The religions we propose to consider *belt the world*. Their *histories stretch back* thousands of years, in addition to which they are *motivating more men today*. Is it possible to listen seriously to them within the compass of a singe book? (ix, emphasis added).

The author next mentions the problem of selection and notes his principle of economy: to do justice to a modest array of perspectives rather than cover, in catalogue fashion, the spectrum of religions. More specifically, his criterion is relevance "determined by sheer numbers, relevance to the modern mind, and universality" (4):

> We live in a fantastic century. I leave aside the incredible discoveries of science, the narrow ridge between doom and fulfillment onto which they have pushed us, and speak only of the new situation among peoples. Lands across the planet have become our neighbors, China across the street, Egypt at our doorstep. Radio and air traffic have shriveled space until the only barrier is cost. Even where plane fare is lacking there is a never-ending stream of books, documentaries, and visitors from abroad. A random issue of a metropolitan daily carries word of yesterday's doings in seventeen countries. We hear on all sides that East and West are meeting but it is an understatement. They are being flung at one another, hurled with the force of atoms, the speed of jets, the restlessness of minds impatient to learn of ways that differ from their own. From the perspective of history this may prove to be the most important fact about the twentieth century. When historians look back upon our years they may remember them not for the release of nuclear power nor the spread of Communism but as the time in which all the peoples of the world first had to take one another seriously....
>
> The change in role this new situation requires of us all—we who have been suddenly catapulted from town and country onto a world stage—is enormous. Twenty-five hundred years ago it took an exceptional man like Socrates to say on his deathbed, "I am not an Athenian or a Greek but a citizen of the world." Today we must all be struggling toward these worlds....
>
> To borrow Nietzsche's image, we have all been summoned to become Cosmic Dancers who do not rest heavily in a single spot but lightly turn and leap from one position to another.... The Cosmic Dancer, the World Citizen, will be an authentic child of his parent culture but related closely to all (6-7).

After an introduction on his point of departure, Huston Smith has individual chapters on Hinduism, Buddhism, Confucianism, Taoism, Islam, Judaism, and Christianity and a conclusion. According to the index, nowhere does he use the term "world religions" again nor does he systematically discuss these religions with reference to the criteria he has posed.

Huston Smith does state that his approach is a rejection of the history of religions; hence, "the scarcity of names, dates, movements, and social crosscurrents" (2). It is also a rejection of comparative religion, for "comparisons among things men hold dear always tend to be odious, those among religions most odious of all" (5). Thus, the general features or values of the worldview are simply presented for the seven religions with the hope that somehow such edification will broaden one's outlook and fundamentally relate one to other people. His approach, then, is basically dialogic, to prepare one for the global village.

R. C. Zaehner uses the term "world religions" two times in the 1959 book he edited, entitled *The Concise Encyclopedia of Living Faiths* (1959). He states that this book "attempts to describe in a brief compass those faiths which have *withstood the test of time* and which must, therefore, correspond to some fundamental need in man" (15, emphasis added). Zaehner mentions "the map of the *world religions*" (16, emphasis added). His main concern is to classify the religions based on geography (Western Religions and Eastern Religions), a classification which, in turn, is based on those originating from Israel and India. The second reference to the term "world religions" is just as casual. He suggests a classification of religions based on prophetic and mystical or immanentist types (elsewhere called by him "wisdom" religions). Then he states that "In Part One which we have called 'prophecy' we present the prophetic tradition as represented by Judaism and the two *world religions*, Christianity and Islam, that derive from it" (19).

Zaehner notes that his book is about *living faiths*, not about primitive religions or "national religions of great cultures that have passed away" (19). Like Huston Smith his reason for focussing on living religions is preeminently pragmatic: they are relevant and focus on them "eliminates the problem of greatly increasing the size of an already considerable volume" (19). As for the actual living religions covered, in Part One under the rubric "Prophecy" besides Judaism, Christianity, and Islam, he includes Zoroastrianism "which has the same 'prophetic' spirit" (19). In Part Two under the rubric "Wisdom" he includes Hinduism, Jainism, Buddhism, and Shintoism ("the national religion of Japan, which seemed to fit best into this position because of the intimate ties that it developed with Buddhism" (19)). He also includes Confucianism ("some account of it seemed necessary ... in order to make the total Chinese picture more intelligible," (19) and Taoism ("the same type as the main Indian stream") (19). Accordingly, the editor's arrangement is both typological (prophecy and meditation/wisdom) and geographical (West and East). His category "world religions" is nowhere described though he does provide a list, namely, Judaism, Christianity, Islam, Zoroastrianism, Hinduism, Jainism, Buddhism, and Shinto.

In 1958 Harvard University inaugurated a new program in the field of religion, not as History of Religion(s), nor Comparative Religion (the titles *au courant* for the discipline), but as "Program in World Religions." Wilfred Cantwell Smith, then a professor at the Institute of Islamic Studies at McGill University, commented on this development the following year in a seminal article entitled "Comparative Religion: Whither and Why?" in the *The History of Religions*, edited by Eliade and Kitagawa. Smith sees the frontiers of the study of religion as a concern with living religions. More precisely, he locates them in the living encounter between persons of diverse faiths rather than in the collection of information about other religions which had been the preoccupation of the field until the world wars:

> Part of the personalization of our studies is evinced in the shift over past decades to a primary interest in the *major living religions of the world*. (The phrase "living religions," which has become current, is itself significant.) Whereas at the turn of the century a typical introductory course in this field would emphasize "primitive religions," and a typical book would address itself to the "nature and origin of religion" (the phrase implicitly postulates that the reality or truth of religion is to be found most purely or most surely in its earliest and simplest forms), today it is normal to give chief or even sole attention to Hindus, Buddhists, and Muslims, along with Christians and Jews — groups that between them constitute the vast majority of today's population, and between them claim most forcefully to represent *religion's highest and truest development*. And whereas once such attention as was given to *the great religions* was primarily to their scriptures and historically to their early, classical phases, today these religions are seen primarily as the faith of present-day groups (37-38, emphasis added).

To support his view of a critical shift of focus to living religions, Smith mentions in a footnote a recent work, *Living Religions of the World* (1956) by Frederic Spiegelberg, and notes that course titles may now contain the term. He mentions in other footnotes Edward J. Jurji's edited volume *The Great Religions of the Modern World* (1946) and a course called Contemporary World Religions at the Divinity School, the University of Chicago, in 1957-1959. But it is Huston Smith's *The Religions of Man* which particularly strikes his attention:

> The same omission of primitives and concern for the *great religions* is true of the recent brilliant text of Huston Smith ... a luminous example of the treatment of religion as the faith of *persons* ... This work is perhaps the first adequate textbook in *world religions*, precisely because it treats religions as human (38, emphasis added).

Next, Smith points to the various issues of *Life* magazine in 1955 which were about the living religions and the fact that they were republished as *The World's Great Religions* (New York, 1957) with a Dutch version entitled *De Grote Gotsdiensten der Wereld* appearing the following year. At this point in his article he speaks about the new Program in World Religions at Harvard and relates all these publications and events to the growing popularity of dialogue as an encounter.

Harvard's Program in World Religions soon took on a new institutional form with the creation of the Center for the Study of World Religions, which was inaugurated in 1960. Writing of this event in an article called "The Harvard Way in the Study of Religion" (1988), William R. Darrow says: "It is noteworthy that this Center has its roots in a devotional encounter with the *great* religious literature of the world by the donors who made it possible.... It is also significant that the Center was placed in the Divinity School, the home of the history of religion" (230, emphasis added).

Radhakrishnan, who according to Eric J. Sharpe (1975), brought together "the concerns of comparative religion with the concerns of world peace, international harmony and universal brotherhood" (258), inaugurated the new center:

> One of the last major public appearances made by Radhakrishnan before his retirement was to deliver an address at the inauguration of the Harvard University Center for the Study of World Religions. This address, entitled *Fellowship of the Spirit* was published in 1961, and reprinted in L. S. Rouner (ed.), *Philosophy, Religion, and the Coming World Civilisation* (1966) — a collection of essays in honour of W. E. Hocking, the architect of *Rethinking Missions*.... "The different religions are to be used as building stones for the development of a human culture in which the adherents of the different religions may be fraternally united as children of one Supreme. All religions convey to their followers a message of abiding hope. The world will give birth to a new faith which will be but the old faith in another form, the faith of all ages, the potential divinity of man which will work for the supreme purpose written in our hearts and souls, the unity of all mankind. It is my hope and prayer that unbelief shall disappear and superstition shall not enslave the mind and we shall recognise that we are brothers, one in spirit and one in fellowship" (260, quoting Rouner).

Radhakrishnan, in his call for a "new faith," may have gone a step beyond Smith's expectations. But it was Smith, especially in his role as director of the Center from 1964, who gave intellectual formulation to what may be termed a growing cultural fashion: focussing on the contemporary aspect of certain religions. In this regard the enterprise was timely. The interest in the "origins" of religion had become passé with the waning of evolutionary theories. Then, too, travel for pleasure, business, and migration as well as media coverage of events around the world were rapidly increasing. The *philosophia perennis* of Ananda K. Coomaraswamy, René Guénon, Aldous Huxley, and others also contributed to this mood.

Scrutiny of the various statements by Wilfred Cantwell Smith suggests that his criteria for the category "world religions" were (1) living, (2) major in the sense that they involved the vast majority of today's population, and (3) great in the sense that they could claim between them to represent religion's highest and truest development. His emphasis on the encounter with religious persons rather than the study of religions per se, however, led to a slightly different kind of list: Hindus, Buddhists, Muslims, Christians, and Jews.

Paul Tillich, in 1961, delivered lectures at Columbia University which were published the following year as *Christianity and the Encounter of the World Religions* (1962). Of these lectures the author says:

> They were not supposed to give embracing answers to the manifold problems raised in the discussion of the subject matter, but to confront the reader with some points of view which I consider decisive for every approach to the central problem. Among them are the emphasis on the characterization of the quasi-religions, the elaboration of the universalist element in Christianity, the suggestion of a dynamic typology of the religions, the dialogical character of the encounter of *high religions*, and the judgement of Christianity against itself as a religion and its ensuing openness for criticism, both from religions in the proper sense and from quasi-religions (vii-viii; emphasis added).

This book, which is mainly about the problem of secularism, does not define the term "world religions" used in the title; it does mention, however, Buddhism, Shintoism, Greek Orthodoxy, Confucianism, Taoism, Hinduism, African tribal religions, and Islam.

Whaling, when contrasting the study of religion in the classical and contemporary periods, notes that:

> In the classical period, there was relatively great stress put upon the data of primal religion, archaic religion, religions of antiquity, and the classical forms of the major living religions.... At the present time, the situation is different. Not only has there been an explosion of knowledge in regard to all the religious traditions of mankind, the greatest relative accumulation of data encompassed the *major living traditions* (1983:18).

Nowhere does Whaling define major religions, much less major living religions. He does say, however, that:

> There are at least two important consequences for the study of religion arising from this increasing interest in the *major living religions* in their contemporary as well as classical forms. In the first place, there is a correlation between the data used by scholars and the approach they adopt towards their studies.... An increasing number of present-day scholars make predominant use of the data of the *major living religions in their contemporary as well as classical forms*. The increasing use of the data of the

major living religions, and the increase of theorising on the basis of those data, constitute a contemporary development that is little remarked but is of obvious long-term significance.... The second consequence relates to the seeming difference within western scholarship in relation to the types of data that are used. We have seen how continental European scholars are more likely to make greater use of the data of the religions of antiquity, the classical forms of the major religions and (to a lesser extent) primal religions, whereas Anglo-Saxon scholars are more likely to use the data of the major living religions in their contemporary as well as classical forms (1983:22).

Whaling goes on to attribute the Anglo-Saxon interest to former imperialism and the presence of immigrants in their societies.

It is striking that *The Encyclopedia of Religion* edited by Mircea Eliade (New York: Macmillan, 1987) does not mention the term "world religions" in the index (volume 16) either separately or under the categories of Religion, Study of Religion, History of Religions, Comparative Religion, or Comparative-Historical method.

Some observations based on the preceding discussion are in order.

1. The decade 1951-61 saw the growing popularity of the term "world religions" in North America, especially in the Boston area, through the writings of Huston Smith, Wilfred Cantwell Smith, and Paul Tillich. The institutional role of Harvard, which initiated first a Program in World Religions, and then a Center for the Study of World Religions, also contributed to the prestige of the term.

2. During this period, the term was often left undefined; occasionally, however, a few adjectives were offered. These were "living," "major," and "great." Only the first was the subject of scholarly reflection. Sometimes, however, a list of religions was provided, as if that defined the category.

3. Several reasons seem to have prompted the use of this term. (a) The desire by the West to solve world problems, be good world citizens (especially in the wake of imperialism and the world wars), and create a peaceful transition to religiously plural societies in the West itself through understanding or dialogue. Hence the emphasis on living religions practised by large numbers of people. (b) The interest in successful religions in terms of spread and continuity; hence the interest in "major" religions. (c) The wish for a convenient selection principle for textbooks to enable a manageable number of religions to be surveyed and give the appearance of being global.

There is a certain overlap of the scope of the term "world religions" with other terms. We have already encountered the term "great religions" and "living religions" in some prefaces and titles. A few more details are provided here. The first English book with the title "great religions" was James Freeman Clarke's *Ten Great Religions: An Essay in Comparative Theology*, written in 1882. In his Introduction he mentions that "most of the

Religions of the World are Ethnic or the Religions of Races"; he goes on to discuss Confucian and Taoist religions, Brahmanism, Buddhism, Zoroaster, and Zend Avesta, the Gods of Egypt, the Gods of Greece, the Religion of Rome, Teutonic and Scandinavian Religion, Jewish Religion, Mohammed and Islam, with a final chapter on the superiority of Christianity. He nowhere justifies the concept of "great" nor his principle of selection; indeed there seems to be none, aside from a primary interest in religions related to the West and an exposure to some other religions. A more explicit use of "great" occurs in the preface of Arnold Toynbee's 1958 book *Christianity among the Religions of the World* (1975).

> This book is a discussion of the attitudes of Christians toward the followers of the other *great living religions*. . . . The writer does not expect to see the *historic higher religions* coalesce into a single religion, and he does not advocate this; but he does put the question whether, in the face of such a formidable and evil opponent [Communism] the *higher religions* ought not now to stand together in preaching the supremely important negative belief that is common to them all (vii, emphasis added).

For Toynbee, the great living religions are the historic "higher" religions. S. G. F. Brandon wrote *Man and His Destiny in the Great Religions* in 1962. This was an historical treatment of a number of religions but did not go later than the High Middle Ages. John Danielou in 1964 edited a book entitled *Introduction to the Great Religions*, which has chapters on the religions of nature, Islam, Buddhism, Hinduism, the religions of Japan, Judaism, and contemporary atheism. This was followed the next year by *A Reader's Guide to the Great Religions* edited by Charles Adams. From his comments in the Preface to the first edition (1965), it seems that the choice of a title was difficult:

> The title chosen for this volume represents a compromise by the editor and was agreed upon only after the expenditure of much effort to find a more satisfactory one. Application of the terms "religion" and "religions" to such diverse phenomena as the cults of noncivilizational peoples in the more remote regions of the earth, on the one hand, and to the highly sophisticated, articulate, and self-conscious piety of the *great traditions* of India, China, and the Middle East, on the other, implies a closeness of connection between the two that is much too simple if it can be accepted at all. . . . There is reason for challenging the use of the adjective "great" in the title in view of the inclusion of a chapter on primitive religions. Objection on this point could perhaps be met by an argument designed to show that the so-called *primitive religions* are, indeed, a *"great"* tradition in virtue of the very extent of their spread through time and space and the numbers of persons who have been affected by them.

Finally, the clarity of the title is compromised by the method of organizing the material of the volume as a whole. One of the chapters deals with a most diffuse group of phenomena that have been designated by the abstraction "primitive religions." Another group of chapters takes distinct religious traditions and treats of them separately and to some extent in relation with one another. Yet a third group of chapters, those dealing with the religions of China and Japan, have been conceived and organized in geographical terms. Although any usefulness this volume may have will not be materially affected by the felicitousness of the title chosen for it, it seems better to acknowledge these reservations about the adequacy of the title from the beginning (reprinted in the second edition, 1977, xvi, emphasis added).

A clue to Adams's sense of classification can be seen in his choice of terms: "great," "noncivilizational," or "primitive." Unlike other authors, however, he expresses his own dissatisfaction with the nomenclature and the organization of his material on the basis of primitive religions, distinct religions, and geography.

The National Geographic Society in 1971 published the *Great Religions of the World*. Krister Stendahl writes in the foreword: "This book is an invitation to marvel at, learn from, and feel the strangeness and attraction of the *great religions of the world*. Given the global oneness, our pluralism is not a liability but an asset. God may be one, but religions are many" (7, emphasis added). Hinduism, Buddhism, Judaism, Islam, and Christianity are covered without any further rationale.

We may conclude this discussion by observing that:

1. In our initial discussion the adjective "great" was but one of three characteristics which, taken together, defined the term "world religions." But it has also been used in a more general way to designate religions considered by the author to be important or "high" or, in an even more general way, to designate a spectrum of religions chosen according to different criteria. Hence its use is even more fluid than the term "world religions."

2. The use of the adjective "great" in titles seems to be disappearing. Perhaps this is on account of a desire to avoid the adjective because it suggests a normative orientation akin to the idea of "high religions" (with its corollary that there are "low" or primitive religions). Although the word "great" is found in descriptions of the term "world religions," the fact that the term "world religions" itself is not so obviously judgemental may contribute to its growing popularity in an age that has no patience with elitism or evolution.

In the next section the term "world religions" will be compared to the phrases "the world's religions" and "the religions of the world." Indeed, if Joachim Wach's use of the compound "world-religions" is a clue, the relation of the two words must have originally been governed by the genitive case. Be that as it may, there is, again, a great deal of overlap between "world religions" and "the world's religions" or the "religions of the world," especially when the adjective "living" is added.

In 1933 R. E. Hume, for instance, wrote *The World's Living Religions: An Historical Sketch*. He discusses eleven religions of the world: Hinduism, Jainism, Buddhism, Sikhism, Confucianism, Taoism, Shinto, Judaism, Zoroastrianism, Islam, and Christianity. In 1963 David G. Bradley published *A Guide to the World's Religions*, which he says is "intended to introduce the reader to the major contemporary religions" (vii). After a chapter on the "religion of primitive peoples" the book is arranged geographically: The Religions of Biblical Lands (Judaism, Zoroastrianism, Christianity, Islam); India (Hinduism, Jainism, Buddhism, Sikhism), and the Religions of China and Japan (Taoism, Confucianism, and Shinto). In 1964 Geoffrey Parrinder wrote *The World's Living Religions*. In the Preface he says:

> This book gives a short and impartial account of the *major religions of the modern world*. Islam is studied first, as it is likely to be the first Eastern religion which the Westerner might meet, and it is less strange to our way of thinking than some Eastern faiths. Then African and some other non-scriptural faiths. Finally Judaism and Christianity are discussed in their history, teachings and diverse branches" (7, emphasis added).

While Hume's list of religions closely resembles that given by authors who speak of "world religions," other authors who speak of "major religions of the modern world," or the "world's living religions" also include some "primitive" or "nonscriptural" religions.

To make matters even more confusing, not all books on the "world's religions" or the "religions of the world" focus on the living religions. In 1969, S. Vernon McCasland, Grace E. Cairns, and David C. Yu authored *Religions of the World*. They said:

> The aim of this book is to present the *major living religions of the world* — the faiths by which the major peoples of the world live at the present time. However, in order to provide an understanding of the living religions, we have found it necessary to consider some of the *religions of the past*.
>
> The order in which we have presented these religions has been chosen primarily on the basis of two principles: the first is phenomenological and has to do with the obvious similarities among some religions: the second is geographical. For example, the religions of Mesopotamia, Egypt, Greece, and Rome all developed in the Mediterranean area and are thus bound by the principle of geography; as contemporary polytheisms they also constitute, phenomenologically, a natural family.... Zoroastrianism, Judaism, Christianity, and Islam, the four great monotheisms, together make one of the most definite families of religions; they are linked with one another by worship of one God, as well as by possession of high moral codes and similar eschatologies. The

geographical bond between them lies in the fact that they all originated in the Middle East.

The kinship of the religions of India stems from the fact that Jains, Buddhists and Sikhs look back to Hinduism as their common mother. But one must go far beyond the frontiers of India to follow the story of Buddhism so we have also been compelled by geography to consider Buddhism as one of the great religions of East Asia, the others being Confucianism, Taoism, and Shinto. . . . We believe that the religion of any people is closely related to its culture and that it can therefore be best understood against the background of its geography, social life, and history (viii, emphasis added).

Once again, it is as if the authors first decided on what religions they wished to include and then created some reasons for their choice, some silly (the inclusion of Confucianism, Taoism, and Shinto because they were important to the story of Buddhism) and some even erroneous (e.g., Buddhism looking to Hinduism as its mother).

Of the same ilk is Geoffrey Parrinder's preface to a volume he edited entitled, initially, *Man and His Gods* (U. K., 1971), and *Religions of the World* (U. S. A., 1971), and later on *An Illustrated History of the World's Religions* (1983), and *World Religions: From Ancient History to the Present*. He says the book

> brings together studies of religions past and present. It seeks to present not only a study of religion in a narrow sense, but a picture of history, geography, social life, current affairs and international relationships. . . . The method adopted here is to provide articles on all the *major* religions, with reference to *minor* ones. . . . The arrangement of chapters must be arbitrary to some extent, but the one that is adopted here aims both at showing something of the development and historical position of the religions, and including a wider range of religions than is generally found in such a comprehensive work. It is sometimes said that *there are eleven living religions*, and these can be noted in the list of contents, running from Ancient Iran to Islam, with China including Confucianism and Taoism as well as Buddhism. But such a division of living and dead, though excluding the virtually extinct religions of ancient Europe and the Near East, ignores those still living faiths of other continents which chiefly remain outside the scope of the *historical religion* (7-8, emphasis added).

The order of the chapters written by various specialists is as follows: Ancient Iran, Hinduism, Jainism, Sikhism, Buddhism, China, Japan, Judaism, Christianity, Islam. Thus, only living "major" religions are covered.

Lewis M. Hopfe also wrote a text in 1976 called *Religions of the World* and said:

The third and most common variety of course in this field is the one that seeks to present an introduction to the *major religions of the world*. Texts for this course usually present some basic material on primitive and early religions and then devote the majority of their pages to describing the historical development and current form of those religions. *Religions of the World* aims to do just that (xi-xii, emphasis added).

Contents of this book include "basic religions" (i.e., archaic and primitive), American Indian religions, Hinduism, Jainism, Buddhism, Sikhism, Chinese Religions, Shinto, Zoroastrianism, Judaism, Christianity, Islam, and Baha'i.

Books (often they are written to be textbooks) sometimes have different titles but fall into one of the categories enumerated above. One is Robert S. Ellwood's 1976 work *Many Peoples, Many Faiths: An Introduction to the Religious Life of Mankind*, which he introduces as follows:

But the study of the religions of the world is no longer a matter of reading about exotic lands to which only the most intrepid travelers have voyaged. In today's pluralistic society and *world community*, almost any faith from anywhere is a presence and an option throughout the world.... This new day in the *encounter* with the religions of the world makes possible a new kind of approach (2-3, emphasis added).

After a first chapter on "Understanding the World's Religious Heritage," he has chapters on: prehistoric and primitive religion, India (Hinduism), Buddhism, religions of China and Japan, religions of the Ancient Near East and Europe (includes religions of Egypt, Mesopotamia, Zoroastrianism, Greece, Rome, Celtic religion, and the religion of the Germanic peoples), and the "Great Monotheistic Religions" (Judaism, Christianity, and Islam). Therefore he has a selection of dead and living religions and organizes them geographically or by type.

By far the most popular textbook has been John B. Noss's *Man's Religions*, which was first published in 1949 and is now in its eighth edition. The author describes his purpose in the preface to the first edition as follows: "an introduction to the world's religions ... [and] a presentation of man's most noteworthy faiths in a time-setting that will do justice to their development as well as to their origins" (reprinted in the fourth edition, xv). He covers primitive and bygone religions (inclusive of prehistoric, primitive and "national religions" by which he means Mesopotamia, Egypt, Greece, and Italy); the religions of India (Hinduism, Jainism, Buddhism, and Sikhism); the religions of the Far East (Taoism, Confucianism, and Shinto); and the religions of the Near East (Zoroastrianism, Judaism, Christianity, and Islam). His classification is largely geographical with "Primitive and Bygone Religions" a potpourri. The eighth edition, released in 1990, has been retitled *A History of the World's Religions*, presumably in the wake of the feminist critique of sexist language (though the promotion folder says that "the new title reflects this continuity and change," that is, the same structure overall but current issues and up-to-date developments). The promotion folder also says:

> Inviting future users "to participate in a continuing dialogue," David S. Noss captures the essence of the success behind *A HISTORY OF THE WORLD'S RELIGIONS*. That is, more than 30 years of discussion and correspondence with believers in the faiths the book presents, and suggestions from literally thousands of teachers and students who have helped shape successive editions. This onging exchange between writer, practitioners, and readers has resulted in the most authoritative and *successful world religions* textbook ever published! (emphasis added).

Here the "World's Religions" and "World Religions" are equated and include the broad terms of primitive, bygone, national, and specific religions of the earlier edition.

Jacques Waardenburg, in his 1973 *Classical Approaches to the Study of Religion: Aims, Methods and Theories of Research*, also implies an equation between the term "world religions" and "religions of the world." He includes the term "world religions" in his "Index of Scholarly Concepts." Only three references to it appear, however, in the volume. (By contrast, there are numerous references to other concepts such as comparative history of religions, comparative religion, comparative study of religion, history of religion(s), phenomenology of religion, science of religion, or just the word religion.) Two of the three references to the term "world religions" in Waardenburg's book are by Waardenburg himself in his Introduction (the other being that of Wach, quoted above).

> The study of the eastern *world religions*, interestingly enough, has been assigned traditionally in the first place to the orientalists, since they were specialists in the literature of the larger Eastern languages. The professional historians of religion before World War II were mostly working—often in connection with biblical studies—on religions that had disappeared. They made comparative studies or were interested in general problems that, characteristically, were more related to the religions of non-literate societies than to the *present-day world religions*. It was relatively rare that a historian of religions would devote himself to the study of one of the *world religions*. Their study was entrusted to those scholars among the orientalists who happened to be interested in the religious aspects of the civilization they studied (58-59, emphasis added).

A thorough study could certainly show to what extent the scholarly images which the West has developed of other religions or of religion in general have been determined by particular trends in its own cultural and intellectual history. In the same way, certain blind spots as well as certain pertinent interests of the scholars of this period in their study of religion can be traced back to the culture in which these scholars were rooted. One pertinent question which may be asked, for instance, is that concerning the scope of attention given to the *present-day world religions*. Strange as it may sound, apart from some significant exceptions, the study of contemporary developments in the larger religions seems to have been relatively neglected, for those scholars of religion who worked on the *major world religions* nearly always studied them in their classical periods and gave only minor attention to the modern and contemporary period (76-77, emphasis added).

In both quotations Waardenburg uses the term "world religions" but does not define it. He does, however, distinguish between "world religions" in general and "present-day world religions"; accordingly, the latter must be a subclass of the former. Waardenburg also implies a distinction between the religions of non-literate societies and the "world religions." And he suggests that historians of religions focus on the former, those who specialize in languages on the latter, especially the classical period. Since his volume is focussed on classical approaches to the study of religion, which were largely European, his lack of perceptive comment on the term "world religions" may be excused, since this has been mainly a development after the mid-twentieth century, that too, largely in North America. (One may argue, of course, that the use of the term for comparative purposes still needs definition to be useful, if not scientific.)

Once again, some observations are in order.

1. The phrase "the world's religions" and its variant "the world's living religions" like the term "world religions" focus on the modern world. It is more common, however, to describe "the world's religions" as "major" rather than "great" and to include religions termed primitive, non-scriptural, Native American Indian, African, etc. This is not the case with the term "world religions," which is often described as inclusive of religions which are living, major, and great.

2. The category "religions of the world" may indicate an even broader sweep and include some religions of the past (usually the religions of Mesopotamia, Egypt, Ancient Greece, and Rome) and more attention on the historical dimension, especially the early period of the religion. But even here there seems to be an interest in understanding religion as a modern adventure if not an interest in the contemporary period per se. Then, too, the terms "world religions" and "religions of the world" may be viewed as equivalent, as is the case with Noss.

3. This takes us full circle. While an attempt has been made to locate some clusters of adjectives as a way of distinguishing categories, the result is by no means unambiguous when we compare the terms world religions, living religions, great religions, the world's religions, and religions of the world.

4. No matter what the nomenclature, though, the modern dimension and the idea of encounter or dialogue is to the foreground.

5. But how many living religions can be studied and how are they to be chosen? Some scholars have used a criterion of "great" or "high" while others have provided a token chapter on religions variously termed "primitive," non-scriptural, and so forth. And some scholars have also included religions of the past (especially those which contributed to Western culture). The sheer scale creates its own problems, at the very least for North American writers of textbooks. Hence the need for selection and some criteria for selection.

6. There is great variation, moreover, among the actual lists of religions offered under these categories.

7. All authors of these books are eager to demonstrate geographical distribution by choosing religions that "have spread" or by suggesting that their own choice of religions is from around the world. (Whole continents such as South America, however, are ignored). In short, there is pressure to be global (albeit in a highly selective way).

8. This fact may be related to the modern agenda of being good world citizens or to the original quest of the history of religion/s: to understand what it means to be religious. Thus, for pragmatic or methodological reasons the study of religion must encompass space and time.

9. Although the term became popular as names of courses and occasionally the titles of books, it has been virtually ignored by historians of the discipline of religion such as Jacques Waardenburg, Eric Sharpe, and Frank Whaling. The most striking omission is by the recent *The Encyclopedia of Religion*.

10. There has been little critical reflection on the term; its reputation rests on usage and unexamined presuppositions.

At this stage, the question must be raised whether the term "world religions" is based only on expediency or whether it can provide a basis for comparisons and generalizations that have heuristic value and can contribute to the study of religion. If the data are examined with this question in mind, a number of anomalies immediately become apparent. To cite just one example, R. C. Zaehner grouped religions geographically (West and East with a focus on the homelands Israel and India respectively) and typologically (prophecy and wisdom). But Zoroastrianism cannot be traced to the Jewish homeland and Shinto is not related to India; Confucianism and Taoism likewise cannot be reduced to a connection with India via Buddhism. And Confucianism has not been classified as a mystical religion.

Such confusion and lack of critical examination makes one wonder whether the term "world religions" does not reflect a larger problem in the discipline and with the scholars themselves. One is reminded of Peter Byrne's critical review "The Theory of Religion and Method in the Study of Religion in the *Encyclopedia of Religion*" (1988). He opines a lack of pattern and editorial direction behind articles in this area and nowhere finds "a clear-sighted characterization of religion for the purposes of the encyclopedia; rather vagueness prevails." Byrne suggests that any decent encyclopedia should have a discussion of "the various types of contemporary definitions of religion and the major issues and distinctions to be faced in adjudicating between them. Thus we read nothing of substantive versus functionalist definitions, family-resemblance versus monothetic definitions, operational versus essentialist definitions, and so forth." (7)

If there remains a difficulty in defining religion as evidenced by the lack of consensus among scholars and exemplified in the most recent encyclopedia, it is predictable that there will be no consensus for the term "world religions," since the word "religion" is involved. Whaling remarks in *Contemporary Approaches to the Study of Religion* (1983) that "clarification of terms and concepts within... more limited areas is important; the advances resulting from such clarifications may contribute to the emergence of a more general view of what is meant by 'religion.'"

And yet this does not seem to be happening. Wilfred Cantwell Smith, who himself was so instrumental in establishing the category "world religions," has in the final analysis been fundamentally hostile to approaching the study of religion through categories. He prefers instead to focus on the living person for whom faith is a constantly changing and ever new experience. Like the early Buddhist theory of momentariness (*ksanavada*) this may have been an effective dialectical means (*upaya*) to force attention on the present. But it also has had the same inherent weakness of seeing categories as provisional, lower forms of knowledge, and ultimately obstructions to right knowledge. Hence they are not worthy of serious examination.

By contrast, category formation is construction, an act of reflective imagination, and a creation for analytic purposes which is based on comparison and generalization involving self-conscious artificulation of choice. According to Jonathan Z. Smith in his *Imagining Religion: From Babylon to Jonestown* (1982):

> The student of religion must be able to articulate clearly why "this" rather than "that" was chosen as an exemplum. His primary skill is concentrated in this choice. This effort at articulate choice is all the more difficult, and hence all the more necessary, for the historian of religion who accepts neither the boundaries of canon nor of community in constituting his intellectual domain, in providing his range of exempla (xi).

Of course, it is category formation which in the final analysis defines the range of exempla, even though the category may be arrived at inductively. At the moment "world religions," if a category at all, is a poorly understood one. A few descriptors such as living, major, and great, and an imaging of the study of religion in textbooks as global, albeit highly selective, hardly serves to illumine the data. Is not the task at hand, then, to come terms with the issues posed by classification?

Category-bashing may occur for a number of reasons today. It may be a dialectical move to focus on the uniqueness of the particular moment. Then, too, it may be a way to make suspect any generalization in the face of specialization.[2] It may be an expression of liberalism, with its distrust of boundaries as limits to freedom. Or, more radically, it may involve deconstruction as the systematic dismantling of all classes and destruction of all boundaries. Whatever the reason, however, the *Weltanschauung* of the postmodern age hardly bodes well for bringing more "class" to the study of religion. The case history of "world religions" is a case in point.

To move beyond our present impasse we should use various methodologies for creating classifications and feel free to experiment with classifications at various levels of generalizations to see what insights they may reveal. It may well be that no one classification will do justice to the material. Perhaps we need Eliade's "patterns" and Wach's concept of the classical. Perhaps it is time to learn something from the social anthropologists and their correlations of variables with a large cross-cultural sample. And perhaps it is timely to look again at the description of the term "world religions" to see if the religions most commonly listed do not have a polythetic set of characteristics that can be correlated with a fundamental historical process or political entity.

My own approach, upon reflection,[3] would be to use a polythetic approach — each class would be defined by a cluster of characteristics, all of which need not be present. For a comparative, historical perspective, my basic categories would be religion, religions of non-state societies (tribes, bands, etc.) and state-religions ("state" being broadly understood as kingdoms, states, empires, and nations at various stages of formation, stabilization, and disintegration). Living and dead would be subcategories of both non-state and state religions. Zoroastrianism, Hinduism, Buddhism, Jainism, Sikhism, Confucianism, Taoism, Shinto, the religions of Mesopotamia, Egypt, Greece and Rome, Judaism, Christianity and Islam, Yoruba and Inca religion, and so on all have formative periods in connection with the "state" experience. A systematic study of them, therefore, should yield a cluster of common characteristics. Again, of these religions, the ones that have endured to the present may yield another set of characteristics. In the final analysis, there should be considerable overlap with the list of so-called "world religions" enumerated by Hume, Huston Smith, and others. More importantly, the cluster of characteristics would provide the rationale of *why* these religions are to be grouped together and the basis for a truly comparative perspective that will generate hypotheses and provide corelations. At that point we may be justified in using the term "world religions" as indicative of a real category.

Notes

1 This essay was written by Wach when he was at the University of Chicago Divinity School. He says in the introduction to the book that this essay (along with the first two) grew out of the experience of teaching and is meant "to stimulate thought on the way in which instruction in our field might be improved" (xiv). From his remarks, it is obvious that Wach did not create the term "world religions" but that it was in use at the Divinity School at the University of Chicago if not elsewhere in North America or was introduced by Wach from continental scholarship. I have not traced its origin beyond Wach.

2 By the mid-80s, according to Darrow: "It is often argued that we are not as comparative as we ought to be and that few comparative theses are written. . . . [Moreover] that which we spend most of our time doing here [is] (learning languages and reading texts) in a way that reminds us of the variety of functions of the word—written, spoken, heard—in the face of a continuing tendency toward a 'logocentrism' that threatens to force forgetfulness of the embeddedness of our texts in communities and in the heart of persons of faith. . . . [Then, too,] it is striking that instruction in the history of religion along the model of History of Religion 101/Humanities II has receded at the very moment of its triumph. There are several reasons for this. Our training has become increasingly specialized. For the most part, we are not called upon to teach courses outside of our areas of specialization. The usual world religions course has declined somewhat as our staple bread and butter course in favor of shorter, more selective and thematic introductory courses, such as the pilgrimage course" (231-32).

3 I first started to wonder about the term "world religions" when Arvind Sharma asked me several years ago to write an introduction for a book he was editing called *Women in World Religions* (1987). Although I knew the term was common, I asked him to clarify its meaning. He referred to a "more or less conventional list" and mentioned Huston Smith's *The Religions of Man* as its *locus classicus*. I did not have much time to worry about category construction, however, for I already had before me a *fait accompli*: my own chapter on women in Hinduism but also chapters on women in Buddhism, Confucianism, Taoism, Judaism, Christianity, and Islam as well as one on women in the religion of the Australian Aborigines. And so the following rationale appeared in the Introduction: "A word about the choice of the expression *world religions*. By world religions is meant primarily the major religions—Hinduism, Buddhism, Confucianism, Taoism, Judaism, Christianity, and Islam—and secondarily the tribal religions, which have been receiving increased attention in their own right. Accordingly, this volume discusses the religions listed above and also one representative of the tribal religions, that of the Australian Aborigines, for purposes of comparison" (Young 1987:2).

Still, I felt uneasy about the term world religions (especially since it was being used in several other books with which I was involved). Hence the present analysis.

References

Adams, Charles J., ed. 1965. *A Reader's Guide to the Great Religions*. New York: The Free Press.

Baird, Robert D. 1971. *Category Formation and the History of Religions*. The Hague: Mouton.

Bradley, David G. 1963. *A Guide to The World's Religions*. Englewood Cliffs, NJ: Prentice-Hall.

Brandon, Samuel George Frederick. 1962. *Man and His Destiny in the Great Religions*. Toronto: University of Toronto Press.

Byrne, Peter. 1988. "The Theory of Religion and Method in the Study of Religion in the *Encyclopedia of Religion.*" *Religious Studies* 24, 1: 3-11.

Clark, James Freeman. 1882. *Ten Great Religions: An Essay in Comparative Theology.* Boston: Houghton.

Comstock, W. Richard, ed. 1971. *Religion and Man: An Introduction.* New York: Harper & Row.

Daniélou, Jean, et al. 1964. *Introduction to the Great Religions.* Notre Dame, Indiana: Fides Publishers.

Darron, William R. 1988 "The Harvard Way in the Study of Religion." *Harvard Theological Review* 81: 2.

Eliade, Mircea, ed. 1987. *The Encyclopedia of Religion.* Vols. 12 and 16. New York: Macmillan.

———. 1969. *The Quest: History and Meaning in Religion.* Chicago and London: The University of Chicago Press.

Eliade, Mircea and Joseph M. Kitagawa. 1959. *The History of Religions: Essays in Methodology.* Chicago: The University of Chicago Press.

Ellwood, Robert S., Jr. 1976. *Many Peoples, Many Faiths: An Introduction to the Religious Life of Mankind.* Englewood Cliffs, NJ: Prentice-Hall.

———. 1977. *Words of the World's Religions: An Anthology.* Englewood Cliffs, NJ: Prentice Hall.

Fu, Charles Wei-hsun and Gerhard E. Spiegler, eds. 1987. *Movements and Issues in World Religions: A Sourcebook and Analysis of Developments Since 1945: Religion, Ideology, and Politics.* New York: Greenwood Press.

Hastings, J. 1908-12. *Encyclopaedia of Religion and Ethics.* 12 vols. Edinburgh.

Hopfe, Lewis, M. 1976. *Religions of the World.* Beverly Hills: Glencoe Press.

Hume, R. E. 1933. *The World's Living Religions: An Historical Sketch.* New York: Charles Scribner's Sons.

Hutchison, John A. 1969. *Paths of Faith.* New York: McGraw-Hill.

Martinson, Paul Varo. 1987. *A Theology of World Religions: Interpreting God, Self, and World in Semitic, Indian, and Chinese Thought.* Minneapolis: Augsburg.

McAfee, Ward. 1983. *A History of the World's Great Religions.* Lanham, MD: University Press of America.

McCasland, S. Vernon, Grace E. Cairns, and David C. Yu. 1969. *Religions of the World.* New York: Random House.

Noss, John B. 1969 (1949). *Man's Religions.* London: Macmillan.

Oliver, James and Christina Scott, eds. *Religion and World History: A Selection from the Works of Christopher Dawson.* Garden City, NY: Image Books.

Parrinder, Geoffrey. 1964. *The World's Living Religions.* London: Pan Books.

———, ed. 1983. *World Religions: From Ancient History to the Present.* New York: Facts on File Publications. Also with the title *An Illustrated History of the World's Religions.* Middlesex, Eng.: Newnes Books. First published in 1971 as *Man and His Gods* in the United Kingdom and as *Religions of the World* in the U. S.

Prozesky, Martin. 1988. "Explanations of Religion as a Part of and Problem for Religious Studies." *Religious Studies* 24, 3 (September): 303-11.

———. 1977. *Religions of the World.* Madras: World Hindu Council.

Severy, Merle, ed. 1978 (1971). *Great Religions of the World*. National Geographic Society.

Sharpe, Eric J. 1975. *Comparative Religion: A History*. London: Duckworth.

Smart, Ninian. 1984 (1969, 1976). *The Religious Experience of Mankind*. New York: Charles Scribner's Sons.

———. 1977. *The Long Search*. Boston: Little, Brown and Company.

Smith, Huston. 1958. *The Religions of Man*. New York: Harper & Brothers.

Smith, Jonathan Z. 1982. *Imagining Religion: From Babylon to Jonestown*. Chicago: University of Chicago Press.

Smith, Wilfred Cantwell. 1959. "Comparative Religion: Whither—and Why?" In *The History of Religions: Essays in Methodology*, edited by Mircea Eliade and Joseph M. Kitagawa, 31-59. Chicago: The University of Chicago Press.

———. 1963. *The Meaning and End of Religion*. New York.

———. 1968. "Traditional Religions and Modern Culture." In *Proceedings of the XIth International Congress of the IAHR*, 55ff. Leiden.

Stendahl, Krister. 1978 (1971). Foreword. *Great Religions of the World*. National Geographic.

Tillich, Paul. 1961. *Christianity and the Encounter of the World Religions*. New York: Columbia University Press.

Toynbee, Arnold. 1957. *Christianity Among the Religions of the World*. New York: Charles Scribner's Sons.

Waardenburg, Jacques. 1973. *Classical Approaches to the Study of Religion: Aims, Methods and Theories of Research*.

Wach, Joachim. 1955. *Types of Religions Experience: Christian and Non-Christian*. London: Routledge and Kegan Paul.

Whaling, Frank, ed. 1983. "Introduction: The Contrast Between the Classical and Contemporary Periods in the Study of Religion." In *Contemporary Approaches to the Study of Religion*. Vol. 1: *The Humanities*. Berlin: Mouton.

Widengren, G. 1971 (1945, 1953). *Religionens warld*. Stockholm. German translation: *Religionsphänomenologie*. Berlin, 1969.

Wilkins, Ronald J. 1979 (1974). *Religions of the World*. Dubuque, IA: Wm. C. Brown Company.

Wilson, J. F. 1970. "Introduction: The Background and Present Context of the Study of Religion in Colleges and Universities." In *The Study of Religion in Colleges and Universities*, edited by Ramsey and Wilson. Princeton.

Zaehner, R. C., ed. 1959. *The Concise Encyclopedia of Living Faiths*. Boston: Beacon Press.

TROISIÈME PARTIE:

Les idées, la réalité

PART THREE:

Ideas and Reality

CHAPTER 12

Anthropological Perspectives on Popular Faith: Catholicism in Brittany[1]

Ellen Badone

Introduction

As my title suggests, this paper comprises three parts. In the first section, I comment briefly on the nature of anthropology and suggest what is offered by an "anthropological perspective" on religion. In the second section, I discuss the notion of the "popular" and question whether there is a difference between popular faith and any other kind of faith. Finally, I illustrate these ideas with some examples from my own research on Catholicism in Brittany.

The Anthropological Perspective

A recent monograph introducing the field of anthropology to non-specialists begins with the questions "What is life? What is the essence of human existence? Of what does experience consist?" (Peacock 1986:1). These fundamental questions that inform anthropological work differ little from those posed by theologians and researchers in the field of religious studies. Anthropology has been defined as "a discipline for understanding humankind in its many facets — holistically" (Peacock 1986:10). The holistic perspective requires that human actions and ideas be viewed in their total context: a marriage custom cannot be studied independently of the economy, a religious ritual must be seen against the background of a people's cosmology and worldview, and contemporary societies need to be understood in the light of their prehistoric past. The anthropologist's focus is on culture, or "the taken-for-granted but powerfully influential understand-

---

Notes and references for this chapter appear on pages 143-44.

ings and codes that are learned and shared by members of a group" (Peacock 1986:7).

In seeking to answer existential questions about the nature of human reality, the anthropologist engages in fieldwork, research on a group of people through participation in their daily lives over an extended period of time. Fieldwork is complemented by consultation of published sources on the history and institutions of the group, in cases where such sources exist. Often, but not always, the community being studied belongs to a cultural tradition that differs widely from the anthropologist's own. During the last two decades, anthropologists have turned increasingly frequently to research "at home," in North America or Western Europe. Even when anthropologists work in their own society, however, they generally choose a social milieu which is foreign to them. Thus, fieldwork involves encounter with an Other. One contemporary anthropologist has applied Paul Ricoeur's definition of hermeneutics to fieldwork, suggesting that the anthropologist achieves "the comprehension of self by the detour of the comprehension of the other" (Ricoeur, quoted in Rabinow 1977:5). As this last statement indicates, the goals of anthropology are not merely to catalogue "different" peoples, but through contrast and comparison to understand ourselves, and ultimately to gain some general insights into the character of human experience.

For the anthropologist, participant-observation fieldwork in an unfamiliar society has been likened to a conversion experience, during which the researcher has "eye-opening encounters, which shatter assumptions held all his life" (Peacock 1986:55). Fieldwork has also been compared to a rite of passage that, "through ordeals and insights, moves the initiate to a new level of maturity" (Peacock 1986:55). In fieldwork, the anthropologist seeks to understand a group of people from the inside out, from the grassroots up, and with respect for the values, customs, and faith of those being studied. The goal of the fieldworker is to see the world "from the native's point of view" (Geertz [1974] 1983; quoted from Malinowski [1922] 1961:25). Like theology and religious studies, anthropological field research, and the writing which follows it, are, as the phrase I have just quoted from Ricoeur suggests, hermeneutic processes, involving constant interpretation and translation across cultural boundaries.

"Popular" "Religion"

At this point, I would like to move from these general reflections about the discipline of anthropology and its parallels with religious studies to consider the ways in which anthropology can help us to understand popular religion. First, however, it is necessary to define what is meant by both the terms "popular" and "religion."

Popular religion is a concept that has recently been criticized in anthropology and history as well as other disciplines involved in the study of religion. As Peter Brown observes, popular religion is frequently "presented as in some ways a diminution, a misconception or a contamination of *un*popular religion" (Brown 1981:19). Anthropology itself has not been immune to this refusal to grant popular religion the status of a meaningful religious field in its own right. Writing in the mid-1950s, anthropologist Robert Redfield (1956) developed the notion of a distinction between great and little traditions, concepts that could be applied to diverse cultural phenomena in complex societies, including art, religion, and medicine. Great traditions, for Redfield "were characteristic of the reflective, literate elite, who invented, elaborated, and refined with infinite subtlety" religious, philosophical and artistic ideas, among others (Brandes 1990:186). Over time, "these products of the great tradition were said to diffuse ... to the supposedly nonreflective, nonliterate and ... rural masses, who selected from among the great tradition elements, reinterpreted them and arrived at a simplified, localized, somewhat distorted version of the great tradition, known as the little tradition" (Brandes 1990:186-87). Although Redfield's ideas initially acted as a catalyst for research on religion in complex societies, it is clear that this is one of the "two-tiered" models of religion which Peter Brown criticizes for their implicit denigration of the popular lower tier, or little tradition (Brandes 1990:187, Brown 1981:18). In addition, the two traditions are presented by Redfield as being discrete, relatively autonomous spheres, linked primarily by a "trickle-down" of ideas from great to little. More recent researchers, building on a perspective developed by historian Carlo Ginzburg in his *The Cheese and the Worms* (1980), have argued that we should instead look for a circular movement of ideas between elite and popular religious culture, with influences moving reciprocally in both directions. Moreover, as anthropologist William Christian has pointed out, in some situations, the same religious style can be shared by all levels of society within a given geographical region, from princes to peasants as well as urban dwellers. For this reason, Christian advocates substituting the term "local" for "popular" religion (Christian 1981).

Christian, who works with historical as well as contemporary materials from Spain, also reminds us that in many cases local or popular religious practices are simply elements of elite, "great tradition" religion that have been preserved in a particular area long after they have become irrelevant for the orthodox religious establishment. An example of this process, also from Spain, is documented by anthropologist Stanley Brandes, who was told in the late 1960s by the villagers of a small parish outside Madrid that their priests were "themselves ... taking religion away from us" (Brandes 1976:23). In the aftermath of Vatican II, "progressive" priests sought to discourage what they perceived as outmoded processions and time-honoured ritual patterns. Paradoxically, these were the same forms of devotion that clerical reformers had laboured to institute at an earlier period, during the Counter-Reformation.

In Christian's view, the term popular religion can only legitimately be used if it refers to "religion as practiced" or lived, in contradistinction to "religion as prescribed" (Christian 1981:178). The anthropological perspective provides a particularly useful point of entry to the understanding of "practice" or "religion as lived." Through fieldwork, anthropologists are placed in a privileged position to listen to the words and observe the actions of those who are living and practising their faith. This kind of information is often difficult to glean exclusively from written sources. Although Ginzburg and other European historians (Ginzburg 1980, 1983; Le Roy Ladurie 1979; Schmitt 1983) have attempted to reconstruct past popular beliefs through recourse to inquisitorial proceedings, such documents are composed of testimony elicited under conditions of duress, and at least in some cases, defendants modified their "stories" to meet the expectations of inquisitors (see, for example, Ginzburg 1983). Likewise, the learned treatises of clerics and theologians present only one side of religion: an idealized vision which may diverge widely from lay experience.

Perhaps the most important contribution which the anthropological perspective can make to illuminating popular religion is the recognition that the religious domain is almost always wider than the sphere accepted by official religious institutions. Referring to Europe, Susan Tax Freeman cautions fellow anthropologists that if we allow "the Church to press on our analyses its own definitions of proper beliefs, parts of the belief system which have not received official sanction are treated as something less than religious. That the personal system of faith may elevate the unsanctioned objects of belief to at least the same level as the sanctioned ones and join them coherently together has either been ignored or is obliterated by the definitions of religion in use" (Freeman 1978:121). In Freeman's view, it is necessary to step beyond the terms of the religious discourse as defined by orthodox religious bodies. Beliefs in phenomena that these institutions would classify as "superstitious," such as healing springs, amulets, and the evil eye, should be interpreted by the anthropologist, in line with "the native's point of view," as "religious" (Freeman 1978:121).

Here, I am finally forced to confront the central question that this volume has set out to explore: what, in fact, is religion? To the 40 thought-provoking definitions of religion offered by Michel Despland (1979:537-42) at the end of his book, I would like to add an anthropological one, that of Clifford Geertz, probably the most prolific anthropological writer on religion and the one who is best known outside the discipline. Geertz proposes that a religion is:

> (1) a system of symbols which acts to (2) establish powerful, pervasive, and long-lasting moods and motivations in men by (3) formulating conceptions of a general order of existence and (4) clothing these conceptions with such an aura of factuality that (5) the moods and motivations seem uniquely realistic (Geertz 1973:90).

For Geertz, as for Max Weber before him, the question of meaning is primary. Without a religious orientation in the world, people are faced by chaos, the feeling that reality is senseless, that evil and suffering are random afflictions lacking in purpose or reason. Religion provides "interpretability" (Geertz 1973:100), by enabling the faithful to see the world against the background of an underlying pattern of broader truths in terms of which misfortune, unexplained events, and evil make sense. Religion, however, does not offer a facile escape into the realm of wish fulfillment. Instead of denying the existence of suffering, Geertz claims that religion provides "models for" the way to suffer, showing "how to make of physical pain, personal loss, worldly defeat, or the helpless contemplation of others' agony something bearable, supportable — something, as we say, sufferable" (Geertz 1973:104). For Geertz, the religious response to what he describes as

> the uncomfortable suspicion that perhaps the world, and hence man's life in the world, has no genuine order at all — no empirical regularity, no emotional form, no moral coherence ... is in each case the same: the formulation, by means of symbols, of an image of such a genuine order of the world which will account for, and even celebrate, the perceived ambiguities, puzzles and paradoxes in human experience (Geertz 1973:108).

Although Geertz's view of religion has recently been criticized for privileging the symbolic dimension of faith and ignoring the relationships of power and domination which shape religious discourses (Asad 1983), I have found his theoretical perspective particularly helpful in interpreting my fieldwork observations. At this point, I would like to move on to a discussion of religion in Brittany, drawing on examples from my research to illustrate some of the theoretical issues about religion and "the popular" that I have explored thus far.

Popular Faith in Brittany

Located at the northwestern tip of France, bordered by the Atlantic and the English Channel, Brittany remained largely a rural peasant region, incompletely integrated with metropolitan France well into the present century. The cultural distinctiveness of the region was enhanced by the widespread use of Breton, one of the Celtic family of languages, which is more closely allied to Welsh than to French. Since the Second World War, however, Brittany has undergone rapid social transformations, involving the mechanization of agriculture, rural depopulation, the improvement of regional, national, and international transportation and communications networks, and the establishment of a fully developed cash economy. Use of the French language now predominates over Breton in most social situations.[2] Nevertheless, despite social change, certain features of Breton culture display important elements of continuity with earlier periods. My own work on Brittany has sought to emphasize this persistence of earlier practices and beliefs as well as their reinterpretation, through a combination of historical research and fieldwork in two Breton communities.

Brittany has long been noted for its devotion to the Catholic Church. Although levels of religious practice have recently decreased, until the 1960s, over 50 per cent of adults in most parts of Brittany classified themselves as regularly practising Catholics, and in certain regions the level of regular Mass attendance exceeded 80 per cent (Lambert 1985:8). The most notably distinctive feature of Breton Catholicism is its preoccupation with eschatological issues and "the cult of the dead." The importance accorded to death in Breton religion and culture may have roots in a pre- or at least non-Christian tradition with parallels in other Celtic regions of Europe. However, the Catholic reform movement of the seventeenth century capitalized on this pre-existing Breton interest in death and the welfare of the souls, simultaneously adapting to and reinforcing such local concerns. During the reforming missions conducted by the Jesuits in seventeenth-century Brittany, eschatology emerged as a primary theme. While similar missionary efforts were carried out contemporaneously in other regions of France and Europe, the Breton missions were particularly successful at inculcating a lasting spirit of reform among local clergy (Croix 1981:1214-15). The missionary approach remained characteristic of Breton clerics until the mid-twentieth century. Until the 1950s, missions marked by preaching on death, the Last Judgement, and the afterlife were a regular feature of parish life in Brittany (Croix and Roudaut 1984:192).

The death-centred discourse of Catholicism in Brittany reveals the reciprocal influences between popular and orthodox levels of the Breton religious system. The already-existent popular preoccupation with death pre-adapted seventeenth-century Bretons to the orthodox teachings of the post-Tridentine church and ensured that those teachings penetrated more deeply into local culture than in other regions of Europe, where similar missions had a less profoundly lasting effect (Croix 1981:1183-86). In turn, the popular Breton "obsession with death"[3] was reinforced and augmented by similar concerns in the orthodox church's missions and regular parochial observances over a 300-year period.

To illustrate more precisely the mutual influences between "religion as practised" and "religion as prescribed" in Brittany, I will start by discussing the example of the *Ankou*, death personified in Breton folk tradition. In the collections of folklorists who worked in Brittany during the nineteenth century, the *Ankou* is depicted as a tall thin man wearing a felt hat and armed with a scythe, or as a skeleton carrying a dart, arrow, mallet, or scythe. In either case, the *Ankou* is a psychopomp. His weapon serves to take away the life of his victims, and it is he who conducts the dying to the otherworld. For this reason, the *Ankou* is frequently represented with a cart, on which he loads his harvest of souls (Le Braz 1928: I:111-16). The figure of the *Ankou* is the best example of a Breton death-related folk tradition which has Celtic antecedents. Parallel personae, the Welsh *angheu* and Cornish *ankow*, exist in parts of Celtic Britain (Croix and Roudaut 1984:83). Literary references mentioning the *Ankou* date to the fifteenth century, and possibly earlier, since the word appears in a marginal gloss commenting upon a ninth-century Latin manuscript. To certain researchers, the fact that the *Ankou* is sometimes depicted with a mallet suggests a possible link with Sucellos, the Celtic god of death, who is associated with the same attribute (Le Menn 1979:8-9, 19-23).[4]

Legends describing encounters with the *Ankou* abound in nineteenth-century Breton folklore. Although some of these popular religious narratives make no reference to official Catholicism, others fuse the two traditions. In *L'histoire du forgeron*, for example, the *Ankou* visits a forge to have his scythe mended on Christmas Eve. The blacksmith has defied orthodox Christian practice by remaining at home to work instead of attending midnight Mass. As soon as his scythe has been repaired, the *Ankou* reveals his identity, and warns the blacksmith to make his confession, for his final hour is at hand (Le Braz 1928: I:132-34). Clearly, this legend reinforces a message of respect for the church's rituals and its orthodox definition of the sacred. Those who ignore clerical ritual and violate the sacred risk instant retribution.

In *L'histoire du forgeron* we see the popular religious tradition incorporating elements of "religion as prescribed." However, official Catholicism in Brittany was equally susceptible to influences from local religion. It is clear that the *Ankou* does not belong in the official Catholic hierarchy of supernatural beings. However, sculpted depictions of this personage are frequently found in association with Breton ecclesiastical architecture, on the exterior walls of churches and ossuaries. Moreover, on occasion, the *Ankou* even penetrated the interior of the church. His skeletal figure decorates the holy water font in one parish, and statues representing him were erected, alongside those of the saints, in two other churches. At present, the visitor to the parish church of Ploumilliau, Finistère, can still see a statue of the *Ankou* prominently displayed.[5]

According to legends recorded in the nineteenth century, an encounter with the *Ankou* presages a forthcoming death. Those who hear his cart passing through their hamlet by night can be certain that one of their neighbours or relatives is about to die. As *L'histoire du forgeron* illustrates, to meet the *Ankou* in person signifies that one's own death is imminent (Le Braz 1928: I:111-63). Bretons today use the same term for such precursors of death as their nineteenth-century predecessors: *intersigne*, or *signe*. The *intersigne* is a sign that links two worlds, the everyday world of the living and the supernatural one of the dead. In addition to visitations by the *Ankou*, other phenomena were regarded by nineteenth-century Bretons as *intersignes*, including the crowing of a cock by night, the howling of dogs, and repeated sightings of magpies around a house (Le Braz 1928: I:1-79).

All of these *intersignes*, and many others, continue to be recognized and discussed in present-day Brittany. It is after a death in the village or family that *intersignes* are remembered and remarked upon, especially if the death is a tragic one: an accidental death or the death of a young person. In such circumstances, there is a special need to situate the event in terms of what Geertz would call the wider religious realities that underlie those of everyday life. In his words, tragic deaths lack "interpretability" (Geertz 1973:100). Those who remain behind to mourn seek a framework within which their grief can be rendered meaningful, and it is just such a framework that reference to *intersignes* provides. The signs that foreshadow a tragic death set it within the context of a predestined pattern controlled by some larger force. As one mother commented after telling me of the *intersignes* she had observed before her 24-year-old son was killed in a cycling accident, "So therefore, there is something supernatural, above us, don't you believe?" Likewise, another woman explained that the *intersignes* she has experienced have convinced her that "there must be a Master. I don't know if it's *le bon Dieu* or another, but I think there must be a Master who forewarns us." This woman is not a practising Catholic, and as her comment suggests, the notion that the hour of death is preordained is only marginally linked to official church doctrine. The "Master" has closer affinities to the *Ankou* than to *le bon Dieu*.

While notions of a "Master" or "something supernatural above us" do not represent a clearly articulated philosophical or theological statement, they nonetheless serve in Geertz's terms, like all religious symbols, to formulate "conceptions of a general order of existence," and images of "a genuine order of the world" (Geertz 1973:90, 108). Paraphrasing Geertz (1973:108), *intersigne* beliefs "deny" that tragic deaths are "inexplicable." *Intersignes* enable the bereaved to glimpse through the apparent chaos of the profane world to an underlying level of reality, what Geertz (1973:112) would call the "really real," where all seemingly random tragedies are revealed as part of a coherent pattern "written in advance" by something greater than ourselves. In terms of the anthropological perspective, *intersigne* beliefs are clearly "religious." Like the official teachings of Catholicism, and perhaps more so for many Bretons, such "popular" notions infuse experience with transcendant significance.

Intersigne beliefs, like the *Ankou*, are elements of Breton popular faith that bear little resemblance to orthodox Catholicism. Other aspects of "religion as practised" in Brittany derive more obviously from the realm of "religion as prescribed." I would like now to discuss two such examples, which illustrate William Christian's observation that "So-called 'little tradition' is often merely 'great tradition' that has taken root in a particular place and lasted longer than its time" (Christian 1981:178).

My first example concerns Catholic ritual for the dying. Until recently, in Brittany as in other parts of the Catholic world, the sacrament of extreme unction served as the rite of passage from the world of the living to that of the dead. Following a modification of Catholic liturgy in 1972, however, extreme unction has been renamed "the anointing of the sick." The new sacrament can be administered to all those of advancing years as well as to victims of serious illnesses or persons about to undergo major surgery. The liturgy explicitly advises against administering the sacrament as a deathbed rite. In contrast to the expiation of sin before death, the liturgy for the anointing of the sick emphasizes themes of physical and spiritual healing (Isambert 1975). In Brittany, the change from extreme unction to the anointing of the sick has not been well received. Many families continue to wait until "the last minute" to summon the priest, regarding his presence as essential at the bedside of a dying relative. Ironically, the post-Vatican II church in Brittany is faced with the task of undoing the work of earlier reforms. Parish registers reveal that the custom of requesting extreme unction was not well established in Brittany prior to the efforts made by the seventeenth-century church to instill regular patterns of receiving the sacraments (Croix 1981:949). Modernizing clergy in present-day Brittany are finding it difficult to eradicate the "religion of fear" centred on death and the afterlife which their counterparts in earlier periods sought to promote.

A second group of death-centred rituals that I found lay Bretons attempting to preserve in the face of clerical reform are the *services de continuation*, early morning Masses held on the first Friday of every month in memory of those from the parish who have died over the preceding year. While "progressive" priests view the *services de continuation* as "vestiges of a religious education that ... placed too much importance on the wrath of God,"[6] many parishioners continue to see them as essential for the salvation of their loved ones. Moreover, these monthly rituals bring together the bereaved into a community, allowing them to share and transcend their individual grief. Following Vatican II, however, rituals such as the *services de continuation* which focus on the afterlife have been discouraged by the Breton clerical establishment in favour of a religious perspective oriented towards ethical action in the present world.

My fieldwork experience clearly bears witness to Christian's suggestion that popular religion tends to remain faithful to religious discourses that have been declared outmoded by orthodox religious institutions. Given that this is the case, should we categorize Breton Catholics and others like them as backward conservatives, obstinately refusing to expand their religious horizons? I would argue that we should not, and to explain why, I would like to return to Geertz. For Geertz, the religious perspective "moves beyond the realities of everyday life to wider ones which correct and complete them.... It is this sense of the 'really real' upon which the religious perspective rests and which the symbolic activities of religion as a cultural system are devoted to producing, intensifying, and so far as possible, rendering inviolable by the discordant revelations of secular experience" (Geertz 1973:112). If religion does indeed operate in this way, how can we expect Bretons or any other people easily to accept religious change? For those who have lived a large part of their lives giving meaning to experience through reference to one set of "wider realities," the kind of intellectual gymnastics required to exchange these for another worldview is difficult to imagine. Thus, I would suggest that the conservatism of popular religion is not merely a reactionary resistance to progress. Rather, it is integral to the essence of all religion — popular or "unpopular." Religion by nature offers an "authoritative" and "inviolable" model of reality. Attempts to alter it, therefore, cannot help but appear contradictory and paradoxical.

Conclusion

Here I would like to draw together the themes I have been exploring throughout this paper and offer some conclusions.

First, I share William Christian's view that the concept of popular religion is only meaningful if we think of it as referring to "religion as practised" rather than "religion as prescribed." This distinction between precept and practice is, in my view, worthwhile to recognize, especially for research in complex societies on religious traditions that have codified doctrines and liturgy, institutionalized bureaucracies, and a specialist class of religious practitioners.

I have chosen, despite the recommendations of Christian and certain other anthropologists and historians, to continue using the word "popular" in describing "religion as practised" in Brittany. I use popular alongside other terms, such as Christian's own local religion, unofficial or informal religion, and folk religion, although the word "folk" evokes many of the same problems as "popular." I use the phrase popular religion cautiously, and I hope, without the implication that the "popular" is somehow less than truly "religious." As my examples from Brittany demonstrate, practices and ideas that the official church would characterize as superstitious are, when viewed against the anthropological definition of the word, "religious."

I also share the view recently expressed by William Christian that the anthropological perspective is particularly useful for the study of popular (or folk) religion. As he notes, popular religion is often closely anchored to particular places or communities, and its subtleties can only be appreciated if the researcher can comprehend through experience the intense links between religion and locality (Christian 1987:371). Moreover, I do not see how else we are to understand "religion as practised" if we do not observe it being practised and engage in dialogue with its practitioners. However, fieldwork observation of "religion as practised" provides only a partial glimpse of the complexity of religion in any given culture. As I hope my own reliance on literate and historical sources as well as fieldwork indicates, the anthropological perspective also requires the researcher to focus on the doctrines and background of the "official" religious tradition. Since the relationship between precept and practice is always a circular and dialectical one, both are integral components of a culture's religious system.

Notes

1 The fieldwork upon which this paper draws was supported by the Social Sciences and Humanities Research Council of Canada, the Wenner-Gren Foundation for Anthropological Research, and by a Humanities Graduate Research Grant and Lowie Scholarship from the University of California, Berkeley.
2 For more detailed discussions of social change in Brittany during the second half of the twentieth century, see Berger (1972), Chevalier (1983), Elégoët (1983), Morin (1970), Segalen (1985), and Badone (1989).
3 This phrase is used by Breton author Pierre-Jakez Hélias (1978:104) to describe his own culture's fascination with the theme of death.
4 However, this link is difficult to establish, since there are no known depictions of the *Ankou* armed with a mallet that pre-date the nineteenth century (Croix 1981:1066-67).
5 Exterior depictions of the *Ankou* on church buildings may be found in the parishes of Ploudiry, Landivisiau, La Roche-Maurice, Brasparts and Lannédern in the *département* of Finistère. The font at the entrance to the parish church of La Martyre, Finistère, is decorated with a figure of the *Ankou*. In addition to the statue in the church at Ploumilliau, a statue of the *Ankou* was formerly located in the church of Saint-Mathieu in Morlaix.
6 Quoted from an interview with a Breton parish priest during fieldwork.

References

Asad, Talal. 1983. "Anthropological Conceptions of Religion: Reflections on Geertz." *Man* 18: 237-59.

Badone, Ellen. 1989. *The Appointed Hour: Death, Worldview and Social Change in Brittany*. Berkeley: University of California Press.

Berger, Suzanne. 1972. *Peasants Against Politics*. Cambridge, MA: Harvard University Press.

Brandes, Stanley. 1990. "Conclusion: Reflections on the Study of Religious Orthodoxy and Popular Faith in Europe." In *Religious Orthodoxy and Popular Faith in European Society*, edited by Ellen Badone, 185-200. Princeton, NJ: Princeton University Press.

―――. 1976. "The Priest as Agent of Secularization in Rural Spain." In *Economic Transformations and Steady-State Values: Essays in the Ethnography of Spain*, edited by J. B. Aceves, E. C. Hansen and G. Levitas, 22-29. Flushing, NY: Queen's College Press.

Brown, Peter. 1981. *The Cult of the Saints: Its Rise and Function in Latin Christianity*. Chicago: University of Chicago Press.

Chevalier, Jacques. 1983. "Les nouvelles conditions de la production agricole." In *L'Ouest, bouge-t-il? Son changement social et culturel depuis trente ans. Synthèse des recherches de l'A. T. P. du C. N. R. S. dans le Grand Ouest*, 81-99. Nantes: Vivant.

Christian, William A., Jr. 1987. "Folk Religion: An Overview." In *The Encyclopedia of Religion*. Vol. 5, edited by Mircea Eliade, 270-74. New York: Macmillan.

―――. 1981. *Local Religion in Sixteenth Century Spain*. Princeton: Princeton University Press.

Croix, Alain. 1981. *La Bretagne aux 16e et 17e siècles. La vie, la mort, la foi.* Paris: Maloine.

———, and Fanch Roudaut. 1984. *Les Bretons, la mort et Dieu. De 1600 à nos jours.* Paris: Messidor - Temps Actuels.

Despland, Michel. 1979. *La Religion en Occident: évolution des idées et du vécu.* Montréal: Fides.

Elégoët, Fanch. 1983. "Populations et structures sociales." In *L'Ouest bouge-t-il? Son changement social et culturel depuis trente ans. Synthèse des recherches de l'A. T. P. du C. N. R. S. dans le Grand Ouest,* 100-14. Nantes: Vivant.

Freeman, Susan Tax. 1978. "Faith and Fashion in Spanish Religion: Notes on the Observance of Observance." *Peasant Studies* 7: 101-23.

Geertz, Clifford. 1974 (1983). "From the Native's Point of View: On the Nature of Anthropological Understanding." In *Local Knowledge: Further Essays in Interpretive Anthropology,* 55-70. New York: Basic Books.

———. 1973."Religion as a Cultural System." In *The Interpretation of Cultures,* 87-125. New York: Basic Books.

Ginzburg, Carlo. 1983. *The Night Battles: Witchcraft and Agrarian Cults in the Sixteenth and Seventeenth Centuries.* Translated by John and Anne Tedeschi. London: Routledge and Kegan Paul.

———. 1980. *The Cheese and the Worms: The Cosmos of a Sixteenth Century Miller.* Translated by John and Anne Tedeschi. Baltimore: Johns Hopkins University Press.

Hélias, Pierre-Jakez. 1978. *The Horse of Pride.* Translated and abridged by June Guicharnaud. New Haven: Yale University Press.

Isambert, François-A. 1975. "Les transformations du rituel catholique des mourants." *Archives de sciences sociales des religions* 20(39): 89-100.

Lambert, Yves. 1985. *Dieu change en Bretagne.* Paris: Cerf.

Le Braz, Anatole. 1928. *La légende de la mort chez les bretons armoricains.* 5th. ed. 2 Vols. Paris: Champion.

Le Menn, Gwennole. 1979. "La mort dans la littérature bretonne." Mémoires de la *Société d'histoire et d'archéologie de Bretagne* 56: 5-40.

Le Roy Ladurie, Emmanuel. 1979. *Montaillou: The Promised Land of Error.* Translated by Barbara Bray. New York: Vintage Books.

Malinowski, Bronislaw. (1922) 1961. *Argonauts of the Western Pacific.* New York: E. P. Dutton.

Morin, Edgar. 1970. *The Red and the White.* New York: Pantheon Books.

Peacock, James L. 1986. *The Anthropological Lens: Harsh Light, Soft Focus.* New York: Cambridge University Press.

Rabinow, Paul. 1977. *Reflections on Fieldwork in Morocco.* Berkeley: University of California Press.

Redfield, Robert. 1956. "The Social Organization of Tradition." In *Peasant Society and Culture,* 67-104. Chicago: University of Chicago Press.

Schmitt, Jean-Claude. 1983. *The Holy Greyhound: Guinefort, Healer of Children Since the Thirteenth Century.* Translated by Martin Thom. Cambridge: Cambridge University Press.

Segalen, Martine. 1985. *Quinze générations de bas-bretons.* Paris: Presses Universitaires de France.

CHAPTER 13

Is it a Crime to be Interdisciplinary? A Different Approach to the Study of Modern Jewish Law

Simcha Fishbane

An expression often used by North American Jews is, "Jews are like everyone else, except more so." And one may not exempt Jewish scholars from the aphorism. The academic study of rabbinic Judaism (in this I include the gamut from the ancient to the modern period) remains primarily a Jewish vocation, and its practitioners in part express through their research what it means for them to be Jewish. In this behaviour Jews resemble their counterparts who engaged in the study of Christianity, or at least this was true until the end of World War II. Who were the scholars in schools of theology? They were believing religious individuals. This does not mean that either set of scholars, Jewish or Christian, intends its scholarship to serve theological ends. These scholars seek to conduct research free from traditional authority, although not from tradition itself. Here lies the fundamental frustration which bothers both realms of scholarship.

This paper will endeavour to uncover some of the problems in the study of Judaism. The emphasis will be placed upon the research of halakhah, Jewish rabbinic law, where I will suggest the application of a methodology that has been successfully employed in the analysis of biblical and ancient Judaism to documents redacted in modern times. In conclusion I will discuss the social context of the Jewish scholar and his scholarship, for the manner in which this scholarship is practised suits the social context of the scholars of Judaica. Moreover, both scholar and scholarship serve implicitly to model for the Jewish community a distinctive definition of Jewish social identity and mapping.[1]

Notes and references for this chapter appear on pages 154-56.

I

Until the period of the *Wissenschaft des Judentums*, almost all Jewish scholarship can be classified as rabbinical or theological both in methodology and goal. The students of the *Wissenschaft* attempted to respond to their modern situation: they intended to provide the academic rationale for the reform of the Jewish tradition, on the one hand, and to demonstrate to Western Europeans Judaism's lofty level of civilization on the other. Geiger, Zunz, and others adopted the model of Liberal Protestant scholarship. Within the area of halakhah they moved from the traditional rabbinic concerns of adjudication to a different emphasis. The *Wissenschaft* scholars placed their emphasis upon issues of Jewish literary culture, placing the primary accent in their studies on biographies of leading Jewish rabbinical authorities. In this fashion data gathered from the halakhic texts were employed to build descriptive historiographies. The texts were surveyed for explicit statements to be taken at face value, as a true and accurate articulation of the realia of Jewish society as well as a repository of historical data-names, dates, and places.

As halakhic study developed in the twentieth century, a small group of researchers, not wanting to be bound either by the rabbinic methodologies (and authority) or the *Wissenchaft* school, increasingly emphasized the social, economic, and political consequences of Jewish behaviour as inferred from these texts. The facts so collected served to answer questions about the history of Jewish communities, how the Jews or the rabbis sought to organize their lives, and how they tried to live within the dominant non-Jewish society.

Various perspectives were utilized. Some scholars began to view the character of all rabbinic law (as applied in a specific era) as a product of human experience. Queries were posed as to how the rabbis at various points in history sought to organize and evaluate human action, given the facts at their disposal (Hass 1985:37). The halakhic material was offered by others as evidence that Jewish adjudicators at different times and places in history reacted to social change. Still other researchers showed an interest in the nature of Jewish legal thinking.

Responsa literature, in which Jews turned to leading rabbinical authorities with questions of realia, provided scholars with an ideal testing ground for emerging socio-economic theories and their associated methodologies. Although the rabbi did not necessarily intend his responsa to be historical documents, the written legal discussions were seen to be reporting on the social historical reality of their author and his society.

The methodological problems faced by this school of scholarship stem from the very way in which questions are formulated. It is at the bottom a matter of the sources available and what we can know from these sources. If one proposes to use responsa alone as a source for historical research, then it is inappropriate to ask about hard social, political, and economic facts. Responsa are not disinterested historical witnesses. They are legal documents which are designed to categorize and adjudicate human actions within the framework of Jewish law. To adequately apply the data in order to reconstruct a picture of a community's social life, the researcher must take into consideration the relationship of the social historical phenomena to the literary sources of the period being considered (Hass 1985:42).

To suggest a social reality based upon ten centuries of responsa[2] is problematic. Each geographical location had its own social concerns, and for this reason one cannot randomly select or collate responsa, or for that matter any halakhic data, on one topic from texts written in different locations. Halakhah must be used synchronically, with several possibilities opened at the same time, as well as diachronically, changing over time. One must only with great caution borrow a text from more than one location and more than one writer to address a topic. While modern researchers of responsa have become aware of these methodological principles, they have not necessarily addressed their consequences. In particular, they have not provided a large-scale synthesis of the cultural environment within which the phenomenon of halakhah can be explained. Often, one piece of the puzzle will be the focus of a particular study while the rest of the picture is ignored.[3]

Not until the middle of the twentieth century was there an attempt by Jacob Katz[4] seriously to apply data of the surrounding non-Jewish as well as the Jewish world to the study of halakhah, primarily through the employment of the responsa literature. Katz's theoretical framework suggests that rabbis' rulings were related to and even dependent upon external social, economic, and political influences, but he does not deal extensively with the personal bias of the individual halakhists.

Responsa are not issued in a vacuum, but are products of particular authors writing at a specific time. The social-historical context of the document must therefore be considered. Knowledge of the literary components of the responsa also provides a valuable means for comprehending and identifying the meaning and message of this literature. Thus, a key to understanding the nature of these differences, as well as why an individual rabbi read the tradition in the manner that he did, may well lie in an investigation of the social-historical context in which the responsum was written and in an examination of the psychological profile of the individual decisor as well as in the study of its "literary components" (Ellinson 1985:98, 103).

Aside from these studies of responsa, modern halakhic research has paid little attention to the developments in this approach to the study of Jewish law. Most traditional students of this literature perceive Jewish law to be a natural continuation from those rabbinical philosophies and rulings which preceded it. They prefer to treat the entire history of halakhah as a seamless unfolding of the divine word of God which Moses received at Sinai, independent of the social context in which it was promulgated and transmitted. To paraphrase a comment of Professor Jack Lightstone (1983:27), these scholars have examined vertical slices of successive strata of Israelite and rabbinic literature, ignoring the synchronic approach in favour of an exclusively diachronic perspective. The imperative to dissect a document as a transmitted product is not considered.

Only during the twentieth century have some scholars of halakhah begun to focus their attention upon individual legal themes.[5] But while the focus has changed, the methodology has not varied from that of earlier halakhists.

II

A major turning point in the study of the history and interpretation of halakhah came in the 1960s, when a group of scholars researching the documents and period of early rabbinism rejected the prevailing assumptions of their predecessors concerning the veracity of rabbinic sources. These scholars went exploring early rabbinic texts, particularly the *Mishnah*, *Tosephta*, and *Midrash*,[6] seeking evidence for the structure and origin of the rabbinic society in late antiquity. It was a search for testimony of the nature and character of these sources.[7]

To accomplish their goal these researchers of early rabbinism adopted a method which might be termed literary structuralism[8] and in doing so they have successfully demonstrated that social and cultural perceptions are communicated through the texts of early rabbinism. Their studies examine the contents, forms, and formulary patterns of these documents. They also dissect their successive redactional forms and examine the meagre social-historical data of the era of late antiquity. In the process these studies demonstrate both what can and cannot be inferred from rabbinic literature of the period. If *Mishnah* can be considered representative of second century Jewish realia, then these students of late-antiquity Judaism are therefore able to search, with their self-developed tools, for implicit intentions which might be communicated by the form of these early rabbinic documents.

It has been convincingly argued that these religious texts reveal socio-cultural evidence, from which these scholars have constructed a model of the rabbinic social system. In their view, these texts contain, in particular, evidence of the cosmologies of their redactors or authors and their close associates. In each document there is evidence of the ideology of the editor.[9] Moreover, these early rabbinic writings can be analyzed in terms of the aims and images that its editors might wish to convey. This shift to systematic study of individual documents does not invite the homogenizing of rabbinic thought, as has been the case with the *Wissenschaft* scholarship, but rather, a comparative history of rabbinic world views.

As mentioned above, the approach employed by this school involves a search for implicit meanings in the texts. To reveal these implicit meanings, the researchers examine the documents' contents, literary structure, traits or patterns, and forms.

By structure I mean in part a closed system, the law-like rules which limit the range of a system's permissible content. A structure imposes meaning upon its own content, and these theorists therefore hold that the structure of a text, apart from its content, speaks primarily for its framer. It is the law-like rules of the documents that convey their socio-cultural meaning.[10]

The form and rhetoric of a text like *Mishnah* appear to be central components of the message being transmitted. The marks which the framers of the document leave on the text will help to identify the locus of inquiry into the intention communicated by the documents themselves.

Thus it is argued that we must first begin a systematic inquiry into rabbinic literature with an analysis which takes the documents with their own divisions as a point of departure. In other words, the scholar, at least initially, restricts his exploration to the confinements of a particular document, such as *Mishnah*. Thus, within the specific text, through structure and form the implicit meaning is revealed, apart from the explicit content of the text as a whole or any other passage.

While examining the individual pericope of the text, the researcher must not ignore "the law-like relationships that can be discovered between the elements of a whole" (Polzin 1972:2). The text must be studied as one whole work, a self-regulated whole document. The content and development of the text represents the mind of its author. One can then decode the language and formulation of the pericope to reveal the writer's implicit message, for the text is at least a self-contained whole, and any study must respect the integrity of its final redaction.

However, one must be wary of employing the above methodology.[11] In *Mishnah*, for example, the framers were concerned with a non-existent world. The document certainly presents opinions about "proper" social behaviour; however, it frankly obscures the social relevance of its content. Therefore, we have no empirical evidence whether people actually behaved in accordance with Mishnaic law. Moreover, our understanding of the *Mishnah's* social reality is further frustrated by its uniqueness. It is similar to no other known contemporaneous text or earlier Jewish document. It stands alone, and therefore must be treated as an intellectual contract, a work of rabbinic imagination and not a work of collective behaviour or the product of situational legislation.

To offer as evidence to *Mishnah* additional rabbinic texts such as *Tosephta* or *Midrash*, which were redacted subsequent to *Mishnah*, is to use a commentator's view to explain the worldview of its author. In addition, these students of late antiquities have their own individual social context to be considered. In the mind of these scholars, if a document is to be interpreted properly, it must be construed within its historical context.

Furthermore, in attempting to explain a document such as *Mishnah*, it has been argued that we must subdue our own biases. We must take care to avoid interpolating our own social values into some other society, where the perspectives within this social matrix might be different than our own. And our caution must be even greater with respect to *Mishnah's* society, for we lack information concerning its community, its social forces, and its institutions.

The approach of the students of this school of scholarship to *Mishnah* is limited. They must rely upon theory and assumptions, often based upon their personal ideological biases, as well as sociological and anthropological conceptions of aspects of contemporary societies.

III

With this cautionary advice in mind, let us proceed to consider modern halakhic texts. Since we are discussing "modern" documents, we are in a position to be better acquainted with the social, political, and religious world of their authors. Thus, the knowledge of the world of the writers of modern halakhic texts is akin to that suggested by the researchers of early rabbinic texts, thereby allowing the scholar a greater understanding of the ideology of the documents' authors. Although this methodology, a literary structuralist approach, has been developed and applied to rabbinic texts of late antiquity, its application to modern halakhah as a whole is sparse, and my extension of this methodology to *Shulkhan Arukh* commentaries is yet to be published.[12]

As example, I have chosen from a larger study to apply this methodology to a book of law, *Mishnah Berurah*, redacted by Rabbi Israel Meir Hacohen Kagan (1838-1933),[13] which almost from the time of its redaction at the turn of the century, became a primary and dominant influence in the lives of the halakhah-observant Jew. This work is a commentary on the basic, fundamental code of Jewish law of the Jewish people, the *Shulkhan Arukh*. It deals with all aspects and situations that govern the life of the observant Jew. The topics cover areas from how to tie one's shoelaces, to sexual behaviour between partners. Rabbi Kagan focussed upon one section of the *Shulkhan Arukh*, titled *Orakh Chaim*. This section deals with day-to-day religious behaviour, beginning with awakening in the morning, prayer, holidays, Sabbath, and fasts.

Rabbi Kagan lived in an era when the Jewish community of Eastern Europe spawned a diversity of religious and secular expressions.[14] The haskalah (Jewish enlightenment) and secular Zionism, among others, induced many observant Jews to shed their halakhically observant behaviour for a more secular way of life. One of the responses of the orthodox community (of which Rabbi Kagan was considered a leading spokesman) to this phenomenon was to attempt to regulate and strengthen its cosmological and social boundaries with respect to both its intra- and extra-communal map. "Communal map" refers to an implicit model of level of group membership. Examples include marriageability, commensality (who can eat in one's house), community worship, and eligibility for positions of prestige and status. Strengthening communal boundaries required an emphasis upon stringent religious, moral, and halakhic behaviour. On the other hand, rabbinical circles feared that if stringency in the law were overemphasized, it might cause Jews to reject the halakhic life-style. This fear was especially rife in an era that offered the Jew alternate religious ideologies. These ideologies did not require its members to remain within the boundaries of halakhah.[15]

Rabbi Kagan's personality, rabbinical role, and communal activities suggest his concern for the religious well-being of the halakhic community.[16] In his introduction to volume one of the *Mishnah Berurah*, in fact, he emphasizes the importance of halakhic observance as a means of guarding the "boundaries" of rabbinic Judaism. An analysis of his *Mishnah Berurah* can reveal fully Rabbi Kagan's ideology concerning the religious tensions of his milieu.

The *Mishnah Berurah* is organized into subparagraphs. Close examination of these subparagraphs reveals that they were compiled mostly through the interpolation of phrases, statements, and paragraphs from various "latter rabbinical" *Shulkhan Arukh* commentaries.[17] This literary form is an accepted and preferred genre for *Shulkhan Arukh* commentaries.[18] Thus, through his employment of this genre, Rabbi Kagan declares his identification with the society represented by the genre, the halakhic-observant community.

While the *Mishnah Berurah* follows the accepted pattern, the adjudicative decision to be lenient or stringent (while not deviating from all "latter rabbinical authorities") was that of Rabbi Kagan. From the topics this commentary discusses, it is unclear in most cases whether they were areas of actual concern for Rabbi Kagan and his contemporaries. Even when he uses expressions as "in our times," in most cases he is quoting a commentary from the previous century. Our knowledge of nineteenth-century Eastern European society may tell us that the concern existed, but the data does not inform us to what extent it was of concern for the halakhic community and Rabbi Kagan. We do, however, observe the pattern that, with topics of concern to his contemporaries, Rabbi Kagan is particularly stringent, while he tends to be more lenient in normative issues.[19]

The biographers of Rabbi Kagan, when discussing the *Mishnah Berurah*, assert that the adjudications offered in this legal work are lenient. Statements employed in the *Mishnah Berurah* in instances of stringent rulings, such as "it is difficult to be accommodative" (Section 247 *Shaar Hatzion* 17), would suggest that the biographers' postulation is substantiated. My investigation of the *Mishnah Berurah* agrees with this reading in cases which are not of special concern for Rabbi Kagan. In those subparagraphs dealing with normative halakhic topics, the author brings together the views of the earlier rabbinical authorities and emphasizes the accommodative rulings. This pattern of adjudication appears normative for the *Mishnah Berurah*.

But a closer examination of the text reveals that in areas of concern for Rabbi Kagan, a divergent rhetorical pattern, one of stringency, is employed. These issues of concern appear in cases that can be identified as modern for the period of the *Mishnah Berurah*. (The identification of modern issues for this period is provided by oral history[20] and/or from the handful of ethnographic studies available.[21]) In these cases, the accommodative ruling is not completely excluded, but it is either subordinated to the stringent decisions or appears as a gloss to the stringent ruling. In those subparagraphs which discuss modern issues and in which Rabbi Kagan adopts a stringent ruling, he employs formularies (which are not direct quotations from other rabbinical authorities) such as "it is the law" (*hu hadin*), "it should be borne in mind" (*da*), and "nevertheless" (*mikol makom*), thereby identifying his social and religious concerns. Often these formularies are also followed by statements which are, again, not quotations from past sources, but rather Rabbi Kagan's own words. An additional rhetorical pattern which suggests Rabbi Kagan's concern is the use of non-Hebrew terminology (i.e., *post meister* for postmaster (Section 247 subparagraph 1) or tea[22] and coffee (Section 318 subparagraph 39), and quoting such formulae as "in our times" (*bezemanenu*) (Section 244 subparagraph 13). This literary pattern is specific to what I identify as areas of concern for Rabbi Kagan.[23]

An additional pattern that manifests Rabbi Kagan's concern are the super-legal (*musar*) materials found in the *Mishnah Berurah*.[24] Through the employment of authoritative sources such as the Bible, as well as expressions that involve the name of God (or the fear of God) interpolated in issues that can be identified as part of the society's realia, Rabbi Kagan emphasizes his concern. Halakhic treatises such as the *Mishnah Berurah* as a rule exclude the use of God's name as well as other ethically persuasive arguments. The sporadic introduction of the super-legal material by Rabbi Kagan in the *Mishnah Berurah*, which can be identified both by content and formularies, reveals to the reader instances where the author felt alarmed. For example, at the close of Section 247, when discussing the laws concerning partnership with a non-Jew on the Sabbath, Rabbi Kagan states:

> He who trusts in God and fulfils the wishes of the Torah rulings "that your ox and ass will rest on Sabbath etc." as the Torah intended, and does not attempt manipulations in regard to Sabbath, shall be contented. Because of this, the Holy One Blessed Be He, will certainly grant him success in his possessions during the six days of work.

This pattern, a realistic issue with super-legal statements, is consistent throughout the *Mishnah Berurah*, thus identifying an area of distress for Rabbi Kagan.

For Rabbi Kagan, as the author of the *Mishnah Berurah*, his own society was threatened with the contaminating influence of secular Jewish movements. He therefore required stringent halakhic behaviour from his followers. He made this strict conduct compulsory by issuing stringent rulings, especially in cases where he felt directly concerned for the state of his own social milieu. At the same time, he appears to portray himself as lenient adjudicator, a position claimed by his biographers. For them, his stringent halakhic rulings are not explicitly identified in situations which troubled Rabbi Kagan. His rigid decisions provided the structure by which he, through the *Mishnah Berurah*, sought to regulate and strengthen the religious and social boundaries of his community.

I have argued that in the case of Rabbi Kagan's *Mishnah Berurah* it is the structure and form of this modern halakhic document which contains meaning beyond that gained from the analysis of any single pericope within it. For the halakhic library in general, the content of a book of Jewish law is not the only agenda of its framer. Thus, the structure and form of the text bears the imprint of the intentions and subconscious aims of its writer.

IV

I have suggested a different approach to the study of modern Jewish law. It might even be termed interdisciplinary. This approach, both in the study of antiquities and of modern Judaism, has been ignored and often rejected by many Jewish scholars. While these Jewish scholars have physically relocated from the seminary to the university, methodologically they are immobile. One may also ask the question, Who benefits by remaining traditional? The answer may be suggested: the contemporary Jewish community, with which modern Jewish scholarship has been intimately linked, for as part of this community and often financially backed by it, these scholars are expected to portray the consensus of what it means to be Jewish. The scholarly picture thus portrays a parallel consensus for all past states of affairs, in which Judaism judaized the best of the surrounding culture, *without assimilating* to it. An evolving normative tradition remained the inviolate, canonical core, which could take on the garb of every successive age — for most contemporary Jews an easy self-serving image of the past. Such is the portrayal of Judaism conveyed by modern Jewish scholars.

Thus, not only the content of scholarship, but its form as well, connotes the mapping of Jewish identity. Are not Jewish scholars refurbished rabbis? The object of scholarship remains the same, the canonical core of texts, each viewed as normative for its age. We therefore are confronted by a circular effect between the community's search for identity and the scholarly world. Each is dependent upon the other while not crossing the traditional boundaries erected.

But there is light at the end of the tunnel! In the university milieu during the past ten years, a number of interesting phenomena have been occurring. First, the close relationship with the non-Jewish scholarly world is having a direct impact upon these Jewish scholars. Methodologies and theories well known and accepted in the study of non-Jewish religions are being convincingly argued and received by Jewish scholars. The strong dawning of new approaches to the study of Judaism has been introduced. Second, one finds an increasing number of non-Jewish students in Ph. D. programs of Judaism. This new group of students are not under the social and religious pressures of the Jewish community. To emphasize my point I turn to the difference in scholarship between Israel and North America. What I have termed the interdisciplinary study of Judaism will not be considered in Israel, while in Canada, for example, I find a ready stage. Moreover, the precise detachment of the orthodox community outside Israel from the rest of the Jewish community has reduced the pressure from scholars. To the ever-growing ultra-orthodox community, the university, and especially the study of the social sciences and religion, is not kosher! Alternately, the non-orthodox Jewish American community seeks a new type of Jewish identification that the interdisciplinary approach might serve.

Abraham Lincoln addressed Congress on the eve of the Civil War with the words, "We cannot escape history." Let scholars be aware that "we cannot escape sociology" — but we must endeavour always to stretch its bounds.

Notes

1 Parts of the opening and concluding sections of this essay have been adapted from a paper delivered by Professor Jack Lightstone at the conference for the Social Scientific Study of Judaism at Concordia University, Montreal Canada, 1989. Professor Lightstone has granted me permission to include his material. I would also like to thank Professor Lightstone for his input in the development of this essay.
2 For an example of such a study see Agus 1970.
3 For an example see Beneth 1922 and Zimmels 1932, who show that the tone of such documents reflects the authors' attitudes toward their own particular interpretations, but they do not consider the social or religious context in which the works were written.
4 Katz 1960.
5 See, for example, Feldman 1968 and Lightstone 1981:99 who review Feldman's work.
6 These early rabbinic documents were redacted during the second to fourth centuries CE. The first was *Mishnah*, a study of Jewish law and redacted in the second century. For a discussion of these texts see Neusner 1981b.
7 The leadership of this form critical movement can be attributed to Jacob Neusner. He summarizes his method in Neusner 1981:79. Also see Green 1983, 1982.
8 This structuralism is not that of Lévi-Strauss. As used in my study it is defined by Robert Polzin (1977), Bernard Jackson (1980) and Jack Lightstone (1979, 1981, 1981b).
9 For example, see Bokser's 1984, study of the Passover seder, Wegner's 1988 study of women in *Mishnah*, and Lightstone 1981 and 1983.
10 For further discussion of form and structure as a means of communication see Lightstone 1979:154; 1983:32.
11 See Green 1983:195-202, who in a detailed discussion of early rabbinic literature cautions the researcher of the shortcomings of this methodology.

12 Fishbane; in my Ph. D dissertation (1988) I provide an in-depth study of the *Mishnah Berurah*. The revised manuscript of my work has been accepted for publication by KTAV Publishing House, New York.
13 For a biographical (or rather hagiographical) report on Rabbi Kagan see Kagan 1983 and Yosheri 1952.
14 For a discussion of these movements, see, for example, Mauler 1971.
15 For a discussion of Eastern European society see Goldscheider and Zuckerman 1984, Luz 1985, and Zaborowski and Herzog 1952.
16 For example, see Douglas 1982 for the influences of biases upon scholarship. Although the problem of bias is common to all disciplines, it has been traditionally ignored in the study of Rabbinic Judaism.
17 Latter rabbinical authorities referred to in Hebrew as *aharonim* are all rabbinical authorities who lived after Rabbi Joseph Karo.
18 For an in-depth discussion of the genre, see Fishbane 1988:29-42.
19 By normative I refer to Rabbi Kagan's analysis of the *Shulkhan Arukh's* statements that are not necessarily directly applicable to nineteenth-century realia.
20 For example, see the ethnographic reports prepared by Margaret Mead which are based upon interviews with immigrants from Eastern Europe to the United States. These documents are housed in the Library of Congress, Washington, DC.
21 For example see Zaborowski 1952 and Luz 1985.
22 The Hebrew term used for tea by commentators quoted by Rabbi Kagan is *"aley yerakot"* (leaves of vegetation).
23 I have shown these literary patterns in depth in my study of the *Mishnah Berurah* in Fishbane 1988.
24 For a detailed analysis of the super-legal materials in the *Mishnah Berurah*, see Fishbane 1990.

References

Agus, Irving. 1970. *Rabbi Meir of Rothenburg: His Life and Works as for the Religious, Legal and Social History of the Jews of Germany in the Thirteenth Century.* Vol. 2. New York: KTAV.

Baneth, Eduard. 1922. "Soziale Motive in der rabbinischen Rechtsplege." In *Festschrift zum 50 jährigen Bestrehen der Hochshule für die Wissenschaft des Judentums.* Berlin: Philo.

Bokser, Baruch. 1984. *The Origins of the Seder.* Berkeley and Los Angeles: University of California Press.

Douglas, Mary. 1982. "The Effects of Modernization on Religious Change." *Ddalus* 111, 1.

Ellinson, David. 1985. "Jewish Legal Interpretation: Literary, Scriptural, Social, and Ethical Perspectives." *Semeia* 34.

Epstein, Isidore. 1925. *The Responsa of Rabbi Solomon ben Adreth of Barcelona.* Routledge.

Feldman, David. 1968. *Birth Control in Jewish Law.* New York: New York University.

Fishbane, Simcha. 1988. "An Analysis of the Literary and Substantive Traits of Israel Mayer Hacohen's Mishnah Berurah," unpublished doctoral dissertation, Concordia University.

―――. 1990. "The Supra-Legal Materials in Israel Mayer Hacohen's Mishnah Berurah." In *Social Scientific Study of Judaism.* Montreal: Concordia University.

Goldscheider, Calvin and Alan Zuckerman. 1984. *The Transformation of the Jews.* Chicago and London: The University of Chicago Press.

Green, William Scott. 1983. "Reading the Writing of Rabbinism: Towards an Interpretation of Rabbinic Literature." *Journal of the Academy of Religion* 51, 2 (June).

Hass, Peter. 1985. "The Modern Study of Responsa." In *Approaches to Judaism in Medieval Times*, Vol. 2, edited by D. Blumenthal. Chico, CA: Scholars Press.

Jackson, Bernard. 1980. "History Dogmatics and Halakhah." In *Jewish Law in Legal History and the Modern World*, edited by Bernard Jackson. Leiden: E. J. Brill.

Kagan, Aryeh Leib. 1983. *Michtive Hachafetz Chaim.* New York: Saphrograph.

Katz, Jacob. 1960. "Al Halakhah v-Derush Kimqor Histori." *Tarbiz* 30, 1 (October).

―――――. 1960b. *Exclusiveness and Tolerance.* London: Oxford.

Lightstone, Jack. 1979. *Yose the Galilean.* Leiden: E. J. Brill.

―――――. 1981. "Problems and New Perspectives in the Study of Early Rabbinic Ethics," *Journal of Religious Ethics.*

―――――. 1983. "Form as Meaning in Halakic Midrash," *Semeia.*

Luz, Ehud. 1985. *Parallels Meet: Religion and Nationalism in Early Zionistic Movement (1882-1904).* Tel Aviv: Oved Publishers.

Mahler, Raphael. 1971. *A History of Modern Jewry.* London: Vallentine, Mitchell.

Mann, Jacob. 1973. *The Responsa of Babylonian Geonim as a Source of Jewish History.* New York: Arno Press.

Neusner, Jacob. 1974. *Understanding Rabbinic Judaism from Talmud to Modern Times.* New York: KTAV.

―――――. 1981. *Method and Meaning in Ancient Judaism*, 3d. series. Chico, CA: Scholars Press.

―――――. 1981b. *Judaism: The Evidence of the Mishnah.* Chicago and London: The University of Chicago Press.

Polzin, Robert. 1977. *Biblical Structuralism: Method and Subjectivity in the Study of Ancient Texts.* Philadelphia: Fortress Press.

Wegner, Judith. 1988. *Chattel or Person.* Oxford and New York: Oxford University Press.

Yosher, Moses. 1952. *The Chafetz Chaim: The Life and Works of Rabbi Israel Meir Kagan of Radin.* New York: Mesoral Publications.

Zaborowski, Mark and Elizabeth Herzog. 1952. *Life is With People: The Culture of the Shtetl.* New York: Schocken Books.

Zimmels, H. J. 1932. *Die Marranen in der Rabbinischen Literatur.* Berlin.

Zunz, Leopold. 1892. *Die gottesdienstliche Vortraege der Juden.* Frankfurt a.M.

CHAPTER 14

Religion, religieux, croyance, imaginaire

Roger Lapointe

L'histoire des religions, comme d'ailleurs toutes les sciences du religieux, développe une terminologie technique hybride et bâtarde dans la mesure où celle-ci englobe, côte à côte avec des termes hétéro-interprétatifs, tels que «société», «histoire», «système», «individu», etc., des termes auto-interprétatifs, issus de la pratique religieuse elle-même, par exemple «église», «charisme», «totem», etc. Les textes scientifiques sur la religion sont effectivement tissés à l'aide de cette double trame.

Sur ce point, les sciences du religieux ne se démarquent pas des sciences humaines en général, lesquelles puisent également dans le langage de tous les jours une bonne partie de leurs expressions linguistiques. Même lorsqu'elles aspirent à un plus grand formalisme, elles se gardent de doubler le langage vulgaire par un jargon ou une algèbre de peur de perdre en lisibilité ce qui serait éventuellement gagné en précision.[1] Les sciences naturelles vont plus loin dans cette direction, mais elles aussi font place aux mots du langage vulgaire soit pour expliquer leurs algorithmes soit pour les rattacher à l'expérience immédiate et au sens commun.[2]

La pression vers la mathématisation et le formalisme, de même que corrélativement l'éloignement du langage vulgaire montrent que ce dernier fait problème lorsque la pensée devient scientifique. Mal dégrossis, les mots ordinaires ne se prêtent qu'imparfaitement à véhiculer une conception rigoureusement objective des choses. Le paléontologue ne fait pas du tout le pédant quand il remplace l'expression «homme» par celles d'«*homo sapiens*», d'«*homo sapiens sapiens*», «*homo neanderthalensis*» et autres semblables. Il cherche simplement à dire exactement ce qu'il veut dire. Ce problème se pose évidemment au scientifique de la religion. Il se pose même à lui avec une acuité spéciale, car, en tant que scientifique et donc

---

Les notes et références concernant ce chapitre se trouvent aux pages 167-68.

incroyant, il doit aller chercher l'objet de sa discipline en dehors de soi-même, chez les praticiens de la religion, dans leur langage à eux.

Le problème, certes, n'est pas insoluble. Le même mot peut recevoir une acception scientifique en sus de son acception vulgaire initiale. Songeons à des termes comme «lune» ou «étoiles», ou encore, pour les sciences humaines, à «rêve» ou à «société». En sciences de la religion, les mots empruntés par les scientifiques au vocabulaire des croyants ont tous été redéfinis plus ou moins radicalement, par exemple «mana» chez M. Mauss ou «charisme» chez M. Weber. Une certaine ambiguïté n'en persiste pas moins et, dans le cas du religieux, cette ambiguïté recouvre même une véritable sporie, car, me semble-t-il, il faut choisir entre comprendre le même mot de l'intérieur ou de l'extérieur, sur le mode émique ou sur le mode étique, par auto ou par hétéro-interprétation, en croyant ou en incroyant. Lorsque l'indigène fait part à l'ethnologue de sa foi au mana, celui-ci y croira ou n'y croira pas.

La foi selon W. C. Smith

Le terme «religion» est clairement émique, auto-interprétatif, croyant. M. Despland (1979) le montre à profusion dans son étude sur *La Religion en Occident*. Parmi les quarante définitions que son enquête a fait émerger une à une, la plupart — non pas toutes — reflètent un point de vue croyant. Le terme est latin originairement et, même si l'étymologie en est incertaine, l'usage en est fortement attesté chez Lucrèce et Cicéron. Lucrèce déjà avait acclimaté le mot dans une perspective externe et incroyante.

W. C. Smith ne conteste pas cela, tout au contraire.[3] Il entérine dûment les principaux faits qui attestent l'emploi du mot «religion» par tous les parlant latin, aussi bien païens que chrétiens. Il pense toutefois que la signification la plus fondamentale, la plus juste et la plus importante du mot «religion» serait de nature adjectivale et non substantive, c'est-à-dire renverrait à une manière de vivre et non à la vie elle-même, plus précisément encore à un état de la subjectivité plutôt qu'à l'incarnation de cette même subjectivité dans la réalité matérielle du monde. Il croit ensuite observer au fil de l'histoire occidentale une progressive dégradation de la religiosité au profit de ce qu'il appelle une réification. La réification serait chose faite à l'époque moderne, mille ans après Lactance, mille cinq cents ans après Lucrèce qui, de longue date, l'avaient amorcée. Désormais, l'expression «religion» évoquerait des phénomènes intellectuels, sociaux, historiques et non plus, sauf de façon indirecte, l'attitude intérieure par laquelle l'être humain se réfère à Quelque chose ou à Quelqu'un de transcendant. Du même coup, elle revêtirait une signification abstraite et générale au lieu de référer à l'expérience concrète de la foi. Aujourd'hui donc, le mot «religion» fonctionnerait à la manière d'une catégorie logique à l'intérieur de laquelle se trouveraient des cas d'espèce tels que le Christianisme, l'Hindouisme, l'Islamisme, ainsi qu'une multitude d'autres désignations en «ismes».

Tout au long de son enquête factuelle et historique — trop brève pour être satisfaisante, en particulier en ce qui concerne le moyen-âge[4] — W. C. Smith ne démontre aucun intérêt spécial à l'égard de la tension qui oppose les intervenants qui disent «religion» de l'intérieur et ceux qui en parlent d'un point de vue externe. Il cite en vrac les uns et les autres. Il ne blâme pas spécialement l'incroyance ou la science moderne pour le glissement réificateur dont le terme «religion» aurait été victime.

Je crois que le profond penseur regarde ici de haut une distinction qu'il juge simpliste et infructueuse.[5] Distinguer les perspectives croyante et incroyante lui paraît relever d'une religion elle-même réifiée et inauthentique; demander à la religion véritable d'être vraie ou fausse trahirait une totale incompréhension de ce qu'est cette dernière. Au sens adjectival en effet, la religion serait une expérience subjective *sui generis* devant être reçue à l'instar de toute autre expérience et qu'il n'y a pas lieu de juger à partir d'un quelconque critère de vérité autre qu'elle-même.

Comme on le sait, W. C. Smith suggère d'appeler «foi» (*faith*) une telle expérience, pour éviter justement de la traiter comme une réalité objective, ce qui est en pratique inévitable lorsqu'on se sert du mot «religion». Les aspects du religieux que ne désigne pas le mot «foi» et que Smith évidemment n'entend pas omettre sans plus, on les exprimerait par des formules comme «*cumulative traditions*», traditions, incarnations sociales, etc.

Il me semble évident que, loin de dominer la distinction entre croyance et incroyance, Smith en fait se situe carrément du côté de la foi. Il ne se contente pas en effet d'identifier dans l'ensemble du phénonène religieux une composante adjectivale qu'on conviendrait d'appeler «foi», il définit la foi en question, il l'adopte et il la préconise. Sur quoi porte l'expérience de la foi? Sur quelque chose ou quelqu'un d'ultime.[6] Semblable expérience de réalités ultimes, Smith (1978:8) la fait sienne au point de se donner à tâche de la concilier avec la science moderne.[7] Entre une telle définition de la foi et un tel engagement à son service il y a, du reste, une liaison essentielle et non pas seulement libre ou contingente. Il va de soi, en effet, pour W. C. Smith (1978:6) que quiconque n'a pas l'expérience d'au moins une religion — je traduis: n'a pas la foi — n'est pas non plus adéquatement équipé pour entreprendre l'étude des phénomènes religieux.[8]

Smith n'exige pas du scientifique qu'il adopte une foi quelconque en un sens confessionnel. Cela équivaudrait à confondre de nouveau la foi elle-même avec ses prolongements historiques et institutionnels. L'expérience religieuse comme telle se ramène pour lui à une disposition universelle, une et la même au coeur de toutes les religions historiques, autrement dit à une sorte d'essence ou de corrélat phénoménologique. À ce titre et à ce niveau, la foi domine l'opposition entre la religion et l'irréligion qui sont des phénomènes concrets et historiques, mais elle ne le fait qu'à la faveur d'une extrême abstraction et, qui plus est, d'une abstraction métaphysique.

On aurait beau jeu ici de retourner contre Smith l'objection d'abstraction et de généralité qu'il soulève contre l'usage du terme «religion», car sa définition de la foi affiche le même statut noétique abstrait et universel. Mais l'argument *ad hominem*, comme il arrive souvent, ne va pas assez loin. Il faut voir surtout que la foi selon Smith se conforme à un autre type d'abstraction que la religion selon les scientifiques. Alors que celle-ci se contente de formaliser des objets empiriques en les réunissant dans une classe logique, celle-là érige la foi en substance intemporelle après l'avoir extraite des contingences historiques. La foi, certes, se mêle aux événements et aux institutions, mais, en elle-même, elle existe à un autre plan, dans l'âme des êtres humains, très précisément dans l'âme humaine considérée en tant qu'elle débouche sur la divinité. Ainsi conçue, la foi est indissociablement une abstraction et une concrétude, une chose abstraite de la matière mais une réalité spirituelle éminemment concrète. Elle échappe, d'une part, à la contingence et à l'histoire, protégée dès lors de toute critique empirique, mais par ailleurs elle dévoile l'horizon d'une vérité supra-empirique qu'elle ne possède pas pleinement tout en existant sous sa dépendance. Voici une phrase où Smith exprime cela sans ambages : «Theology is part of the traditions, is part of this world. Faith lies beyond theology, in the hearts of men. Truth lies beyond faith, in the heart of God» (Smith 1978 :185).

La foi selon le scientifique

Élaborée à l'aide d'un tel concept de la foi, l'histoire comparée des religions que mènerait W. C. Smith serait, il va de soi, une opération théologique. Je ne lui apprends rien sans doute là-dessus. Je ne lui en fais pas reproche non plus. Il ne s'agit pas d'étiqueter ou de stigmatiser.

J'estime seulement que Smith le théologien se trompe sur sa propre foi et également sur la foi des autres croyants. Il se trompe sur le point très aigu et très pertinent en histoire des religions de prendre en compte ce qui arrive à la foi lorsqu'elle se *compare* à une autre. L'histoire des religions s'est nommée lucidement et significativement l'histoire *comparée* des religions, attirant l'attention sur ce que les premiers praticiens considéraient justement comme décisif, c'est-à-dire le fait pour les chrétiens de se confondre avec les non-chrétiens au sein d'une classe unique et englobante. Une telle opération impliquait une relativisation du Christianisme et la chose a été dûment remarquée.

On a moins remarqué que les religions s'étaient comparées entre elles, bien avant que ne naisse l'histoire comparée des religions. On ne l'ignorait pas malgré tout et, l'eût-on ignoré, le magistral ouvrage de H. Pinard de la Boullaye (1922) l'aurait rappelé à tout le monde.

L'aspect des choses qui, à mon sens, n'a pas reçu la considération qu'il méritait, aspect qui touche à l'existence réelle de la foi, qui appartient à la foi elle-même dans la mesure où celle-ci est consciente de soi-même, cet aspect tient justement à la comparaison que le croyant institue avec une autre foi que la sienne à partir du moment où il entre en rapport avec cette dernière. Et cela arrive inévitablement un jour ou l'autre. Un jour vient donc où, dans la paix ou dans la guerre, un groupe de croyants en rencontre un autre. Hérodote voyage et observe que les Égyptiens vénèrent d'autres divinités que les Grecs. Les Montagnais voient débarquer sur les rives du Saint-Laurent des missionnaires jésuites qui leur enseignent un Dieu et un Ciel fort différents de ce qu'ils concevaient traditionnellement de la divinité et de l'au-delà. Avant une telle rencontre, chacune des religions concernées pouvait tranquillement abonder dans son propre sens, c'est-à-dire bloquer sa croyance propre avec la vérité pure et simple. Il ne pourrait plus en être ainsi une fois le contact établi, une fois que, par la force des choses, la comparaison aurait été instituée.

Pour comparer en effet, il faut tout d'abord réunir dans une même classe les objets de la comparaison. Si j'entends comparer des chiens et des chats, il est nécessaire que j'inclue tout d'abord les uns et les autres dans la catégorie englobante de l'animal, à moins que ce soit celle de quadrupède, de vivant ou de chose. Or, *toute catégorisation est en même temps une relativisation*. Aucun membre de la classe n'est *sui generis*, au moins sur le point qu'il a en commun avec les autres et grâce auquel il est regroupé avec eux.

Ainsi, les Grecs cultivés qui comparaient leurs propres dieux à des dieux étrangers relativisaient par le fait même leur croyance. Ils avaient des dieux, mais d'autres peuples aussi en avaient, assimilables aux leurs (Rudhard 1987:21-22). Semblablement, les Montagnais ou les Hurons rétorquaient aux missionnaires, lorsque la dialectique insistante de ceux-ci les poussaient au pied du mur, que sans doute le Ciel dont ils parlaient était bon pour les chrétiens, mais que, pour eux, la survie après la mort consisterait en ce que leurs âmes rejoindraient les âmes des ancêtres.[9]

Qui dit pourtant relativisation dit équivalemment *atténuation de la foi*. Dès que le croyant compare sa croyance à une autre et que, indissociablement, il met une foi distincte de la sienne sur le même plan que la sienne, il admet implicitement qu'il ne possède pas la pleine et entière vérité, que sa version des choses n'est pas sans plus la réalité des choses. Même si, l'instant d'après, il poursuit la comparaison en soutenant que seuls ses dieux sont réels, que son idée de l'au-delà correspond seule à ce qu'est réellement l'après-vie, bref que sa religion est la seule vraie, il n'aura maintenu la certitude de sa foi qu'à condition d'avoir triomphé du doute et donc de l'avoir expérimenté; il aura de la sorte associé à la foi ce qui la contredit, c'est-à-dire le manque de foi, l'incroyance.

La dose minimale d'incroyance, qui est inhérente à l'acte comparatif lui-même, ne représente que le premier degré d'une échelle dont le degré terminal se trouve dans l'incroyance. Lucrèce déjà en son temps en était proche. Les sciences humaines d'aujourd'hui sont animées par une incroyance principielle, aussi longtemps du moins qu'elles demeurent elles-mêmes et ne se mâtinent pas de philosophie ou de théologie. Elles sont dans la même mesure inconciliables avec la foi. L'incroyance totale qu'elles recèlent subvertit radicalement la crédibilité même de la foi.

Entre le degré minimal et le degré maximal il y a place pour une infinité de positions intermédiaires qui sont toutes autant de combinaisons entre la croyance et l'incroyance. La foi selon W. C. Smith, pour ne retenir que ce cas, résulte d'un comparatisme tous azimuts entre les religions du monde et de l'histoire. Elle représente une adhésion religieuse ferme à une réalité transcendante. Toutefois, cette adhésion ferme s'accompagne d'une non-foi non moins ferme à l'égard de ce que Smith appelle les traditions et qui pourtant constitue l'objet de leur foi pour l'immense majorité des croyants. Ainsi fonctionne la comparaison pour ce théologien contemporain. Elle ne le conduit pas à défendre le Christianisme contre les religions non-chrétiennes, ainsi que l'avait fait Lactance. Le pluralisme et l'oecuménisme qui sont de mise aujourd'hui interdisent un tel chauvinisme. Le comparatisme de Smith le conduit à identifier une conviction commune à toutes les religions, conviction présente en elles, même lorsqu'elles n'en ont pas pleinement conscience, conviction qui en outre par bonheur coïncide avec celle que le théologien entretient personnellement.

Soit, W. C. Smith fait de la théologie. Je n'aurais guère fait progresser nos débats, si je m'étais proposé de souligner pesamment ce qui doit être clair pour tout le monde. Je voulais démontrer que la *foi selon W. C. Smith est en même temps une non-foi* même lorsqu'elle est dissociée des traditions dans lesquelles elle s'incarne historiquement. Le théoricien peut sans doute séparer abstraitement la foi elle-même de ses mises en oeuvre concrètes — quoique ce procédé soit à mon sens discutable — mais il ne peut dissocier la foi ainsi définie de l'opération rationnelle par laquelle il l'a séparée et qui est une opération de comparaison. Or, ainsi que nous venons de le montrer, toute comparaison est une relativisation et toute relativisation de la foi injecte à celle-ci une dose plus ou moins forte de non-foi.

C'est évidemment la dernière chose que Smith me concédera. Il a échafaudé précisément sa théorie en vue de mettre à part un objet de foi qui échapperait à toute relativisation. S'il conseille d'écarter le mot «religion», c'est que celui-ci lui semble renvoyer inévitablement à des croyances toujours impures, toujours entachées d'incroyance.

Dans l'hypothèse cependant où j'aurais raison de soutenir que même la foi selon Smith, tout authentique qu'elle soit, se trouve mêlée à la non-foi, il faudrait convenir que le grand déploiement stratégique auquel il a recours pour expulser du discours scientifique le terme «religion» s'avère être finalement sans objet, car, pas plus que le mot «religion», le mot «foi» ne désigne une croyance parfaitement pure et pleinement étanche. Dans la foi comme dans la religion, il y a la dose minimale d'incroyance qu'apporte avec soi l'opération même de la comparaison.

Il resterait à supposer que la foi peut échapper à la comparaison, dans le sens par exemple où certains textes de la Bible tiennent Yahvé pour incomparable,[10] où dans le sens où Karl Barth a mis la foi chrétienne à part des religions,[11] ou encore dans le sens apparemment visé par W. C. Smith où la foi existe toujours à la faveur d'une expérience singulière. Mais affirmer de Yahvé qu'il est incomparable, c'est encore le comparer à des divinités qui ne font pas le poids; considérer le Christianisme comme une foi et non comme une religion, c'est comparer la foi à la religion; souligner l'existentialité de la foi par l'usage de termes généraux ne peut évidemment se faire qu'à travers la comparaison de plusieurs expériences individuelles.

À l'interne

Donnons-nous donc tranquillement le droit d'employer le mot «religion».

La sagesse d'une telle décision, j'aimerais la manifester tout d'abord en montrant à grands traits comment les religions ont géré l'irréligion qui les habitait. Ce faisant, nous déborderons l'aire occidentale à laquelle se confine l'enquête de M. Despland sur la religion telle que pensée et telle que vécue. Nous incluons, bien sûr, l'Occident, nous travaillons du sein de notre culture où le terme «religion» est apparu et s'est imposé. Par ailleurs, nous ne nous limitons pas à l'Occident, car nous sommes d'avis que le mot «religion» représente encore le meilleur terme pour exprimer verbalement les phénomènes religieux non-occidentaux, précisément dans la mesure où il a un contenu comparatiste, plus précisément encore dans la mesure où, en tant qu'issu d'une comparaison, il dénonce dans toute religion, la présence de la non-religion, dans toute foi la présence de la non-foi. Autrement dit, il insinue à l'intérieur même de la croyance quelque chose déjà de ce qu'on doit penser d'elle du point de vue scientifique, mais qu'elle ne peut reconnaître sans se détruire, à savoir qu'elle relève en fin de compte de l'imaginaire.

Dans la mesure où le comparatisme qu'instituent les religions emporte une inévitable concession à l'incroyance, les religions se trouvent paver la voie à l'étude scientifique des religions du sein même de leur autocompréhension.[12] La dose d'incroyance qu'elles s'injectent, toute petite qu'elle soit, les met en position d'entrevoir la vérité sur elles-mêmes, d'apercevoir obscurément qu'elles procèdent de l'imaginaire et non de la réalité factuelle.

Il me semble que les religions qui ont franchi cette étape de la comparaison et qui en conséquence ont commencé à voir un peu plus clair en elles-mêmes ont fait sa part à l'imaginaire suivant deux modalités contrastantes. Certaines l'ont reconnu en soi, d'autres hors de soi. L'Hindouisme a logé à l'intérieur de soi-même la part d'imaginaire qu'il avait appréhendée. De la sorte, il démontrait une grande lucidité scientifique, mais il s'interdisait d'aller jusqu'au bout de cette logique. Déjà aux temps védiques, la religion de l'Inde a résulté d'une comparaison ou d'un brassage entre différentes traditions. Or, la multiplicité des dieux et des déesses a été vécue, comme on le sait, sur le mode de l'intégration et de l'harmonisation. Ils et elles étaient tous et toutes vrais. Mais différentes formules ne peuvent être vraies simultanément à moins que chacune ne soit jugée quelque peu fausse et inadéquate. Le pluralisme ne va pas sans un certain scepticisme. Il faut donc penser que le polythéisme hindou comporte un certain taux d'incroyance, autrement dit qu'il inclut la conscience plus ou moins claire que l'objet de la croyance n'est pas tout à fait factuel et qu'il est enrobé par une couche plus ou moins épaisse d'imaginaire. Les dieux inférieurs ne sont que des avatars des grands dieux et les grands dieux eux-mêmes n'ont guère de réalité face au Brahman. Les dieux hindous doivent à leur déficit entitatif de se maintenir les uns à côté des autres, tout comme le font les fantasmagories de l'imagination.

Par la place qu'elle fait à l'imaginaire à l'intérieur de son auto-compréhension, la religion hindoue anticipe sur le point de vue rationnel de la science. Cette scientificité naissante demeure pourtant sans lendemain. Joue à ce point la loi qui régit toute croyance: elle ne peut pénétrer sa propre nature imaginative et onirique sans se détruire elle-même. Au nom de cette loi, la scientificité incluse dans l'Hindouisme ne pourrait jamais qu'être partielle. En fait, elle ne dépasserait pas la rationalité métaphysique du Vedanta. Le Bouddhisme, qui allait plus loin, serait considéré comme hétérodoxe.

Le Judaïsme et le Christianisme ont mis hors d'eux-mêmes l'imaginaire qu'ils ont discerné dans le religieux en vertu de ce qu'on appelle leur exclusivisme. Ayant comparé les dieux des autres nations au sien, le peuple juif des temps bibliques a constitué la classe des dieux, classe à laquelle le sien appartenait, et, de la sorte, a relativisé sa croyance. Affublé de ce nom commun – Dieu, El – Yahvé n'a pas le monopole de la vérité. Au lieu toutefois d'intégrer les divers dieux comme l'Hindouisme ou comme le polythéisme en général, le Judaïsme a mis le sien à part de tous les autres et lui a accordé l'exclusivité de la vérité et de la réalité. «Tu n'auras pas d'autres dieux que moi» (Ex 20,3). «Car toi tu es Yahvé Très Haut sur toute la terre, surpassant de beaucoup tous les dieux» (Ps 97,9). Si, parmi tous les dieux, Yahvé était le seul vrai et réel, les autres n'étaient donc qu'erreur et néant. Leur apparente réalité ne pouvait être rien d'autre qu'une illusion et un prestige de l'imagination.

Le Christianisme a pratiqué le même genre de comparatisme. Il s'est proclamé vraie et unique religion face à toutes celles qu'il avait commencé par inclure dans la même classe logique que la sienne. L'Islam n'a pas procédé autrement, quoi qu'en dise W. C. Smith. Selon la foi coranique, Allah est seul vrai et rien ne doit lui être associé. «Allâh! Il n'y a pas de Dieu sinon Lui, Le Vivant L'Existant par lui-même!» (Mahomet, II:256). Il est vrai cependant que Mahomet se sent solidaire d'Abraham, de Moïse et de Jésus. Il ne se dissimule pas qu'Allah, le seul vrai Dieu, est également adoré par les Juifs et les Chrétiens, quoique de façon imparfaite. Il donne par là l'impression d'être plus comparatiste – Smith dit même: singulièrement – que les autres fondateurs de religion. Il l'est certes de façon originale, il l'est même de façon généreuse, mais il ne tranche pas sur les autres par le fait même de l'être. Moïse comparait son Dieu à celui de Pharaon, Jésus se comparait à Moïse et ses disciples le compareraient à Dieu lui-même. Mahomet institue en fait une double comparaison, l'une qui rapproche Judaïsme, Christianisme et Islam dans le sillage de la religion abrahamique,[13] l'autre qui oppose en bloc cette foi monothéiste à la malcroyance polythéiste. L'incroyance se trouve rejetée toute entière hors de la croyance, car, d'une part, le polythéisme ne se combine évidemment pas avec la foi en Allah, mais d'autre part, Yahvé et la Trinité chrétienne non plus, sauf dans la mesure où ils s'identifient avec Allah. Le mot *din* à cet égard n'effectue par lui-même aucune percée spectaculaire dans le champ religieux.[14] Il exprime en arabe une prise de conscience qui affecte immanquablement les religions au moment où elles se comparent à une autre.

En mettant l'imaginaire affectant le religieux hors de soi, c'est-à-dire dans les religions concurrentes, le Judaïsme, le Christianisme et l'Islam faisaient moins scientifique que l'Hindouisme, car ils restaient complètement aveugles à l'imaginaire qui les habitait.[15] Par ailleurs, ils instauraient une situation où l'incroyance pourrait aller jusqu'au bout de son projet puisqu'ils constituaient la notion d'illusoire et d'imaginaire en rapport avec les religions païennes. Un jour viendrait où eux aussi seraient pris à revers par une instance pleinement factuelle et seraient agrégés sans plus à la classe des pseudo-réalités qu'ils avaient eux-mêmes instituée.

Ce jour se lèverait au XVIIIe siècle avec le rejet par les philosophes de la religion révélée. Les philosophes eux-mêmes seraient débordés et le comparatisme strictement scientifique serait à terme mis au point.[16]

Pour le comparatisme strictement scientifique, le religieux ne comporte pas seulement, en soi (Hindouisme) ou hors de soi (Monothéismes), une dose plus ou moins forte d'imaginaire. Il est de part en part non factuel.

Du dehors

Après avoir observé comment les choses se passent à l'interne, sortons du domaine de la foi, situons-nous dans la non-foi et, en somme, accomplissons de la sorte un mouvement que les religions elles-mêmes avaient amorcé.

C'est le mot «religion» qui offre la plus grande commodité pour apporter au dehors ce qui se trouve au départ à l'intérieur. Inventé par l'auto-compréhension croyante, forgé par le travail de la comparaison, il renvoie à une catégorie qui comprend les religions que l'on connaît, la sienne incluse, et, si on néglige la voie suivie par l'Hindouisme et en général le polythéisme, on a grâce à lui la possibilité de nommer de l'extérieur l'objet qui s'était d'abord nommé de l'intérieur. Du point de vue chrétien, les religions non chrétiennes sont tout de même des religions (fausses) et ce même mot (religion) qui les désigne ne peut pas ne pas refluer de quelque manière sur l'idée que le chrétien se fait de sa religion (vraie). L'ambivalence du terme «religion» peut certes engendrer de la confusion, mais cette même ambivalence rend possible la transition de l'auto- à l'hétéro-interprétation avec le maximum de garantie.

Une fois en possession d'un concept qu'aucune religion particulière ne contrôle exclusivement, l'observateur remet nécessairement en question le découpage que les religions opèrent dans l'objet religieux. Alors que les religions sont appelées par les exigences de la vie sociale à définir une orthodoxie, autrement dit un religieux authentique, par rapport auquel diverses croyances ou pratiques religieuses apparaissent comme inauthentiques, le théoricien, dégagé de la pratique, ne manque pas de s'apercevoir que l'inorthodoxe et l'inauthentique ne sont si sévèrement réprimés qu'en raison même de leur ressemblance avec la vraie religion. Là où la direction ecclésiastique déclare : c'est de la magie et non de la religion, le théoricien pourra juger bon de conjoindre sous l'appellation générale de religieux et l'orthodoxe (religion) et l'inorthodoxe (magie). Là où cette même direction ecclésiastique soutient que la philosophie relève de la raison et non de la foi, de nouveau le théoricien pourra être conduit à inclure ce qui passe pour être du non-religieux dans la catégorie du religieux.

J'estime qu'on a besoin ici d'un autre terme : «religieux». Il s'agit d'un adjectif substantivé et qui généralise encore davantage que le substantif, loin donc de nous faire retourner à l'adjectivalité de la religion au sens de W. Cantwell Smith.

Parler de «religieux», c'est déjà échapper aux limites de l'approche confessionnelle. Ce n'est pas pour autant échapper à toute forme de théologie, libérale notamment ou oecuménique. La théologie libérale dévie toujours peu ou prou de la stricte orthodoxie. Quant aux théologies mondiales ou oecuméniques, elles transcendent délibérément les frontières de chaque religion particulière. Dans les deux cas cependant, une option de foi régit l'ensemble du discours, l'Oméga par exemple chez Teilhard de Chardin, le *Someone* chez W. C. Smith. Pour quiconque voudrait s'interroger sur le religieux en général, il serait nécessaire de le comparer avec les croyances qui lui ressemblent et qui pourtant se distinguent de lui, les idéalisations et les valorisations tout particulièrement, sans exclure les positions extrêmes et antithétiques de la folie et de l'art.

Il me paraîtrait utile d'affecter le mot «croyance» au sens strict pour désigner une telle classe où, côte à côte avec le religieux, se trouveraient les multiples formes d'inventions imaginatives, qui de tout temps ont toujours constitué pour leur part la civilisation.

Reste un dernier ensemble de faits pertinents : les rêves. À partir des rêves éveillés que sont les croyances, on est infailliblement renvoyé aux rêves proprement dits. La catégorie englobante devrait ici s'appeler «l'imaginaire». Il faut en effet se rendre jusque-là. Les sociétés primitives nous l'imposent pour lesquelles l'expérience onirique a représenté la voie par excellence de la révélation religieuse. Semblablement les sciences humaines, particulièrement la psychologie selon laquelle l'objet religieux n'est rien d'autre qu'une projection imaginative de la conscience.

Voilà donc comment il faudrait conduire sa pensée et son langage pour développer adéquatement les sciences humaines de la religion. D'abord, ne pas craindre d'employer le mot «religion», ensuite le compléter par «religieux», «croyance», et «imaginaire».

Religion/religieux/croyance/imaginaire forment une *séquence* rigoureusement concentrique où les diamètres progressivement plus grands résultent de l'opération comparatiste et où l'explication définitive s'obtient à l'intérieur du cercle le plus vaste.

Religion — religieux croyance — imaginaire forment également une *dichotomie* puisque l'usage scientifique et incroyant doit prendre le relais de l'usage croyant au passage du religieux à la croyance.

Finalement la suite religion — religieux — croyance — imaginaire peut s'interpréter comme une *dérive* dans la mesure où la foi n'existe pas à l'état pur mais se mâtine toujours de doute, de tromperie, de rationalité.[17]

Notes

1 V. Pareto se méfiait du langage vulgaire au point de désirer le remplacer par des symboles purement techniques, mais il a reculé devant les énormes difficultés de communication qui s'ensuivraient. (Pareto 1968:55-56.)
2 Il y a donc à cela des raisons de fond, i.e., théoriques, notamment la limitation interne des formalismes, et non seulement des raisons pédagogiques ou vulgarisatrices.
3 Voir Smith 1978.
4 Smith 1978:31-32. Compléter par le ch. 8 de M. Despland où l'auteur fait remonter au treizième siècle la première *territorialisation* de la *christiana religio*.
5 Pour mieux l'écarter, il la caricature dans des termes que lui-même appelle cyniques : «All religions are, to the believer, equally true; to the philosopher, equally false; and to the politician, equally useful» (Smith).
6 «Faith is concerned with something, or Someone, behind or beyond Christianity, or Buddhism» (Smith 1978:13).
7 Comment concilier, demande-t-il, «the precious heritage of ultimates at the heart of the world's faiths» [et] «the hard won heritage of scholarship and science?» (Smith 1978:8).
8 «All should concede this much, that a person who has not seen the point of any one religion is not in the best position to generalize about the significance of them all» (Smith 1978:6).
9 «Et quand nous leur preschons un Dieu créateur du Ciel et de la terre et de toutes choses; de mesme quand nous leur parlons d'un Enfer et d'un Paradis, et du reste de nos mystères; les opiniastres respondent, que cela est bon pour nostre Pays, non pour le leur; que chaque Pays a ses façons de faire» (de Brébeuf 1972:34).
10 Voir là-dessus Labuschagne (1966).
11 Les églises en tant qu'institutions étant incluses dans ce que Barth appelle «religion». «Religion et grâce s'opposent comme la mort et la vie, écrivait-il dans le *Römerbrief*». Cité dans Bouillard (54). Bouillard note plus loin : «Organisation de la religion, l'Église recèle la même ambiguïté» (Bouillard 1957:60).
12 L'histoire comparée des religions s'est développée en Occident, donc à partir d'une auto-compréhension chrétienne. «L'histoire des religions, comme discipline, est née d'une constatation ancienne . . . : les autres (sous-entendu : les non-chrétiens) ont eux aussi des religions. . . . Il a fallu en outre qu'à cette constatation . . . vienne

s'ajouter le projet (conçu à la fin du XVIIIe siècle) de considérer la possibilité d'une étude non confessionnelle des phénomènes appelés religieux» (Borgeaud 1986:65).

13 «Et qui aura de l'aversion pour la religion d'Abraham, si ce n'est celui qui est insensé?» (Mahomet II:124). «Dites: 'Nous croyons à Allâh et à ce qui nous a été révélé, et à ce qui a été révélé à Abraham, à Ismaël, à Isaac, à Jacob et aux Tribus, et à ce qui a été apporté à Moïse et à Jésus'» (Mahomet II:130).

14 Quoi qu'en dise Smith (1978:ch. 4).

15 L'Islam fait moins de place à l'imaginaire que le Christianisme, moins même que le Judaïsme, ainsi que le sort fait récemment au roman de Salman Rushdie l'a dramatiquement illustré. La foi coranique baigne dans la clarté et non dans le mystère. Voir là-dessus Lapointe (1981).

16 Car la métaphysique est elle-même de type religieux, une version savante du religieux aux antipodes de la magie, version populaire de ce même religieux. Voir là-dessus Lapointe (1988).

17 Sur l'ensemble de cette problématique, notamment a) l'étude incroyante de la religion, b) la religion parmi les croyances, voir Lapointe (1989).

Références

Borgeaud, Ph. 1986. «Le problème du comparativisme en histoire des religions». *Revue européenne des sciences sociales* 72: 59-75.

Bouillard, H. 1957. *Karl Barth*. Théologie 38. Paris: Éditions Montaigne, 1.

De Brébeuf, Jean. 1972 (1635). *Relations des Jésuites*. Montréal: Jour.

Despland, Michel. 1979. *La religion en Occident. Évolution des idées et du vécu*. Montréal: Fides.

Labuschagne, C. J. 1966. *The Incomparability of Jahweh in the Old Testament*. Pretoria Oriental Series 5. Leiden.

Lapointe, Roger. 1981. «La situation herméneutique du Coran.» *Studies in Religion/Sciences religieuses* 10: 311-19.

———. 1988. *Socio-anthropologie du religieux. I La religion populaire au péril de la modernité*. Genève: Droz.

———. 1989. *Socio-anthropologie du religieux. II Le cercle enchanté de la croyance*. Genève: Droz.

Mahomet. 1958. *Le Coran*. Trad. E. Montet. Paris: Payot.

Pareto, Vilfredo. 1968 (1917-19). *Traité de sociologie générale*. Oeuvres complètes 12. Trad. P. Boven. Genève: Droz.

Pinard de la Boullaye, H. 1922. *L'étude comparée des religions. I Son histoire*. Paris: Beauchesne.

Rudhart, J. 1987. «Considérations sur la diversité des croyances religieuses et sur le changement des notions de valeur». *Revue européenne des sciences sociales* 74: 14-23.

Smith, W. Cantwell. 1967. *Questions of Religious Truth*. London: Victor Gollancz.

———. 1978 (1962). *The Meaning and End of Religion*. San Francisco: Harper & Row.

CHAPTER 15

Foi et religion : une relecture sémiologique

Raymond Lemieux

Dans la mesure où les sciences de l'homme *construisent* leur objet en *déformant le réel* (selon le mot de Bachelard 1969) pour lui donner le statut épistémologique de réalité et l'introduire dans les modes contrôlés du langage, le champ religieux représente pour elles une région limite. Il est celui où les êtres humains travaillent les frontières de leur univers et de leur capacité d'imaginer le monde. Il est celui où, à travers la mise à la raison du cosmos et de la vie, ils côtoient l'altérité, l'incontrôlable, l'irrationnel. On ne peut donc se surprendre que les objets et les signifiants du monde religieux restent souvent ambigus et évanescents. Et pour cela même, le champ religieux est un des plus difficiles qui soit pour l'investigation des sciences de l'homme.

Un symptôme bien révélateur de cette difficulté se présente dans les rapports qu'instituent les sciences religieuses (disciplines théologiques et analytiques confondues) entre les concepts de *religion* et de *foi*. Chacun des deux termes, en effet, peut recevoir une multitude de définitions, au point de faire l'objet de véritables glossaires (Despland 1979). Parfois ces définitions s'opposent, mais elles peuvent aussi bien se compléter, s'emprunter des éléments de signification, voire même renvoyer tout bonnement un terme à l'autre. Observer leurs relations, telles qu'enregistrées par la littérature savante, serait un objet de thèse passionnant pour un épistémologue. Quels systèmes de différences, et par voie de conséquence, quelles logiques de pensée, définissent les concepts de *religion* et de *foi* quand ils sont mis en regard l'un de l'autre?

Dans le texte présenté ici, je voudrais tenter de donner à ce contentieux une problématique plus opérationnelle, non pour à mon tour produire l'utopie d'un nouvel ensemble de définitions irrévocables, mais tout simplement pour tenter de voir jusqu'à quel point, à toutes fins pratiques, ce couple de termes peut devenir scientifiquement utile et constituer les

---

Les notes et références concernant ce chapitre se trouvent aux pages 189-91.

éléments d'un discours contrôlable, sinon toujours contrôlé, en désignant des réalités différenciables et repérables les unes par rapport aux autres. Dans un premier temps, je retracerai donc quelques éléments de l'histoire particulière de cette démarche, telle qu'elle s'est présentée dans ma trajectoire intellectuelle personnelle. J'essaierai de saisir comment s'y est élaborée, par la force des choses, sinon sous forme de projet conscient, une certaine problématique des rapports entre foi et religion. Dans un deuxième temps, je tenterai de jeter une autre lumière sur cette problématique, en déplaçant quelque peu ses perspectives initiales pour y introduire des éléments de sémiologie contemporaine. Enfin dans un troisième temps, j'esquisserai quelques pistes de recherches qui me semblent prometteuses.

La religion comme limite des sciences de l'homme

On me pardonnera d'utiliser comme base de réflexion une trajectoire intellectuelle personnelle. Qu'on se rassure immédiatement, ce faisant il s'agit simplement d'illustrer un processus de construction problématique commun. Une trajectoire intellectuelle, collective ou individuelle, ne peut se constituer que dans un ensemble de transactions constantes avec la culture. Quelle qu'elle soit, pourvu qu'on se donne la peine de l'analyser, elle devient révélatrice des influences, voulues ou non, acceptées ou rejetées, conscientes ou inconscientes, provenant de cet environnement. La trajectoire évoquée ici, nous fournira des indicateurs pour identifier des problèmes qui, la plupart du temps, la dépasse largement. Considérons-la comme un *terrain* d'observation, parmi bien d'autres possibles, mais qui a l'avantage d'être disponible à court terme.

La foi, intouchable sociologique

Au Québec, comme en Europe (Poulat 1989) et aux États-Unis (on lira pour ce pays le tout récent numéro de *Sociological Analysis* à l'occasion de son cinquantième anniversaire), les sciences empiriques de la religion sont nées de préoccupations religieuses. À une époque où l'institution catholique commençait à prendre conscience de l'effritement de l'unanimité culturelle et des appartenances communautaires qu'elle avait codifiées jusque-là, elle a voulu se donner, à bon droit, certains instruments de diagnostic de sa situation. Est alors née, avant même la Révolution tranquille, une *sociologie religieuse* inspirée directement des travaux de l'école française, elle-même naissante, dont ceux de Gabriel Lebras (1945; 1956).

Sans bouder théoriquement les développements qualitatifs, mais motivée d'abord par des observations quantitatives concernant les pratiques religieuses, surtout dominicales, cette *sociologie religieuse* a entériné tout naturellement les concepts et les catégories de l'univers religieux dont elle dépendait: celui du catholicisme de l'époque. Bref, il s'agissait moins pour elle de décrypter la culture religieuse des Québécois que de diagnostiquer (le terme lui-même laissant voir la part de valeurs investies dans l'entreprise, puisqu'il évoque la maladie et la santé) les forces et faiblesses de la présence de l'Église dans la société.

Sociologie religieuse, elle était, au sens encore plus strict, *sociologie catholique*. Et en cela, on aurait pu lui appliquer très exactement les caractéristiques que donnaient à leur association, à la même époque, les présidents successifs de l'*American Catholic Sociological Society* :

> Il existe une telle chose qu'une sociologie catholique, énoncent-ils, parce que la sociologie n'est pas une science exacte dans le plein sens du mot. Son mode d'investigation, son traitement des données, ses conclusions dépendent fréquemment de la pensée et de la philosophie de l'investigateur. Certes pouvons-nous apprendre beaucoup de ceux dont les approches sont différentes des nôtres. Ils ont une contribution importante à apporter au champ de la méthode et de la recherche. ... Cependant, notre vision de l'homme diffère de la leur, aussi les données colligées dans l'étude des relations entre les hommes seront-elles souvent interprétées différemment. Les principes sociaux ne peuvent être séparés des pratiques sociales. La théorie sociale ne doit pas être en variation par rapport aux principes fondamentaux.[1]
>
> Les catholiques possèdent un corps de vérité pour servir de guide dans l'étude de la théorie sociale et, à cause de cela, la société ne peut être pour eux un organisme sans but ni finalité, ni ne peut être en elle-même un but ou une finalité.[2] (Gallagher 1938; Mundie 1940, dans *Sociological Analysis* 1989, notre traduction).

Il n'y a rien là de bien original. Nous tenons à en faire état, cependant, parce qu'il nous semble qu'autrement on ne peut comprendre les rapports qui vont s'établir, en contre-coup, entre la pensée théologique communément admise, elle-même avant tout pensée ecclésiastique, et l'approche scientifique des phénomènes sociaux. On comprendra alors que les sciences de la religion naissantes dans ce contexte seront assez lourdement marquées, voire handicapées. Ce handicap est celui de toute discipline intellectuelle tentant de se développer dans un univers idéologiquement lourd : tributaires d'une distance déjà organisée entre le sujet observateur et l'objet observé, distance réglée par des principes immuables, elle n'est pas en mesure de *construire* son propre mode de distanciation, c'est-à-dire de se donner un point de vue spécifique. Les sciences humaines appliquent alors au champ religieux des *techniques* de recherche; elles n'ont pas à leur disposition de véritables méthodes d'analyse. Et dès que quelqu'un tente un pas dans ce sens, il est renvoyé à la subjectivité de ses postulats, c'est-à-dire au champ polémique de la croyance et de l'incroyance.

Comment s'est manifesté concrètement ce handicap? Très simplement : il y a, dans le domaine religieux, des questions intouchables, un ensemble de réalités à propos desquelles la science, quelle qu'elle soit, ne saurait rien dire, bref, des *objets qui échappent à l'observation*, et partant à la construction scientifique. Quels sont ces objets? Ceux de la *foi*. On peut bien, certes, observer et analyser les *manifestations religieuses*. Elles sont, précisément, des manifestations, c'est-à-dire des *données à voir* et elles s'offrent, vraisemblablement, au décryptage empirique. Jamais on ne touchera, cependant, le noyau dur de la foi. Voilà en gros une des premières leçons qu'on m'ait faites quand, jeune chercheur, j'ai été engagé par le Centre de recherches en sociologie religieuse de l'Université Laval, en 1965.

On voit déjà se dessiner ainsi une distinction hautement opératoire entre *religion* et *foi*. Qu'opère-t-elle cependant, sinon une stratégie institutionnelle, *ecclésiastique*, consistant à retirer certains objets arbitrairement du champ de l'analyse scientifique? Quand on parle ainsi de foi, en effet, qu'évoque-t-on sinon des *objets* de foi, c'est-à-dire, pour être clair, des discours dogmatiques, des énoncés de vérité et, par approches progressives sinon directement, des rituels, des directives ecclésiastiques, des normes institutionnelles, des positions d'autorité et des modes d'organisation sociale? En bout de course, puisque l'Église est mystère de foi, l'observation sociologique ne saurait en dire grand'chose, non plus que de ses modes de fonctionnement. Et sous les attentes de diagnostics concernant sa présence à la société, on veut surtout cacher à l'observateur ce qui ne saurait lui être montré.

Discours pervers, évidemment, qui piège à leur insu ceux-là mêmes qui le tiennent. La sociologie — et certes l'ensemble des disciplines de sciences humaines — vont devoir apprendre à le contourner puisque, c'est là leur fondement, elles voudront se donner les outils de reconstruction de *tout objet*. Tout objet en effet, qu'il soit de foi ou de religion, puisqu'il est objet, ne peut-il être vu sous l'angle relatif de sa valeur sociale, psychique ou autre, comme participation au fonctionnement de la société, à la construction de l'identité individuelle, ou autrement? Certes la science, en cela, est réductrice : elle reconstruit l'objet selon un point de vue particulier. Elle ne change rien à son réel, mais elle le regarde dans une perspective qui, à l'instar de tout regard humain, est réduite.

Religion sans foi, foi sans religion

Pour se développer dans un tel environnement, les sciences de la religion devaient commencer par déplacer les regards convenus sur leur objet. Ce travail, pourtant, elles n'ont pas été seules à le poursuivre. Déjà dans les années soixante, dans le sillage de Vatican II, se dessinait une *glasnost* ecclésiale produisant des effets remarquables dans le discours des théologiens eux-mêmes. Nous avons rencontré, de leur part, un certain nombre de textes qui, sans nécessairement être majeurs, traitaient du problème de la foi et de la religion d'une façon directement pertinente pour notre propre travail et y apportaient des perspectives nouvelles. Nous pouvons aujourd'hui les considérer comme des balises de notre itinéraire.

Le premier d'entre eux est un petit texte de Pierre-André Liégé. Dominicain, prédicateur invité régulièrement aux *Carêmes* de l'Université Laval, il développe le thème de *la religion qui n'est pas la foi*, dénonçant des attitudes religieuses qui, quoique bien conformes aux normes institutionnelles, peuvent fort bien être aussi des caricatures d'acte de foi. On y reconnaîtra, bien sûr, de vieux thèmes prophétiques: la dénonciation du pharisaïsme, de la prière des lèvres mais non du coeur, etc. Au-delà de la portée pastorale de ce texte, il faut pourtant lui reconnaître aussi une portée épistémologique. Celle-ci lui vient, non pas du fait qu'il réactive la distinction entre *foi* et *religion*, mais du fait qu'il en déplace les termes, et ceci au coeur même d'un projet théologique et pastoral, c'est-à-dire d'une réflexion *interne* sur l'Église. Il ne s'agit pas seulement d'y proposer la religion comme l'avatar analysable d'une foi hors de portée, mais d'indiquer que cette «foi» elle-même, quand elle se manifeste, ne va pas de soi. Les rapports entre *religion* et *foi* deviennent dès lors plus complexes que ce que l'épistémologie naïve des discours institutionnels peut laisser penser.

À la même époque, il nous faut aussi signaler un deuxième texte, celui de François Roustang (1966), intitulé «Le troisième homme». Exactement à l'inverse de celle de Liégé, la démarche du jésuite Roustang lui est pourtant complémentaire. Il découvre tout d'abord, dans sa génération, un nombre de plus en plus grand d'hommes et de femmes qui, pour toutes sortes de raisons, délaissent la «religion», c'est-à-dire les pratiques réglées et considérées comme normes de l'appartenance à l'Église, dont bien sûr, en premier lieu, la pratique dominicale. Cet «éloignement» de l'Église visible et officielle, remarque-t-il également, peut très souvent s'accompagner d'un engagement accru au service de l'humanité et cela parfois au nom même des «valeurs» chrétiennes qu'on a intériorisées dans l'enfance mais que, précisément, on ne croit plus retrouver dans l'institution. Ce qui ne va pas sans paradoxe, puisque se développe alors une redécouverte de la foi comme quête, mais d'une foi sans religion, d'un christianisme sans église, celui, nous dit-il, du *troisième homme*.

Religion sans foi, foi sans religion, voilà les deux frontières d'un territoire qui commence à se dessiner, celui d'un ensemble de rapports problématiques de la foi et de la religion. La plupart des questions qu'il faut se poser, dès lors, proviennent évidemment des ambiguïtés propres à la définition des termes. Qu'est-ce que la religion? Et surtout, qu'est-ce que la foi?

La foi au coeur déchiré de la raison

Sur le terrain, nos propres recherches nous ont fait voyager bien souvent d'un extrême à l'autre. N'est-ce pas à une religion sans foi, par exemple, que nous invite un système scolaire fondé sur la confessionalité officielle, mais dans lequel ni les maîtres, ni les élèves, ni les parents ne sont capables de former les noyaux de communautés chrétiennes effectives d'une part, et où la catéchèse même se donne le plus souvent comme la proposition d'une religion culturelle, voire d'une «religion civile» (Bellah 1967), sorte de rite de passage qu'il faut avoir accompli pour accéder à la base des «valeurs» communes? (Lemieux 1970; 1988; Milot 1989).

Dans le même temps cependant, une troisième rencontre nous a été capitale: celle de Michel de Certeau. Historien des XVIe et XVIIe siècles, anthropologue, philosophe, psychanalyste et théologien, Michel de Certeau a tenu de façon constante, en filigrane de sa propre trajectoire intellectuelle, une réflexion qui, en même temps que recherche épistémologique, s'avère un questionnement fondamental sur le christianisme. Nous pouvons déjà en saisir la portée par le caractère évocateur de ses titres: *L'étranger ou l'union dans la différence* (1969), *L'absent de l'histoire* (1973), *La rupture instauratrice ou le christianisme dans la culture contemporaine* (1971), *La faiblesse de croire* (1977), *Le silence de l'absolu. Folles et fous de Dieu (1979)*, *La fable mystique XVIe-XVIIe siècle* (1982). L'enjeu, à la fois *théologique* et *épistémologique* de tous ces textes et de bien d'autres, tient dans une question simple, question énoncée dans les débuts mêmes son oeuvre: y a-t-il une *parole* possible du croyant, une parole qui dise quelque chose de son expérience originale, celle de l'*altérité* (1967)? Autrement dit, quelles sont les *possibilités du langage d'assumer l'Autre?*

Le problème des limites, ici, n'est plus posé en termes d'exclusion, la foi ou la religion, la religion sans la foi ou la foi sans la religion. Il se pose comme question-force au coeur même de la pratique du langage, c'est-à-dire dans la capacité de l'être humain de faire société, de coexister avec d'autres. On le voit, cet être humain, rencontrer l'étranger et en faire figure de l'étrange, rencontrer la différence et en faire figure de mystère. S'en dégage une problématique qui constitue, à son tour, une façon radicale de *faire de la théologie*.

La confrontation à l'oeuvre de Michel de Certeau a été signifiante dans notre propre itinéraire dans la mesure où, à la fin des années soixante-dix, nous nous interrogions de notre côté sur les rapports multivariés entre les sciences humaines et la théologie. Ces rapports, on le sait, sont le lieu d'un certain nombre de difficultés et d'ambiguïtés. Nous ne nous y attarderons pas puisqu'il nous est arrivé d'en traiter ailleurs (1987). La première de ces difficultés, cependant, vient du fait que dans l'importation des concepts, méthodes ou résultats, d'une discipline vers une autre (ici des sciences vers la théologie mais l'inverse peut aussi être vrai), il arrive trop souvent qu'on oublie la valeur spécifique de ces concepts, méthodes ou résultats, telle que produite dans leur lieu d'origine.

Les traditions théologiques contemporaines, en France comme aux États-Unis, nous ont habitué à un large recours aux sciences humaines. Ces dernières, en certains cas, ont pris la relève du rôle qu'on attribuait autrefois à la philosophie comme *ancilla theologiae*. Il n'y a rien à redire là-dessus: c'est le droit le plus strict de n'importe quelle discipline intellectuelle de recourir à d'autres pour assurer la construction de son discours. Intellectuels ou charbonniers, nous ne parlons jamais qu'avec les mots des autres.... Cependant garder dans l'implicite, *mettre entre parenthèses* les valeurs qu'ont, dans leur propre bouche, les mots des autres, provoquer des problèmes : avec les mêmes mots, on ne dit pas nécessairement les mêmes choses.

Les sciences tiennent sur l'être humain un discours de vérité *relative* : elles n'en parlent que dans la mesure où leur méthode, le contrôle de la distance qu'elles instituent avec cet être humain devenu pour elles *objet*, leur permet d'en parler. Or elles sont inlassablement renvoyées, par cette méthode, à un agnosticisme radical, un agnosticisme qui est, tel que Weber lui-même l'a posé (1959), la condition première de leur honnêteté. Rien ne leur permet d'induire, pour l'être humain, un quelconque salut. Faire autrement serait très exactement se prendre pour d'autres, c'est-à-dire pour un discours de désir, un discours de foi.... C'est là la règle la plus radicale de leur production de valeurs et le fondement même de leur éthique.

À partir de là, la rencontre des sciences et des pratiques théologiques ne peut se résoudre que dans une *confrontation* constante de leurs interprétations (Geffré 1984). Si l'herméneutique, dans le sillage de Paul Ricoeur (1955; 1965; 1969) est devenue de son côté un autre support majeur de la recherche et de la réflexion théologique dans le monde contemporain, ce n'est pas sans rapport avec la pratique des science humaines qui s'effectue par ailleurs : voilà que s'offre au philosophe, et par conséquence au théologien, une possibilité de gestion originale du contentieux science/foi (Malherbe 1985).

Sans rien bouder, ni de la science ni de la philosophie dont elle respecte les exigences au maximum, la démarche théologique de Michel de Certeau ne peut être réduite à aucune de ces deux tendances, cependant. Au lieu d'opposer raison et foi, elle inscrit l'acte de foi comme celui d'un sujet, au coeur même de la rupture que constitue pour lui la conscience, scientifiquement construite et vécue comme destin inéluctable, de sa fragilité dans le monde, c'est-à-dire dans l'acte même de sa raison. Elle se présente ainsi, certes, comme une théologie radicale, non pas une théologie d'école, mais un rapport à l'intelligence qui, tout en restant irrémédiablement insatisfait du langage qui est le sien, et se donnant comme tâche de critiquer tout langage, ne se privant pas d'utiliser pour cela tout outil pertinent, s'inscrit néanmoins au coeur du langage.

Une telle problématique conduit à interroger les limites mêmes du langage pour y chercher, non plus des mécanismes et des articulations logiques, mais le projet de sens dont elles témoignent. On s'intéressera dès lors précisément à ces lieux où le langage n'a plus de sens, où il révèle son *impuissance* : la jouissance, la folie, la violence, la mort, mais aussi la mystique, la poésie, la musique, la peinture et l'architecture, de même que l'affectivité et le désir. Se profile ainsi, et on le verra très bien dans l'étude des grands mystiques tels Jean de la Croix, Thérèse d'Avila, Maître Eckhart, Angelus Silesius, un autre rapport à l'acte de foi, rapport qui, sans s'inscrire dans des compte-rendus langagiers qui en contrôleraient les tenants et aboutissants, fait néanmoins trace dans le langage et dans l'histoire.

Autrement dit l'acte de foi, tel qu'on peut le retrouver dans l'histoire et tel qu'il s'inscrit dans l'expérience, fût-ce l'expérience du rien, est ce travail de l'être humain pour aller, par le langage, au delà du langage. Dans les limites du langage, il se met alors en quête de l'illimité, pour faire jouer dans le langage non seulement les catégories objectives que celui-ci met à sa disposition, telles que véhiculées par la culture, mais sa subjectivité elle-même, c'est-à-dire son désir d'exister et dès lors de rencontrer l'altérité. Ainsi l'acte de foi (qu'il faut bien sûr distinguer du corpus des «vérités» dites de foi qui en sont des institutionnalisations) apparaît quand le langage n'a plus de sens. Et il consiste à continuer de travailler le langage pour lui faire porter, toujours plus loin, du sens.

Le statut de la fiction : croyances et imaginaire religieux

La sémiologie, nous dit Saussure, est cette discipline appelée à étudier «la vie des signes au sein de la vie sociale» (1972:33). N'est-ce pas précisément de ce dont il s'agit dans tout ce système de transactions entre les concepts de *foi* et de *religion*, tel que nous venons de relever? Ce sont là, bien sûr, des signes : on les utilise dans la mesure où on *veut dire* quelque chose. Ils ne se comprennent qu'à travers la syntaxe qui organise et règle leurs relations, entre eux-mêmes, avec d'autres signes, avec le monde. Ils ne sont pas réductibles à un contenu déterminé. Au lieu de cela, ils produisent de la valeur, c'est-à-dire de la coexistence entre les êtres humains. Le signe, derrière son fonctionnemnet immédiat, cache et révèle, en même temps, tout un monde de forces et de désirs qui transitent par lui pour rendre effectif leur «message».

Toute disjonction sémantique, telle que celle qui s'instaure de la mise en rapport foi/religion, renvoie ainsi à un ordre. C'est par cet ordre qu'elle fait sens. Nous appellerons cette production de sens son «opération sémantique».

La religion comme opérateur sémantique

La notion même de *religion*, en Occident, évoque le rapport (au moins possible sinon effectif) avec un autre, une altérité. Or cette altérité, posée comme réelle, est évidemment du domaine de l'intouchable. La religion, ainsi considérée, est un *opérateur sémantique* particulièrement redoutable :

> Toutes les croyances religieuses connues, dit Durkheim, qu'elles soient simples ou complexes, présentent un même caractère commun : elles supposent une classification des choses, réelles ou idéales, que se représentent les hommes, en deux classes, en deux genres opposés, désignés généralement par deux termes distincts que traduisent assez bien les mots de *profane* et de *sacré*. La division du monde en deux

domaines comprenant, l'un tout ce qui est sacré, l'autre tout ce qui est profane, tel est le trait distinctif de la pensée religieuse (1960, 50).

Cette division du monde peut se dire dans des termes diversifiés : l'ici et l'ailleurs, le relatif et l'absolu, le touchable et l'intouchable, etc. Il est évident, en ce sens, que la production même de la distinction entre *foi* et *religion*, objets de foi et manifestations religieuses, actes de foi et propositions religieuses, *est une production religieuse*. Elle consiste, très précisément, à *diviser le monde* en deux domaines dont l'un se donne comme intouchable, c'est-à-dire à toutes fins pratiques figure du sacré, tandis que l'autre, la notion même de «religion», devient une figure paradoxale du profane, puisque qu'on admet alors qu'elle désigne et représente un champ de construction humaine.

La mise en regard des termes *foi* et *religion* traduit ainsi une sorte de déplacement de la conscience religieuse, propre d'ailleurs à la modernité. Au lieu d'accepter un sacré envahissant, monopolisateur du champ religieux et ne laissant au profane que des miettes, elle repousse le sacré dans ses derniers retranchements : le noyau dur qui ne saurait jamais être réduit aux épiphénomènes de la culture. Mais c'est toujours le même *fonctionnement* de la conscience religieuse qui est en cause, en ce que cette conscience est productrice d'une cohérence (*quibus cohaerent homines*) là où se trouverait inévitablement, autrement, le chaos.

Or c'est précisément cette opération — et non pas d'abord les *objets* qu'elle met en circulation — qui fait l'enjeu fondamental des *sciences* de la religion. Elle se propose, en effet, comme l'opération *civilisatrice* par excellence, celle par laquelle le monde, pour les êtres parlants qui l'habitent, finit par prendre sens et par *s'imposer comme sens*, inaugurant à la fois l'ordre spirituel et l'ordre politique. Autrement dit, les sciences de la religion sont appelées à se préoccuper non pas d'abord de ce en quoi les religions sont des productions culturelles relatives, mais de ce en quoi elles sont inévitables dans l'histoire et le développement de l'humanité. Or précisément, elles sont inévitables en ce qu'elles instituent, dans cette histoire et ce développement, un *acte de foi* qui, chaque fois qu'on le rencontre, les dépasse.

Les sciences de la religion, ainsi considérées, se préoccupent de ce en quoi les religions, même si leurs adeptes se contredisent, même si leurs objets s'excluent les uns les autres, sont nécessaires à l'humanité, de ce en quoi, comme disait Marx, «la critique de la religion est toujours à reprendre», «l'essentiel reste à faire» (Labica 1978) parce que les fondements mêmes de la conscience de la condition humaine sont de l'ordre du mythe. Elles sont, en ce sens, un appel radical à la raison pour qu'elle pousse toujours plus loin ses investigations (De Diéguez 1989) mais sans se laisser prendre, à son tour, par le mythe d'une raison toute puissante qui parviendrait enfin au terme de son travail. La nécessité de la critique de la religion correspond à la nécessité de la religion elle-même : elle ne peut pas ne pas être. On ne peut en effet envisager la condition humaine, dans sa relativité même, qu'en se demandant comment elle se donne conscience d'elle-même en se mirant au regard d'un absolu, c'est-à-dire *en se figurant l'absolu qui la regarde.*

Certes la religion, selon la proposition durkheimienne, ne peut être mise en adéquation avec le sacré (ou mieux dit : le sacré ne peut se réduire à la religion). Elle suppose cependant un rapport au sacré, c'est-à-dire à un réel non seulement subjectif, produit de l'incapacité de l'être humain à tout connaître, à tout contrôler, mais *objectif*, ayant une existence en soi, indépendante du rapport entretenu avec lui.

Si l'Autre, qui ainsi constitué mérite bien l'hommage de la majuscule, possède une existence en soi, substantielle et objective, il va sans dire qu'il passe à l'ordre de l'inconnaissable radical. L'opération sémantique de la religion est aussi un acte de connaissance du monde. Dans cet acte de connaissance, l'Autre prend la place épistémique du *réel*, ce qui continue sans cesse d'échapper au langage et se définit, précisément, par son impossible appréhension par les signifiants du langage. Pourtant, si la religion est bien l'opérateur sémantique que nous venons de décrire, divisant le monde en sacré et profane selon les modes les plus divers dans les différentes cultures, elle *institue*, chaque fois, un rapport concret entre l'Autre et le même, l'Ailleurs et l'ici, l'intouchable et le manipulable, le sacré et le profane. Institution (*in-stare*), elle porte l'Autre dans le langage. Et elle le fait, précisément, en accommodant pour lui, dans le langage, les catégories de l'intouchable.

Elle *manifeste*, c'est-à-dire ramène au visible ce qui serait autrement invisible, selon le sens même du mot chrétien *sacrement*. Bien sûr, on convient facilement qu'elle ne rende pas justice à la totalité de l'Autre, qu'elle n'en épuise en rien le sens, qu'elle n'en soit jamais qu'une approche liée aux possibilités de la culture. Il en reste néanmoins que c'est de l'Autre qu'elle parle, que c'est avec Lui qu'elle institue une relation, toujours sublime.

L'instance de l'imaginaire

Comment, dès lors, sortir de l'ordre religieux pour comprendre le religieux ? Poser ainsi la question de la méthode est un piège. C'est un peu comme prétendre sortir du langage pour comprendre le langage. Pour ce faire, il faut plutôt tenter de décrire et d'analyser comment opère le langage, et accepter de rendre compte de cette tentative dans un discours qui est lui-même production de langage et l'objet possible d'une enquête similaire sur son propre fonctionnement. Serait-ce dire qu'on ne sort jamais complètement du religieux? Prétendre le faire serait utopique si tant est qu'il est, comme nous venons de le poser, de l'ordre du nécessaire.

Quelques règles simples, pourtant, sont disponibles pour nous aider à prendre distance, au moins provisoirement. On les retrouvera dans n'importe quel traité d'analyse du langage. On sait, par exemple, que le signe n'épuise pas la signification. Il indique plutôt qu'il ne définit, ce pourquoi d'ailleurs il faut sans cesse prendre soin de le définir quand on veut lui donner, dans l'utilisation concrète, une opérationalité spécifique. De même, dans l'ordre de la langue comme dans tout ordre symbolique, de la musique jusqu'aux mathématiques, un signifiant renvoie toujours à un autre signifiant. Il ne se comprend pas en lui-même mais par la place qu'il *désigne* dans l'univers des possibles du langage. Il s'inscrit dans cet univers comme la possibilité d'y repérer un certain nombre de différences et de similitudes qui en définissent la *valeur* propre.

Un champ sémantique comme celui du religieux est d'abord un univers déterminé de signes. Il est tributaire de limites, le plus souvent arbitraires, qui définissent les frontières de son inclusion et de son exclusion et, à l'intérieur de ces limites, instaure un ordre de valeurs, c'est-à-dire un échange rendu possible précisément par le jeu des différences et des similitudes qui y sont instituées. Un champ sémantique, ainsi considéré, est une mise en scène du monde qui s'effectue par des signes indiquant chacune des valeurs relatives qui s'y instaurent. Nous pouvons le considérer comme un théâtre. On y trouve, comme sur la scène théâtrale, une mise en ordre, des rideaux ou des décors qui déterminent l'ici et l'ailleurs, les coulisses, l'*obscène* qui ne saurait être montré puisque c'est là que se définissent les règles mêmes de la mise en scène. Mais cela n'est là que pour rendre possible un jeu, jeu scénique (mais ne parle-t-on pas aussi de la *scène sociale*), au cours duquel des drames se nouent et se dénouent constamment pour donner à l'existence sa dimension de vérité.

Le champ sémantique, ainsi instauré, inaugure l'instance de l'imaginaire. Qu'entend-on par ce terme? Rien d'autre que le fait que *la représentation du monde n'est pas le monde* et que, justement, elle ne saurait jamais en épuiser le sens. Le monde que l'on pense n'est pas celui que l'on vit : sinon, penser la mort équivaudrait à mourir. On voit bien qu'alors il n'y aurait plus de scène, plus de représentation, plus de sens, mais effet de réel déniant aux acteurs mêmes qui y seraient pris tout espace de liberté, aliénation du sujet (auteur, interprète ou spectateur) dans le non-sens.

Comprendre le monde (et c'est là, avons-nous vu, l'enjeu d'un opérateur sémantique), c'est le rendre à l'instance de l'imaginaire. Déjà, remarquons-le, cette instance de l'imaginaire est présente chez Saussure, à la base même de la linguistique générale : le concept, avance-t-il en substance, est le produit d'un signifiant phonique et d'une *image* acoustique et la langue ne fait rien d'autre que transformer en *figures* déterminées des matériaux phoniques et acoustiques. Autrement dit, l'imaginaire est une condition première de la mise en forme du monde que constitue le langage et des possibilités de communication qu'il instaure.

L'instance de l'imaginaire, dès lors, c'est bien l'instance de la fiction, mais d'une fiction aussi *nécessaire* à la vie que l'air qu'on respire parce que, pour vivre *ensemble*, nous ne saurions nous en passer. C'est grâce à elle que prennent consistance les valeurs que nous échangeons les uns avec les autres et qui tissent notre vie quotidienne. Et nous ne saurions penser le monde, c'est-à-dire l'approprier comme un ordre de valeur *manipulable*, sans le faire passer ainsi par l'instance de l'imaginaire.

De la vérité de la fiction

L'instance de l'imaginaire est celle où le monde fait signe. Elle nous introduit d'emblée à la réalité de la société. Qu'est-ce qu'une société, en effet, sinon un *ensemble* d'individus en interaction, c'est-à-dire une totalité qui se donne à appréhender comme telle? Changer la société, dès lors, c'est en travailler l'imaginaire, c'est-à-dire lui faire admettre quelque chose de ce qui, jusque là, lui était étranger. C'est ce qu'a bien compris la publicité, parmi d'autres intervenants dans ce sens : «l'essentiel de la communication visuelle, dit Umberto Eco, se fonde moins sur l'énonciation proprement dite de prémisses et de lieux communs que sur la présentation d'un iconogramme dans lequel la prémisse, sous-entendue, est *évoquée à travers la connotation* du champ topique» (1972, les italiques sont de nous). C'est ce qu'ont mis en oeuvre, bien avant elle, les religions.

Mais cette fiction, notons-le, n'a elle-même de valeur que dans la mesure de ses *effets* de vérité. Il ne s'agit pas pour elle de rendre compte du réel, mais de rendre possibles une coexistence et un commerce entre les êtres imaginants. Effets de vie, puisqu'elle instaure par là les conditions mêmes de la *survie*, non seulement de l'espèce mais aussi des individus, comme interdépendance des êtres humains entre eux dans une même culture, c'est-à-dire une même scène socio-sémantique.

La nécessité de l'imaginaire n'altère en rien son caractère de fiction. Pourtant, elle inaugure un rapport qui, pour être paradoxal, n'en est pas moins essentiel avec la vérité. Certes la vérité de l'image a finalement peu à voir avec l'Autre, le réel qu'elle représente. Au contraire, l'image la plus mensongère, l'*idole*, est précisément celle qui se donne pour le réel de ce qu'elle représente. Les traditions abrahamiques, en Occident, ont de ce point de vue mené une longue lutte contre cette propension irrecevable de l'image, lutte qui à certaines époques a conduit à un refus radical de toute image et souvent à leur destruction : Dieu ne se donne pas à voir, aussi ne peut-on le représenter; Il parle, Il écrit, Il se donne à *croire*. La vérité de l'image réside donc dans un autre lieu que dans la matérialité de sa représentation. Elle est, dirons-nous, de l'ordre du désir.

La métaphore théâtrale, ici encore, peut nous permettre de mieux comprendre. Au théâtre, un drame se joue sur scène et a, pour chacun de ses spectateurs, des effets de vérité. Plus encore, chacun d'eux, en acceptant d'entrer dans la logique de la mise en scène, est mobilisé émotivement et se met à vivre – tout en restant, bien sûr, assis dans son fauteuil – les émotions, les états d'âme que lui procure le déroulement du jeu. Qu'est-ce à dire? La vérité du théâtre ne réside pas dans le fait que le jeu se donnerait pour le réel de la vie. La mise en scène, au contraire, garantit la séparation, parce qu'elle enclôt l'espace délimité du jeu, du construit par rapport au donné. La vérité du théâtre lui vient du fait que tout le monde sait que ce qui se déroule sur scène est fictif. Pourtant du lieu de cette fiction, chaque spectateur est appelé à *reconnaître* quelque chose de sa vie, à se reconnaître participant, non pas du drame qui se déroule sur scène, mais d'un autre drame dont les éléments sont mis en lumière par celui qui se déroule sur scène, d'un autre drame dont il est appelé, sur le champ, à interpréter le sens. Autrement dit le théâtre, comme d'ailleurs tout art, ouvre un champ herméneutique, non seulement pour l'interprète au sens restreint du terme, l'acteur sur scène, mais aussi et souvent plus encore pour le spectateur qui devient, en transitant par cette mise en regard de l'autre scène, interprète de sa propre vie.

Ce qui se joue dès lors pour le spectateur, dans l'émotion ressentie et la mobilisation de son être, c'est bien le désir d'être reconnu dans son propre drame, ou, autrement dit, la vérité même de son désir d'être au monde en tant que sujet.

Ce n'est certes point un hasard si, en Occident, c'est la religion qui a donné naissance au théâtre, à travers la *représentation des mystères*, tant au moyen-âge chrétien que dans la Grèce antique. Les religions comme le théâtre et, aujourd'hui toutes les formes banalisées de culture de l'image (qu'il faudra encore apprendre à critiquer), *travaillent* l'imaginaire : elles mettent en scène ce qui permet à l'être humain de mieux comprendre et assumer sa situation concrète et rapportent cette dernière à une autre scène. Elles lui demandent ainsi, quasi obsessionnellement, de mettre à jour son désir.

Bien sûr elles peuvent aussi le pervertir. C'est ce qu'elles font quand elles se donnent comme une *réification* des valeurs qu'elles mettent en jeu. Elles se présentent alors comme des lieux de pouvoir et de savoir, des lieux totalitaires qui assujettissent le désir au lieu de le libérer. Autrement dit, elles font en sorte qu'il n'y ait plus de désir possible qu'en épousant le jeu tel que mis en scène. Celle-ci n'est plus une évocation de la réalité humaine; la réalité humaine en devient la réalisation. Ce n'est certes pas ce que nous entendons quand nous évoquons la *nécessité* de l'imaginaire. Pourtant la transformation des jeux de désir en jeux de pouvoir en est un avatar toujours possible et très souvent observable.

Quoi qu'il en soit, la religion et l'image, même quand elles sont des outils d'oppression, font signe.

L'opération de l'acte de foi

Si nous avons fait de la religion un champ sémantique, ce n'est pas pour lui dénier du sens mais bien pour montrer qu'elle est, essentiellement, un lieu de production de sens. Ce faisant cependant, tout ce qu'elle produit, y compris bien sûr la distinction entre *religion* et *foi*, est de l'ordre de l'objet transitoire, de la fiction, provisoire mais nécessaire pour que le désir d'être au monde de l'être humain prenne consistance. C'est là ce qu'on peut tirer, nous semble-t-il, d'une première lecture sémiologique du champ religieux : la construction d'un monde de représentations qui permettent aux êtres humains de vivre.

Autrement dit la religion produit, elle aussi, des *objets*. Elle le fait, notamment, sous le terme de *croyances*. Qu'est-ce qu'une croyance, en effet, sinon un *énoncé*, c'est-à-dire un fait de langage, qui pose une réalité extérieure au sujet parlant, réalité ayant une existence indépendante mais susceptible de l'influencer dans le déroulement de sa vie, l'amenant à prendre position, affirmative ou négative, vis-à-vis d'elle, bref capable de le *mobiliser* (Lemieux et Milot 1990). On retrouve, dans cet univers des croyances, tout ce que nous avons dit jusqu'ici de l'imaginaire : l'impératif de cohérence, qui seul permet à la construction du monde de prendre sens, c'est-à-dire d'intégrer chacun de ses éléments à une place qui lui est propre; la capacité d'exclure et d'inclure, de désigner l'étrange par rapport au familier, l'ailleurs par rapport à l'ici; la nécessité qu'il en soit ainsi, parce que sans elle le monde, précisément, n'aurait pas de sens; l'utilité pour la vie quotidienne elle-même, les questions embarrassantes étant désormais élaguées de celle-ci. Les croyances, comme n'importe quel objet, circulent entre les êtres humains. Elles leur permettent de faire société en se donnant comme lieux de ralliement, signes d'identité personnelle et collective. Elles sont, en cela, facteurs de culture.

L'art de croire

Certes on ne saurait réduire aux croyances ainsi définies tout le champ sémantique du croire. On croit d'abord quelqu'un, objecterait-on alors avec raison, et non à quelque chose. C'est dire autrement cela même que nous avons avancé plus haut, à savoir que l'enjeu de l'imaginaire est bien le désir, c'est-à-dire le travail de l'intersubjectivité, et non pas une quelconque concordance avec le «réel».

Il faut distinguer, pour mieux avancer dans ce sens, entre *l'art de croire*, impératif de toute vie en société, et les objets de croyance que cet art met en scène. Quand un être parlant s'adresse à un autre, en effet, il demande essentiellement à ce dernier de le croire. Et il se pose lui-même comme *croyable* sous son regard. Il le fait d'autant plus que rien de son dire, pour l'autre, n'est évident. C'est là une leçon que nous apprend chaque jour la pratique du langage : quand on a le sentiment d'être compris, on s'arrête normalement de parler. C'est dans la mesure où on pense être incompris — c'est-à-dire dans la mesure où les mots qu'on emploie sont toujours équivoques, où ils laissent toujours traîner derrière eux un non dit — qu'on continue de parler, et surtout que cette parole se transmue en dialogue où prennent place des *interlocuteurs*. Moins on se comprend, oserait-on avancer, plus on se parle. ... La structure la plus élémentaire de la socialité repose ainsi, sur un inter-questionement où la réalité du *je* ne peut prendre consistance que dans la mise en regard du *tu*, dans une éthique de la coexistence (Ricoeur 1984) où on pousse sans cesse plus loin le questionnement de l'autre (*quaestio* : question, quête). Plus on devient conscient de la relativité du langage, de son impuissance à dire le réel, plus on parle... à moins de fermer la porte au désir et, dès lors, de se taire.

C'est dans ce creux, bien sûr, que se structure l'acte de croire : il s'accorde au *crédit* donné à l'autre. On a beau parler la même langue, les mots qu'on emploie sont lourds, pour chaque interlocuteur, des expériences de vie qui les chargent de valeurs différenciées. Chacun entend l'autre du lieu de son histoire particulière et les mots ne font sens, pour lui, que dans cette histoire qui ne peut en rien être l'histoire de l'autre. Autrement dit, quand on entend l'autre, on comprend, structurellement, autre chose que ce qu'il *veut* dire puisque le lieu de l'écoute n'est jamais celui de l'énonciation. Le référent commun, le code du langage, certes révèlent quelque chose du désir, mais ils en cachent aussi la plus grande partie. Ils peuvent d'aileurs toujours être travestis dans le mensonge : faire croire à l'autre ce qu'on ne saurait réaliser avec lui, un désir d'être qui n'existe pas, tel que le démontre, par exemple, la fable de Don Juan (Felman 1980). La communication humaine, ainsi considérée, relève de l'*impossible* : elle ne peut jamais être complètement réalisée, elle est toujours en marche, en recherche de continuité. Dans cet impossible, on ne peut que se croire, croire les uns les autres, se faire crédit mutuellement du désir d'être ensemble, pour continuer de s'écouter et de se questionner de façon à aller plus loin dans le sens même de ce désir.

L'acte de croire fait partie des structures les plus élémentaires de la socialité. On le retrouve, de l'expérience de la naissance à celle de la mort comme condition première de la possibilité de *survivre* (Lemieux 1982) à sa propre coupure avec le monde. Il en est tellement ainsi qu'il n'y a pas, à vrai dire, de relations humaines qui ne reposent sur une mise en scène du croyable. Quand, dans un espace de socialité donné, un des interlocuteurs devient incroyable, cet espace est irrémédiablement appelé à éclater et devient, concrètement, espace impossible. Toute société se fonde, ainsi, sur ce que Michel de Certeau appelait déjà, en 1977, la *faiblesse de croire*, c'est-à-dire le fait que le *croire* habite les manques à être de l'intersubjectivité.

Le travail de la raison

Les *croyances*, on le voit bien, n'épuisent pas le croyable. Pas plus que les mots n'épuisent le désir. On ne peut les considérer non plus comme des *expressions* pures et simples du croyable. Loin de là, c'est parce qu'elles n'arrivent jamais à *exprimer*, à rendre compte parfaitement de tous les enjeux du croyable, que sans cesse on les produit comme objets transitoires et provisoires de l'intersubjectivité. Loin d'être les réalisations du désir — ce en quoi elles continuent pourtant de se donner — elles sont les symptômes du manque, ce en quoi, face au désir, elles deviennent des *médiations*.

Peut-être est-ce là ce qui peut expliquer avec le plus d'acuité théorique l'extraordinaire foisonnement de croyances dont les sociétés dites postindustrielles font montre, foisonnement qui a tant étonné ceux qui, dans ces sociétés, avaient déjà conclu à la mort du religieux. Certes ces croyances sont elles-mêmes en grande partie celles d'une *religion séculière*, épiphanie de l'humanisme séculier (Marty 1976:14) qui sublime les forces cosmiques, l'ordre supposé du monde, le moi intériorisé, voire les enjeux sociaux et sotériologiques de la paix, de l'amour, de la justice, et du savoir.

Si nos sociétés produisent ainsi beaucoup de croyances, peut-être est-ce dû au fait qu'elles sont très proches de l'expérience du non-sens, de l'expérience du rien. Il en est, en effet, de cette expérience comme de celle de la mort: ne pouvant rien contre elle, *on en érige les symboles pour constamment les détruire*. Et sans doute nos sociétés ne sont-elles pas très différentes, là-dessus, des sociétés anciennes.

On comprend pourquoi, dit Mircea Eliade (1957), le même schéma initiatique — souffrances, mort et résurrection (re-naissance) — se retrouve dans tous les mystères, aussi bien dans les rites de puberté que dans ceux qui donnent accès à une société secrète; et pourquoi le même scénario se laisse déchiffrer dans les bouleversantes expériences intimes qui précèdent la vocation mystique (chez les primitifs, les «maladies initiatiques» des futurs chamans). L'homme des sociétés primitives s'est efforcé de vaincre la mort en la transformant en rite de passage. En d'autres termes, pour les primitifs on meurt toujours à quelque chose qui n'était pas essentiel; on meurt surtout à la vie profane.

Il s'agit, dans un système de croyances, qu'il soit collectif et institutionnel, tel celui des religions *dénommées* (celles qui ont pignon sur rue), individuel, tel celui qu'on retrouve maintenant dans les enquêtes d'opinion, ou encore diffus, sous-terrain, implicite, tel celui dont cherche à rendre compte le concept de *religion invisible* (Luckmann 1967), de *répondre* à l'expérience du manque. Cette réponse consiste à proposer des objets susceptibles de combler le manque à vivre et, bien sûr, à rendre possible la vie en lui donnant un sens, voire en le lui imposant. Là où la vie n'a pas de sens, là où la communication humaine renvoie inlassablement au risque du désir (croire l'autre), on lui donne des *objets à croire* qui permettent de faire, pour un temps au moins, l'économie de ce risque. Que ces objets se présentent comme des mythes fondateurs, tels que les ont proposés les grandes traditions religieuses civilisatrices, qu'ils soient des étais de l'existence fragile de l'individu sécularisé (Milot 1989), il y est question de *survie*.

Si le sens, en effet, est produit, il n'est jamais acquis. Il est toujours à reconstruire. Or c'est là précisément qu'entre en scène le *travail de la raison*. Nous ne nous attarderons pas longtemps à celui-ci, sinon pour dire qu'il est tout aussi nécessaire à la religion que celle-ci est nécessaire à la vie. En effet, il consiste à renvoyer le mythe et les croyances à leur caractère de construction de l'esprit, c'est-à-dire à la *vérité qui leur est propre*. Là où le mythe se donne comme pérenne, c'est la raison seule qui peut le renvoyer à son éphémérité. Là où les croyances se donnent comme des objets nécessaires, c'est la raison seule qui peut les renvoyer à leur relativité. Or ce faisant, elle est appelée à les *déconstruire*, c'est-à-dire à montrer ce en quoi ces réalités, comme tout autre réalité humaine, sont tributaires d'un mode de construction. La raison *décrit (describere)* ce qui s'écrit, *démontre* ce qui se montre. Si elle aussi est appelée à produire à son tour des modèles, qui ne sont jamais eux-mêmes que des fictions provisoires, ces modèles sont moins ceux de l'objet que ceux du *mode de production* de l'objet.

Quand nous disons «renvoyer la religion à vérité qui lui est propre», il ne s'agit pas pour nous d'en réduire la problématique à celle d'une dichotomie *vérité / mensonge*. Bien au contraire, il s'agit de la renvoyer à son niveau de vérité essentiel et inévitable, qui n'est pas celui d'une quelconque concordance de l'objet (imaginaire) avec le réel, mais celui du désir dont il témoigne. Or cette vérité du désir, précisément, elle ne peut venir à la lumière que *dans la mesure de la déconstruction* de l'objet, c'est-à-dire quand l'objet avoue son manque à dire le désir que, pourtant, il porte au monde. Autrement dit, pour reprendre la problématique qui a été la nôtre au point de départ, c'est à partir du moment où l'imaginaire religieux est renvoyé à son statut propre, à partir du moment où le doute s'inscrit dans ses constructions les plus solides, que l'acte de foi devient possible comme acte de *croire* conscient de lui même.

Opérationaliser le concept de foi

La question qui nous reste à poser, au terme de ce parcours, est de celles que nous n'aurions osé poser au point de départ mais qui deviennent maintenant possibles : peut-on donner une valeur opératoire au concept de *foi*? Autrement dit, peut-on désigner par ce concept une réalité observable et analysable?

Il semble bien que non, si on s'en tient à ses modes de construction religieux. Tant que le travail de la pensée religieuse produit le concept de foi comme la désignation d'un intouchable, il est évident qu'il le fait sortir de tout champ empirique. Si la foi est ce qui s'exclut de la religion, elle ne peut certes qu'échapper aux sciences de la religion. En tant que désignation d'un ensemble d'*objets*, le signifiant *foi* n'a pas de valeur empirique : ou bien ces objets sont de simples objets religieux qui, par toutes sortes de stratégies de langage, se disent autrement, ou bien ils sont effectivement hors de portée de la connaissance et on ne peut rien en dire.

Si on se donne la peine de déconstruire le mode de production même de la distinction entre *foi* et *religion* et de saisir comment il fonctionne en tant que mode de production religieux de sens du monde, on peut alors obtenir un concept de foi qui commence à être opérationnel. Ce concept devient cependant un concept purement formel, un signifiant nécessaire certes, mais lui-même sans contenu nécessaire. Les cultures lui donnent, inlassablement, des contenus. Il désigne une place vide que toutes sortes d'*objets* peuvent venir combler, toujours d'une façon provisoire. Le lieu de la foi, ainsi compris, n'est pas celui d'un ensemble d'objets, c'est celui d'un ensemble de pures potentialités : l'ensemble *nécessaire* des potentialités du monde, oserait-on avancer. Il ne *représente* rien, en lui-même, mais actualise plutôt ce qui est, pour le sujet, de l'ordre d'une expérience : l'assumation du monde où il se trouve mis au défi d'accepter l'autre.

Autrement dit, l'acte de foi que nous pouvons ainsi repérer est celui qui se traduit dans un risque : en terme de *connaissances* il est l'acceptation de ne rien savoir sur le monde et de continuer à miser sur le sens. Il ne saurait se justifier d'aucune évidence; au contraire, il a comme condition préalable l'abandon des évidences. Il n'est pas l'abdication de la raison; au contraire il se supporte du travail de désillusion que poursuit cette dernière, sachant, avec elle, qu'il n'est pas de produit de la raison qui ne soit, lui aussi, porteur d'illusions. Il est ce en quoi l'être humain se justifie de continuer de vivre quand plus rien n'est évident, quand il a épuisé les offres de sens de l'imaginaire. Bref l'acte de foi commence quand l'imaginaire se met lui-même à craquer, quand le miroir, qui ne renvoie jamais que les reflets de ceux qui le contemplent, cesse d'être fidèle pour laisser voir dans les infractuosités de sa surface, l'inconnu. Autrement dit quand, dans la désillusion, l'imaginaire commence à se donner pour ce qu'il est : rien qu'une quête, fragile, de l'autre.

On dira que cette position est bien morose. Pourtant c'est elle qui a présidé, dans l'histoire de l'humanité, à toutes les grandes créativités religieuses. On la trouve à l'aube des traditions judéo-chrétiennes, notamment, dans cette invention d'un Dieu qui ne se voit ni ne saurait se dire, qui ne se manifeste jamais que dans l'après-coup, mais dont on reconnaît la voix, dont on est appelé à entendre la parole... un Dieu qui jamais ne se *représente* mais donne sans cesse son écriture, l'histoire même du monde, à interpréter. Elle n'est pas étrangère, on le voit, aux traditions théologiques elles-mêmes, comme interprétation du *sensus fidei*, dont elle refuse pourtant les propensions réifiantes. On la trouve à profusion, de même, dans l'expérience des mystiques, quand dans la nuit obscure plus rien ne tient, sinon le choix réactualisé de demeurer fidèle à l'inconnu : *volo* (De Certeau 1982 : 225ss).

Mais là où il est plus impératif encore d'apprendre à en saisir la réalité, c'est sans contredit dans l'expérience contemporaine et commune. Celle-ci, en effet, propose désormais aux êtres humains une conscience du monde dont plusieurs traits sont inédits.

Tout d'abord, elle se présente comme expérience constante du relatif. Après la *crise de la modernité*, cette crise où l'absolu de la religion s'est opposé à l'absolu de la raison, il semble qu'on passe maintenant à un temps d'incertitude. La raison, comme prétention au salut du monde, a cessé d'être croyable : elle a conduit à trop de désillusions politiques, économiques et sociales. Elle doit revenir à la vérité qui lui est propre, celle du relatif. La science elle-même apprend à se concevoir comme structurellement falsifiable, relative, voire anarchiste dans ses formations (Chalmers 1987). La religion, marquée par la critique historique, est elle aussi acculée au risque de l'interprétation : «comprendre le texte de l'Écriture, ce n'est pas s'approprier une vérité qui serait derrière un texte, mais rejoindre la 'proposition de monde' auquel renvoie le texte» (Geffré 1990 : 14 référant à Ricoeur 1986). En conséquence, toutes ces formations de l'esprit qui ont pendant un temps prétendu à des vérités définitives, quoique concurrentielles, sont renvoyées à leurs mythes fondateurs.

Ensuite, cette conscience contemporaine est celle du tragique de l'existence : Auschwitz certes l'a marquée profondément, mais aussi, et de façon récurrente les Goulags, le spectacle interminable de la mort, de l'injustice et de la violence avec laquelle elle doit accepter de vivre, violence non seulement collective qui, telles les guerres, opposent les communautés humaines les unes aux autres, mais tout aussi sauvage et *sans raison*, celle de la détresse émotionnelle des individus, cet détresse qui cherche à se résoudre dans la folie, le suicide et les passages à l'acte psychotiques.

La conscience contemporaine ne peut désormais échapper à l'expérience du non-sens.

Si l'on ajoute à cela l'éclatement de l'imaginaire religieux lui-même, marqué non seulement par la pluralisation des langages due au côtoiement de traditions autrefois étrangères, mais plus profondément encore, par leur déchirure interne, on a tous les ingrédients d'une culture où les questions de sens deviennent lancinantes. Nous ne développerons pas ici cette dimension puisque nous avons eu l'occasion de le faire ailleurs (Lemieux et Milot 1990). Disons simplement que, renvoyant à la conscience individuelle l'appropriation du sens du monde, dans ce que certains ont appelé la «religion à la carte» (Bibby 1988), cette nouvelle conscience religieuse qui n'est plus réglée par les grandes institutions devient elle-même un lieu d'expérience de l'aléatoire. On y est appelé à changer constamment, à mesure que les expériences de la vie se déroulent, de champ d'interprétation du monde, de champ de certitudes... et l'histoire de sa propre vie risque alors de devenir, pour l'individu, celle d'une cohérence difficile, c'est-à-dire une histoire qu'on ne peut plus raconter à d'autres, un *lien indicible* (Lemieux 1990).

L'expérience religieuse, comme l'expérience du monde, renvoie désormais à l'éphémère. On s'y expose sans cesse à l'insatisfaction. Elle représente, pour les hommes et les femmes d'aujourd'hui, un des déclencheurs majeurs de la conscience du non-sens. Et inversement, comme l'avance Bernhard Welte (1988), cette *expérience du rien*, désormais si répandue, devient un lieu privilégié d'expérience religieuse, c'est-à-dire de questionnement, inéluctable, sur le sens du monde.

Ne rencontre-t-on pas là les conditions propices à l'acte de foi?

Il faudrait évidemment poser ici à nouveau la question de la «foi du charbonnier», non plus cependant en termes de classes sociales (ignorant versus savant), ni, encore moins, en termes d'hétérodoxies et d'orthodoxies. Il faut la poser dans la mesure où il n'y a pas d'imaginaire plus apte qu'un autre à exprimer le désir d'être au monde des humains, dans la mesure où il n'y a pas d'imaginaire sûr, mais où tout imaginaire, unifié ou éclaté, réglé ou anarchique, est un essai de survie, c'est-à-dire une tentative de cohérence, provisoire et transitoire, qui porte à l'autre, pour un temps, le désir. Tous les imaginaires (toutes les croyances) sont respectables, même quand on n'en comprend pas les articulations logiques, parce que derrière eux se profilent des sujets en quête d'identité. Mais l'acte de foi, précisément, consiste aussi à détruire les idoles, c'est-à-dire à reconnaître cette quête en refusant les propensions terroristes de l'imaginaire, en renvoyant ce dernier à la vérité qui lui est propre, celle d'un objet transitoire, quoique nécessaire. Or ces propensions terroristes, on les trouve, elles aussi, partout.

Conclusion

Cette expérience de l'éphémère est désormais devenue commune à nos pratiques intellectuelles, de la psychanalyse (il n'y a pas d'objet qui comble le désir, mais au contraire tout objet est fait pour le tromper) jusqu'à l'histoire des religions (il n'y a pas de mythe qui, mesuré à l'aune de l'histoire, ne soit précaire). Nous l'avons retrouvée ici à partir de la pratique du langage, en considérant le champ religieux comme un champ sémantique. Nous aurions pu le faire tout aussi bien, et cela n'a pas été sans incidences dans notre inspiration première, à partir du champ théologique lui-même, dans son inlassable tentative de rendre compte de la foi des communautés croyantes, acculé qu'il est sans cesse, en cela, à aller plus loin, à dépasser les formulations qui, pour un temps, en ont expliqué quelque chose. Le discours théologique cependant, quand il s'attaque à ces questions, le fait en *fidélité* (*fides quaerens* . . .). Pour démontrer les mécanismes de construction de cette fidélité elle-même, il lui faut encore se déplacer, et tenter l'aventure de l'*intellectum*.

Mais, comme l'avançait Claude Geffré, le théologien n'est-il pas «celui qui croit assez en Dieu pour faire sienne l'interrogation humaine dans ce qu'elle a de plus radical»? (1984). Croire en Dieu, dès lors, n'est évidemment pas s'attacher à une de ses images, mais le poser en signifiant, toujours à reconsidérer, de l'incommensurable désir dont il devient le répondant. Mais dire Dieu, c'est aussi, inévitablement, l'imaginer ... et accepter, c'est là que la phrase citée prend sens, l'effraction constante de cet imaginaire par le travail de la raison. Autrement dit, c'est précisément quand il se heurte au non-sens que le travail théologique commence.

Nous n'avons pas voulu rester sur ce terrain théologique, pourtant riche, parce que nous avons voulu rendre l'acte de foi à son statut épistémologique (facteur de connaissance) et culturel (facteur de vie sociale). Il n'appartient pas en exclusivité, à ce niveau, aux *croyants* ni aux religions établies. Il fait sauter toute frontière entre *vraies* et *fausses* religions qui se définiraient ainsi par les contenus de leur imaginaire. La fausse religion serait plutôt celle qui se donne dans l'exclusivité absolue de ses signifiants, en refusant de considérer la quête des autres.

Nous avons trouvé la foi, dans un premier temps, au coeur déchiré de la raison. Nous la retrouvons maintenant comme *quête*, c'est-à-dire espace ouvert à la découverte de l'autre et signifié, essentiellement, dans le geste transitoire d'aller vers lui. Or quel est ce geste sinon celui qui consiste à exprimer quelque chose de l'altérité? C'est-à-dire à puiser, parmi ses signifiants, ceux qui sont susceptibles de signifier, fût-ce passagèrement, une rencontre possible, et à faire transiter le *croire* par les *croyances*? L'acte de foi peut dès lors être considéré comme l'acceptation de vivre (ou *survivre*) dans le non-sens de l'histoire, la relativité de l'imaginaire et la déconstruction même du religieux : accepter de vivre avec les fictions provisoires du monde en sachant que ce sont là des fictions provisoires.

Notes

1 «There is such a thing as a Catholic sociology, for sociology is not in the full sense of the word an exact science. The method of investigation, the assembling of data, the conclusions drawn depend frequently upon the thought and philosophy of the investigator. Certainly we can learn much from those whose approach is different from ours. They have much to contribute in the field of method and research... Our estimate of man differs from theirs, so that the data collected from the study of the relationships of man will often be interpreted in a different way. Social principles cannot be divorced from social practice. Social theory must not be at variance with fundamental principles. Our philosophy, our faith, and the teachings of the Church must be kept in view as we engage ourselves in the study of social phenomena.»
2 «Catholics have a body of truths to serve as guides in the study of social theory and, because of this, society for them can never be a goal-less or purposeless organism, nor can society be an end or purpose in itself.»

Références

Bachelard, Gaston. 1969. *La formation de l'esprit scientifique*. Paris : Librairie philosophique J. Vrin.
Bellah, Robert N. 1967. «Civil Religion in America». *Daedelus* 96, 1 (Winter).
Bibby, Reginald. 1988. *La religion à la carte*. Montréal : Fides. Traduction de *Fragmented Gods : Poverty and Potential of Religion in Canada*. Toronto : Irwin.
Chalmers, Alan F. 1987. *Qu'est-ce que la science? Récents développements en philosophie des sciences : Popper, Kuhn, Lakatos, Feyerabend*. Paris : Éditions La Découverte.
De Certeau, Michel. 1967. «La parole du croyant dans le langage de l'homme». *Esprit* (octobre) : 455-73.
———. 1969. *L'étranger ou l'union dans la différence*, Paris : Desclée de Brouwer.
———. 1971. «La rupture instauratrice, ou le christianisme dans la culture contemporaine». *Esprit* (juin) : 1177-1215.
———. 1973. *L'absent de l'histoire*. Coll. «Repères». Paris : Mame.
———. 1977. «La faiblesse de croire». *Esprit* (avril-mai) : 231-45.
———. 1979. «Le silence de l'absolu. Folles et fous de Dieu». *RSR (Recherches de sciences religieuses)* 67, 4 : 525-46.
———. 1982. *La fable mystique XVIe-XVIIe siècle*. Paris : Gallimard.
De Dieguez, Manuel. 1989. *Le combat de la raison*. Paris : Albin Michel.

Despland, Michel. 1979. «Quarante idées de religion». Dans *La religion en Occident : évolution des idées et du vécu*, 537-42. Montréal : Fides.

Durkheim, Émile. 1960. *Les formes élémentaires de la vie religieuse*. 4e éd. Paris : Presses universitaires de France.

Eco, Umberto. 1972. *La structure absente*. Paris : Mercure de France.

Eliade, Mircea. 1957. *Le sacré et le profane*. Coll. «Idées». Paris : Gallimard.

Felman, Shoshana. 1980. *Le scandale du corps parlant*. Paris : Seuil.

Geffré, Claude. 1984. «Théologie chrétienne». In Paul Poupart, *Dictionnaire des religions*. Paris : Presses universitaires de France.

———. 1990. «Révélation et expérience historique des hommes». *Laval théologique et philosophique* 46, 1 (février) : 3-16.

Labica, Georges. 1978. «Sur la constitution et le sens de la critique marxiste de la religion». Dans *L'apport de la théorie et de la méthode marxiste à l'étude des religions*, 1-15. Dirigé par Jacques Maitre. Travaux et documents, VI. Paris : Centre d'études sociologiques.

Lebras, Gabriel. 1945. *Introduction à l'étude de la pratique religieuse en France*. Paris : Presses universitaires de France.

———. 1956. *De la morphologie à la typologie*. Tome 2 des *Études de sociologie religieuse*. Paris : Presses universitaires de France.

Lemieux, Raymond. 1970. «Catéchèse objective, catéchèse culturelle et catéchèse enseignée». *Social Compass* 17, 3 : 403-23.

———. 1982. «Pratique de la mort et production sociale». *Anthropologie et société* 6, 3 : 25-44.

———. 1987. «Théologie, science et action : les enjeux du discours pastoral». *Laval théologique et philosophique* 43, 3 (octobre) : 321-38.

———. 1988. «Les défis contemporains de l'enseignement religieux». Dans *Le défi de l'enseignement religieux. Problématiques et perspectives*. Dirigés par Marcel Aubert, Micheline Milot et Réginald Richard. *Cahiers de recherches en sciences de la religion* 9 : 227-38.

———. 1989. «Une question d'interprétation : les rapports entre les sciences humaines et la théologie dans l'action pastorale». Dans *L'interprétation, un défi de l'action pastorale*, 175-96. Dirigé par Jean-Guy Nadeau. *Cahiers d'études pastorales* 6. Montréal.

———. 1990. «Vieillir, une question de sens?» *Revue internationale d'action communautaire*.

Lemieux, Raymond et Micheline Milot (dir.). 1990. *Les croyances des québécois. Esquisses d'une approche empirique*. Québec, *Cahiers de recherches en sciences de la religion*, 10.

Liégé, Paul-André. 1965. «La religion qui n'est pas la foi». *Parole et mission* 31 (octobre). Reproduit également par André Godin, *Cours de psychologie religieuse*, Québec : Institut de catéchèse de l'Université Laval (octobre) : 20-29.

Luckmann, Thomas. 1967. *The Invisible Religion : The Problem of Religion in Modern Society*, New York : Macmillan.

Malherbe, Jean-François. 1985. *Le langage théologique à l'âge de la science. Lecture de Jean Ladrière*. Coll. «Cogitatio fidei» 129. Paris : Cerf.

Marty, Martin E. 1976. *A Nation of Behavers*. Chicago and London : The University of Chicago Press.

Milot, Micheline. 1989. «De la transmission de la religion. Rapports famille-école», thèse de doctorat en psychopédagogie, Université Laval.

Poulat, Émile. 1989. «La C. I. S. R., de la fondation à la mutation. Réflexions sur une trajectoire et ses enjeux», Conférence d'ouverture à la XXe Conférence internationale de sociologie des religions, Helsinki, 21-25 août 1989. Dactylographié.

Ricoeur, Paul. 1955. *Histoire et vérité*. Paris : Seuil.

———. 1965. *De l'interprétation*. Paris : Seuil.

———. 1969. *Le conflit des interprétations*. Paris : Seuil.

———. 1984. «Avant la loi morale : l'éthique». *Encyclopaedia Universalis*, supplément *Les enjeux*, 42-45.

———. 1986. «Herméneutique philosophique et herméneutique biblique». Dans *Du texte à l'action*, 119-37. Paris : Seuil.

Roustang, François. 1966. «Le troisième homme». *Christus* 13 (octobre) : 561-67.

Saussure, Ferdinand de. 1972. *Cours de linguistique générale*. Paris : Payot (1925).

Sociological Analysis. 1989. «Historical Documents». 50, 4 : *Fiftieth Anniversary Special Issue*.

Weber, Max. 1959. *Le savant et le politique*. Coll. 10/18 134. Paris : Plon.

Welte, Bernhard. 1988. *La lumière du rien. La possibilité d'une nouvelle expérience religieuse*. Traduit de l'allemand par Jean-Claude Petit. Montréal : Fides.

CHAPTER 16

Prolégomènes à une définition sémiotique de la religion

Jacques Pierre

Introduction

S'étonnera-t-on jamais de ce qu'un débat, né pour ainsi dire avec notre discipline et lané avec celle-ci, ait perduré sous différentes formes à travers toute son histoire et qu'aujourd'hui encore il en départage les clans épistémologiques ? Le débat entre ce que Wilhem Dilthey (1927:204-56) appelait lui-même les approches explicative et compréhensive n'est pas nouveau en effet et, depuis l'émancipation simultanée au XVIIe siècle de la méthode scientifique et de l'objet humain hors du tronc commun du discours théologico-philosophique, a connu de nombreux avatars. À vrai dire, chaque génération a eu ses protagonistes et lancé ses propres hérauts à l'assaut des arguments de l'adversaire. De Schleiermacher à Wilfred Cantwell Smith (Gusdorf 1988), on ne compte plus ceux qui ont revendiqué contre positivisme et structuralisme de tout acabit la prégnance d'une dimension existentielle dans l'intelligence du phénomène religieux. Et de Karl Marx à Edmund Leach, on ne compte plus ceux qui leur ont répondu. La dispute entre Heidegger et Carnap, celle entre Ricoeur et Lévi-Strauss (Ricoeur 1969; Lévi-Strauss 1963:628-53) ou entre Durand et Greimas (Durand 1979:85-114; 1984a:42-61; Greimas 1966:56-58) martèlent de loin en loin l'irréductibilité du problème et l'impossibilité de le trancher dans un sens ou dans l'autre.

L'entêtement mutuel à s'insurger contre l'élision ou l'introduction de la «subjectivité»[1] dans l'étude du phénomène religieux a emprunté trop de légitimations philosophiques différentes pour qu'il s'agisse du simple avatar d'un système de pensée quelconque, d'une conséquence logique d'une problématique philosophique particulière destinée à s'évanouir dès lors que, par un effet de mode, elle sortirait de l'actualité. Le débat est trop

---

Les notes et références concernant ce chapitre se trouvent aux pages 206-208.

ancien pour qu'il ne soit pas lié à la constitution de l'objet sinon à la structure même de la discipline. Il y a ici un souci d'une autre nature auquel il faut acquiescer pour lui-même. Or, la définition de la religion que nous proposerons ici veut faire son lit de cette problématique. C'est-à-dire qu'elle refuse de choisir et préfère remonter jusqu'à la bifurcation instauratrice de ce débat pour en penser le lieu. Elle entend donc proposer une définition du phénomène religieux qui éclaire et dénoue le débat par sa source, et permette de penser ensemble le formalisme de l'un et la requête existentielle de l'autre.

Pour ce faire, il nous faudra considérer la religion comme appartenant essentiellement à la sphère du langage et la concevoir comme *une fonction de celui-ci*. Non pas, bien entendu, le langage limité à la sphère verbale et écrite des «langues naturelles», mais le langage conçu dans son amplitude maximale comme un système de sens. Les productions de l'esprit, les délires de l'imagination symbolique ont en effet une forme assignable porteuse d'un sens. L'organisation spatiale d'une cathédrale, par exemple, a une signification; la séquence des gestes du prêtre qui y préside un culte a aussi une signification, et sans doute la même que l'architecture où il officie. C'est dire que la forme du signifié est détachable de son support expressif et peut être Prolégomènes à une définition sémiotique analysée pour elle-même. En sorte que les moyens sémiotiques mis en oeuvre pour analyser les structures d'une oeuvre écrite en langues naturelles peuvent être rigoureusement les mêmes que ceux employés à l'étude de l'architecture, de la musique ou de la religion. Nous n'entendons pas ici mettre en oeuvre la sémiotique (Greimas 1966, 1970, 1979; Hjelmslev 1971a, 1971b) sur un objet concret mais faire jouer quelques-uns des concepts de l'épistémologie sémiotique pour éclairer le débat entre explication et compréhension, montrer le role de la religion dans le langage et proposer une définition conséquente de celle-ci.

Forme, substance et langage

La sémiotique distingue dans le langage une «forme» et une «substance». L'un et l'autre termes ne sont pas nouveaux. Mircea Eliade dans son *Traité d'histoire des religions* (1966:344) emploie pour désigner la classification et l'étude des formes symboliques le terme de morphologie. On sait aussi depuis Aristote que la forme est ce qui garantit l'identité et la permanence des êtres. La forme informe la plasticité d'une matière ou d'une substance et ce faisant, lui confère une identité. En revanche, il revient à la substance de manifester cette forme. Nulle forme donc qui ne soit manifestée par une substance; et nulle substance, en retour, qui apparaisse sans être «informée». L'un et l'autre se présupposent mutuellement.[2]

En sémiotique, ces termes ont reçu une définition opératoire. Dans une structure, appartient à la forme ce qui est invariant; par opposition à ce qui est variable et qui appartient à la substance. Prenons l'exemple de la voyelle /o/. Cette voyelle a une forme verbale stable et reconnaissable en dépit de ses innombrables prononciations. Un /o/ est un /o/ qu'il fût prononcé par une personne avec l'accent traînant de la région montréalaise ou avec celui, plus vif et pointu de la ville de Québec. Cette stabilité de la forme est garante de la possibilité de communiquer. Quant à l'accent fluctuant et changeant, il est toujours singulier, relève de la substance et s'oppose à la généralité de la forme. Il est une variable subordonnée à l'invariant de la forme. Si tant est que le signifiant soit ici seul concerné, comme dans notre exemple, la forme relève en linguistique de la phonologie; et la substance, elle, de la phonétique.

Or cette distinction forme/substance vaut également pour le signifié. Une substance sémantique est productrice de significations dans la mesure où elle a une forme. Soit par exemple la catégorie /haut/ vs /bas/ ou /mâle/ vs /femelle/ : ces deux termes catégoriels informent un axe sémantique. Ils organisent le continuum du sens et catégorisent le monde. Sans eux, une région de l'expérience resterait inarticulée et ne pourrait se nommer. Par sa forme, le langage a ainsi pour fonction de quadriller l'expérience et de l'organiser dans une vision du monde. La forme de ce quadrillage est stable et reconnaissable : elle constitue pour ainsi dire le lieu commun d'une culture, ce qui permet à ses membres de communiquer entre eux et de se comprendre. En ce sens, elle est objective et objectivable.

Quant à la substance de ce quadrillage, elle constitue au contraire quelque chose d'absolument singulier. Elle est l'expérience du monde elle-même, la charge inextricable de réalité et d'affectivité à laquelle renvoient les mots. Les choses ne nous sont jamais indifférentes; le temps n'est pas homogène; l'espace n'est pas partout le même. Choses, temps et espace sont porteurs de prégnances affectives qui les dilatent et les contractent dans notre perception. C'est ainsi que le temps à attendre l'objet aimé est plus long que celui passé auprès de lui. Tel intermezzo de Brahms a un air, c'est-à-dire une forme reconnaissable. Mais l'interprétation qui le manifeste, elle, est toujours singulière. Elle a eu lieu une seule fois. Et rien, ni personne ne pourra ressusciter la subtile coloration qu'elle a prise ce jour-là de la fin d'un amour, d'un crépuscule hivernal ou de la naissance d'un fils. Car c'est là ce qui relève de la substance. L'étude formelle de cet intermezzo ne saurait donc restituer l'expérience sans laquelle cet air ne serait qu'une coquille vide. Inversement, la paraphrase émue de cet instant ne saurait rendre compte de la rigueur esthétique de sa construction. Il ne suffit pas d'être ému pour émouvoir.

C'est pourquoi cette intériorité de la signification qui est revendiquée pour elle-même par de nombreux analystes, tant en sciences de la religion qu'en études littéraires, relève d'une aperception de la substance du signifié. Tandis que, à l'opposé, les approches structurales et plus formalisantes qui traitent la signification comme des jeux d'emboîtement reposent plutôt sur la forme de celui-ci (Pierre 1986 : 107). Le sémantisme dynamique des images auquel, par exemple, réfère Gilbert Durand (1984 :

410-43) est mobilité herméneutique de la substance. Et la singularité de celle-ci procède de ce que, comme Héraclite le disait, le flux du devenir n'est jamais pareil à lui-même. La «compréhension» est alors docilité à ce flux et participation au sémantisme de la substance. On comprend le texte en le prolongeant jusqu'à nous par la paraphrase herméneutique comme il en serait d'un canal dont on allongerait le lit pour en être irrigué et baigné. L'herméneutique est création continue.

À l'inverse, l'approche «explicative» d'un Lévi-Strauss manie des formes syntaxiques vides, délestées de leur charge existencielle et explore simplement leurs règles de concaténation.

L'inscription référentielle

Il faut pour assigner un nom à chaque chose, pour lui attribuer des déterminations et lui donner une forme sémantique, il faut, dis-je, un *cadre référentiel*.

Ce système de coordonnées peut aisément se comparer à un jeu de construction offert à l'ingéniosité d'un enfant pour créer des simulâcres d'objets et copier le monde. Il s'y trouve un nombre limité de pièces standardisées et assez élémentaires dont la combinaison plus ou moins élaborée permet l'organisation et la schématisation de l'expérience. Si tant est que cette boîte comporte un nombre illimité de pièces standardisées et réparties dans un petit nombre de catégories, elle constitue un «cadre référentiel».

Or le processus d'apprentissage à travers lequel passent les enfants à l'école repose toujours sur la mise en place de tels «cadres référentiels». On apprend à compter de 1 à X, puis on commence à additionner les chiffres et à les soustraire. L'ensemble des nombres entiers est de la sorte une boîte de pièces que les opérations arithmétiques permettent de combiner dans des constructions de plus en plus savantes. Et cette boîte de pièces nous permet d'affirmer qu'il y a là devant nous X objets, que ces objets se divisent eux-mêmes en X parties que l'on peut additionner, multiplier ou soustraire. Il y faut absolument ce «cadre référentiel»: il est préalable à toute organisation de l'expérience et à toute saisie des déterminations du monde.

Il s'agit certes là d'un cadre référentiel assez spécialisé puisque les seules déterminations qu'on peut y assigner aux objets sont numériques. Mais nous savons qu'il y en a d'autres. L'arithmétique est en effet une excroissance des prédicats numéraux et ordinaux de la langue. Comme telle, on peut la considérer comme une spécialisation ou un sous-ensemble du «cadre référentiel» global que constittue le langage. Les choses, le monde, n'ont par conséquent de déterminations, quelles qu'elles soient, que pour autant qu'elles sont quadrillées par ce cadre référentiel qui permet de les décrire.

Représentons-nous une surface blanche couverte de taches noires irrégulières. Et nous dirons : Quelle que soit l'image qui en résulte, je puis toujours en donner la description approximative qu'il me plaira, en couvrant la surface d'un filet fin adéquat à mailles carrées et dire de chaque carré qu'il est blanc ou noir. De cette manière j'aurais donné une forme unifiée à la description de la surface. Cette forme est arbitraire, car j'aurais pu tout aussi bien me servir d'un filet à mailles triangulaires ou hexagonales et obtenir un résultat non moins satisfaisant. Il se peut que la description au moyen d'un filet à mailles triangulaires eût été plus simple : c'est-à-dire que nous pourrions décrire la surface à l'aide d'un filet plus grossier à mailles triangulaires avec plus d'exactitude qu'à l'aide d'un filet plus fin à mailles carrées (ou inversement), etc. À ces différents filets correspondent différents systèmes de la description de l'univers. La mécanique détermine une forme de la description de l'univers, du fait qu'elle dit : Toutes les propositions de la description de l'univers doivent être obtenues d'une manière donnée à partir d'un nombre de propositions données — les axiomes mécanistes. Par là elle fournit les pierres pour la construction de l'édifice de la science et elle dit : quelque édifice que tu veuilles construire, il faudra que ce soit toujours d'une manière quelconque, au moyen de ces pierres-là et seulement au moyen de ces dernières (Wittgenstein 1972 :163-64).

Songeons par exemple à la grille des méridiens et des parallèles : ce quadrillage géométrique de l'espace, rendu nécessaire par le développement de la navigation et l'expansion des empires coloniaux européens, a permis d'attribuer des références à tous les points de l'espace géographique, de les situer les uns par rapport aux autres et de tracer par conséquent les parcours entre ces points. De praxis aléatoire soumise aux fluctuations imprévisibles des choses, à l'opacité vertigineuse d'un inconnu que l'on tente désespérément d'interpréter par des systèmes divinatoires ou de se concilier par des sacrifices aux divinités qui incarnent et assument en quelque sorte l'arbitraire du monde, la navigation devient une praxologie.[3] Les continents ont alors une forme, les côtes un pourtour et un dessin, les villes un emplacement par le fait de ce système référentiel. Autrement, tout n'est que substance désorganisée, sans feu ni lieu, mer des Sargasses et shéol où le grand serpent primordial abolit convulsivement entre ses anneaux la possibilité de s'orienter et de distinguer.

Or ce que l'on peut dire de l'organisation géographique vaut aussi pour la culture dans son ensemble. Objets, gestes, valeurs de la culture n'ont de consistance et de signification qu'en tant qu'une forme y est discernable. Notre expérience émerge en effet de l'indistinction de la substance, d'une immersion sans reste dans la matrice de l'expérience et dans le tourbillon des impressions que si elle trouve dans le langage un point d'appui, une trame qui en supporte et fixe le dessin. Il y faut d'abord la césure d'une ligne, d'une discontinuité pour qu'apparaissent l'avant et l'après, l'en-deçà et l'au-delà. Car la césure d'une ligne, une seule, l'irruption d'une seule discontinuité dans la belle unanimité blanche de l'innocence originelle suffit pour que le temps et l'espace commencent de se délier et de s'organiser. En psychogénèse, la distance par rapport au sein, le délai dans la satisfaction du premier besoin introduit d'emblée une discontinuité et par là même, une forme dans l'expérience primordiale. Tout le reste en découlera. La psychanalyse l'a bien montré : il suffit que ce premier noeud soit mal assuré pour que le tissage, plus tard, au moindre choc, se défasse et que le sujet sombre dans la psychose.

Le cadre référentiel fonde donc l'identité de toutes choses dans la culture, assure la captation de la substance dans une forme. Il cadastre la substance et lui assigne des déterminations. Il permet de dire des choses sur le monde. Il est le fondement. Rien ne saurait être sans lui ou hors de lui. S'évanouit-il que tout le reste disparaît avec lui et se disperse dans l'abîme vague. Tous les récits de genèse, toutes les cosmogonies passent par cette mise en place d'un cadre référentiel.

L'amarrage référentiel

Ce cadre référentiel est un dispositif classificatoire qui permet de répartir les différences. Encore faut-il que ce cadre soit stable. Non seulement dans son organisation interne — une règle qui ne change pas avec les cas qu'elle traite — mais dans sa localisation externe. Il faut que le cadre référentiel soit amarré au monde qu'il prétend quadriller. Que dire en effet d'une grille qui serait vagabonde et instable, qui errerait librement sur la disposition des objets, désignant alternativement le même objet par une coordonnée et par une autre : que le mot pomme, par exemple, soit indifféremment un fruit, un livre saint et une façon de se moucher ?

La métrique ne saurait donc être complètement idéale. Il faut qu'elle s'incarne dans un corps qu'elle promeut à l'exemplarité. Le mètre, par exemple, fut longtemps une mesure en platine placée dans un coffre à Paris à l'abri des variations de température et d'humidité pour rester intact, et pour que tous les autres, le mètre de bois de l'instituteur, le mètre de corde du géomètre, puissent unanimement y référer et identiquement en procéder. Il faut que le cadre référentiel soit amarré au monde, qu'il y ait en lui un point fixe et permanent planté en quelque sorte dans la substance et depuis lequel le cadastre puisse ensuite se déployer sur la substance.

C'est pourquoi il y a dans tout cadre référentiel une décision instauratrice d'une marque sur le monde où forme et substance s'intersectent. Le système des méridiens est ordonné au point 0 de Greenwich. Ce point serait-il nomade et mobile que toutes les coordonnées se mettraient du même coup à osciller avec lui. Villes, côtes et détroits ne seraient plus localisables.

C'est pourquoi aussi la fondation d'une construction commence invariablement par le dépôt d'une première pierre — celle qu'on appelle la «pierre d'angle» — ou la mise en terre d'un piquet d'arpentage qui marque l'intersection du plan idéal et de l'espace concret d'érection. Cette première pierre posée, ce premier piquet fiché, le plan est en quelque sorte épinglé à la surface du monde. Tout le reste pourra en découler. L'arbitraire du premier geste fondateur assumé, il n'y a plus après que la nécessité formelle d'un plan qui se réalise peu à peu dans la matière et dicte l'emplacement des matériaux. Toutes les entreprises de création d'un monde et par conséquent de déploiement d'un cadre référentiel commencent ainsi par la fondation d'un centre. Après quoi, les quatres points cardinaux peuvent être disposés et avec eux le séjour des ancêtres, ceux des bons et des mauvais esprits; après quoi on peut décider ce qui est bon et mauvais, ce qui est comestible et ce qui ne l'est pas, quand les semailles doivent être mises en terre, quand les hommes doivent partir à la chasse, etc. Le récit de la réception du décalogue par Moïse sur le Sinaï est intaurateur non seulement d'un point de référence privilégié dans la cartographie, mais il est fondateur aussi de toute la socialité et de l'être-ensemble des tribus hébraïques rassemblées en Canaan.

Toutes les religions comportent ainsi un centre, une origine - objet hors du commun, événement singulier et extraordinaire, initiative d'un dieu — qui ponctue la monotonie et l'homogénéité de la substance pour y inscrire une première discontinuité à partir de laquelle le cadre référentiel pourra se déployer.

> Au commencement, Dieu créa le ciel et la terre. Or la terre était vague et vide, les ténèbres couvraient l'abîme, l'esprit de Dieu planait sur les eaux.
> Dieu dit: «Que la lumière soit» et la lumière fut. Dieu vit que la lumière était bonne, et Dieu sépara la lumière et les ténèbres.
> Dieu appela la lumière «jour» et les ténèbres «nuit». Il y eut un soir et il y eut un matin : premier jour (Gen. 1 :2-5).

Sans ce point 0 qui amarre le référentiel au monde, on ne saurait rien dire du monde; ou plutôt toutes choses et leur contraire pourraient être dites simultanément.[4]

> «Malheureusement, la moutarde n'est pas un oiseau», fit remarquer Alice.
> «Exact, comme d'habitude, reconnut la Duchesse; quel plaisir que de vous entendre expliquer tout d'une manière si limpide!»
> «C'est, je *pense*, un minéral», dit Alice.
> «Bien sûr que c'en est un, confirma la Duchesse, qui semblait disposée à approuver tout ce que disait Alice. Il y a une grande mine de moutarde, tout près d'ici. Et la morale de ceci, c'est: «Il ne faut jamais juger les gens sur la *mine*.»

«Oh! je sais maintenant! s'écria Alice, qui n'avait pas prêté attention à cette dernière phrase. C'est un végétal. Cela n'en a pas l'air, mais c'en est un.»

«Je suis tout à fait de votre avis», répondit la Duchesse; «et la morale de ceci, c'est: Soyez ce que vous voudriez avoir l'air d'être; ou, pour parler plus simplement: Ne vous imaginez pas être différente de ce qu'il eût pu sembler à autrui que vous fussiez ou eussiez pu être en restant identique à ce que vous fûtes sans jamais paraître autre que vous n'étiez avant d'être devenue ce que vous êtes» (Carroll 1979:168-69).

L'événementialité du fondement

Il ne saurait donc y avoir de structure, c'est-à-dire de conjonction entre une forme et une substance sans ce point immobile et primitif.

Or cette singularité dont dépend le cadre référentiel et le fondement de toute signification, est elle-même le fruit d'un pur acte d'assertion. Il ne tient pas sa légitimité d'autre chose que de l'événementialité. Rien dans ce point n'est nécessaire; tout en lui est accidentiel. C'est pourquoi nous appelons «événement» cette intersection de la forme et de la substance. À la question: Qu'est-ce qui fonde ce fondement? Qu'est-ce qui légitime le fait que le méridien X passe par Montréal? Nous devons donc répondre: Rien. Rien si ce n'est l'ordonnancement du cadre référentiel lui-même et le fait que le point 0 passe par Greenwitch en Grande-Bretagne. Mais que ce point passe par Greenwitch, cela, rien ne saurait le justifier absolument. Il s'agit d'un acte politique complètement arbitraire. Il fut posé là par la puissance coloniale anglaise pour des raisons tout à fait contingentes qui ressortissent davantage d'une conjoncture politique transitoire où la Grande Bretagne avait la suprématie des mers, pouvait se considérer comme le centre du monde et par conséquent comme le pôle référentiel; que d'une essence[5] nécessaire et éternelle dont les humains auraient eu la révélation en quelque commencement du monde. Le fondement est sans fondement. Les mots ne tiennent aux choses que par le fil ténu d'un éclat de rire. Tout le langage, toute la signification se découpe ainsi sur fond d'abîme.

C'est pourquoi cette prise de conscience est invariablement un moment d'angoisse: nous y sommes acculés à notre finitude et à notre mortalité, c'est-à-dire au sans fondement. Les signes de notre vie ne sont pas éternels et notre identité ouvre sur le vide. Le Même est adossé à l'Autre. Au-delà de cet «événement», ou mieux, quelque part en lui, par le fait de sa singularité, de son absence de déterminations, s'ouvre l'impensable de l'origine.

C'est ainsi qu'il faut penser l'événement comme une singularité, un point d'intersection entre la forme et la substance, limitrophe de l'identité et de l'altérité. L'événement ou la singularité de ma naissance, par exemple, marque le moment où ma présence s'est exhaussée depuis la béance de l'absence. C'est-à-dire que je viens d'un lieu où je n'étais pas; je me reçois de l'Autre. J'existe pour autant qu'à travers la singularité de mon origine, la différence afflue jusqu'à moi.

Il en est de même dans la religion : le fondement est événementiel. Les fondateurs de Rome ont suivi un taureau et ont fait le voeu de le sacrifier et d'édifier la ville à l'endroit où l'animal s'arrêterait pour brouter l'herbe. Le devin africain qui jette en l'air une poignée de cailloux et lit ensuite la volonté des ancêtres dans leur disposition sur le sol fonde le sens sur un événement aléatoire. Dans tous les cas, c'est une parole reposant sur la contingence. C'est pourquoi cette parole qui fonde, manque à sa propre origine. C'est pourquoi dans la tradition juive, par exemple, le temple de Jérusalem, centre du monde par excellence et amarrage du cadre référentiel, est posé sur le shéol.

L'essence de la religion : le rapport à l'événement

Nous dirons que le «mystique» est l'essence du discours religieux. Non pas le mysticisme au sens où nous entendrions cette relation privilégiée au divin mise en oeuvre par des individus d'exception. Nous voulons plutôt dire «l'élément mystique» présent dans les discours religieux de toute nature — qu'il soit juridique, cosmologique, liturgique ou technologique — dès lors qu'ils sont rapportés à leur origine et à leur fondement; dès lors qu'en eux l'événement est problématisé. Cessent-t-ils de l'être que tous ces discours se sécularisent comme la modernité nous en offre l'exemple. Le caractère anonyme ou général du point de vue observant ne vise d'ailleurs rien moins que la banalisation de «l'événement». Le gain formel et opératoire de ce discours se fait alors par la mise entre parenthèses de la question ontologique solidaire de cet «événement».

Inversement, on peut dire que «l'élément mystique» est amovible de tous ces discours. Il n'est pas une aire de discours; il est l'événement du langage, c'est-à-dire la problématisation et le rapport à son fondement[6] mystique se déleste si volontiers de la phraséologie théologique ou du lyrisme poétique pour confiner au silence. C'est pourquoi aussi une expérience religieuse infiniment fugace et transversale à tous les discours perdure au 20ᵉ siècle en dépit de l'écrasante domination des rationalismes de toutes sortes (Ménard et Miquel 1988; Eliade 1973:197-232; 1971: 222-48; 1986:15-42; Simoneau 1982).

Or ce concept de «mystique» nous vient paradoxalement de l'oeuvre de Ludwig Wittgenstein[7] et de l'un des fameux énoncés qui concluent le *Tractatus Logico-philosophicus*. «Ce qui est mystique, affirme-t-il, ce n'est pas comment est le monde, mais le fait qu'il est» (Wittgenstein 1972:173).

Par là, Wittgenstein délimite le domaine qui relève des sciences naturelles, commises comme elles le sont à l'intelligence du «comment est le monde», c'est-à-dire à «ce qui se dit», et celui, indicible, de la mystique qui contemple «ce qui se montre».

> 6.522 — Il y a assurément de l'inexprimable. Celui-ci se *montre*, il est l'élément mystique (Wittgenstein 1972:176-77).

Le sens, la signification peut se dire; mais l'événement de la signification, lui, en tant qu'il la met en place et en constitue le fondement, ne peut être dit. Il est sans déterminations. Il est le fondement sans fondement. Le «mystique» relève alors de l'indicible parce qu'il concerne le fondement du langage. Le langage servant de cadre référentiel à la nomination de toutes choses, il ne saurait lui-même être pensé. Il est impossible de sortir du langage pour le penser plus originairement. Il n'y a pas de méta-langage. Tout au plus, arrivons-nous à longer l'impossibilité de sortir du langage.

Ce qui se dit appartient alors aux énoncés du langage; il se tient à l'intérieur de sa clôture. Or «ce qui se montre», institue cette clôture. Il ne saurait donc être décrit par le langage puisqu'il est présupposé par le langage. La forme appartient à l'ordre du dicible, mais l'événement se montre. «Ce qui se montre», c'est le pur acte d'assertion qui dispose le cadre référentiel du langage et permet de dire le monde. «Ce qui se montre», c'est l'amarrage événementiel de la forme à sa substance.

Prétendre donc, comme nous le faisons, que «l'élément mystique» est l'essence de la religion, c'est dire que la religion est essentiellement tenue dans le langage d'assumer le «ce qui se montre». Elle est indifférente à «ce qui se dit» — cosmologie, anthropologie, psychologie. Elle n'est qu'accessoirement liée à ces aires de discours et peut à la limite s'en défaire complètement quand elle confine, comme chez Jean de la Croix, au silence et au ravissement. La cosmologie moderne est autonome et n'a nulle besoin de faire intervenir des considérations mythologiques pour comprendre l'univers. Mais il suffit qu'elle pose à nouveau la question du fondement ou de l'origine pour qu'elle redevienne une contemplation de «ce qui se montre» et retrouve des accents religieux.[8]

La religion a donc pour fonction de gérer ce que le cadre référentiel — c'est-à-dire le fondement — a de sans fondement. La religion est postée sur la limite et assure le voisinage du Même avec l'Autre. Sentinelle de la totalité, elle est gardienne de tous les seuils; elle assure le passage rituel entre les états. Elle reçoit les nouveaux-nés depuis le non-lieu d'où ils nous arrivent; elle reconduit les morts jusqu'aux frontières de la totalité. Elle fait transiter les êtres de l'enfance à l'âge adulte, de l'état profane à l'état sacré par-dessus l'abîme de l'informe et de l'inommé.

> 6.5 — Le sentiment du monde en tant que totalité constitue l'élément mystique (Wittgenstein 1972:173).

Avoir le sentiment du monde en tant que totalité limitée signifie donc que nous en pensons l'«événement». La totalité limitée du monde est la clôture du cadre référentiel: avoir le sentiment de cette totalité c'est entendre ce que ce cadre référentiel a d'arbitraire et de contingent, et ce faisant, le découper sur le fond de son altérité. La religion est donc vigie sur les limites de la totalité. Poste entre chiens et loups, sur les murailles de la cité et sur le parvis de la nuit, aux confins de l'empire, elle écoute distraitement les bruits animés de la ville derrière elle, l'éclat des voix et des jeux dont ce soir elle est séparée. Mais tournée aussi vers la nuit qui s'ouvre autour de la ville, elle prête oreille à sa rumeur et essaie d'en déchiffrer le murmure.

Événement et singularité

Voilà des métaphores pour dire le lieu et le temps de l'événement: gardien des seuils, vigie, passeur entre des rives et en même temps foyer, centre du monde, pierre d'angle. Toutes ces métaphores tournent autour d'une singularité, c'est-à-dire une grandeur morphologique qui n'a pas de déterminations.

Or, sont aussi hiérophaniques dans l'expérience, les êtres singuliers. Les commencements et les fins sont des moments singuliers: ils bornent la temporalité. Les moments intersticiels qui coupent dans le continuum de l'existence et en délimitent les cycles en sont aussi. Les centres sont des singularités: là où on érige le sanctuaire, le temple, là où passe l'*axis mundi*. La périphérie est une singularité. Des jumeaux, un albinos, un animal difforme, une très haute montagne se singularisent aussi parce qu'ils sont hors catégorie, parce que leur condition d'exception défie en quelque sorte le système classificatoire et l'empêche de leur assigner une place. Mary Douglas a bien montré dans son essai sur la souillure (Douglas 1981) que le tabou procédait simplement d'une incapacité de situer un être dans l'une ou l'autre des cases du découpage culturel. Le pangolin, par exemple, est frappé d'un interdit alimentaire chez les Lele.

> Par son existence, il contredit toutes les catégories animales courantes. Il possède des écailles comme les poissons, mais il grimpe sur les arbres. La femelle ressemble plutôt à une lézarde pondeuse d'oeufs qu'à une mammifère, mais elle allaite ses petits. Ce qui est plus significatif encore, c'est que, contrairement aux autres petits mammifères, elle donne naissance à un seul petit à la fois (Douglas 1981:180).

Le pangolin est donc non seulement un animal «singulier» mais une singularité dans le système de cases.

Mary Douglas toutefois n'a pas montré *le rôle instaurateur de cette singularité par rapport au dispositif classificatoire du cadre référentiel*. En étant limitrophe, la singularité institue la clôture de la totalité. Elle est «l'événement du cadre référentiel»: «ce qui ne peut être dit» parce que hors catégories ou antérieure à celles-ci. Spatialement, cette singularité est au centre et à la périphérie. Elle instaure un centre en déployant le cadre référentiel autour de son événement, et marque la limite ou la circonférence de ce même cadre en montrant ce qui dans l'événement échappe aussi au cadre et le nie. Au centre, l'événement sert de source au cadre référentiel; à la périphérie, il lui sert de repoussoir. Dans les deux cas et de façon complémentaire, il l'instaure comme totalité. Le cadre référentiel commence et finit avec l'événement de cette singularité. Il s'en reçoit et s'y perd.

Conclusion

Fondée sur l'étude d'une telle singularité indicible et ineffable, la position de notre discipline ne manque pas d'être paradoxale à son tour. En tant que science, notre discipline prétend au général; or, son objet est absolument singulier. Et, comme chacun sait, il ne peut y avoir de science du singulier. Tels sont du moins les termes du dilemme que pose Wittgenstein.

> 6.53 — La juste méthode de philosophie serait en somme la suivante : ne rien dire sinon ce qui se peut dire, donc les propositions des sciences de la nature — donc quelque chose qui n'a rien à voir avec la philosophie — et puis chaque fois qu'un autre voudrait dire quelque chose de métaphysique, lui démontrer qu'il n'a pas donné de signification à certains signes dans ses propositions. Cette méthode ne serait pas satisfaisante pour l'autre — il n'aurait pas le sentiment que nous lui enseignons de la philosophie — mais *elle* serait la seule rigoureusement juste.
>
> 6.54 — Mes propositions sont élucidantes à partir de ce fait que celui qui me comprend les reconnaît à la fin pour des non-sens, si, passant par elles, — sur elles — par-dessus elles, il est monté pour en sortir.
>
> Il faut qu'il surmonte ces propositions; alors il acquiert une juste vision du monde.
>
> 7. — Ce dont on ne peut parler il faut le taire (Wittgenstein 1972 : 176).

Mais ce dilemme est-il incontournable? Wittgenstein soutient au cours de cette première période de sa vie que ce qui saurait être «dit» relève exclusivement des sciences de la nature. C'était la période de sa vie où il fondait avec Bertrand Russell le positivisme logique et donnait naissance au célèbre cercle de Vienne.

Mais Wittgenstein s'est très tôt rendu compte que beaucoup de choses n'appartenant pas aux sciences de la nature s'entêtaient à être dites et ne semblaient pas pour autant dépourvues de sens. Il s'est intéressé alors à ce qu'il a appelé, dans la deuxième période de sa vie intellectuelle, les «jeux de langage». Wittgenstein découvre que le langage a une consistance pour lui-même et que beaucoup de choses dans notre aperception du monde et dans notre façon de poser les problèmes en sciences de la nature en dépendent.

Ce faisant, entre le silence et le discours des sciences de la nature, seul autorisé à dire ce qui se dit, il ouvre une troisième voie dans laquelle il engagera la philosophie analytique.

Nous avons fait la même chose. Fût-elle dépendante d'une singularité indicible, la religion parle. Elle est sens et événement du sens : c'est-à-dire que la singularité sur laquelle se fonde la religion en bordant le langage regarde à la fois dedans et dehors, en tant qu'elle regarde au dehors du langage, elle est expérience de l'ineffable, expérience du «ce qui se montre». De cette expérience, il n'est pas possible de parler. Une science ici est impossible. Mais regarde-t-elle à l'intérieur du langage que la religion appartient alors au domaine dicible du Même. Comme telle, par son appartenance au langage, elle est alors chose de science. Elle laisse des traces tangibles — rituels, architectures, statuaire — qui sont analysables avec des moyens sémiotiques. Le totem, par exemple, est un poteau qui supporte les chapiteaux du cadre référentiel. À ce titre, il constitue l'événement du sens. Mais il porte aussi une inscription, c'est-à-dire un sens où cosmologie, taxinomie animale et généalogie familiale s'entrecoupent et tissent l'étoffe de la culture. Or cet entrelac de sens est analysable : l'anthropologie l'a suffisamment montré.

C'est là une première façon de répondre au paradoxe constitutif de notre discipline. Mais cette réponse n'est pas complètement satisfaisante en ceci que, séparant le sens de son événement, elle oscille entre le mutisme de la mystique et un sens séculier que rien ne distingue essentiellement du sens qu'on retrouve ailleurs dans le langage que ce fût, par exemple, dans un roman ou dans une pièce de théâtre. Certains analystes ont conclu en effet à une absence de spécificité sémiotique du langage religieux.[9] Or, eu égard à la nécessité qu'il y a pour nous de définir la religion, une telle conclusion est embarrassante. Cette première approche est certes capable, comme elle l'a bien montré, de produire d'importants dividendes analytiques et d'éclairer le phénomène religieux, mais elle ne peut le définir. Une large partie de la recherche s'en contentera volontiers, mais ce ne saurait être là toute la recherche; en tout cas, pas la recherche portée par un souci fondationnel. Il faut donc penser ensemble le sens et son événement. Mais comment?

Cette singularité, avons-nous dit, n'a pas de déterminations intrinsèques, mais comporte tout de même une fonction par rapport au sens. Et cette fonction peut être analysée.[10] Dans la mesure, en effet, où la religion est à la fois sens et événement, dans la mesure où elle est solidaire de la singularité, elle assure le voisinage de l'identité et de l'altérité dans une structure : nous l'avons déjà dit. Mais cet adossement de l'identité et de l'altérité dans la singularité signifie qu'elle ouvre et ferme à la fois la structure. Elle ferme la structure sur son identité et l'ouvre sur son altérité. *La singularité est ainsi postée au lieu précis de la structure où intervient la morphogénèse de celle-ci.* Elle ne conduit pas la morphogénèse : elle ne détermine pas un contenu d'identité et d'altérité. Les mécanismes en sont ailleurs. Elle se contente ici de désigner à l'attention l'événementialité du sens, c'est-à-dire le fait que le sens est soumis lui aussi au devenir.

On sait, par exemple, l'importance de la catégorie du «pur» et de «l'impur» dans l'étude de la religion. Mais qu'est-ce qu'être pur? C'est n'être que soi, replié sur soi-même et coïncider exactement, sans surplus ni déficit, avec le site de son être. Nulle étrangeté dans cette pureté, nulle contamination de la différence : la structure est recluse sur elle-même. Or, la religion ici assure cette fermeture de la béance. Elle la légitime. La parole de Dieu est ici dictée de la Loi; le Sacré est stase apollinienne.

L'impureté, au contraire, procède d'une structure vacante, complètement aliénée à elle-même où on entre et on sort sans s'essuyer les pieds. Le dehors traverse librement le dedans et finit par s'y abolir. La religion assure alors l'ouverture de la béance. Elle la légitime encore, mais autrement : elle invoque cette fois, à travers l'ivresse ou la transe, la parole d'un autre dieu, Dyonisos.

Placée donc à la jointure de l'altérité et de l'identité, la religion est solidaire du pur et de l'impur en assurant tour à tour la fermeture et l'ouverture de la structure. C'est dire qu'elle a pour fonction spécifique dans le langage d'en *gérer la béance*. Elle donne à voir et/ou détourne de ce qui «se montre» dans l'événement du sens.

Pour une part, la religion réconcilie donc avec l'altérité qui insiste à travers notre finitude. Elle laisse dans la lumière ce que le fondement a de sans fondement, prévient la forclusion de l'identité sur elle-même et le travestissement conséquent de l'altérité en symptôme.

Mais la religion tient aussi l'identité en sa sauvegarde. L'amarrage du cadre référentiel au monde ne tenant sa légitimité que du pur acte d'assertion d'un sujet individuel ou collectif, la religion lui permet d'en occulter l'arbitraire derrière une temporalité originelle et essentielle. Elle transforme de la sorte la contingence en nécessité. Le sans-fondement du fondement est rattrapé dans un fondement anté-historique qui encercle l'abîme d'une boucle plus lointaine, plus retorse et plus imperméable au devenir. L'abîme devient montagne. L'identité a alors une assise et peut livrer d'autre guerre que celle de sa légitimité. L'identité a une caution transcendante qui lui permet d'avancer sans continuellement se retourner pour assurer sa provenance. Le père a précédé le fils et lui témoigne, par son désir de lui, d'une légitimité par-delà sa naissance. Le fils peut alors consacrer ses forces à l'édification de la cité. Il a pour appuyer le levier de sa vie l'assise du fondement.

Notes

1 Il faut entendre ici le terme «subjectivité» dans une acception beaucoup plus large qu'en psychologie. À vrai dire, la «subjectivité» désigne ici «l'instance énonciative» (Heidegger 1964).

2 D'un point de vue ontologique, la forme présuppose la substance. D'un point de vue fonctionnel, la substance présuppose la forme. Nous avons là deux niveaux épistémologiques distincts dont il faut déplier l'enchevêtrement et distinguer les enjeux pour éviter de créer de faux problèmes.

3 Précisons que le système des méridiens n'a pas surgi *ex nihilo*, là où il n'y avait rien, pour suppléer à une absence totale de système de coordonnées. Ces systèmes divinatoires dont nous avons parlé n'étaient pas dénués de tout fondement empirique et de valeur opératoire. Preuve en est bien que la navigation n'a pas commencé avec le système des méridiens. Mais disons que le cadre référentiel qu'il constituait s'est

avéré de moins en moins fonctionnel à mesure que les horizons du monde qu'il avait charge de quadriller ont été repoussés par la curiosité des explorateurs et l'appétit de gain des marchands.
4 La psychose n'est en effet rien d'autre que cette dérive du langage sur le monde. Il y a certes un cadre référentiel — c'est pourquoi il est possible au paranoïaque de discourir et de discourir même assez systématiquement — mais ce discours est délirant et dénué de fondement référentiel parce que privé d'amarrage.
5 Faut-il ajouter pour achever de nous convaincre que la marine française, rivale de la marine britannique dans sa tentative de quadriller le monde et d'étendre partout son réseau d'influence, faisait passer le méridien 0 par Paris?
6 C'est pourquoi, il est impensable qu'une société puisse être entièrement et essentiellement sécularisée.
7 Ludwig Wittgenstein est fondateur du positivisme logique et du célèbre Cercle de Vienne.
8 Nous sommes particulièrement frappé à cet égard de l'actuelle floraison des discours de physiciens sur la place de Dieu dans la cosmologie (Delumeau et al. 1989; Sibony 1989; Trinh Xuan Thuan 1989).
9 C'est ce que nous confiait Jean Delorme, exégète reconnu et praticien de la méthode sémiotique sur les textes bibliques, au cours d'une conversation en 1983.
10 Cette fonction est même susceptible de recevoir un traitement formel. Le structuralisme s'y intéresse. On sait par ailleurs qu'un domaine des mathématiques qu'on appelle la topologie s'y intéresse aussi. Il est évidemment impossible dans le cadre d'un tel article d'exposer avec quelque minutie l'une ou l'autre de ces méthodes de traitement formel des singularités. Il suffit de souligner qu'elles existent (Thom 1978).

Références

Carrol, Lewis. 1979. *Tout Alice.* Paris : Garnier-Flammarion.
Delumeau, Jean. 1989. *Le savant et la foi. Des scientifiques s'expriment.* Paris : Flammarion.
Dilthey, Wilhem. 1927. *Gesammelte Schriften.* Bd. VII. Leipzig.
Douglas, Mary. 1981. *De la souillure.* Paris : François Maspero.
Durand, Gilbert. 1979. «Les chats, les rats et les structuralistes». Dans *Figures mythiques et visages de l'oeuvre,* 85-114. Paris : Berg.
———. 1984a. *L'imagination symbolique.* Paris : PUF.
———. 1984b. *Les structures anthropologiques de l'imaginaire.* Paris : Dunod.
Eliade, Mircea. 1968. *Traité d'histoire des religions.* Paris : Payot.
———. 1971. *La nostalgie des origines.* Paris : Gallimard.
———. 1973. *Aspects du mythe.* Paris : Gallimard.
———. 1986. *Briser le toit de la maison.* Paris : Gallimard.
Greimas, Algirdas-Julian. 1966. *Sémantique structurale.* Paris : Larousse.
———. 1970. *Du sens.* Paris : Seuil.
——— et Courtès, J. 1979. *Sémiotique. Dictionnaire raisonné de la théorie du langage.* Paris : Hachette.
Gusdorf, Georges. 1988. *Les origines de l'herméneutique.* Paris : Payot.
Hjelmslev, Louis. 1971a. *Prolégomènes à une théorie du langage.* Paris : Minuit.
———. 1971b. *Essais linguistiques.* Paris : Minuit.
Heidegger, Martin. 1964. *Lettre sur l'humanisme.* Paris : Aubier-Montaigne.

Lévi-Strauss, Claude. 1963. «Réponses à quelques questions». *Esprit* 11 :628-53.
Ménard, G. et C. Miquel. 1988. *Les ruses de la technique*. Montréal : Boréal.
Pierre, Jacques. 1986. «Herméneutique». In *Dictionnaire raisonné de la théorie du langage*. Tome 2, 107. Paris : Hachette.
Ricoeur, Paul. 1969. *Le conflit des interprétations*. Paris : Seuil.
Sibony, Daniel. 1989. *Entre dire et faire*. Paris : Grasset.
Simoneau, J.-P. 1982. *Sécularisation et religions politiques*. La Haye/New-York : Mouton.
Thom, Ren. 1978. *Morphogénèse et imaginaire*. Paris : Lettres modernes.
Trinh, Xuan Thuan. 1989. *La mélodie secrète*. Paris : Fayard.
Wittgenstein, Ludwig. 1972. *Tractatus logico-philosophicus*. Paris : Gallimard.

CHAPTER 17

W. C. Smith, Hermeneutics, and the Subject-Object Syndrome

John C. Robertson, Jr.

Introduction

One of our leading historians of religions, Wilfred Cantwell Smith, has happily ventured far beyond the chronicling and describing of the world's religious traditions to advance some rather bold and arresting ideas concerning the nature of religious belief itself and its study, ideas of philosophical and theological significance. In this paper, I wish to consider, if only in a very preliminary and programmatic way, some of his key ideas against the background of certain post-Enlightenment philosophical developments, especially in hermeneutic theory.

Relativization of Subject-Object Schema

The great philosopher A. N. Whitehead, who was as aware of the complexity of things as anyone, once shrewdly suggested that we should, in considering matters of import, first seek simplicity and then distrust it. He averred that the venerable and seemingly self-evident (in the West at least) substance-accident schema was one such useful but finally dubious simplification. It is obviously useful for certain practical purposes to think in terms of "vacuous actualities" upon which one can hang incidental adjectives and predicates, but it is misleading to think that such a way of construing things finally suffices as a metaphysical description of the nature of reality itself.[1]

I wish to suggest for the purposes of this discussion that the subject-object schema is another such simplification.[2] The terms "subject" and "object" and "subjectivity" and "objectivity" are of obvious and proven worth for some purposes. But I am arguing here that we will do well to distrust their capacity finally to penetrate and render intelligible our

---

Notes and references for this chapter appear on pages 222-23.

deepest and most profound experiences, perhaps, especially, our religious experiences.

Some historical perspective will lend support to the argument, for it turns out that the subject-object schema itself, as we understand it, is fairly recent. Although most of us assume, most, if not all of the time, that the interactions between human beings and their surroundings have always implied the subject-object relation and that our ancestors have understood the terms "subject" and "object" to mean either exactly or approximately what we ordinarily mean by them today, such happens not to be the case. That the assumption is so natural to us, however, is testimony to the influence of the Enlightenment, more precisely to the success of the philosophical revolution generated by Descartes and Kant. For if all languages, at least all Western languages, have implied a distinction between subjects and objects and, if all philosophy, in the West anyhow, has thought of being itself in these terms, it is nevertheless the case that people have not always understood these terms, subject and object, as we do today. As a matter of fact, our understanding of the terms exactly inverts their meanings in the antecedent tradition. The history of these terms has been traced for us by Rudolf Eucken in his *Main Currents of Modern Thought* (1912), and subsequently the matter has been analyzed penetratingly by Martin Heidegger in *What is a Thing?* (1967). The medievals, both Eucken and Heidegger observe, employed "subjective" and "objective" as technical terms and in opposing senses. The word "*subjectum*" meant "that with regard to which all the remaining things first determine themselves as such" (Heidegger 1967: 105). In other words, it meant then about what we mean now by "subject matter": i.e., that about which we are thinking and speaking, that which is the controlling centre of our discourse. And, by contrast, "the word '*objectum*' denoted what one casts before (oneself) in mere fantasy: e.g. when one imagines a mountain of gold" (Heidegger 1967: 105). But with the celebrated "Copernican revolution" in Western consciousness—focussed as it was first in Descartes and then in Kant—a mutation in the meanings of the terms occurred. Now the experiencing, imagining, thinking ego becomes the subject and that which the ego experiences, thinks, imagines, has opinions and beliefs about becomes the object. This shift in meaning, while anticipated earlier and elsewhere, observes Eucken, becomes complete only when:

> the words were assimilated into the German language (through the Wolffian school of philosophy). At first the terms *subjektivisch* and *objektivisch* ... were not used outside this school. It was the Kantian philosophy which first brought them into common use, and at the beginning of the nineteenth century they were widely employed. It was entirely owing to German influence that their new meanings became general, and at first they were frequently regarded as strange.[3]

"It was Coleridge, that great popularizer of the Kantian transcendental philosophy in England," adds James Brown, "who first introduced his fellow countrymen to the terms 'subjective' and 'objective' in their new (i.e., current) meanings" (Brown 1962:19, parenthesis added).

In light of the above, it is not altogether surprising that in the post-Kantian era—especially in the English-speaking world — pride of place has been accorded to objects in the subject-object relation, and the word "objective" has become eulogistic and the word "subjective" derogatory. In a way this is strange, inasmuch as for Kant objects were largely constituted by the creative activity of the subject and thus were dependent upon it, and Heidegger was only being Kantian when he later maintained that objectivity is a "project" or achievement of existing *Dasein*: something the self does or achieves. This side of Kant, however, has not been the side that has been most noticed in the English-speaking world. What has been more influential has been Kant's insistence that the indispensable condition of real knowledge is *anshauung*—sensuous intuition or, if you prefer, sense experience of external objects. And Kant's summary phrase "concepts without percepts are empty" has become well known to and generally accepted by the literate public, while numerous hardboiled philosophers have moved from regarding claims to knowledge not based on sense data as nonsensical (in a technical and in principle tolerant sense), to regarding them simply as nonsense (as in "damned nonsense!").

Kant, however, was less narrow and more sophisticated than this. Despite the impression an initiate might gain from the English-speaking reception of Kant, the justly venerated philosopher wrote more than one *critique*, and in the preface of even the first he wrote these all too neglected lines: "Human reason has this peculiar fate that in one species of its knowledge it is burdened by questions which, as prescribed by the very nature of reason itself, it is not able to ignore, but which, as transcending all its powers, it is also not able to answer" (1933:7).

In other words, in Kant's view, human experience is a mansion of *many* rooms, and the human spirit may be thought to intimate dimensions and spheres of being which quite transcend that sphere studied by the natural sciences, even if these intimations do not quite qualify as knowledge in the most rigorous sense. More specifically, Kant recognized that in addition to the drive for scientific knowledge, human life also has to do with morality, aesthetics, and religion, and he tried to give due place in his comprehensive philosophy to them all.

Kant's Subjectivization of Morality, Aesthetics, and Religion

If, however, objects and objectivity dominate Kant's account of cognition, the subject and subjectivity dominate his accounts of morality, aesthetics, and religion. It is well known that Kant's account of morality intentionally and strictly prescinds from empirical questions and seeks to answer the question "What ought I to do?" entirely from an analysis of reason itself.

Thus Kant is a formalist in ethics. He contends, in the *Fundamental Principles of the Metaphysics of Morals* (*Grundlegung*, 2d ed., 1785:13)[4] that an action's moral significance is constituted "not in the purpose to be attained by it, but in the maxim in accordance with which it is decided upon." This is so, Kant reasons, because success in attaining ends is not wholly within one's own control, hence one's actions cannot be judged according to their effects. What can be judged, however, are one's intentions; one can measure the maxims or controlling principles of an action against the requirements of the moral law. One does this by asking whether one could willingly universalize the subjective principle of one's own actions as a law for everyone, thus applying the test of the famed "categorical imperative." The upshot is a morality grounded entirely in the moral being of the moral agent or subject, that is, an autonomous ethic.

Kant's account of aesthetics is less familiar than his account of morality. Kant takes up the topic of aesthetics systematically in his third critique, *The Critique of Judgement*. There he seeks to exhibit (among several things) the presence in human existence of an aesthetic capacity, or sense of beauty, quite distinct from the human moral and theoretical capacities. And consistent with his approach in the two previous critiques, he tries to provide a "transcendental justification" for aesthetics; that is, he seeks to demonstrate the a priori conditions of the possibility of our experiencing beauty. He does not think that one can find such a justification in the presence of an aesthetic *rule* or objective *principle*; if there were such, then disputes about beauty could be decisively settled in a way that they in fact are not. Kant cannot believe, however, that aesthetics is simply a matter of empirical generalization as to what most people just happen to call beautiful. Rather he argues, it is rooted in a "subjective principle," a subjective but very real and universal feeling. It is *subjective*, Kant allows, because in the aesthetic experience nothing is actually known of the object claimed to be beautiful; all that is known is that there is a feeling of a very distinct pleasure, the pleasure of beauty. But this feeling of beauty is quite real; Kant argues that it is firmly rooted in the mutual suitability of the representation of the object and our faculties of knowledge. It coheres naturally with the free play of human imagination and understanding. Hence, Kant's position is that the principle of aesthetic judgment falls in between being either a rigorous rational adherence to or application of a stateable rule or a merely accidental agreement about matters of taste.

In making the above argument, Kant powerfully challenges the hegemony of objectivism and scientific knowledge; aesthetic experience, like moral experience, is a distinct domain of life. But there is this to note: Kant's vindication of the aesthetic experience is won at the very high price of denying to aesthetic experience any *cognitive* import. For, to repeat, aesthetic experience imparts no knowledge whatsoever of the object. Nor, for that matter, does it — as *aesthetic* experience — have any interest in receiving information about its object from any other source. This is why, by the way, Kant has a reasoned and strong preference for *natural* rather than *artistic* beauty. In the former case there is no danger of corrupting the aesthetic experience through consideration of non-aesthetic ends, whereas in the latter case there is; for example, in contemplating a beautiful building one may also consider the *practical* purposes the building is meant to serve, whereas no one would be bothered by such concerns while contemplating a sunset or snowflake.

Kant's subjectivization of aesthetics coheres with the basic dualism he posits in distinguishing so radically between the order of nature and the order of spirit; that is, the order of nature is mechanistically determined, whereas in the order of spirit freedom prevails. How the two orders could be mutually related is a major problem in Kant, a problem explored in *The Critique of Judgement* but perhaps never entirely solved to Kant's own satisfaction or that of his more critical followers. Simply to put aesthetics and morality on one side of a divide and cognition on the other is never entirely satisfying.

This dualism, with the subjectivization of aesthetics which it allows and indeed promotes, was in any case obviously anticipated by the scientists and some of the most notable philosophers (the British Empiricists) of the period just prior to Kant. For example, John Locke, influenced by Newton, is famous for distinguishing between primary and secondary qualities. (Descartes had done so even earlier.) The latter refer to such things as colours, sounds, tastes, odours, texture. The former refer to such things as magnitude, shape, and motion. The primary qualities are what science studies, and the relationship between them is what constitutes the natural order. This order, however, for all its self-sufficiency, is somehow experienced by our minds, an event which generates in our minds sensations which are, in the last analysis, qualities of the mind itself. These sensations, which are called the secondary qualities, are then projected onto the external order of nature. Thus the illusion is created that these qualities, which are in fact products of the mind, actually belong to the external world. In other words, the external world, the world of objects if you like, is interpreted to have qualities which are really not its own.

Whitehead satirizes the resulting situation by remarking that:

> (On this philosophy) nature gets credit which should in truth be reserved for ourselves; the rose for its scent; the nightingale for his song; and the sun for his radiance. The poets are entirely mistaken. They should address their lyrics to themselves, and should turn them into odes of self-congratulation on the excellency of the human mind. Nature is a dull affair, soundless, scentless, colourless; merely the hurrying of material, endlessly, meaninglessly (1962:55, parentheses added).

I have called attention to the subjectivization of morality and aesthetics in Kant. Very brief mention can and should be made of his treatment of religion. The mention can be brief because Kant's treatment of religion is of a piece with his treatment of morality. For Kant, religion is essentially, as someone has said, "only morality tinged with emotion." Kant distinguishes, in effect, as did much liberal theology after him, between the kernel and the husk of religion, the *kernel* being the experience of the moral law (as a divine command). The *husk*, on the other hand, consists of the external trappings and packaging of the kernel: the Biblical stories, the ecclesiastical institutions, the sacraments, the cultic practices, and so on. These things have religious value, not in themselves, but only as they evoke within us a sincere, inward response. That response is nothing more or less than obedience to the moral law, which is no external thing but is the very law of our own being. Revelation and positive religion, properly understood, do not present us with anything new; rather they *re-present* to us, in a colourful, dramatic, and forceful way—and therefore in a way that appeals to the imagination—the moral law that has been given to us from the beginning, simply by virtue of our natures as rational human beings. This could even be said of the central figure of Christianity, Jesus. Jesus is not thought by Kant to give us new knowledge or to do anything for us which we could not do for ourselves. Jesus only serves, in the last analysis, as the occasion for our renewed self-knowledge and renewed effort to obey the moral law within (as Jesus himself is portrayed as doing).

Gadamer's Critique of Kant and His Own Proposal

Whitehead likens philosophical reflection to "the flight of an aeroplane. It starts from the ground of particular observation; it makes a flight in the thin air of imaginative generalization; and it again lands for renewed observation rendered acute by rational interpretation" (Whitehead 1960:7). When Kant's accounts of human experience are brought back to the ground of actual practice, how does it go? Only relatively well, answers H. G. Gadamer, the chief theoretician of contemporary hermeneutical philosophy. Gadamer applauds Kant for challenging the reduction of human spirituality to the mere reception of sense data. He applauds Kant's attempt to vindicate the moral, religious, and aesthetic dimensions of life. However, Gadamer is less impressed with Kant's performance than his intention. Kant's account of moral, aesthetic, and religious experience, in a word, avoids the bear of objectivism (the hegemony of natural science) only to fall under the spell of the witch of subjectivism. Kant saves these domains of experience, only at the price of overly subjectivizing them.

Gadamer does not discuss Kant's related accounts of morality and religion in any great detail, or at least as extensively as he does Kant's account of aesthetics.[5] This is partly, no doubt, because of Gadamer's own special interests. It could also be, however, because Gadamer sees the same problem illustrated in each domain. In any case, however, Gadamer pays Kant's aesthetic theory the compliment of seeing it as decisive for the development of eighteenth-century and indeed subsequent aesthetic theory. But he regards this influence as ambiguous at best, simply because it does not correspond to human experience: to the experience of art, first of all, but then also just to human experience itself. "Aesthetic consciousness," Gadamer writes, is an "abstraction" from what actually happens when we encounter a work of art (1989:81). (By "abstraction" Gadamer means not that it is wrong, but that it is only partially right: it captures something but leaves out other, important things, hence falsifying the complete, concrete reality.)

Gadamer writes: "it cannot be doubted that the great ages in the history of art were those in which people without any aesthetic consiousness and without our concept of 'art' surrounded themselves with creations whose function in religion or secular life could be understood by everyone and which gave no one solely aesthetic pleasure" (1989:81).

In this, Gadamer is challenging Kant's "purification" of aesthetics. Historically, people have not had such pure aesthetic experiences when they produced and experienced great works of art. Art for them has been characteristically a focus of multiple dimensions of life. Complex causes have been served and complex truths have been revealed in actual paintings, music, sculpture, poetry.

Of course, Kant would admit that this has been so *with art*. This is, in fact, precisely the reason that Kant privileges natural over artistic beauty: natural beauty is purer, being freer of other interests. Gadamer, however, follows Hegel in challenging Kant's privileging of nature over art. The moral interest in natural beauty that Kant had portrayed so enthusiastically, Gadamer writes, "retreats behind the self-encounter of man in works of art. In Hegel's magnificent *Aesthetics* natural beauty exists only as a 'reflection of spirit'" (1989:58). In other words, *contra* Kant, the experience of beauty in nature is coloured by, dependent on, and inferior to the experience of beauty in art. The experience of beauty in nature is derivative and that of art basic. And the experience of art is less pure than Kant would have it.

Nor is this "impure" character of our experience of art merely an historical accident, on Gadamer's account. Gadamer, drawing on the phenomenological findings of the early Heidegger, argues against the primacy of pure perception of anything and in favour of the necessarily mixed basic perception of all things (Gadamer 1989:90ff.). One does not simply experience, one experiences something. And one does not simply experience something, one always, in the first instance, anyhow, experiences what one experiences *as this or that*. In other words, no one simply experiences, say, a patch of colour; one experiences a silver coin or a red bird. One is able to experience, say, a mere patch of silver or red through a subsequent and fairly sophisticated act of abstraction. Similarly, one never, in the first instance, experiences "pure," unmixed beauty; one experiences something that one understands to be this, and not that, as beautiful. Neither the work of art nor, derivatively, nature is "only an empty form, a mere nodal point in the possible variety of aesthetic experiences," a mere occasion for a subjective aesthetic experience (Gadamer, 1989:95). The work of art, and derivatively, nature encounters us as a something, and our experience of it is constituted by how we understand it, what we take it to be: "understanding belongs to the encounter" (Gadamer 1989:100). As a something, it is a something in and for itself and not just for us, and as such it demands to be taken account of. And this is just what Kant's subjectivized aesthetics, for all its purity and elegance, fails adequately to do. When one truly encounters (or is encountered by!) a work of art, it simply will not do to think of the work, the "aesthetic object," as a mere occasion for the exercising of one's own wonderful potential for beauty (almost as if one encountered the object and enjoyed oneself). One will not do justice at all to our experience of art *as it actually happens* if one thinks of it in this way.

As an alternative way of understanding this experience, Gadamer proposes that we consider the phenomenon of play (Gadamer 1989:101-34). If this seems a strange model in terms of which to understand the experience of art, contrary to Gadamer's manifest determination to overcome the limitations of the subjectification of aesthetics, this is likely because we are still inclined to think of playing itself as a merely subjective behaviour or disposition. Drawing upon the phenomenological investigations of Johann Huizinga, however, Gadamer argues that play is a relational and reciprocal event; play is not *simply* a matter of inner attitude (even if is *also* this). Nor is it even primarily something which we *do*, although play does involve our activity, often our strenuous activity. Play rather, in a mysterious way, has its own identity, essence, dynamics, and tendencies—in a word, its own life. We may begin by simply playing, but then we become drawn into the game. We say we are playing a game, but it is just as true to say that, after awhile, the game is playing us, or playing itself out, in and through us. We quickly lose our initial status as the subjects of the play; the play exercises its *own* agency. In play there is a to-and-fro, backward and forward, tug and pull movement; there is a dance-like rhythm. Gadamer writes, "The structure of play absorbs the player into itself, and thus frees him from the burden of taking the initiative, which constitutes the actual strain of existence" (1989:105). There is a sense, he continues to explain, in which "the game masters the players," in which the game is the true subject, charming the players and holding them in its spell, "draw(ing) (them) into play and keep(ing) (them) there" (1989:106). Thus "(t)he player experiences the game as a reality that surpasses him" (1989:109). This, *precisely this*, is what makes play, although often strenuous and demanding, essentially renewing and refreshing and thus re-creative. The ego, with its will, while not entirely set aside or suppressed, is nevertheless "sublated" (*aufgehoben*) in play; it is transformed: by being taken *out* of itself and taken *up* into something that transcends itself.

Now it is this game phenomenon, Gadamer contends, which serves as the needed paradigm for understanding the human experience of art. The work of art does not lie before us passively as an *object* to be manipulated and studied. (One thinks of Wordsworth's lines about the "meddling intellect" that "mis-shapes the beauteous forms of things . . . murder[ing] to dissect," etc.). Nor do we stand before the work of art in splendid solitude with our merely *subjective* experiences. Of course, there is a sense in which, say, a painting, is an *object*; it can be weighed, measured, transported, analyzed. And when I stand before the painting, an observer will notice that I am a *subject* with subjective reactions. But these are "abstractions" from the experience itself.

Nor as abstractions are they entirely false. They do, however, hide more than they reveal. In the concrete and authentic experience of art, the art work emphatically does *not* passively lie at our disposal. Nor does it confront us as an ink blot might. Rather, the art work confronts with an integrity of its own. Thus, standing over against us, it challenges our customary ways of seeing and understanding ourselves, our neighbours, and our world. It tears us out of our everyday context. It presents us with its own way of understanding and construing the world. Of course, we may or may not choose to make this construal of the world our own. In a true encounter with a work of art, however, we must somehow at least take account of what is presented. Nor will we ever be *entirely* the same after such an encounter.

One will recall that our original concern was with experience in general and the suitability of the subject-object schema in rendering it. I have drawn attention to Gadamer's account of the experience of art, primarily because it is a dominant topic in his own work. Although he does attend to other dimensions and domains of experience, for example, the moral and religious, it is in discussing the experience of art that he is most expansive. Whatever all his reasons, his procedure has certain advantages. If aesthetic experience, which so many since Kant regard as entirely subjective, actually can be shown to transcend the subjective-objective polarity altogether, then the gate is open for challenging the hegemony of the subjective-objective schema in other areas as well. The aptness of the comparison of art to play supports this challenge.

W. C. Smith on the Study of Faith Expressions

Now let us turn from Kant and Gadamer to consider some of W. C. Smith's thoughts concerning religious faith. Smith's negative comments on "objectivism" are the easiest to understand. His *The Meaning and End of Religion* (1964) is a sustained, radical, and arresting critique of the very word "religion," as an unwarranted, unhelpful, and indeed misleading reification of the word "religious" which properly qualifies persons in the act of faith-ing. Elsewhere and repeatedly Smith argues against scholars of religion who study their subject matter at arm's length, so to speak, and philosophers of religion who make the double mistake of assuming that certain detached statements of belief can capture the essence of religion and that the meaning and truth of such statements can be impersonally determined. In short, Smith argues against the assumption of the omnicompetence of the natural scientific orientation in disciplines such as Religious Studies which, in effect, have to do with persons not things (e.g., 1977:30).

Similarly, he argues against the confusion of faith and belief. Faith is a deeply personal act; "belief," which once, like "faith" meant "holding dear" or pledging allegiance, has now been debased into meaning something like imagining or having an opinion about. For this reason, Smith contends, it is a blunder to treat religious utterances as though they were beliefs in this modern sense of the word (e.g., 1977:52ff. and 1979:viii and 105ff.). In addition to treating highly personal utterances as though they were quasi-scientific statements, such objectifying procedures tend to abstract religious language from the dynamics of historical contexts and processes (1981:28). One can understand religious language and behaviour, if at all, only by seeing them in connection with persons in historical communities (1981:58). If one fails to do this, one not only errs intellectually but also runs the risk of antisocial and destructive behaviour (1981:58).

However, if Smith is far removed from a positivistic objectification of religion, how close is he to a Kant-like *subjectification* of personal faith? Uncomfortably close, it might well seem.

In *The Meaning and End of Religion*, Smith argues that the important thing is not "what one believes but that one has been granted the gift of believing" (1964:124). One's "religiousness" is the main thing (1964:125). One is reminded of the U. S. President Eisenhower's comment (often criticized by theologians) that he wanted only people in his government who believed, though he did not care much in what. That is to say, it is not always clear that for Smith faith has an "object," or aims at something or someone. Many statements could be cited to suggest that it does not, on his account. Faith, he tells us, is a "quality of ... life" (1964:125; see also 1979:12 and 129). It is "something in and of itself, not explicitly directed to an object," he writes (characterizing the New Testament position apparently with approval) (1977:90). Faith is a (sort of self-contained) virtue like courage (1977:93). Faith is not about an *object* of consciousness; it is itself a *form* of consciousness (1981:93). "Religious life is at heart a matter not of creed but of character and conduct," he continues (1981:145).

Perhaps the pages that most put one in mind of Kant on aesthetics come in the first chapter of *Towards a World Theology* (1981). There one finds Smith's fascinating account of the circulation of the custom of using prayer beads and holiday greeting cards from culture to culture. Roman Catholics learned to use rosary beads in about 1000 A. D. from Muslims, who in turn had learned the custom from the Hindus. Moreover, certain stories, doctrines (devil, hell, heaven, etc.) and practices (asceticism) have similarly circulated, Smith tells us. This circulation phenomenon, Smith suggests, might well encourage one to prescind from the content of the stories and doctrines as things to be believed in favour of using them rather as instruments of faith, or put differently, as occasions for exercising one's capacity for piety. One recalls Schleiermacher speaking of "striking up the music of one's religiousness" (and Barth's scornful retort!). Does this not seem to suggest a subjectification of religion that is the exact counterpart to Kant's subjectification of aesthetics?

Before we get very deep into *Towards a World Theology*, however, we find Smith explicitly denying "the proposition that the (only) alternative to objective is the subjective" (1981:59). Smith suggests a *third alternative*: "I would submit that in addition to the subjective ... and to the objective ... there is a *third position*, which subsumes both of these and goes beyond them ... I call it corporate critical self-consciousness" (1981:59, emphasis added).

Smith defines this "corporate critical self-consciousness" as knowledge from the standpoints of both observers and participants (1981:59). For example, one — or perhaps a team of Hindu and non-Hindu scholars — would strive for an account of, say, Hinduism that would be sufficiently comprehensive, even-handed, nuanced, sensitive, and sophisticated to do justice to the experiences of both those faithfully participating in the Hindu tradition *and* those who critically observe it from without, that is, of both insiders and outsiders (1981:66). Such an effort would take us "forward to a larger vision" than that provided by the blinkered and one-eyed approaches so dominant in Religious Studies currently (1981:70).

There is, then, no doubt that Smith wishes, in such going "forward," to go beyond the old subjective-objective opposition. Nor is there room for significant doubt that he does in fact succeed in doing this. At least he succeeds in transcending the disjunction of *either* subjective *or* objective in favour of an inclusive both ... and.

Another Possibility

While I do not wish to detract in the least from the nobility and ingenuity of this proposal of Smith's, I do suggest that there are resources in Smith's writings for yet another way of transcending the subjective-objective schema, a way more radical and profound than the one explicitly proposed by Smith. This would be a way that goes beyond the opposition in question by sublating it and thereby moving on to a higher level.

What I have in mind is this. In addition to the many passages in the Smith *corpus* which support a subjectivistic account of religion, there are other passages which suggest the possibility of what one might call a dialogical account. By the former I mean an account according to which personal faith is an interior affair and by the latter an account according to which personal faith is relational. I have already cited some of the many passages in Smith that illustrate and support the former account. I wish now to draw attention to a few of the many that do the same for the latter account.

In *The Meaning and End of Religion*, Smith says: "To be a participant in a religious movement is to recognize that that movement *points to something or someone beyond itself*" (1964:118, emphasis added). He continues: "If we would comprehend (religious people) we must look not at their religion but at the universe, so far as possible through their eyes" (1964:125).

Now I am quite aware that Smith is emphatically opposed to reducing religious faith to the having of opinions about states of affairs. Nevertheless, it is one thing to correct an over-intellectualization or a falsely conceived intellectualization of faith, and entirely another to empty faith, to make faith out to be something entirely non-cognitive or, if one prefers, non-intuitive or non-apprehending. Sometimes one is not clear about Smith's position on this matter. But it would certainly seem that the visual metaphor in the sentence quoted just above implies some sort of apprehension of "something" and thus some sort of relationship to "it." After all, one does not ordinarily just see or look; one sees someone or something or else looks for him, her, or it. The visual metaphor is used in various forms, by Smith, in many places. (It contrasts with the idea that faith is only an inward quality, like courage, for example). Some examples: faith is described as an insight (1977:79), a "recognition, insight, the capacity to discern" (1977:79), a "seeing the point (of a man dying on a cross)" (1977:79, parenthesis added), a "seeing that life and the universe do indeed have a point—a cosmic point; and that man can be grasped by it and be transformed" (1979:133). Faith involves "insight and response" (1979:159). Further: "To understand the faith of Buddhists, one must not look at something called Buddhism. Rather one must look at the world, as far as possible, through Buddhist eyes" (1981:47).

Now my suggestion, in conclusion, is this. In addition to combining and including subjective and objective accounts of religious phenomena, as Smith urges, there is also the possibility of transcending the subject-object schema altogether in what I have called "dialogue." This is certainly not to negate or even minimize Smith's proposal. It is, however, to say that we can and should go beyond it—and to do so in a way for which there are grounds, even if underdeveloped, in Smith himself.

Human faith-ing and the traditions thereby generated, can surely be studied in many different ways. But just as surely, one must surely admit that one has not done justice to religious texts, events, or persons—one's "subject matter"—until one lets them say something to one about "something."

On the wall in front of me just now there is a copy of a Mathias Grunewald painting "The Crucifixion": John the Baptist points a long finger at the figure on the cross; in the background are the words "I must decrease and he must increase." To be sure, one could validly study John in any number of "objectifying" ways. One also could allow John to trigger one's own subjective, inward processes. But one finally, I believe, does justice to John only by attending not to John but to the one to whom John points. And then one finds that the mission of *that* person was to point to and to represent a "Reality" beyond himself, that within which we all, it is claimed, "live, move and have our being." One could, and scholars do, focus on Jesus as an object of study of one sort or another. But Christians themselves will insist that such study reaches its term only when something like this happens:

> As we come to Jesus and seek to learn from him, we discover some strange effects he has upon us. He will not "stay put," at arm's length. We may try to hold him "out there" and speculate about him—then suddenly and somehow, the relationship changes and *he* becomes the inspector and judge and assessor of *our* existence.... We inquire of him about his opinions and teachings ... then, suddenly and somehow, this relationship of inquiry is turned about and he becomes "the way, the truth, and the life" for *us*. We look to him as exemplar—then discover that he is pointing us past himself to God, with the demand that we put God's kingdom and his righteousness above all else in life and death. (We) discover that he is confronting us with (God's gift and summons) (Outler, 1989:49).

I have quoted a Christian's testimony. One finds similar testimony from Buddhists, Muslims, Hindus, et. al.: do not look *at* me but *with* me, and attend to what I see and say and not to me and my seeing and saying.

To be sure, dialogue cannot have as its condition a prior commitment or agreement to walk the same path as one's dialogue partner. But it does require a willingness to let the other speak to one, to address one, to hear something new and perhaps even disorienting from the other, to allow the other to put one at risk. And, if the testimony quoted above is at all to be trusted and if Gadamer's phenomenology of dialogue is at all adequate, then such openness will lead one into a (game-like) situation concerning which the language of "subjective" and "objective" is only a partially valid "abstraction." The terms are neither totally adequate for faith itself nor for the in-depth study of faith and its expressions.

Conclusion

At the risk of anti-climax, I wish to suggest that, if this essay is at all persuasive, one could conclude that further comparative work of Gadamer and Smith would be useful. Hermeneutical philosophy might well help make more explicit and cogent Smith's deepest intentions; Smith's historical work would provide an empirical touchstone and storehouse of illustration for philosophical theory. It is a virtue of Smith's, I find, that his work is more philosophical than that of most historians and, of course, much more historical than that of most philosophers, and therefore richly rewards close study by both.

Notes

1 The schema fails to do justice to the processive and relational character of actual entities, Whitehead contended. As the etymology of the word itself suggests, "substance" implies an identity complete and unchanging beneath the process of becoming. And "accident" seems to miss the truth that relationships and contexts enter into the very constitution of a thing (Whitehead 1962:53ff. and 115ff.).
2 Whitehead also mistrusted it; he tried, awkwardly and unsuccessfully perhaps, to correct the defects of "subject" by introducing the word and idea "superject" (Whitehead 1962:149).
3 Quoted by James Brown 1962:19.
4 Quoted in W. H. Walsh's article on Kant in: Edwards (1967: vol. 3, 317).
5 See, however, Gadamer (1989:143; 1987:189-202; and 349-60).

References

Brown, James. 1962. *Kierkegaard, Heidegger, Buber, and Barth: Subject and Object in Modern Theology*. New York: Collier.

Gadamer, Hans-Georg. 1987. *Gesammelte Werke: Neuere Philosophie II*. Tübingen: J. C. B. Mohr (Paul Siebeck).

———. 1989. *Truth and Method*. 2nd rev. ed. Translation revised by Joel Weinsheimer and Donald G. Marshall. New York: Crossroad.

Heidegger, Martin. 1967. *What Is a Thing?* Translated by W. B. Barton, Jr. and Vera Dentsch. Chicago: Henry Regnery.

———. 1977. *Basic Writings*, edited and introduced by David Farrell Krell. New York: Harper & Row.

Kant, Immanuel. 1933. *Critique of Pure Reason*. Translated by N. K. Smith. 2nd ed. London: Macmillan.

———. 1960. *Religion Within The Limits of Reason Alone*. Translated by Theodore M. Greene and Hoyt H. Hudson, with a new essay, by John R. Silber, "The Ethical Significance of Kant's *Religion*." New York: Harper and Brothers.

———. 1964. *Critique of Judgement*. Translated and introduced by J. H. Bernard. New York: Hafner.

Outler, Albert C. 1989. "Through Jesus Christ, Our Lord." In *Albert Outler, The Preacher*. Nashville: Abingdon Press.

Smith, Wilfred Cantwell. 1964. *The Meaning and End of Religion*. New York: Macmillan.

———. 1967. *Questions of Religious Truth*. New York: Charles Scribner's Sons.

———. 1977. *Belief and History*. Charlottesville, VA: University Press of Virginia.

———. 1979. *Faith and Belief*. Princeton, NJ: Princeton University Press.

———. 1981. *Towards a World Theology: Faith and the Comparative History of Religion*. London: Macmillan.

Walsh, W. H. 1967. Article on "Kant." In *The Encyclopedia of Philosophy*. Vol. 3. Paul Edwards, Editor-in-Chief. New York: Macmillan and The Free Press.

Whitehead, Alfred North. 1960. *Process and Reality: An Essay in Cosmology*. New York: Macmillan.

CHAPTER 18

In Search of an Open Concept of Religion

Jacques Waardenburg

Discussing the concept of religion among people interested in religion, for whom the word evokes something and has some subjective meaning, resembles discussing the concept of money among exchange dealers, the concept of power among politicians, or the concept of affection among lovers. How then can we distance ourselves from such experiences and, when doing research in the wide field of religion, conceptualize religion in such a way that it can become a subject of empirical research, a field in which various disciplines and approaches can be applied, leading to improved scholarly knowledge of it, that is to say, knowledge of general validity?

Many attempts have been made in pursuit of this aim. Since the eighteenth-century Enlightenment both in England and in Germany religion has been studied, analyzed, and reflected upon in many ways. Histories have been written of individual religions and of religion as such, starting from what were considered to be its primal forms. Comparisons between religious data have been made, both within a specific culture area and across different cultures. Social and other contexts have been taken into account, and the problem of the meaning of religious phenomena and religions has haunted generations of scholars.

Many attempts have been made to delineate religion, for instance, by stressing its connection with the transcendent realities about which the religions themselves speak, or by focussing on its sacred quality, or the experience it provides of something sacred, opposed to the secular qualitiy of life in modern societies. Innumerable attempts have been made to define religion. Mircea Eliade, in the line of Rudolf Otto and classical phenomenologists of religion, gave the concept a metaphysical and even ontological direction contrasting with the positivistic approaches, which

---

References for this chapter appear on pages 239-40.

he considered to be reductionist. And some twenty-five years ago, Wilfred Cantwell Smith proposed to replace it, arguing that the concept of religion does not provide an adequate framework or model to study religious matters. He presented his case eloquently, and his name figures as a kind of permanent reference in any discussion on the concept of religion, including this very conference.

Since the moment when religion became a subject of empirical investigation, different motivations and intentions have inspired this research, varying from the simple desire to control religion to the wish to be spiritually enriched, from realistic assessments of what religions have brought to mankind to projects of involving religions in attempts to improve the condition of humanity, in particular in the fields of justice and peace. Outside the realm of scholarship proper, scholarly findings have been used to support ideologies critical of or apologetic towards religion, or to provide a basis for ideological presentations of various religions. If knowledge leads to power, at least certain kinds of power, knowledge of religion and religions brings this power in its own way, if not to the scholars, then to those who use their knowledge either for better or for worse. Consequently, the current debate about the concept of religion is not as innocent as it may seem; knowledge and insight about religions and religion may serve the human quest for truth, but they may also veil truth when used ideologically.

When keeping to scholarly work and refraining from ideologization, the first rule is for us to be attentive to our data, be they texts, works of art, or direct observation of people. The ability to read, see, and observe correctly, and to question intelligently what has been read, seen, and observed is, in my view, the basic requirement in our field of studies. It should, however, be accompanied by an effort to interpret and to explain what has been read, seen, and observed, particularly in our field, its religious aspects or features. One way is to inquire about the meaning of these religious features in given contexts for the people concerned. The question is neither what such things mean to us "personally" nor what this meaning is when taken in isolation, but rather how to discover what these things meant or mean to the people concerned, within the society in which they live, and to interpret their expressions correctly when a choice of meanings present themselves. The reason why I stress so much the risk of ideological manipulation of religious matters is precisely that ideologies destroy the very ability to observe and interpret correctly what people "outside" the "ideological circle" mean when they express themselves. The present paper, pleading for an open concept of religion, is mainly concerned with this problem.

Another way is to inquire on a more theoretical level how and why sacralizations arise, religious meaning patterns develop, and religious systems function in human societies, for instance by making life bearable, providing it with meaning, and orienting it towards the future. We shall leave aside these more general questions in this paper.

For the most part I shall refer to Islam (with which I am most familiar) and ways of conceptualizing it as a religion. In the second part, I shall suggest that the principle of using what will be called an open concept of religion is not only fruitful in Islamic studies but can be applied to the study of other religious subjects, too. The conceptualization of religion which I propose, however, goes very much against current ways of representing religions, derived as they are, largely, from theological or philosophical schemes developed in the West, or from particular theories evolved in empirical disciplines such as history, sociology, and cultural anthropology, also developed in the West. Over against current conceptualizations we urgently need, for the sake of good scholarship, a conceptualization of religion which is not linked to a specifically Western kind of philosophy and a specifically Western kind of culture. It should promote accurate observation and correct interpretation of religious data and allow inquiries on a more theoretical level, without imposing foreign schemes of interpretation. It should serve interpretations of religious matters which are at worst less ethnocentric than most current ones and at best of universal validity.

The Case of Islam

When analyzing the ways in which different researchers of Islam have interpreted Islam as a religion, one cannot but be struck by their variety; it becomes less and less easy to recognize one common scholarly image of the religion of Islam. The differences can be explained in part by differences in disciplines, data studied, and questions raised. They are also due, however, to the different values and loyalties adhered to by the researchers themselves and the circles in which they move. A certain deconstruction of established scholarly images of Islam, which could also be applied to established Muslim images of it, is helpful in order to clear the way for fresh and innovating research. Taking this deconstruction of images for granted, we find ourselves confronted with the problem of conceptualization as soon as we refrain from applying the norms and values applied in earlier images, representations, and conceptualizations. How, then, should we represent Islam as a religion?

It has usually been assumed that what makes Islam a religion is its claim to be based, through the Quran as revealed *âyât* (verses, meaning also "signs," "symbols"), on revelation from beyond. This has been elaborated by Muslim *'ulamâ'* who have taken it to mean that Islam is the true religion as far as it is based on the true "roots" or bases of religion (*'usûl al-din*), the first two of which are the Quran and the *Sunna* (Tradition). From a detached and observing, scholarly point of view, however, it is more correct to say that it is the Muslims' *belief* in the Quran as revelation, and in Islam as the absolute religion, which makes it into a religion. In other words, Islam is not, without further ado, a religion in itself: scholarly speaking it is only a religion for those people who consider and believe it to be so in the present and have done so in the past. In other words, it is the interpretation, in particular the religious interpretation, which makes it into a religion.

This interpretation may be explicit, for instance when Muslims testify to their faith in the Quran as the Word of God, or express the belief that Islam is a "heavenly" or revealed religion. But it may also be latent, the acceptance of the religious claim of Islam being simply implied in the recognition of some religious authority which affirms Quran and Islam to be revealed. Anyone who accepts such an Islamic authority and does not deny this religious claim can be assumed to accept it as well. Nowadays there are many Muslims who basically consider Islam as a social system or an ideology, but who do not explicitly deny the authoritative statement that it is a religion, even a religion based on revelation. It will clarify the basic issues and the ensuing discussion if we can agree that, speaking in scholarly terms, it is subjective intentions which make certain entities into "religions." Such intentions can be explicit or implicit, of a more personal or a more social nature. However this may be, Islam is only a religion for those who hold it to be so.

It has also usually been assumed that religions are more or less specific entities which can be delineated from each other, have an impact on their believers, and have their own history. In fact, however, what are called religions in everyday speech appear from a detached, scholarly view as rather broad cultural traditions. Such religions sometimes refer to persons with inspired religious visions and religiously inspired actions (as Islam refers to Muhammad), but very often this origin is unknown or put in mythical terms (like many popular customs in different regions of the world of Islam). It is not the whole cultural tradition which is considered to be equally religious. Rather, within the overall cultural tradition certain specific elements are distinguished by being considered to carry an extra meaning which often has religious quality. Such elements are more than just ordinary facts: they function as signs or symbols capable of conveying particular meanings which the ordinary facts are not able to. They are of particular interest to us insofar as they can also convey religious meanings. Such elements remain part of the given cultural tradition as a whole and have an important function in it. Around such "religious," sacralized elements within the cultural tradition there tend to develop "sub-cultures" on a local level which possess their own communication networks; people are especially concerned with them, and institutions maintain and develop them. This has been the situation in all traditional Muslim societies and cultures where there has not yet been a clear separation between "religion" and "culture." Any conceptualization of religion must be able to take this form of religion into account.

Muslim religious leaders, scholars, and specialists will speak of certain of these religious elements as "the religion," "true Islam," about which they then develop ideas and a normative concept of how Islam should be practised and believed as a religion. But looking from a distance and with scholarly detachment one immediately sees the difference between this normative Islam and Islam as it is practised (*Islam vécu*), between the normative concept of religion of the Muslim *'ulamâ'* and the descriptive concept of religion encompassing everything that given Muslim communities consider to be part of their religion. In such descriptive accounts of practised Islam it is not possible to make a valid separation between the religious and non-religious or cultural elements in the life and practice of a Muslim community, or even a Muslim person. There are, moreover, considerable differences between Muslim communities and between individual Muslims. Certain more "religious" Muslims will tend to interpret the whole of life in spiritual or religious terms, according to which anything for them may possess a religious or spiritual meaning. For many other Muslims only certain elements in the given cultural tradition, for instance Quranic verses and ritual practices, have a clearly religious character and function as religious signs and symbols. Only those who have received a religious education and studied religion have a distinct concept of what Islam as a religion is, or rather, should be; to them it will always be a normative entity, since they have learned how Islam ought to be. Most other people, however, have no clear concept about it: they just practise. Our conceptualization of Islam as a religion should take into account this state of affairs.

What is to be called "religion" in Islam, then, is neither as well defined and simple nor as static as many handbooks written by Muslims and non-Muslims alike would have the reader believe. Not only is there the intricate connection between the religious and cultural aspects we have just alluded to, but reality is much less static than the books suggest. With the enormous changes in the cultural traditions of Muslim societies in the various culture areas of the Muslim world over the last hundred years, the religious "subcultures" of these cultural traditions have been forced to change considerably, too. Some of them, like the following of holy men and membership of certain *tarîqas*, have gone down. Others, like voluntary associations and certain fundamentalist and activist groups like the Muslim Brotherhood, have increased in number and prestige. Some of their representatives want to impose their religious views on society and the state as a whole, and develop from a religious subculture to a political power.

In this perspective, the study of Islam as a religion is largely the study of the religious elements of the great tradition as well as of the small cultural traditions of Muslim societies. Here particular attention must be paid to the way in which specific groups and persons at present or in the past have interpreted these elements and drawn conclusions from them for their social and political action. From this angle the proclamation of the Bâb and the self-manifestation of Bahâ Ullâh in the cultural traditions and the religious expectations of their time in nineteenth-century Iran are just as interesting as the recognition of the divine right of Shah Ismâ'îl at the beginning of the sixteenth and Khomeiny at the turn of the 1980s. And when we study *fiqh*, *kalâm*, or *tasawwuf* from this angle, it is the particular interpretations and applications, with their underlying religious visions and orientations, which are of interest. In order to notice the often subtle varieties, one should be thoroughly familiar both with the broad cultural tradition within which these Islamic religious sciences have developed and with their particular histories.

To summarize our argument up till now: Islam is only a religion and things are only religious in Islam for the simple reason that all Muslims or particular groups of Muslims consider them as such; the religious elements of Islam are distinguished by their particular sign and symbol character, but they are primarily part of a great or small tradition in Islam; around particular religious elements certain groups may assemble and develop religious subcultures with their own life and activities within the broader cultural tradition; the study of Islam as a religion is largely the study of the religious interpretations given of those elements of the tradition which have a sign and symbol character.

Islam as a Sign and Symbol System

In the foregoing, an outline has been given of the way I suggest that we should conceptualize Islam as a religion, in order to fulfill the scholarly prerequisites mentioned earlier. I would like to develop this further in the following six points, which may serve as a starting point for more detailed descriptive accounts:

1) We assume that Islam as a religion consists of an infinite number of elements (including Quran texts, *hadîths*, rituals, and so on) which function as units of one semantic system. With the help of these elements, Muslims can enter into a specific kind of discourse with each other, especially with regard to anything essential for social and personal life, where they seek to establish the appropriate norms and values. Given the system and the elements constituting it, Muslims of all times and places make up a sort of commonwealth. The religious elements constitute a kind of communication system, making communication between Muslims as Muslims, on the basis of Islam, possible – leading to an Islamic discourse.

2) Such an Islamic discourse operates with the help of the elements mentioned above, among which Quranic texts and *hadîths* have priority and enjoy a special authority. But many non-verbal elements, like common worship and ritual customs, also provide a framework of communication, too, as forms of symbolic communication.

3) Different problems may be discussed in different ways. When familiar problems arise, for instance, they can be discussed in terms of the well-known Islamic system, and solutions can be found on the pattern of earlier solutions to similar problems in the past. New problems, however,

present a challenge. They can be discussed sometimes in terms of the Islamic system and "Islamic" solutions can be proposed in this way, as for instance, Khomeiny did. But they can also be discussed in new terms, on the basis of a system different from the Islamic one. This was what Mustafa Kemal, for instance, did in Republican Turkey, basing his solutions on the principles of secularism and Turkish nationalism. A third possibility, which constitutes a sort of middle way, is to discuss new problems in terms which combine the Islamic and another more modern system. This was the method adopted, for instance, by Gamal ' Abd al-Nâsir in Egypt, who based his solutions largely on the principles of Arab socialism and Arab nationalism but used an Islamic vocabulary to present them.

4) Islam represents a multi-interpretative system of signs and symbols. That is to say, its elements as well as the connections between particular elements, can be interpreted in different ways, and a variety of responses to given problems are possible, using different elements and also different interpretations of these elements and of the system as a whole. As a sign and symbol system Islam is before all else a prescriptive system, providing norms and models for right action. Although in principle many interpretations of the system are possible, in the course of history certain interpretations have prevailed, and even nowadays the number of interpretations of Islam and its elements, though larger than a hundred years ago, is restricted to certain models only. Yet, in the absence of an infallible spiritual authority, Islam, and particular elements of it, can be interpreted and applied in a great variety of ways.

5) Behind new interpretations and applications of (elements of) the Islamic sign and symbol system, as well as behind adherence to older interpretations and applications, lie specific material interests, psychological motivations, and spiritual intentions. These may range from the most banal political motives stemming from the lust for power to an idealism which projects a utopia beyond the present-day world, and perhaps even highly spiritual intentions in which the world of facts as such is hardly taken into account. They mostly represent hidden concerns at deeper levels among the people concerned.

6) Much of the "Islamic" meaning currently discovered or assigned to life, and the world in general, is the result of an interaction between, on the one hand, the interests, motivations, and intentions of particular persons and groups and, on the other, the Islamic sign and symbol system. In the social discourse involved constant reference is made to elements of the Islamic system, which provide what are felt to be "Islamic" meanings. Much of the present-day revitalization of Islam on a semantic level consists of assigning Islamic meanings to specific present-day situations and events.

The Interpreters and Their Interpretations

Just as a language offers the words available for use in speech, the Islamic system offers its available signs and symbols from which meaning patterns can be constructed and communicated. The people who appeal to the system with their particular interests, motivations, and intentions play an active part, for it is thanks to them that interpretations and applications occur. In the case of Islam it is not sufficient to study the system as a closed, self-contained entity. Due attention must be paid to its interpreters and the various interpretations they give. Our conceptualization of Islam should take this subjective aspect of the interpreters and their interpretation into due account. We shall illustrate this with a specific example from recent history: the Iranian Islamic revolution.

1) In order to understand and explain the reasons why Islam has been interpreted as it has been in Iran before and after January 1979, one needs to be competent on at least two levels. On the one hand, one needs to know the schools of Islamic thought and action within the cultural tradition of Iran since, say, World War II. On the other hand, one needs to be familiar with the social, economic, and political situation of Iran in the sixties and seventies and the implications of this for different groups: the 'ulamâ', the bazaar, the intelligentsia and civil servants, the farmers, the urban proletariat, and last but not least, the Shah and the government.

2) On this basis we should trace the major problems with which various groups of the population were confronted at the time and the way in which they became more sensitive to certain elements of the Islamic system in its Shî'î variety. Which alternatives existed in response to the official government policy and where did Islam provide alternative meaning patterns to this government policy whenever it was felt to be oppressive? What do documents of the period teach us about the expectations and intentions current among the higher and lower ranking 'ulamâ', about the intellectual groups around Shariati discovering alternative social and political doctrines in Islam, and about the people celebrating the *Muharram* ceremonies which symbolize the sufferings of the innocent for the sake of justice?

3) We need to ascertain, in the growing tension between the government, symbolized by the Shah, and the people who felt increasingly oppressed politically and deprived economically, which values became most relevant and which norms were most appealed to (justice, democracy, freedom from foreign intervention). How were these norms and values derived from interpretations of the Quran, particular *akhbâr*, examples from Islamic history?

4) Which different interpretations and applications of Islam were presented during the crucial decades before the revolution and in the years immediately following it? What new ideas were written or preached by the

'ulamâ', thought out by the "lay" intellectuals, proclaimed by the poets, received from Iranian authors abroad?

5) Which cultural and religious expressions of the period before the revolution, including art and literature, can tell us something of what was going on among the people at the time? What could be said openly and what was censured, and by whom?

Questions like these should always be asked, but they are particularly relevant to our understanding and explaining of the Islamic revolution in Iran. Historians and political scientists writing about the period tend to concentrate on the changeover of power. Yet the massive appeal and recourse to Islamic and other norms in protest against a government considered to be un-Islamic, even satanic, turned out to be a powerful historical force, guided by the *'ulamâ'*, and an invincible instrument in the hands of determined religious leaders. I am still looking for a study of the Islamic revolution from this perspective, which urges a revision of older conceptualizations of Islam as a religion.

The interesting thing about the example of the Iranian revolution, as in the struggle for independence from colonial domination, is that the blending of religion and politics, a religious sign and symbol system and its political application, does not constitute a problem for the observer who becomes aware, at such moments of collective action, that the Islamic system lends itself to both political and religious readings. This constitutes also a confirmation of the validity of our approach: not to look for norms and values which would be contained in Islam per se, but for the readings and applications of the Islamic sign and symbol system and specific attitudes and actions deriving from them.

It is not only in revolutions and wars, however, but also in quieter times that elements of the Islamic sign and symbol system are read as a guidance for life, including forms of conduct, or taking action at critical moments. Islamic studies have often concentrated on the objective side of Islam: the elements of the system and their history. Much less attention has been given to the subjective aspect of the interpreters and their interpretation. Yet it is by paying attention to the weight of social and personal subjectivity in Muslim societies, both in thought and in action, that we become aware of the powerful appeal of inspired preachers and charismatic persons and of Quranic texts, prophetic sayings, and other elements of the Islamic sign and symbol system, often simultaneously.

In retrospect it seems rather strange and one-sided that so much has been said about Islam's impact on the life of individual Muslims and Muslim communities and relatively little about the ways in which such individuals and communities actively read and apply elements of Islam, or about the ways in which they respond to their own situation by appealing to Islam. One reason for this state of affairs may be that in former times Islam was not itself a subject of reflection. People may just have followed the path of established traditions and blindly obeyed the literal meaning of often-quoted Quranic textes. Another reason may be that former generations of Islamicists saw the adherents of Islam, and perhaps of any religion, as more or less passive objects of the impact of a religious system. However this may have been, with the growth of literacy and social development and the evident use of Islam for widely differing aims and political purposes, the majority of Muslims can no longer be considered as passive objects of their religion and its leaders, but rather as victims of political pressures.

It is time now to come back to our starting question: How to envisage and conceptualize Islam as a religion? Our answer has arisen out of the practice of Islamic studies: by using a model which allows for an objectively given sign and symbol system and subjective interests, motivations, and intentions we are able, in principle, to discover various meanings, including religious ones, which specific elements of the Islamic sign and symbol system have had and have for particular individuals and groups who have recourse to it, giving their particular interpretations of it in specific situations and circumstances. If this is true for the conceptualization of Islam as a religion, we can move on to a more abstract level and ask what kind of concept one should have of religions in general. Would the concept developed for Islam be of general validity?

Conceptualizing Religions

Throughout the history of the scholarly study of religion, efforts to arrive at a general concept of religion appear to have moved between two poles. On the one hand religion has been clearly defined in advance. Its conceptualization was a preliminary to the search for and interpretation of relevant facts. This may be called the rational option, which also served to legitimate *Religionswissenschaft* as an autonomous discipline.

On the other hand religion has been conceptualized according to the nature of the religious data discovered; this may be called the empirical option, for instance in the search for the most primitive forms of religion, as practised in cultural anthropology up to World War I. And for less scientifically minded thinkers a third option has existed: to arrive at a general concept of religion on the basis of the contemporary Western (European or American, Protestant or Catholic, humanist or socialist, and so on: in a word, ethnocentric) concerns with religion in the West. This third option, which has been adopted by most Western theologians and missionaries or others applying Christian theological schemes to data outside Christianity, has been particularly harmful to the study of religious data. Indeed, by stressing a particular form of religion highly valued in the West (for instance, myticism or liberal modernist attitudes) they have not only prevented themselves and others from really observing the religious expressions and practices of other people, but have also tended to ideologize their preferred form of religion, with the aim of revitalizing other religious traditions along the same lines. Since the effect of this third option is to exclude an open observation of people as they really are, with or without religious expressions, we may speak here of a "closed" concept of religion. What we are looking for is just the contrary: an "open" concept of religion which allows us to see and observe as much religion as possible, without remaking it in our image.

The question of the most adequate concept of religion thus boils down to the following problem: if we are interested in discerning the religious qualities which certain data have or have had for certain people or groups of people, what kind of conceptualization does most justice to them, from which of the two poles should it be derived, and where is the concept of religion situated between the two poles mentioned above? I would like to submit for your consideration, as a solution to this extremely relevant problem, the conceptualization I have just described for the case of Islam.

This conceptualization consists of a formal structure encompassing those elements of a cultural tradition which for the religion's adherents are distinguished by some kind of religious meaning, just as some numbers in a telephone book have special significance for individual subscribers. These elements, in given circumstances, can be called upon to supply meaning in the widest sense of the word, including religious meaning.

This is the objectively given sign and symbol system: a structure not particularly linked to Western culture and religion, and I think, of general, if not of universal, validity. It should be filled out concretely with the data of the various religions, preferably but not exclusively, by scholars coming from the cultural traditions in question. This formal structure, which considers religion as a semantic system, is a rational postulate near the first of the poles described.

This formal structure must be supplemented by what I would like to call the subjective reality of groups and individuals who, out of their subjective interests, motivations, and intentions, address themselves to those elements of the semantic system which appear to be particularly meaningful to them. These interests, motivations, and intentions express themselves sometimes by the creation of new religious data, but mostly by interpreting and applying elements of the given sign and symbol system in particular ways. These interpretations are both the subject of extensive and intensive research and the stuff of experienced religion (*religion vécue*). This concept of experienced religion and the study of it through the manifold interpretations to which it leads is an empirical datum near the second of the poles just described.

Our proposed conceptualization of religion, as a sign and symbol system on the one hand, and as a set of interpretations (of the system as a whole, of particular elements of it, and ultimately of experienced reality as such) on the other, tries to connect the rational and empirical poles. It is adequate in as far as it is able to discover all references to signs and symbols recognized in a given cultural tradition. And with it we find ourselves in a field of tension between the objective, semantic aspect of a given religion and the subjective, experienced aspect of it. Religion comes into existence through the creative tension between these two; otherwise we are dealing, not with religion, but with culture.

What, now, are the benefits of such an open concept of religion for the study of religions other than Islam, for which we have already demonstrated its usefulness?

Some Wider Applications

What kinds of problems come into focus, and can be treated and to some degree solved, when we proceed with our proposed conceptualization of religion? We have to do here with research problems, because our sole concern is that of scholarly research, without a hidden political, theological, or ideological agenda, at least as far as I am aware. If later analysis were to disclose any such hidden aims and purposes, our procedure should be rid of them immediately.

I would like to demonstrate the usefulness of our approach to three broad areas of research in religious studies: (1) the study of interpretative processes; (2) the study of presentations and representations of religions; (3) the study of interactions.

The Study of Interpretative Processes

To have access to present-day Muslim discourses on Islam the notion of interpretation is a key (Roff 1987). Books, articles, and speeches on Islam become relevant and interesting when we pay attention to what is said and what is not said, to those elements of Islam which are mentioned and those which are not, to the interpretations given, not only of particular Quranic texts and *hadîths*, but also of particular concepts and problems. The rise and further history of Muslim movements becomes a particularly interesting subject of research when we ask which intentions and motivations were underlying them in the specific context of their beginnings and during their further development (Bayat 1982, Waardenburg 1988).

Within religious traditions, and with regard to religious matters generally, interpretative activity is going on constantly. Most obviously, the leadership at a given time and place have to interpret the given religious sign and symbol system as a preceding generation did or mostly with certain innovations. The transfer of a given sign and symbol system to a following generation or to people outside the given community and their appropriation of it implies particular forms of interpretation for pedagogical or missionary aims. Already the use of media of whatever kind confronts the people with certain choices bearing on the interpretation of what they want to hand over. Less obviously but probably more effectively, at the grassroot level a number of adaptations and interpretations are made by preachers, monks, healers, and others who have some kind of religious authority in the eyes of the people and are not directly subservient to the official religious and political leadership. This range of constant interpretations and reinterpretations implies a certain dynamic process which becomes visible precisely if we study it in terms of the proposed open concept of religion.

New interpretations are often based on particular intentions leading to the construction of mental, spiritual, or religious universes different from those of preceding generations or other groups. At a given time and place, the necessities of life cause particular attitudes to be taken towards life and the world which, in the course of time, lead to a particular cultural and religious tradition. Then, through war or other catastrophes, radical changes in the infrastructure of a society, and psychological crises, such tradition is discovered or comes to be seen, as "past" reality, no longer relevant to present-day life. This discovery is made, not by those more reflecting people who have always known about the relative character of their culture and religion, but rather, by those who have become more or less a product of them and who, for various reasons, are confronted anew with certain basic realities of life which they cannot interpret satisfactorily through them. This is a kind of ending of the interpretative process which means a threat to the given religion.

The Study of (Re)Presentations of Religions

Islamic studies received a new impulse when the representation of Islam to Muslims and its presentation to non-Muslims became the subject of research and when such presentations and representations were explained in terms of the interests of the community and the context within which it lives (Smith 1963).

Our proposed approach and conceptualization can make a valuable contribution to the study of what may be called the mental constructs of "religions." People have conceptions of the religion to which they belong (or do not belong), of different religions, and of religion in general. The reasons why people make such conceptions are always connected somehow or other with their sense of identity. Nowadays, religions of all kinds all over the world are presented to people and conceived by them to express, not only the truth by which they (should) live, but also their communal and personal identitiy.

To inquire how particular people or groups of people represent to themselves the particular sign and symbol system to which they belong is an important field of research. It cannot but lead to further inquiry into how these religions are represented both to adherents and to non-adherents by their official representatives or other authoritative figures. Besides the sign and symbol system itself, the cultural tradition and the social context, certain material interests, psychological motivations, and spiritual intentions play an important role.

Since a plurality has appeared within given traditions, cultures and societies have become more differentiated. Internal discussions have taken place within religions and ideologies which, because of prevailing authority and power structures, had previously been more homogeneous. All these differentiations and personalized expressions lend themselves very well to be studied as so many varied interpretations and applications of the given sign and symbol system.

The Study of Interactions

Increasing communication has favoured contacts between Muslims and other believers. In general, this leads to increased interaction and possible dialogue on religious matters, and such interaction has become subject of scholarly research (Waardenburg 1984a:1).

The proposed open concept of religion appears to be particularly suitable for the investigation of interactions between people of different spiritualities. The point of reference in a spirituality may be a given broader or narrower religious sign and symbol system to which an individual adheres. It may also combine elements from different sign and symbol systems in a more or less original and creative way. In any case, any spirituality is characterized by strong spiritual intentions.

Questions like the following present themselves. What happens in the concrete situations where interaction between people of different spiritualities occurs, who are the actors and what are their aims? How do they speak about the world, their own traditions, and themselves? To which extent are they open to "others"? Should the actors be described in terms of their respective "confessions," or is this insufficient and should they be described in terms which do justice to the spiritual aspects of the communication which they aim at and in part achieve?

It may very well be, indeed, that such interaction between people of different spiritualities finally transcends the two traditions and sign and symbol systems represented. Consequently, it must be understood not in terms of them but in terms of a new system which arises as the result of the communication, in a process of transformation leading to new signs and symbols and to new meanings of the old ones.

This opens up a fascinating area of research, the constructs which result from interaction and which are further elaborated to pursue this interaction in the future and to guide and direct it. The nature and use of such new signs and symbols in order to promote interreligious dialogue, but also the resistance they meet in the established traditions and the possibility that they are used for new kinds of social action, calls for intensive research. I am convinced that our approach and conceptualization can make a contribution to such research.

Conclusion

The starting point of our analysis is the assumption that religious phenomena are phenomena that are interpreted religiously, and that religions are entities composed of such phenomena that are interpreted religiously too. Our analysis assumes that religion can very well be studied fruitfully by paying attention to all the interpretations involved. This implies an interest in problems of meaning (Ricoeur 1976) and hermeneutics (Wood 1975), although old-trodden paths have to give way to new, secret routes (Waardenburg 1973, 1974, 1978, 1979). The concept of religion that we use in our scholarly work is of capital importance (Waardenburg 1984b:2).

In our time, when changes, not only material but also mental, are so great we, as scholars, are privileged to be able to ask new questions and have the opportunity to arrive at new ways of understanding. Subjects such as those discussed in this paper are customarily treated as isolated pieces of empirical research. We need to consider them as problems which have an inner coherence on a more theoretical level.

References

Bakhash, Shaul. 1985. *The Reign of the Ayatollahs: Iran and the Islamic Revolution*. London: I. B. Tauris.

Bayat, Mangol. 1982. *Mysticism and Dissent: Socioreligious Thought in Qajar Iran*. Syracuse, N. Y.: Syracuse University Press.

Ricoeur, Paul. 1976. *Interpretation Theory: Discourse and the Surplus of Meaning*. Fort Worth, TX: The Texas Christian University Press.

Roff, William R., ed. 1987. *Islam and the Political Economy of Meaning: Comparative Studies of Muslim Discourse*. Berkeley and Los Angeles: University of California Press.

Smith, Wilfred Cantwell. 1963. *Modern Islam in India: A Social Analysis*. Lahore: Sh. Muhammad Ashraf.

―――. 1963. *The Meaning and End of Religion: A New Approach to the Religious Traditions of Mankind*. New York: Macmillan.

Waardenburg, Jacques. 1973. "Research on Meaning in Religion." In *Religion, Culture and Methodology*, edited by Th. P. van Baaren and H. J. W. Drijvers, 110-36. The Hague and Paris: Mouton.

―――. 1974. "Islam Studied as a Symbol and Signification System." In *Humaniora Islamica*. Vol. 2, 267-85. The Hague and Paris: Mouton.

―――. 1978. *Reflections on the Study of Religion, Including an Essay on the Work of Gerardus van der Leeuw*. The Hague and Paris: Mouton.

―――. 1979. "The Language of Religion, and the Study of Religions as Sign Systems." In *Science of Religion: Studies in Methology*, 441-57 and 482-83, edited by Lauri Honko. The Hague and Paris: Mouton.

―――. 1984a. "Muslims and Other Believers: The Indonesian Case. Towards a Theoretical Research Framework." In *Islam in Asia*. Vol. 2: *Southeast and East Asia*, 24-66. Jerusalem: The Magnes Press, The Hebrew University.

―――. 1984b. "Über die Religion der Religionswissenschaft." In *Neue Zeitschrift für Systematische Theologie und Religionsphilosophie* 26: 238-55.

―――. 1988. "Muslim Enlightenment and Revitalization. Movements of Modernization and Reform in Tsarist Russia (ca.1850-1917) and the Dutch East Indies (ca.1900-1942)." In *Die Welt des Islams* 28: 569-84.

Wood, Charles M. 1975. *Theory and Understanding: A Critique of the Hermeneutics of Joachim Wach*. Missoula: Scholars Press.

Appendice

Appendix

Wilfred Cantwell Smith:
A Chronological Bibliography

Compiled by Richard T. McCutcheon

1936. "Canadian Youth Congress." *Canadian Forum* 16 (July): 16-18.
1943. *Modern Islam in India: A Social Analysis.* Lahore: Minerva. Rev. ed., London: V. Gollancz, "1946" (*sic* 1947). Reissued: Lahore: Sh. M. Ashraf, 1963, 1969; New York: Russel & Russel, 1972; and pirated edition, Lahore: Ripon, 1947 (with a spurious chapter "Towards Pakistan" by an unknown hand). New edition: New Delhi: Usha, 1979.
1944. "The Mughal Empire and the Middle Class: A Hypothesis." *Islamic Culture* (Hyderabad) 18: 349-63.
1944. "Objective Tests in History." *The Punjab Educational Journal* (Lahore) 29: 309-13, 336-45. Reprinted in *Education* (Lucknow) 24, 2: 53-60.
1945. "Achievement Tests in History." *Education* (Lucknow) 24, 1: 57-62.
1946. "Lower-Class Uprisings in the Mughal Empire." *Islamic Culture* (Hyderabad) 20: 21-40.
1947-48. "The Muslim World." *One Family*, 2:27-32. 2 vols. Toronto: Missionary Society of the Church of England in Canada.
1948. "The Azhar Journal; Survey and Critique." Ph. D., Princeton University.
1950. "Hyderabad: Muslim Tragedy." *Middle East Journal* 4: 27-51.
1950. "The Comparative Study of Religion: Reflections on the Possibility and Purpose of a Religious Science." *McGill University, Faculty of Divinity, Inaugural Lectures*, 39-60. Montreal: McGill University. Reprinted as "On the Comparative Study of Religion." In *Ways of Understanding Religion*, edited by Walter H. Capps, 190-203. New York: Macmillan, 1972.
1951. "The Muslims and the West." *Foreign Policy Bulletin* (New York) 31, 2 (October): 5-7.
1951. "Islam Confronted by Western Secularism: (A) Revolutionary Reaction." In *Islam in the Modern World: A Series of Addresses Presented at the Fifth Annual Conference on Middle East Affairs, Sponsored by the Middle East Institute*, edited

by Dorothea Seelye Franck, 19-30. Washington: Middle East Institute. Translated into Arabic (1953).
1951. *Pakistan as an Islamic State*. Lahore: Sh. M. Ashraf (sic 1954).
1952. "Modern Turkey—Islamic Reformation?" *Islamic Culture* (Hyderabad) 25, 1: 155-86. Reprinted in abridged form, with comments: *Die Welt des Islams*, N.F. 3 (1954): 269-73. Translated into Turkish (1953).
1953. "Pakistan." In *Collier's Encyclopaedia*.
1953. "The Institute of Islamic Studies (McGill University]." *The Islamic Literature* (Lahore) 5: 173-76.
1954. "The Importance of Muhammad (review article)." *The Canadian Forum* (September): 135-36.
1955. "The Intellectuals in the Modern Development of the Islamic World." In *Social Forces in the Middle East*, edited by Sydney Nettleton Fischer, 199-204. Ithaca: Cornell University Press.
1955. "Propaganda (Muslim)." In *Twentieth Century Encyclopaedia of Religious Knowledge*, 2:767-68. Grand Rapids: Baker.
1956. "The Place of Oriental Studies in a Western University." *Diogenes* 16: 104-11. Translated into French (1956), German (1957), and Spanish (1958).
1956. "Ahmadiyyah" and "Amir Ali, Sayyid." In *Encyclopaedia of Islam* (new edition). Leiden and London: E. J. Brill. Translated into French (1956).
1956. "The Christian and the Near East Crisis." *The British Weekly*, 20 December, 5. Reprinted in *The Presbyterian Record* (Toronto) 82, 1 (January): 16-17.
1956. *The Muslim World*. Pamphlet, Current Affairs for the Canadian Forces series, 10, 4. Ottawa: Bureau of Current Affairs, Department of National Defence, 26 pp. Translated into French (1956).
1957. "Islam in the Modern World." *Current History* 32: 321-25. Reprinted in *Enterprise* (Karachi), January 4, 1958; *Morning News* (Karachi), April 12, 1959.
1957. "Independence Day in Indonesia." *The McGill News* (Winter): 23-24.
1957. *Islam in Modern History*. Princeton: Princeton University Press. Reissued: London: Oxford Univesity Press, 1958; New York: New American Library (Mentor Books), 1959; London: New English Library (Mentor Books), 1965; Princeton and London: Princeton University Press (Princeton Paperback), 1977. Taped for Recording for the Blind, Inc., Washington, 1973. Translated into Arabic (pirated, 1960; authorized, 1975), Swedish (1961), French (1962), Indonesian (1962-1964), German (1963), and Japanese (1974). Portions translated into Urdu (1958-59, 1960) and Arabic (1960).
1958. "Aga Khan III." *Encyclopaedia Americana*.
1958. "Law and Ijtihad in Islam: Some Considerations on Their Relation to Each Other and to Ultimate and Immediate Problems." *Dawn* (Karachi), 5 January 1958. Reprinted in *Pakistan Quarterly* (Karachi), 8: 29-31, 63; also in *International Islamic Colloquium Papers*, 29 December 1957-8 January 1958, 111-14. Lahore: Punjab University Press, 1960. Translated into Urdu (1958); Arabic (1960).
1959. "Some Similarities and Differences Between Christianity and Islam." In *The World of Islam: Studies in Honour of Philip K. Hitti*, edited by James

Kritzech and R. Bayly Winder, 47-59. London: Macmillan. Translated into Urdu (1964).

1959. "Comparative Religion: Whither — and Why?" In *The History of Religions: Essays in Methodology*, edited by Mircea Eliade and Joseph M. Kitagawa, 31-58. Chicago: The University of Chicago Press, 1959. Translated into Urdu (1962), Japanese (1962), and German (1963). Chapter 8 of *Religious Diversity: Essays by Wilfred Cantwell Smith*, edited by Willard G. Oxtoby. New York: Harper & Row. Hereafter: *Religious Diversity*.

1959. "The Christian and the Religions of Asia." In *Changing Asia: Report of the Twenty-Eighth Annual Couchiching Conference: A Joint Project of the Canadian Institute on Public Affairs and the Canadian Broadcasting Corporation*, 9-16. Toronto: Canadian Institute on Public Affairs. Reprinted in *Occasional Papers*. Department of Missionary Studies, International Missionary Council (World Council of Churches), London, 5 (April 1960); under the title, "Christianity's Third Great Challenge." *Christian Century* 77 (27 April 1960): 505-08; also in abridged form in *The Beacon* (London) 39 (1962): 337-40.

1960. "The YMCA and the Present." *Bulletin* (National Council of Young Men's Christian Associations of Canada, Toronto) 34, 4 (June): 3-5.

1960. "India, Religion and Philosophy: Islam." In *Encyclopaedia Americana*. Reprinted in *India, Pakistan, Ceylon*, rev. ed., edited by Norman Brown, 104-07. Philadelphia: University of Pennsylvania Press; London: Oxford University Press, 1964.

1961. "Modern Muslim Historical Writing in English." In *Historians of India, Pakistan and Ceylon*, Historical Writing on the Peoples of Asia, 1, edited by C. H. Philips, 319-31. London: Oxford University Press.

1962. "The Comparative Study of Religion in General and the Study of Islam as a Religion in Particular." In *Colloque sur la sociologie musulmane: Actes, 11-14 septembre 1961*, 217-31. Bruxelles: Publications du Centre pour l'étude des problèmes du monde musulman contemporain.

1962. "Iblis." In *Encyclopaedia Britannica*.

1962. "The Historical Development in Islam of the Concept of Islam as an Historical Development." In *Historians of the Middle East*, Historical Writing on the Peoples of Asia, 4, edited by Bernard Lewis and P. M. Holt, 484-502. London: Oxford University Press.

1962. *The Faith of Other Men*. Toronto: Canadian Broadcasting Corporation. Enlarged edition. New York: New American Library, 1963. Reissued: New York: New American Library (Mentor Books), 1965; London: New English Library (Mentor Books), 1965; New York and London: Harper & Row (Torchbook), 1972. Translated into Swedish (1965), Korean (1989). Pp. 105-28 in abridged form = Chapter 1 in *Religious Diversity*.

1963. "The 'Ulama' in Indian Politics." In *Politics and Society in India*, edited by C. H. Philips, 39-51. London: George Allen & Unwin.

1963. *The Meaning and End of Religion: A New Approach to the Religious Traditions of Mankind*. New York: Macmillan. Reissued: New York: New American Library (Mentor Books), 1964; London: New English Library (Mentor Books), 1965; San Francisco: Harper & Row, and London: S.P.C.K., 1978; Philadelphia: Fortress Press, 1990. Translated into Korean (1990).

1963. "Druze." In *Encyclopaedia Britannica*.
1964. "Koran (Qur'an)." In *Encyclopaedia Britannica*.
1964. "Mankind's Religiously Divided History Approaches Self-consciousness." *Harvard Divinity Bulletin* 29 (October): 1-17. Translated into German (1967). Chapter 6 of *Religious Diversity*.
1965. "Non-Western Studies: The Religious Approach." In *A Report on an Invitational Conference on the Study of Religion in the State University, Held October 23-25, 1964 at Indiana University Medical Center*, 50-62. Comments and discussion follow, 62-67. New Haven: The Society for Religion in Higher Education.
1965. "Secularism: The Problem Posed." *Seminar* 67: 10-12.
1965. "The Concept of Shari'a among some Mutakallimun." In *Arabic and Islamic Studies in Honor of Hamilton A. R. Gibb*, edited by George Makdisi, 581-602. Leiden: E. J. Brill.
1965. "The Islamic Near East: Intellectual Role of Librarianship." *Library Quarterly* 35: 283-94. Discussion follows, 294-97. Reprinted in *Area Studies and the Library*, edited by Tsuen-Hsuin Tsien and Howard W. Winger, 81-92 (92-95). Chicago and London: The University of Chicago Press, 1966.
1965. *Modernization of a Traditional Society*. Bombay, Calcutta: Asia Publishing House. Pp. 1-22 in abridged form = Chapter 5 of *Religious Diversity*.
1966. "Religious Atheism? Early Buddhist and Recent American." *Milla wa-Milla* (Melbourne) 6: 5-30. Reprinted in *Comparative Religion: The Charles Strong Trust Lectures 1961-70*, edited by John Bowman, 53-81. Leiden: E. J. Brill.
1967. "The Mission of the Church and the Future of Missions." In *The Church in the Modern World: Essays in Honour of James Sutherland Thomson*, edited by George Johnson and Wolfgang Roth, 154-70. Toronto: The Ryerson Press.
1967. *Questions of Religious Truth*. New York: Charles Scribner's Sons; and London: V. Gollancz, 1967. Translated into Japanese (1971). Pp. 39-62 in abridged form = Chapter 2 of *Religious Diversity*.
1968. "Traditional Religions and Modern Culture." In *Proceedings of the XIth International Congress of the International Association for the History of Religions. Vol. 1: The Impact of Modern Culture on Traditional Religions*. Leiden: E. J. Brill. Chapter 4 of *Religious Diversity*.
1969. "The Crystallization of Religious Communities in Mughul India." In *Yad-Name-ye-Iraini [sic]-ye Minorsky*, Ganjine-ye Tahqiqat-e Irani, no. 57; Publications of Tehran University, no. 1241, edited by Mojtaba Minova and Iraj Afshar, 197-220. Tehran: Intisharat Daneshgah.
1969. *Orientalism and Truth: A Public Lecture in Honor of T. Cuyler Young, Horatio Whitridge Garret Professor of Persian Language and History, Chairman of the Department of Oriental Studies*. Princeton: Program in Near Eastern Studies, Princeton University, 16 pp. (Pamphlet.)
1969. "Secularity and the History of Religion." In *The Spirit and Power of Christian Secularity*, edited by Albert Schlitzer, 33-58; discussion follows, 59-70. Notre Dame: The University of Notre Dame Press.
1969. "Participation: The Changing Christian Role in Other Cultures." *Occasional Bulletin* (Missionary Research Library, New York) 20, 4: 1-13. Reprinted in *Religion and Society* 17, 1: 56-74; also in abridged form in *Mis-*

sion Trends No. 2, edited by Gerald H. Anderson and Thomas F. Stransky, 218-29. New York: Paulist Press and Grand Rapids: Eerdmans, 1975. Chapter 7 in *Religious Diversity*.

1970. "The End is Near." Annotated translation from Urdu of Siddiq Hasan Khan, reputed author, *Iqtirab al-Sa'ah*. Published anonymously in *Muslim Self-Statement in India and Pakistan 1857-1968*, edited by Aziz Ahmad and G. E. von Grunebaum, 85-89. Wiesbaden: Otto Harrassowitz.

1970. "University Studies of Religion in a Global Context." In *Study of Religion in Indian Universities: A Report of the Consultation Held in Bangalore in September, 1967*, 74-87. Bangalore Press, n.d. (*sic* 1970).

1971. "A Human View of Truth." *Studies in Religion* 1, 1: 6-24. Reprinted in *Truth and Dialogue: The Relationship between World Religions*, edited by John Hick. London: Sheldon Press, 1974; *Truth and Dialogue in World Religions: Conflicting Truth Claims*, 20-44. Philadelphia: Westminster Press, 1974, with a new addendum, "Conflicting Truth-Claims: A Rejoinder," 156-62.

1971. "The Study of Religion and the Study of the Bible." *Journal of the American Academy of Religion* 39, 2 (June): 131-40. Chapter 3 of *Religious Diversity*.

1973. "On Dialogue and Faith." A rejoinder to E. S. Sharpe (see Sharpe review article) *Religion* 3: 106-14.

1973. "Programme Notes for a Mitigated Cacophony." *The Journal of Religion* 53, 3 (July): 377-81. A review article of R. C. Zaehner, *Concordant Discord* (1970).

1973. "'The Finger That Points to the Moon': Reply to Per Kvaerne." See Kvaerne review article, *Temenos* 9: 169-72.

1974. "World Religions." *Christian Century* 91 (January): 16.

1974. "Objectivity and the Humane Sciences: A New Proposal." *Transactions of the Royal Society of Canada*, Series 4, 12: 81-102. Reprinted in *Symposium on the Frontiers and Limitations of Knowledge / Colloque sur les frontières et limites du savoir*, edited by Claude Fortier, et al., 81-102. Ottawa: Royal Society of Canada. Chapter 9 of *Religious Diversity*.

1974. "Religion as Symbolism." Introduction to *Propaedia*, part 8, "Religion." *Encyclopaedia Britannica*, 15th ed. Vol. 1, 498-500. Chicago: Encyclopaedia Britannica. Translated into Korean (1990).

1975. "Methodology and the Study of Religion: Some Misgivings." In *Methodological Issues in Religious Studies*, 1-25. Discussion follows, 25-30. Further discussion: "Is the Comparative Study of Religion Possible? Panel Discussion." With Jacob Neusner and Hans H. Penner, 95-109. Smith's rejoinder, 123-24, edited by Robert D. Baird. Chico, CA: New Horizons Press.

1976. "Arkan." In *Essays on Islamic Civilization Presented to Niyazi Berkes*, edited by David P. Little, 303-16. Leiden: E. J. Brill. Translated into Turkish (1977).

1976. "Faith and Belief (Some Considerations from the Islamic Instance)" and "Faith and Belief (Some Considerations from the Christian Instance)." *Al-Hikmat: A Research Journal of the Department of Philosophy* (University of the Punjab, Lahore) 6 (*sic* 1976): 1-20, 21-43.

1976. *Religious Diversity: Essays by Wilfred Cantwell Smith*, edited by Willard G. Oxtoby. New York: Harper & Row, 1976. Chapter 1 reprinted in *Chris-*

tianity and Other Religions, 87-107, edited by John Hick and Brian Hebblethwaite, 87-107. Glasgow: William Collins, 1980.
1976. *The Role of Asian Studies in the American University.* The plenary address of the New York State Conference for Asian Studies, Colgate University, 10-12 October. Hamilton, NY: Colgate University, 13 pp. (Pamphlet.)
1976-77. "Interpreting Religious Interrelations: An Historian's View of Christian and Muslim." *Studies in Religion* 6, 1: 515-26.
1977. *Belief and History.* Charlottesville: The University Press of Virginia.
1977-78. "The University." *Dalhousie Review* 57: 540-49. Review article of Murray Ross, *The University: The Anatomy of Academe*, New York, 1976.
1978. "An Historian of Faith Reflects on What We Are Doing Here." In *Christian Faith in a Religiously Plural World*, edited by David G. Dawe and John B. Carmen. Maryknoll, NY: Orbis Books.
1978. "Divisiveness and Unity." In *Food/Energy and the Major Faiths*, edited by Joseph Gremillion, 71-85. Maryknoll, NY: Orbis Books.
1979. "Tauhid and the Integration of Personality." *Studies in Islam* (Quarterly Journal of the Indian Institute of Islamic Studies, New Delhi) 16: 127-28. Discussion follows, 128-29.
1979. "Thinking About Persons." *Humanitas* 15 (May): 147-52.
1979. "The Explosion in the Moslem World: A Roundtable on Islam." Participant in a roundtable discussion on the Moslem world during the USA hostage crisis. *The New York Times*, 11 December, 16-17.
1979. *Faith and Belief.* Princeton: Princeton University Press. Reissued 1987.
1980. "Belief: A Reply to a Response." See Wiebe review article. *Numen* 27 (December): 247-55.
1980. "Aziz Ahmad 1913-1978." Portrait. *Transactions of the Royal Society of Canada*, Series 4, 18: 43-46.
1980. "The True Meaning of Scripture: An Empirical Historian's Non-reductionist Interpretation of the Qur'an." *International Journal of Middle Eastern Studies* 11 (July): 487-505.
1981. *Towards a World Theology: Faith and the Comparative History of Religion.* Philadelphia: The Westminster Press. Reissued; London: Macmillan and New York: Orbis Books, 1989 (*sic* 1990).
1981. "Understanding Islam." *Funk & Wagnalls New Encyclopaedia 1981 Yearbook*, 22-35. New York: Funk and Wagnalls.
1981. "Faith as Tasdiq." In *Islamic Philosophical Theology*, edited by Parvis Morewedge, 96-119. Albany: State University of New York Press, n.d. (*sic* 1981).
1981. *On Understanding Islam: Selected Studies.* The Hague: Mouton.
1981. "An Attempt at Summation." In *Christ's Lordship and Pluralism*, edited by Gerald H. Anderson and Thomas F. Stransky, 196-203. Maryknoll, NY: Orbis Books.
1981. "History in Relation to Both Science and Religion." *Scottish Journal of Religious Studies* 2: 3-10.
1982. "Islamic Studies and the History of Religions." In *Essays in Islamic and Comparative Studies: Papers Presented to the 1979 Meeting of the American Acad-*

emy of Religion, edited by Isma'il Raji al Faruqi, 2-7. N.p.: International Institute of Islamic Thought, 1402.

1983. "Responsibility." In *Modernity and Responsibility: Essays for George Grant*, edited by Eugene Combs, 74-84. Toronto: University of Toronto Press.

1983. "Traditions in Contact and Change: Towards a History of Religion in the Singular." In *Traditions in Contact and Change: Selected Proceedings of the XIVth Congress of the International Association for the History of Religions*, edited by Peter Slater and Donald Wiebe, 1-23. Waterloo, ON: Wilfrid Laurier University Press.

1984. "The Modern West in the History of Religion." *Journal of the American Academy of Religion* 52 (March): 3-18.

1984. "On Mistranslated Booktitles." *Religious Studies* 20: 27-42.

1984. *Islam dawr-i hazir men (muntakhab-i mazamin)*, edited by Mushiru-l-Haqq. Delhi: Maktabah'-i Jami'ah. A collection of Smith's published articles, translated into Urdu with an introduction by the editor.

1984. "Philosophia, as One of the Religious Traditions of Humankind: The Greek Legacy in Western Civilization, Viewed by a Comparativist." In *Différences, valeurs, hiérarchie: Textes offerts à Louis Dumont*, edited by Jean-Claude Galey, 253-79. Paris: Éditions de l'École des Hautes Études en Sciences Sociales. Maison des Sciences de l'Homme—Bibliothèque.

1984. "The World Church and the World History of Religion: The Theological Issue." *Catholic Theological Society of America: Proceedings* 39: 52-68.

1985. "Introduction." In *India and the West: The Problem of Understanding—Selected Essays of J. L. Mehta*, Studies in World Religions 4, xiii-xvii. Chico, CA: Scholars Press.

1987. "Muslim-Christian Relations: Questions of a Comparative Religionist." *Journal Institute of Muslim Minority Affairs* (London) 8: 18-21.

1987. "Symbols in Religion." In *Symbols in Life and Art: The Royal Society of Canada Symposium in Memory of George Whalley / Les Symboles dans la vie et dans l'art: la Société Royale du Canada, colloque à la mémoire de George Whalley*, edited by James A. Leith, 89-104. Montreal: McGill-Queen's University Press for the Royal Society of Canada. Revised version, "Symbolism in World Religions and in Inter-Religious Discourse." *World Faiths Insight*, New Series 16 (June): 2-19.

1987. "Taking Goodness Seriously." *University of Toronto Bulletin* 40, 21 (29 June): 13. Convocation Address, University of Toronto.

1987. "Theology and the World's Religious History." In *Toward a Universal Theology of Religion*, edited by Leonard Swidler, 51-72. Maryknoll, NY: Orbis Books.

1987. "Idolatry: In Comparative Perspective." In *The Myth of Christian Uniqueness: Toward a Pluralistic Theology of Religions*, edited by John Hick and Paul F. Knitter, 53-68. New York: Orbis Books.

1987. "Theology and the Academic Study of Religion." *The Iliff Review* (Denver, Colorado) 44, 3 (Fall): 9-18.

1988. "Mission, Dialogue, and God's Will for Us." *International Review of Mission* (Geneva) 78: 360-74.

1988. "Transcendence." *Harvard Divinity Bulletin* 18, 3: 10-15.

1988. "Shall the Next Century be Secular or Religious?" In Tenri International Symposium '86: *Cosmos, Life, Religion: Beyond Humanism*, 125-51. Tenri, Japan: Tenri University Press. Originally published in Japanese (1988).

1989. "Scripture as Form and Concept: Their Emergence for the Western World." In *Rethinking Scriptures: Essays from a Comparative Perspective*, edited by Miriam Levering, 29-57. Albany: State University of New York Press.

Wilfred Cantwell Smith: A Bibliography of Review Articles

Boutin, Maurice, Charles Davis, and Norman King. "Trois approches récentes dans l'étude des religions." *Science et Esprit* 35, 3 (1983): 325-51.

Burrell, David. "Faith and Religious Convictions: Studies in Comparative Epistemology." *The Journal of Religion* 63: 64-73.

Cobb, John B., Jr. "Smith's World Theology: An Appreciative Critique." Unpublished paper presented at the Claremont Graduate School, at a conference entitled "Toward a Philosophy of Religious Diversity," Claremont, CA, 23-24 September 1981.

Conn, Walter E. " 'Faith' and 'Cumulative Tradition' in Functional Specialization: A Study in the Methodologies of Wilfred Cantwell Smith and Bernard Lonergan." *Studies in Religion* 5 (1975-76): 221-46.

Doyle, D. M. "Objectivity and Religious Truth, A Comparison of Wilfred Cantwell Smith and Bernard Lonergan." *Thomist* 53, 3 (1989): 461-80.

Duchesne-Guillemin, J., J. Glasse, and H. Sunden. "The Meaning and End of Religion: A Symposium." *Harvard Theological Review* 58 (October 1965): 432-51.

Florida, Robert E. "Theism and Atheism in the Work of W. C. Smith." Unpublished manuscript, Brandon University, April 1986.

Franck, F. "The Basic Constituent." *The Eastern Buddhist* 13 (1980): 115-26.

Frank, Richard M. "Ambiguities of Understanding." Review of "On Understanding Islam: Selected Studies." *Journal of the American Oriental Society* 106, 2 (April-June 1986): 313-21.

Geertz, Clifford. "Conjuring with Islam." *The New York Review* (27 May 1982): 25-28.

Gilkey, Langdon and Huston Smith. "Wilfred Cantwell Smith; Early Opus and Recent Trilogy." *Religious Studies Review* 7 (October 1981): 298-310.

Grant, Colin. "Smith's Discovery and The Ethics of Belief." *Studies in Religion* 13, 4 (1984): 461-77.

Gualtieri, Antonio Roberto. "Faith, Tradition, and Transcendence: A Study of Wilfred Cantwell Smith." *Canadian Journal of Theology* 15 (April 1969): 102-11.

―――. "Can We Know the Religious Faith of Others?" *Religion and Society* 20, 3 (1973): 6-17.

―――. " 'Faith, Belief and Transcendence' According to Wilfred Cantwell Smith." *Journal of Dharma* 6 (1981): 239-52.

Hick, John. "Introduction." In *The Meaning and End of Religion*, ix-xviii. New York: Harper & Row, 1978.

Horne, J. R. "Wilfred Cantwell Smith's Qualified Pluralism." *Scottish Journal of Religious Studies* 9, 1 (Spring 1988): 40-52.
Horvath, T., P. Slater, and D. Wiebe. "Three Responses to 'Faith and Belief': A Review Article." *Studies in Religion* 10, 1 (1981): 113-26. Includes an editorial note by W. C. James.
Horvath, Tibor. "Three Views of Christianity." *Journal of the American Academy of Religion* 6 (1982): 97-109.
Hutchison, John A. "Faith and Belief—Some Critical Reflections on the Thought of W. C. Smith." Unpublished paper presented at the Claremont Graduate School, at a conference entitled "Toward a Philosophy of Religious Diversity," Claremont, CA, 23-24 September 1981.
Isenberg, S. R. "Comparative Religion as an Ecumenical Process." *Journal of Ecumenical Studies* 24, 4 (1987): 616-43.
Isvaradevan, R. "Interreligious Understanding: Wilfred Cantwell Smith's Approach." *Bangalore Theological Review* 20 (1988): 43-57.
Kumar, P. Pratap. "Religion and Theology: Issues in W. Cantwell Smith's *Towards a World Theology*." *Bangalore Theological Forum* 15 (1983): 151-62.
Kvaerne, Per. "'Comparative Religion: Whither—and Why?' A Reply to Wilfred Cantwell Smith." *Temenos* 9 (1973): 161-68.
Long, Eugene Thomas. "Cantwell Smith's Proposal for a World Theology." *Faith and Philosophy* 4 (January 1987): 3-12.
Meynell, Hugo. "The Idea of a World Theology." *Modern Theology* 1, 2 (1985): 149-61.
Netland, Harold. "Exclusivism, Tolerance, and Truth." *Missiology: An International Review* 15, 2 (April 1987): 77-95. Reprinted in *Evangelical Review of Theology* 12 (July 1988): 240-60.
Oxtoby, Willard G. "Editor's Introduction." In *Religious Diversity*, vii-xxiv. New York: Harper & Row, 1976.
Pruett, Gorden E. "History, Transcendence, and World Community in the Work of Wilfred Cantwell Smith." *Journal of the American Academy of Religion* 41, 4 (1973): 573-90.
Rajashekar, J. Paul. "The Challenge of Religious Pluralism to Christian Theological Reflection." *LWF Report* No. 23-24 (January 1988): 9-23.
Sharpe, E. J. "Dialogue and Faith." *Religion* 3 (1973): 89-105.
Slater, Peter. "Review Essay: Three Views of Christianity." W. C. Smith, N. Smart, and W. Clebsch. *Journal of the American Academy of Religion* 50 (1982): 97-109.
Smart, Ninian. "Scientific Phenomenology and Wilfred Cantwell Smith's Misgivings." In *The World's Religious Traditions: Current Perspectives in Religious Studies—Essays in Honour of Wilfred Cantwell Smith*, edited by Frank Whaling, 257-69. Edinburgh: T. & T. Clark, 1984.
Stenger, Mary Ann. "The Problem of Cross-Cultural Criteria of Religious Truths." *Modern Theology* 3, 4 (1987): 315-32.
Swearer, Donald K. "How Do We Teach Religion?" *Theology Today* 40 (1983): 319-25.
Wainwright, William J. "Wilfred Cantwell Smith on Faith and Belief." *Religious Studies* 20 (1984): 353-66.

Welker, Michael. "'Unity of Religious History' and 'Universal Self-consciousness': Leading Concepts or Mere Horizons on the Way Towards a World Theology?" *Harvard Theological Review* 81 (October 1988): 431-44.

Wiebe, Donald. "The Role of 'Belief' in the Study of Religion." *Numen* 26 (December 1979): 234-49.

Wilfred Cantwell Smith: Festschrift, Dissertations, etc.

Bollinger, Gary Allen. 1981. "Personal Faith and Interfaith Encounter." Ph.D., Claremont Graduate School.

Buckalew, Ronald William. 1987. "A Return of the Servant: Kenotic Christ and Religious Pluralism in the Thought of Raimundo Panikkar and Wilfred Cantwell Smith." Ph.D., Union Theological Seminary in Virginia.

Doyle, Dennis Michael. 1984. "The Distinction between Faith and Belief and the Question of Religious Truth: The Contributions of Wilfred Cantwell Smith and Bernard Lonergan." Ph.D., Theology, Catholic University of America.

Hughes, Edward J. 1985. "The Global Philosophy of Wilfred Cantwell Smith: An Experiment in Intercultural Thought." Ph.D., Philosophy of Religion, Claremont Graduate School.

―――. 1986. *Wilfred Cantwell Smith: A Theology for the World*. London: SCM Press. Reviews: Ursula King, *The Expository Times* 98, 4 (January 1987): 124; Alan Race, *Theology* 90 (March 1987): 159-60.

Jones, Richard J. 1988. "Wilfred Cantwell Smith and Kenneth Cragg on Islam: Their Contrasting Implications for a Theology of Religion and a Theology of Mission." Ph.D., Trinity College, Toronto.

Nicholson, Wayne Isaac. 1978. "Toward a Theology of Comparative Religion: A Study in the Thought of Hendrik Kraemer and Wilfred Cantwell Smith." Ph.D., The Southern Baptist Theological Seminary.

Rasiah, Iswaradevan. 1984. "The Contribution of Wilfred Cantwell Smith to Inter-Faith Understanding." Th.D., Boston University School of Theology.

Tadsen, Sister Rose. 1985. "Jesus Christ in the World Theology of Wilfred Cantwell Smith." Ph.D., Theology, University of St. Michael's College.

Wallace, Raymond P. 1989. "Reference, Method, and Religious Pluralism: 'The Encyclopedia of Religion and Ethics' and 'Die Religion in Geschichte und Gegenwart.'" Ph.D., Graduate Theological Union.

Whaling, Frank, ed. 1984. *The World's Religious Traditions: Current Perspectives in Religious Studies—Essays in Honour of Wilfred Cantwell Smith*. Edinburgh: T. & T. Clark. Review: Jeffrey R. Limm, *Journal of Ecumenical Studies* 23, 1 (Winter 1986): 156.

SR SUPPLEMENTS

Note: Nos. 1 to 8, 10, 13, 15, 18 and 20 in this series are out of print.

9. *Developments in Buddhist Thought: Canadian Contributions to Buddhist Studies*
Edited by Roy C. Amore
1979 / iv + 196 pp.

11. *Political Theology in the Canadian Context*
Edited by Benjamin G. Smillie
1982 / xii + 260 pp.

12. *Truth and Compassion: Essays on Judaism and Religion in Memory of Rabbi Dr. Solomon Frank*
Edited by Howard Joseph, Jack N. Lightstone and Michael D. Oppenheim
1983 / vi + 217 pp.

14. *The Moral Mystic*
James R. Horne
1983 / x + 134 pp.

16. *Studies in the Book of Job*
Edited by Walter E. Aufrecht
1985 / xii + 76 pp.

17. *Christ and Modernity: Christian Self-Understanding in a Technological Age*
David J. Hawkin
1985 / x + 181 pp.

19. *Modernity and Religion*
Edited by William Nicholls
1987 / vi + 191 pp.

EDITIONS SR

Note: Nos. 1, 3, 6 and 9 in this series are out of print.

2. *The Conception of Punishment in Early Indian Literature*
Terence P. Day
1982 / iv + 328 pp.

4. *Le messianisme de Louis Riel*
Gilles Martel
1984 / xviii + 483 p.

5. *Mythologies and Philosophies of Salvation in the Theistic Traditions of India*
Klaus K. Klostermaier
1984 / xvi + 552 pp.

7. *L'étude des religions dans les écoles : l'expérience américaine, anglaise et canadienne*
Fernand Ouellet
1985 / xvi + 666 p.

8. *Of God and Maxim Guns: Presbyterianism in Nigeria, 1846-1966*
Geoffrey Johnston
1988 / iv + 322 pp.

10. *Prometheus Rebound: The Irony of Atheism*
Joseph C. McLelland
1988 / xvi + 366 pp.

11. *Competition in Religious Life*
Jay Newman
1989 / viii + 237 pp.

12. *The Huguenots and French Opinion, 1685-1787: The Enlightenment Debate on Toleration*
Geoffrey Adams
1991 / xiv + 335 pp.

13. *Religion in History: The Word, the Idea, the Reality / La religion dans l'histoire : le mot, l'idée, la réalité*
Edited by / Sous la direction de Michel Despland and/et Gérard Vallée
1992 / x + 252 pp.

14. *Sharing Without Reckoning: Imperfect Right and the Norms of Reciprocity*
Millard Schumaker
1992 / xiv + 112 pp.

DISSERTATIONS SR

1. *The Social Setting of the Ministry as Reflected in the Writings of Hermas, Clement and Ignatius*
   Harry O. Maier
   1991 / viii + 230 pp.

STUDIES IN CHRISTIANITY AND JUDAISM / ÉTUDES SUR LE CHRISTIANISME ET LE JUDAÏSME

Note: No. 1 and Vol. 1 of No. 2 in this series are out of print.

2. *Anti-Judaism in Early Christianity*
   Vol. 2, *Separation and Polemic*
   Edited by Stephen G. Wilson
   1986 / xii + 185 pp.
3. *Society, the Sacred, and Scripture in Ancient Judaism: A Sociology of Knowledge*
   Jack N. Lightstone
   1988 / xiv + 126 pp.
4. *Law in Religious Communities in the Roman Period: The Debate Over* Torah *and* Nomos *in Post-Biblical Judaism and Early Christianity*
   Peter Richardson and Stephen Westerholm
   with A. I. Baumgarten, Michael Pettem and Cecilia Wassén
   1991 / x + 164 pp.

THE STUDY OF RELIGION IN CANADA / SCIENCES RELIGIEUSES AU CANADA

1. *Religious Studies in Alberta: A State-of-the-Art Review*
   Ronald W. Neufeldt
   1983 / xiv + 145 pp.
2. *Les sciences religieuses au Québec depuis 1972*
   Louis Rousseau et Michel Despland
   1988 / 158 p.

COMPARATIVE ETHICS SERIES / COLLECTION D'ÉTHIQUE COMPARÉE

Note: No. 1 in this series is out of print.

2. *Methodist Education in Peru: Social Gospel, Politics, and American Ideological and Economic Penetration, 1888-1930*
   Rosa del Carmen Bruno-Jofré
   1988 / xiv + 223 pp.

Available from / en vente chez:

Wilfrid Laurier University Press
Wilfrid Laurier University
Waterloo, Ontario, Canada   N2L 3C5

Published for the
Canadian Corporation for Studies in Religion/
Corporation Canadienne des Sciences Religieuses
by Wilfrid Laurier University Press

www.ingramcontent.com/pod-product-compliance
Lightning Source LLC
Chambersburg PA
CBHW051422290426
44109CB00016B/1402